Reading Dickens Differently

Reading Dickens Differently

Edited by Leon Litvack and Nathalie Vanfasse

WILEY Blackwell

This edition first published 2020
© 2020 John Wiley & Sons Ltd

All rights reserved. No part of this publication may be reproduced, stored in a retrieval system, or transmitted, in any form or by any means, electronic, mechanical, photocopying, recording or otherwise, except as permitted by law. Advice on how to obtain permission to reuse material from this title is available at http://www.wiley.com/go/permissions.

The right of Leon Litvack and Nathalie Vanfasse to be identified as the authors of the editorial material in this work has been asserted in accordance with law.

Registered Offices
John Wiley & Sons, Inc., 111 River Street, Hoboken, NJ 07030, USA
John Wiley & Sons Ltd, The Atrium, Southern Gate, Chichester, West Sussex, PO19 8SQ, UK

Editorial Office
The Atrium, Southern Gate, Chichester, West Sussex, PO19 8SQ, UK

For details of our global editorial offices, customer services, and more information about Wiley products visit us at www.wiley.com.

Wiley also publishes its books in a variety of electronic formats and by print-on-demand. Some content that appears in standard print versions of this book may not be available in other formats.

Limit of Liability/Disclaimer of Warranty
While the publisher and authors have used their best efforts in preparing this work, they make no representations or warranties with respect to the accuracy or completeness of the contents of this work and specifically disclaim all warranties, including without limitation any implied warranties of merchantability or fitness for a particular purpose. No warranty may be created or extended by sales representatives, written sales materials or promotional statements for this work. The fact that an organization, website, or product is referred to in this work as a citation and/or potential source of further information does not mean that the publisher and authors endorse the information or services the organization, website, or product may provide or recommendations it may make. This work is sold with the understanding that the publisher is not engaged in rendering professional services. The advice and strategies contained herein may not be suitable for your situation. You should consult with a specialist where appropriate. Further, readers should be aware that websites listed in this work may have changed or disappeared between when this work was written and when it is read. Neither the publisher nor authors shall be liable for any loss of profit or any other commercial damages, including but not limited to special, incidental, consequential, or other damages.

Library of Congress Cataloging-in-Publication Data
Names: Litvack, Leon, editor. | Vanfasse, Nathalie, editor.
Title: Reading Dickens differently / edited by Leon Litvack and Nathalie
    Vanfasse.
Description: First edition. | Hoboken, NJ : Wiley-Blackwell, 2020. |
    Includes bibliographical references and index.
Identifiers: LCCN 2019025694 (print) | LCCN 2019025695 (ebook) | ISBN
    9781119602224 (paperback) | ISBN 9781119602231 (adobe pdf) | ISBN
    9781119602248 (epub)
Subjects: LCSH: Dickens, Charles, 1812–1870–Criticism and interpretation.
    | Dickens, Charles, 1812–1870–Influence.
Classification: LCC PR4588 .R35 2020 (print) | LCC PR4588 (ebook) | DDC
    823/.8–dc23
LC record available at https://lccn.loc.gov/2019025694
LC ebook record available at https://lccn.loc.gov/2019025695

Cover Design: Wiley
Cover Image: *Dickens Selfie* © Michael Fenner 2019

Set in 10/12pt STIX Two by SPi Global, Pondicherry, India
Printed and bound in Singapore by Markono Print Media Pte Ltd

Contents

List of Figures *vii*
Notes on Contributors *ix*
Acknowledgements *xiii*
Abbreviations *xv*

Introduction *1*
Leon Litvack and Nathalie Vanfasse

Part I   Reconfiguring Dickens   *13*

1 **Dickens's Burial in Westminster Abbey: The Untold Story** *15*
   Leon Litvack

2 **A Tale of Two Brothers: Reading Differently Dickens's French Revolution** *47*
   Lillian Nayder

3 **Parallel Lives, Converging Destinies: Charles Dickens and Thomas Babington Macaulay** *61*
   David Paroissien

4 **Decent Restraint Spurned: Dickens, Penal Policy and Conflict at Cold Bath Fields Prison, 1846–1850** *75*
   Neil Davie

Part II   Reincorporating Dickens   *93*

5 **A Somatic Experience of Dickens's Fiction** *95*
   Georges Letissier

6   **Dickens and Lawrence: Mimicry, Totemism, Animism**   *113*
    Michael Hollington

7   **Wreckage and Ruin: Turner, Dickens, Ruskin**   *125*
    Jeremy Tambling

8   **Boz without Phiz: Reading Dickens with Different Illustrations**   *149*
    Chris Louttit

Part III   Resetting Dickens   *165*

9   **Speculation and Silence: Reading Dickens by Instalment in Time, at the Time and for Our Time**   *167*
    Pete Orford

10 **Dickens Touches the Sky: Urban Exploration and London's Greatest Author**   *185*
    Gillian Piggott

11 **Dickens as Icon and Antonomasia in *Assassin's Creed*: Syndicate**   *207*
    Francesca Orestano

12 **From Movable Book to iPad App: Playing *A Christmas Carol***   *223*
    Claire Wood

Index   *243*

List of Figures

Figure 1.1	Telegram from Charley Dickens to George Holsworth, 9 June 1870	16
Figure 1.2	Arthur Penrhyn Stanley (1815–1881)	18
Figure 1.3	Frederick Locker (1821–1895; later Locker-Lampson)	19
Figure 1.4	The Grave of Charles Dickens in Poets' Corner (1870)	28
Figure 1.5	First page of Dickens's funeral fee account, Westminster Abbey Funeral Fee book, 1811–1899, folio 233	30
Figure 1.6	Second page of Dickens's funeral fee account, Westminster Abbey Funeral Fee book, 1811–1899, folio 234	31
Figure 1.7	John Everett Millais, *Charles Dickens After Death* (1870)	35
Figure 1.8	Death registration certificate for Charles Dickens, 12 June 1870	36
Figure 7.1	Joseph Mallord William Turner, *Bridge of Sighs, Ducal Palace and Custom-House, Venice: Canaletti Painting* (1833)	128
Figure 7.2	Robert Brandard, engraving of Turner's *Rain, Steam and Speed* (1844)	131
Figure 7.3	Joseph Mallord William Turner, *Slavers throwing overboard the Dead and Dying – Typhon coming on* ("*The Slave Ship*") (1840)	137
Figure 7.4	Joseph Mallord William Turner, *The Wreck Buoy* (c. 1807; reworked 1849)	138
Figure 7.5	James Tibbits Willmore, engraving of Turner's *The Fighting Téméraire* (1839)	140
Figure 8.1	Fred Barnard, drawing in undated letter	154
Figure 8.2	Fred Barnard, plate depicting (L to R) Esther, Caddy Jellyby and Mrs Jellyby (1873)	155
Figure 8.3	Fred Barnard, plate depicting (foreground L to R) Mr Gridley, Miss Flite; (background L to R): Inspector Bucket (seated), George Rouncewell, Phil Squod, Mr Jarndyce (seated), Esther Summerson, Richard Carstone (1873)	155

List of Figures

Figure 8.4	Fred Barnard, plate depicting Lady Dedlock (1873)	156
Figure 8.5	Fred Barnard, "Jo" (1873)	158
Figure 8.6	Fred Barnard, Miss Jennie Lee as "Jo"; Theatre Royal Edinburgh poster (1885)	159
Figure 9.1	Characters' appearances in the monthly numbers and chapters of *The Mystery of Edwin Drood*	177
Figure 9.2	Character presence in the first monthly number of *The Mystery of Edwin Drood*	178
Figure 9.3	Character presence in the first three monthly numbers of *The Mystery of Edwin Drood*	178
Figure 9.4	Character presence in the first six monthly numbers of *The Mystery of Edwin Drood*	179
Figure 9.5	Twitter feed for Eugene Wrayburn (@OMF_Eugene), from *Our Mutual Friend Reading Project*	182
Figure 11.1	The Twins Jacob and Evie Frye, from *Assassin's Creed: Syndicate*	210
Figure 11.2	Thames River prospect, at Westminster Pier, from *Assassin's Creed: Syndicate*	210
Figure 11.3	Palace of Westminster from high elevation, surveyed by Evie (L), and Jacob (R), from *Assassin's Creed: Syndicate*	212
Figure 11.4	Dickens wax figure at Madame Tussauds, London	213
Figure 11.5	Visual representation of Dickens, from *Assassin's Creed: Syndicate*	215
Figure 12.1	Cover image from Chuck Fischer's *A Christmas Carol: A Pop-Up Book* (2010)	225
Figure 12.2	London street scene, from Chuck Fischer's *A Christmas Carol: A Pop-Up Book* (2010)	227
Figure 12.3	"Come to Life" panorama from *Stories from Dickens for Boys and Girls* (1935)	231
Figure 12.4	"Marley was dead," screen capture from Charles Dickens's *A Christmas Carol*: For the iPad	234
Figure 12.5	Scrooge in his counting-house, from Charles Dickens's *A Christmas Carol*: For the iPad	235
Figure 12.6	Stave One pop-up, featuring Marley's Ghost, from Chuck Fischer's *A Christmas Carol: A Pop-Up Book* (2010)	236
Figure 12.7	Stave Four pop-up, featuring the Ghost of Christmas Yet to Come, from Chuck Fischer's *A Christmas Carol: A Pop-Up Book* (2010)	237

Notes on Contributors

NEIL DAVIE is Professor of British History at Lyon Lumière University, France. He has published widely on the history of penal policy, crime and criminology, and has also written on the history of science and women's history. He is the author of *Tracing the Criminal: The Rise of Scientific Criminology in Britain, 1860–1918* (2005) and *The Penitentiary Ten: The Transformation of the English Prison, 1770–1850* (2017). He is currently working on a study of the origins of Dartmoor Prison during the Napoleonic Wars.

MICHAEL HOLLINGTON is a retired Professor of English and Comparative Literature, who has held chairs in France and Australia and elsewhere. He currently lives and works in Scotland as an independent scholar. Although primarily a Dickensian (author of *Dickens and The Grotesque* and books on *David Copperfield*, *Great Expectations* and *A Tale of Two Cities*), he has published widely on Modern literature, including books on Whitman, Mansfield and Grass, and essays on D.H. Lawrence. He is currently working on *Dickens Among the Modernists*.

GEORGES LETISSIER is Professor of English Literature at Nantes University, France. He has three areas of speciality: Charles Dickens, Ford Madox Ford, and contemporary British fiction. His recent publications include "Our Mutual City: The Posterity of the Dickensian Urbanscape," in *Dickens and the Virtual City* (2017), and "Between the English Nuvvle and the Novel of Aloofness: Charles Dickens's Proto-(High) Modernism," in *Beyond the Victorian/Modernist Divide* (2018).

LEON LITVACK is Professor of Victorian Studies at the Queen's University of Belfast, Northern Ireland. He is Principal Editor of the Charles Dickens Letters Project (dickensletters.com), and a world authority on Dickens manuscripts, handwriting and photographic portraits. His numerous publications have revolved around historical and visual approaches to the author. This has led him to produce intricately researched studies on Dickens's interest in Australia and the convict experience; his passion for education; his lifetime reading; his intimate knowledge of the topography of London and southeast England; his life at his home,

Gad's Hill; his photographic portraits and the cultivation of celebrity; his methods of composition; and his journalism. He is the author of the comprehensive annotated bibliography of *Dombey and Son*, and is currently working on the authoritative Oxford edition of *Our Mutual Friend*.

CHRIS LOUTTIT is Assistant Professor of English Literature at Radboud University in Nijmegen, the Netherlands. His main area of interest is mid-Victorian fiction and its popular reception and afterlives; his current Dickensian research focuses on the work of later illustrators such as Fred Barnard. He is the author of *Dickens's Secular Gospel: Work, Gender, and Personality* (2009), and numerous articles in the *Dickens Quarterly*, *Book History*, *Critical Survey*, *Gothic Studies* and *Neo-Victorian Studies*.

LILLIAN NAYDER is Professor of English at Bates College. Her books include *Wilkie Collins* (1997), *Unequal Partners: Charles Dickens, Wilkie Collins, and Victorian Authorship* (2002) and *The Other Dickens: A Life of Catherine Hogarth* (2011). She has edited the volume on *Dickens, Sexuality and Gender* for Routledge (2012). In 2016, she guest curated the exhibition "Discovering Catherine" at the Charles Dickens Museum in London. She is currently writing a group biography of Dickens and his three brothers.

FRANCESCA ORESTANO is Professor of English Literature at Milan University. She is the author of books on John Neal (*Dal Neoclassico al Classico*), on the picturesque (*Paesaggio e finzione*) and on visual studies (*La parola e lo sguardo*). She has edited *Dickens and Italy* and *Dickens's Signs, Readers' Designs*, and has written on *Little Dorrit* for *The Oxford Handbook of Charles Dickens*. She works on the reception of Dickens in Italy, as well as on John Ruskin and Virginia Woolf. Her work on literature and chemistry is forthcoming in *Cahiers Victoriens et Edouardiens*.

PETE ORFORD is Lecturer in English Literature at the University of Buckingham, and Course Director for the University's MA by Research in Charles Dickens Studies, which is run in conjunction with the Charles Dickens Museum. His most recent publication is *The Mystery of Edwin Drood: Charles Dickens' Unfinished Novel and Our Endless Attempts to End It* (2018). He is the creator of *The Drood Inquiry* (www.droodinquiry.com) and has coordinated several online reading groups of Dickens's novels. He is currently editing *Pictures from Italy* for the Oxford Dickens.

DAVID PAROISSIEN is Professorial Research Fellow at the University of Buckingham, and Emeritus Professor of English, University of Massachusetts, Amherst. His recent publications include "Dickens the Novelist, Carlyle the Historian, and Dickens, Carlyle and the French Revolution," in *The Fiction of History* (2015), and "History and Change: Dickens and the Past," in *The Oxford Handbook of Charles Dickens* (2018).

GILLIAN PIGGOTT is Associate Professor of English and Humanities at the American University of Afghanistan. She is an expert on Dickens and her interests encompass nineteenth-century literature; British theatre; adaptation; literature and film; representations of the city; and philosophy and literature. She is the author of the monograph *Dickens and Benjamin* (2012) and of a number of articles, including "Dickens and Chaplin"; "Dickens and Postcolonialism"; "Neo-Victorianism in Film"; and "Dickens and Drama."

JEREMY TAMBLING is Professor of Literature at the Warsaw University of Social Sciences and Humanities; he has previously held Chairs at Manchester and the University of Hong Kong. His most recent books are *Dickens, Dante, and the Dance of Death* (2019) and *Histories of the Devil: From Marlowe to Mann and the Manichees* (2017). He is editor of the *Palgrave Encyclopaedia of Urban Literary Studies*. His current project concerns Dante's *Paradiso*.

NATHALIE VANFASSE is Professor of English at Aix-Marseille Université, France. Her first monograph, entitled *Dickens entre normes et déviance*, was shortlisted for the 2008 prize of the SAES/AFEA (French MLA). Her second monograph, entitled *La Plume et la route: Charles Dickens écrivain-voyageur* (2017), was awarded the 2018 book prize by SELVA (Société d'Etude de la Littérature de Voyage du monde Anglophone).

CLAIRE WOOD is a Lecturer in Victorian Literature at the University of Leicester. She is the author of *Dickens and the Business of Death* (2015), a Trustee of the Dickens Society and a member of the Editorial Board for *Dickens Quarterly*. Her research interests include Victorian death culture, materiality and afterlives. Her current research explores different forms of death comedy in the work of Dickens and other nineteenth-century writers.

Acknowledgements

The editors and authors wish to thank the following, without whose kind assistance the completion of this research would not have been possible: Freddie Alexander, Malcolm Andrews, Jen Baker, Galia Benziman, Joel Brattin, Jill Campbell, Rebecca Carpenter, Melinda Creech, Mary Crickard, the Dean and Chapter of Rochester, the Dean and Chapter of Westminster, Clematis Delaney, Duane DeVries, Maxime Durand, Michael Fenner, Jennifer Ide, Elizabeth James, Juliet John, Lisa Johnson, Diarmuid Kennedy, Aoife Leahy, Patrick Lonergan, Nancy Metz, Steve Nye, Leonee Ormond, Jeremy Parrott, Emily Parsons, Bob Patten, Matthew Payne, Nathan Pendlebury, Louisa Price, Dominic Rainsford, Kathy Rees, Andrew Rootes, Michael Slater, Chris Sutherns, Judyta Szacillo, Isabel Torres, Paul Vita, Tom Wingate and Janet Wood.

The editors would also like to extend special thanks to the team at Wiley, in particular Catriona King, Nicole Allen, Giles Flitney, Sakthivel Kandaswamy and Richie Samson, for their belief in the project, and the practical advice and assistance offered during the final editing and publication.

Abbreviations

Note: References to Dickens's fictional works will be indicated in the text by abbreviated title (see below) and chapter number, or book and chapter number (in the cases of *Great Expectations, Our Mutual Friend* and *A Tale of Two Cities*). References to Dickens's letters will be indicated in the text by volume and page number from the Pilgrim edition.

AN   Dickens, Charles (1842/2000) *American Notes for General Circulation*. Ed. Patricia Ingham. Penguin Classics. Harmondsworth: Penguin.
BH   Dickens, Charles (1852–1853/1998). *Bleak House*. Ed. Stephen Gill. Oxford World's Classics. Oxford: Oxford University Press.
BR   Dickens, Charles (1841/2003). *Barnaby Rudge*. Ed. Clive Hurst. Oxford World's Classics. Oxford: Oxford University Press.
C   Dickens, Charles (1844/2006). *The Chimes*. Ed. Robert Douglas-Fairhurst. In *A Christmas Carol and Other Christmas Books*. Oxford World's Classics. Oxford: Oxford University Press.
CC   Dickens, Charles (1843/2006). *A Christmas Carol*. Ed. Robert Douglas-Fairhurst. In *A Christmas Carol and Other Christmas Books*. Oxford World's Classics. Oxford: Oxford University Press.
CH   Dickens, Charles (1845/2006). *The Cricket on the Hearth*. Ed. Robert Douglas-Fairhurst. In *A Christmas Carol and Other Christmas Books*. Oxford World's Classics. Oxford: Oxford University Press.
DC   Dickens, Charles (1849–1850/2008). *David Copperfield*. Ed. Nina Burgis. Oxford World's Classics. Oxford: Oxford University Press.
DS   Dickens, Charles (1846–1848/2001). *Dombey and Son*. Ed. Alan Horsman. Oxford World's Classics. Oxford: Oxford University Press.
GE   Dickens, Charles (1860–1861/2008). *Great Expectations*. Ed. Margaret Cardwell. Oxford World's Classics. Oxford: Oxford University Press.
LD   Dickens, Charles (1855–1857/2012). *Little Dorrit*. Ed. Harvey Peter Sucksmith. Oxford World's Classics. Oxford: Oxford University Press.

Letters	The Pilgrim Edition of *The Letters of Charles Dickens* (1965–2002). Ed. Madeline House, Graham Storey, Kathleen Tillotson et al. 12 vols. Oxford: Oxford University Press.
MC	Dickens, Charles (1843–1844/2009). *Martin Chuzzlewit*. Ed. Margaret Cardwell. Oxford World's Classics. Oxford: Oxford University Press.
OCS	Dickens, Charles (1840–1841/2008). *The Old Curiosity Shop*. Ed. Elizabeth M. Brennan. Oxford World's Classics. Oxford: Oxford University Press.
OMF	Dickens, Charles (1864–1865/2008). *Our Mutual Friend*. Ed. Michael Cotsell. Oxford World's Classics. Oxford: Oxford University Press.
OT	Dickens, Charles (1837–1838/2008). *Oliver Twist*. Ed. Kathleen Tillotson. Oxford World's Classics. Oxford: Oxford University Press.
PP	Dickens, Charles (1836–1837/2008) *The Pickwick Papers*. Ed. James Kinsley. Oxford World's Classics. Oxford: Oxford University Press.
TTC	Dickens, Charles (1859/2008). *A Tale of Two Cities*. Ed. Andrew Sanders. Oxford World's Classics. Oxford: Oxford University Press.

Introduction
Leon Litvack and Nathalie Vanfasse

> ... *that very word, Reading, in its critical use, always charms me*
> (*Our Mutual Friend,* book 3, chapter 10)

"Reading Dickens Differently" may seem a truism. One might well ask: how can different readers not have distinct and idiosyncratic interpretations of Dickens's work? Moreover, from a narrower academic perspective, how could any scholarly essay or book not professing to offer a new light on Dickens's work hope to be published? The bold assertion which predicates this volume stems from other considerations – namely the realisation that we can no longer take for granted the broad readership and traditional scholarly interest in Dickens, who was once an indisputable part of a universally shared Western heritage. While the author's association with Christmas is still an important part of his widespread appeal, this does not necessarily translate into a unanimous familiarity with his texts among the general public, or a continued interest in the critical strategies and pervasive certainties that have been the mainstay of Dickens studies since the 1970s – if not before. The present volume's claim to read Dickens differently also stems from concerns about the very future of reading and interpreting literary texts. Scholars have bluntly voiced disturbing questions concerning the purpose of literature (Compagnon 2007), or the place it holds in our cultures and societies (Citton 2010). These anxieties extend to the print medium itself, which is described by Robert Coover, in an essay provocatively entitled "The End of Books," as "a mere curiosity of bygone days destined soon to be consigned forever to those dusty unattended museums we now call libraries" (1992).

Scholarly endeavour itself has also been called into question. Well-known critics such as Harold Bloom (2000) and Tzvetan Todorov (2007) have bemoaned the excessively interpretive and professional turn taken by the study of literature in the twenty-first century, and the way it seems to have cut readers off from what

Reading Dickens Differently, First Edition. Edited by Leon Litvack and Nathalie Vanfasse.
© 2020 John Wiley & Sons Ltd. Published 2020 by John Wiley & Sons Ltd.

these critics consider as more spontaneous and existential readings. Indeed Stephen Best and Sharon Marcus argue for an abandonment of criticism: they maintain that an "immersion in texts" can facilitate an "attentiveness to the artwork itself as a kind of freedom"; they add that in relinquishing the "demystification" offered by criticism, "we might grope toward some equally valuable, if less glamorous, state of mind" (2009, pp. 16, 17). This denunciation has given rise to two kinds of reactions: some focusing on why one should continue to read literature (Hillis Miller 2002), and others insisting that one should continue not just to read but also to engage in critique in a more innovative manner that does not necessarily seek to unlock some truth concealed in a text. Alternative strategies for "doing" criticism have been offered by, for example, Citton (2007), Jouve (2010), Schaeffer (2012) and Felski (2015). Anker and Felski succinctly outline the problem:

> There is little doubt that debates about the merits of critique are very much in the air and that the intellectual or political payoff of interrogating, demystifying, and familiarizing is no longer quite so self-evident. Even those who insist on the continuing salience and timeliness of critique are now often expected to defend and justify what was previously taken for granted. (2017, p. 1)

The present volume endeavours to offer several ways forward, by means of critiques that demonstrate how innovative strategies for reading Dickens differently can excite new generations of literary aficionados, and can assist in revising and refreshing the ways in which more experienced readers approach the Victorian author's texts. Interdisciplinarity and diachrony are at the core of this project, which brings together approaches that are microhistorical, legal, political, penological, corporeal, intertextual, visual, conversational, social, ambulatory, perilous, ludic, technological and tactile.

Thus, rather than take refuge in the narrow confines in which many established scholars were originally trained, this collection of essays endeavours to address head-on the problem of critique's running "out of steam" (Latour 2004, p. 225). It provides space for some of the new voices and perspectives on Dickens that seek to "associate the word *criticism* with a whole set of new positive metaphors, gestures, attitudes, knee-jerk reactions, habits of thoughts" (Latour 2004, p. 247; emphasis original). While it is true that any scholarly endeavour on Dickens is likely to have as its impetus "Reading Dickens Differently," this volume purports to push the boundaries of current thinking about the author.

The innovative interests and research methods represented by the authors brought together in this project combine with – rather than replace – traditional interpretive practices of literary studies. They build upon the history of reading and of reading practices, delineated by critics such as Blasselle (1998) or Cavallo and Chartier (2001), and upon book history in the West, as discussed by Barbier (2012).

They follow Hans Robert Jauss's reception studies (1982), in that they analyse the meaning or interpretation of Dickens's work by different groups of readers, as well as the evolution of these readings over time. The work by Stanley Fish (1980) and Wolfgang Iser (1980) on the implied reader, and the studies by Normand Holland (1975) and David Bleich (1975, 1978) on actual readers, also provide a theoretical background for this collection of essays. So does the research on the sociology of reading by Jacques Leenhardt and Pierre Jozsa (1982), in whose view reading establishes an exchange between two world visions, each of which is transformed in the process. This book draws on Umberto Eco's theories on the role of cooperative interpretation in reading (1979), and on the work of Michel Picard (1986), who considered reading as a game whose stakes are high, and in which the reader/player is deeply involved in the process and takes significant risks. Rules, according to Picard, organise the complex relations between readers and fiction, and the process of reading resembles an adventure on which readers embark. *Reading Dickens Differently* capitalises upon the arguments of N. Katherine Hayles (1999, 2012) and Jay Clayton (2003), about how a digital environment can endow texts with innovative features that influence reading and interpretation practices. The essays in this volume resonate in spirit with other recent explorations of different forms of reading, such as Stephen Best and Sharon Marcus on "surface reading" (2009); Franco Moretti and Matthew Jockers on "distant reading" (Moretti 2013; Jockers 2013); and Daniel Shore's call for a new "cyberformalism," that foregrounds a qualitative linguistic approach to digital archives (2018).

The book is organised into three parts. The first, entitled "Reconfiguring Dickens," offers four case studies that address central – though under-researched or overlooked – aspects of Dickens's life, and avail of recent developments and trends in biographical studies (see Renders et al. 2017; Magnússon 2017), to offer corrections and reshapings of received opinion. They display intimate and open-minded critical acumen about their common protagonist, and each performs a forensic examination of evidence, in order to demonstrate the creative possibilities inherent in challenging canonical views of the author.

Leon Litvack uses previously undiscovered archival material to reassess our knowledge (gained particularly from John Forster and close family members) regarding Dickens's death and burial, and to read these events with fresh insight. This essay employs recent developments in critical biography – particularly a multi-disciplinary approach (Hamilton 2014, p. ix) – involving analysis of documentary evidence, visual images, financial accounts, ecclesiastical protocol and funerary custom to yield results previously unimagined by those who have written more traditional literary biographies. Litvack demonstrates how a microhistorical emphasis, which reduces the scale of observation (see Peltonen 2014, pp. 110–114), and thus facilitates the examination of minute details in the crucial period 9–13 June 1870, reveals a different narrative from the one promoted by John Forster in his authoritative *Life of Charles Dickens* (1872–1874). Litvack's essay offers an "untold story" of almost Dickensian mysteriousness, 150 years after the events.

Lilian Nayder proposes a completely new understanding of *A Tale of Two Cities* in the light of the complicated relationship between Dickens and his youngest brother, Frederick, who went on trial in 1859 before the Court for Divorce and Matrimonial Causes. The essay, which also reduces the field of study to focus on a particular familial crisis (see Magnússon 2017), examines the intricacies and complications of the relationship between the two Dickens brothers, to demonstrate how the author wove this thorny biographical episode into the plot of his historical novel. This rich source material, including personal letters and reports of legal proceedings, provides unexpected insight into Dickens's inspiration for his text, and on his representation of the French Revolution. Conversely, it also allows the novel's plot to be viewed through a new biographical-cum-historical perspective, thus yielding a new reading of Dickens's life itself.

David Paroissien's contribution demonstrates how a seemingly minor gap in our knowledge of Dickens's otherwise well-documented biography – namely his daily life as a Parliamentary reporter in the 1820s and 1830s – can shed capital light upon his later career as a writer of fiction. While working at the Palace of Westminster as a reporter for the *Mirror of Parliament*, Dickens came into contact with one of the most prominent historians of his time: Thomas Babington Macaulay. This occurred at a unique moment in the history of nineteenth-century Britain: the agitation for the First Reform Act – a time when Parliamentary debate was particularly animated. The young Dickens, perched in the gallery looking down upon proceedings, was most assuredly a reader of the political life of his time: he saw and heard key debates from a vantage point that shaped his political ideas and his view of history. Indeed, Macaulay's influence (together with that of Thomas Carlyle) spread to Dickens's notions about the writing of history and historical novels. *Barnaby Rudge* in particular resonates with echoes of Macaulay, who induced Dickens to read history differently, by focusing less upon political trends and more upon the social – and indeed the anecdotal.

Neil Davie uses fresh evidence from prison archives and reports of legal proceedings to provide a fuller understanding of Dickens's complex and paradoxical engagement with penal policy throughout his life. The research on the "silent" and "separate" systems, and on the situation at Cold Bath Fields Prison in London, emphasises an evolution in Dickens's artistic concern with imprisonment. The essay also reveals new sources of inspiration for the author's journalistic contributions – especially his article "Pet Prisoners" (1850). As in other studies in this section, the use of private correspondence, as well as official reports and newspaper accounts, sheds new light on Dickens's personal circumstances, and confirms the value of the biographical "turn" in reassessing previously assured accounts (Renders et al. 2017, p. 10).

The second section of this volume, entitled "Reincorpotating Dickens," achieves its ends by employing physical and visual strategies to assess bodily sensations, facial contours, physiognomies and visual stimuli. New readings are offered through interdisciplinary and intertextual lenses, focusing on neuropsychology and a corporeal phenomenology of Dickens's work; Modernist rereadings incorporating mimicry, totemism and animism; a reassessment of the importance of painting and visual rendering to Dickens's textual representations; and an investigation of the inextricable link between a particular pictorial style of illustration and the reader's understanding of the text. All of these reading strategies build upon such research as that by Malcolm Andrews on public readings and performance (2006), as well as on arguments concerning literature as a form of praxis (Albrecht et al. 2018). Here, however, the performance is reversed: it does not involve the author as a reader, but rather the individual consumer of Dickens's texts who, in some instances, becomes a performer in the attempt to effect alternative readings. In the wake of the studies by Marielle Macé on reading and being, and the styling of existence (2011, 2016), this section connects reading to ways of life and styles or ideas (including shapes, modes, regimes and allures; see Macé 2016, p. 1) that can be seen as performances delineating forms of authorship. The essays range from the analysis of the somatic (or corporeal) dimensions of reading in the essays by Georges Letissier and Michael Hollington, to renewed visual reading of Dickens's work in the contributions by Jeremy Tambling and Chris Louttit. They build upon Nicholas Dames's groundbreaking study of the affective physiology of Victorian novel reading, which injects the activity with dramatic "passion" (2007, p. 42).

Letissier builds upon reader-response theory to rethink the reading of Dickens's work through the connections between body and text, in what Pierre-Louis Patoine calls an "empathetic reading" (2015). Letissier uses this critic as a starting point, to develop a corporeal phenomenology of reading the Victorian author's work, involving bodily stimuli, phantom sensations, voices and heartbeats emanating from the text – not to mention dissociations of consciousness and even skin and muscular sensations. This innovative mode of reading draws on neuropsychology, among other scientific disciplines, to provide a radically reconceived idea of reading, based on physiological novel theory and somatic theory.

Michael Hollington's essay partakes of hermeneutical strategies centred around a reconfiguration of the Victorian body – to paraphrase Peter Capuano (2015). It picks up on the idea of corporeal reading to explore a particular "rewriting" of Dickens – D.H. Lawrence's *The Lost Girl* (1920) – in a familiar context: that of an ostensible Modernist repudiation of Victorian convention, which nevertheless draws copious sustenance from its rejected sources. The distinctively new feature involves a performative engagement, in three ways, with some cardinal Dickensian themes: the first, a pronounced capacity for mimicry, and a preoccupation with voice in the creation of, and differentiation between, characters; the second, an appreciation of the resemblances between human physiognomies and the facial contours of animals such as birds – particularly ravens, of which Dickens was particularly fond; the third, an "animistic" treatment, relating people and things in satirical ways. Hollington identifies *The Lost Girl* as the most important site of Dickensian engagement for Lawrence.

Kinaesthetic readings of Dickens's work take on another, more visual, dimension in the contributions by Jeremy Tambling and Chris Louttit. Tambling demonstrates that John Ruskin's writing encourages a reading of Dickens's work that reshapes the novelist's art through the work of the painter J.M.W. Turner. Tambling explores a "Turneresque" Dickens, who manages to produce through his very style images that parallel those of the painter; the effect is felt in the "French road" chapter in *Dombey and Son*, which functions as Dickens's textual version of the painting *Rain, Steam and Speed* (1844). A sensation similar to that produced in watery, illuminatory works like *The Slave Ship* (1840) and *The Wreck Buoy* (1807, 1849) may be felt in the escape scene in *Great Expectations*. Conversely, Tambling argues, Ruskin's writing on Turner highlights the similarities between Turnerian images of London and Dickensian verbal renderings of the city. Both writer and artist delight in the depiction of ruins and wreckage; the dissolution of solid forms and structures and the return to shapeless primeval landscapes are, Tambling argues, at the heart of both their representations, as they strive to reach beyond appearances. Paradoxically, Ruskin's reading of Dickens's work failed to capture some of proto-Modernist features that he identified so aptly in Turner's painting, because those features were even more unsettling in Dickens's writing; the result, the essay concludes, is that Ruskin unconsciously shunned them, but, ironically, needed them to inform his critique of Turner.

Chris Louttit picks up on the idea of reading Dickens's visuality, tackling the novels through illustrations and, more particularly, through images that have been neglected, in the Household Edition published after Dickens's death. These depictions show how the illustrator Fred Barnard adapted his visuals to the new public taste of the 1860s and 1870s (which had outgrown the work of Phiz), and how in turn these updated illustrations interacted in a different manner with the original text. Louttit's study not only foregrounds the incompleteness of Dickensian texts without their illustrations; it also raises the question of readings induced by posthumous illustrations that Dickens did not oversee: these images yielded new interpretations of the text that resonate with their time. In these evocative interpretations of Dickens's work (more numerous than those of earlier illustrators), images become essential to the understanding of particular passages – particularly of a novel like *Bleak House*. The essay also examines the possibility of exploring these visual renderings of Dickens's work even further, with the assistance of digital tools that make this field of research available to a wider range of viewers/readers, thus providing incentives to study illustrations in innovative ways. This section of *Reading Dickens Differently* moves away from a "symptomatic reading" that focuses on a meaning that is "hidden, repressed, deep, and in need of detection and disclosure," (Best & Marcus 2009, p. 1) and towards a "surface reading" that embodies a "pure, untranslatable sensuous immediacy," focusing on the immediately "evident" and "perceptible" in the text and its accompanying visualisations (2009, pp. 10, 9).

The final section of this collection picks up on the idea of "surface reading," while turning its attention to the ever-evolving field of new media technologies (see Wardrip-Fruin & Montfort 2003; Lister et al. 2009). It concentrates on digital platforms, social media, interactive applications and virtual/augmented reality, and on how their use has fostered cutting-edge readings and appreciations of Dickens. These essays raise essential questions for readers in the twenty-first century, concerning how new media affect continuity and change in reading Victorian authors; immersion in texts and their representations; reader's perspectives (whether physical or ideological); social forms, user-generated content and commentary on narrative; gameplay; and the technological shaping of everyday life (see Lister et al. 2009, pp. 44–50, 114–124, 176–178, 221–224, 286–306, 254–265).

Pete Orford's contribution on the online reading of Dickens's work builds on the research of Jay Clayton (2003) concerning Dickens's presence in cyberspace. The essay outlines an interactive, communal and social strategy with respect to online reading by instalments that takes it far beyond existing projects, like that conceived by Robyn Warhol (n.d.), which does not allow for reader feedback. The projects Orford discusses demonstrate that reading Dickens online proves distinctly different from reading him in the nineteenth century, as the monthly parts first appeared. While the internet may, in some ways, recreate the experience of Victorian instalments, this research demonstrates that readers do not approach the text in the same anticipatory ways as their forbears: they look ahead, and often peek at the text's resolution; they bring their twenty-first-century concerns and contexts to bear upon discussions; they welcome the open-endedness of an unfinished work like *Edwin Drood*; and they embrace the extra-textual fluidity made possible through the game-playing of social media. Thus Orford's essay usefully explores the experience of reading a text in the making. It also resorts to computational data sampling in order to measure the significance of characters, and this, along with the digitisation of Victorian serial novels, highlights the growing importance of digital humanities in reading Dickens differently. However, the digital experiences depicted in this volume differ from Moretti's conceptions of "distant reading" (2013) or Matthew Jockers's macroanalysis (2013), in that they do not resort to mass data, but instead apply statistical tools to close reading in order to demonstrate textual complexity, and to identify sites that compete for readers' attention.

Like Orford, Gillian Piggott explores ways of reading that were at least partly characteristic of Dickens's own time; but she adds an innovative layer, through an exploration of twenty-first-century recreational trespassing in the built environment. The strategies and trajectories of urban explorers, or "Urbexers," are usefully and evocatively compared to Dickens's perambulations across London. The association between Urbex and the internet is evident in its very terminology, which refers to "infiltration" or "place-hacking," thus introducing new media technologies – particularly augmented/virtual reality video – into its practice. Many aspects of Dickens's metropolitan writing are of interest to Urbex: his ability to create incessant movement and variety; the pictorial, aural and even moving images he conjures up in his fiction; his obsession with representing the vertiginous experience; his fascination with speed; the minute delineation of urban space, with all its strange enigmatic points of connection and disconnection and the continual re-enchantment of the everyday. Piggott proposes Urbex, which forges furtive yet intimate connections with the city, as a new form of reading that facilitates the investigation of sites situated beyond boundaries; thus this analysis reveals, as Dickens's work does, the hidden aspects of cities.

Francesca Orestano considers reading as game-playing, and looks at a recent video game involving Dickens's world. Her essay examines *Assassin's Creed: Syndicate*, launched in 2015 by Ubisoft Entertainment, and the way it transposes and reprocesses Dickens in a new medium adapted to the expectations of a twenty-first-century online community. Reading Dickens is transposed into playing a game involving the author as a character, and also as a metonymy for the entire context and atmosphere of Victorian London. This supposedly Dickensian décor draws on a wealth of historical visual documentation, used by the creators of the game to make it seem as accurate and realistic as possible; images from the game enhance this conception for the reader. In some ways the presence of Dickens resembles the efforts by John Wall and others at North Carolina State University to recreate the world of John Donne and his sermons at St Paul's Cathedral in 1622, in the Virtual St Paul's Cathedral Project (see Wall 2014, n.d.); here, however, the creators of *Assassin's Creed* are less interested in the particularities of Dickens as a producer of texts, and more in him as an evocative representative of his age. In *Assassin's Creed* there is an emphasis on well-researched, stunning visuality, which far outstrips that of the St Paul's project; it also embodies the somewhat eerie elements of ghosts and simulacra. Dickensian fiction is condensed into the pure action and electrifying urban exploration which the players actively control. The Victorian past and the present of the twenty-first century are conflated in this new digital narrative form, which reinvents the ancient tradition of epic writing, with its heroic characters and scale.

Claire Wood also concentrates on visualisations – this time of *A Christmas Carol*, in the form of a pop-up book and an iPad app, both conceived by the American artist Chuck Fischer. The essay investigates the possibilities that such visualisations of the *Carol* have for drawing "reader-interactors" into the story and prompting them to reflect on their own capacities for transformation. Wood demonstrates that the movable components – whether in engineered paper or in electronic form – compel readers to adopt a hybridised mode of engagement; those who engage with the text in these innovative ways become, Wood argues, active participants in Scrooge's reformation.

The enduring value of this final section lies in the fact that while taking into account recent technological tools or games, the strategies employed encourage readers to become aware of broad concerns surrounding the consumption and interpretation of canonical literary texts, that will stand up to scrutiny long after we forget about Twitter, iPads and Urbex. The essays exemplify how, in order to merge with our digital culture, the forms literary reading can adopt involve the creation of "a new set of players, locations, rituals, and use values for reading literary fiction" (Collins 2010, p. 3). In this set-up, the players have an enhanced role in the creative process: reading becomes less a matter of uncovering hidden meanings and structures, and more of a "translation" of Dickensian texts into exciting new arenas (Felski 2016, p. 218).

Reading Dickens Differently revitalises our perception of Dickens and his work, and offers alternative strategies for engaging with a Victorian author and his texts. Taken together, the 12 essays enhance ideas about "curating the humanities": a strategy for "guarding, protecting, conserving, caretaking, and looking after" texts that might, without fresh consideration and recurrent use, slip into oblivion (Felski 2016, p. 217). Such a nurturing attitude also applies to the critic, who, according to Latour, looks after a critique that is "constructed" and is "fragile and thus in great need of care and caution" (2004, p. 246). To carry the metaphor of curation a bit further, Stephen Greenblatt usefully distinguishes between the "resonance" of a museum object, that must "reach out beyond its formal boundaries to a larger world," and the "wonder" an object excites, stopping a viewer in his or her tracks, "to convey an arresting sense of uniqueness, to evoke an exalted attention" (1991, p. 42). Dickens and his works can do both, and nowhere is this more apparent than in the recent exhibitions mounted by the Charles Dickens Museum in London, including "Charles Dickens: Man of Science" (2018) and "Global Dickens: For Every Nation on Earth" (2019). The displays and associated programmes of activities actively seek out new audiences, forge new connections with other institutions and tell stories that inspire visitors to remark, for example, that "few realise that [Dickens] was also one of his era's great scientific communicators" (Shepherd 2018, p. 361), and that "Dickens' depictions of medical conditions were not only acutely observed but also sometimes pre-empted professional recognition" (Moore 2018, p. 392). This volume has the capacity to do the same, in reassessing Dickens so as to highlight his resonance and his wonder.

In order to facilitate the relevance and excitement necessary for reading Dickens differently, what is ultimately required from scholars and readers alike is a change in disposition, in the way described by Christopher Castiglia in his essay entitled "Hope for Critique?" He argues that we must move away from the gravitas inherent in the "habituation" of current critical practice, with its "transcendent" claims of objectivity, and towards an "imaginative idealism" called "hopefulness." In this way, Castiglia believes, scholars can develop "more inventive and experientially diverse" strategies for the assessment of texts and authors. Criticism can thus be freed to occupy "an imaginative space coexisting with and perpetually troubling the imperative here and now within which new ideals, new versions of the real, can be envisioned." He concludes: "Some dispositional change is necessary for critique to get a second wind, to bring to the surface the imaginative idealism that has always been criticism's greatest strength and best hope" (2017, pp. 213, 216,

218, 226). *Reading Dickens Differently* offers such dispositional hopefulness, and allows new sensations, new interrogations and new aspirations in the study of this most iconic of authors to take root, and ultimately, to flourish.

References

Albrecht, Delphine, Bionda, Romain, Borloz, Sophie-Valentine, et al. (2018). *Faire littérature. Usages et pratiques du littéraire (19e–20e siècles)*. Lausanne: Archipel Essais.

Andrews, Malcolm (2006). *Charles Dickens and His Performing Selves: Dickens and the Public Readings*. Oxford: Oxford University Press.

Anker, Elizabeth S., & Felski, Rita (2017). Introduction. In Elizabeth S. Anker & Rita Felski (Eds.), *Critique and Postcritique* (pp. 1–28). Durham, NC & London: Duke University Press.

Barbier, Frédéric (2012). *Histoire du livre en Occident*. Paris: Armand Colin.

Best, Stephen & Marcus, Sharon (2009). Surface Reading: An Introduction. *Representations*, 108(1), 1–21.

Blasselle, Bruno (1998). *Histoire du livre: À pleines pages*. Paris: Gallimard.

Bleich, David (1975). *Readings and Feelings: An Introduction to Subjective Criticism*. Urbana, IL: National Council of Teachers of English.

Bleich, David (1978). *Subjective Criticism*. Baltimore, MD: Johns Hopkins University Press.

Bloom, Harold (2000). *How to Read and Why*. New York: Scribner.

Capuano, Peter J. (2015). *Changing Hands: Industry, Evolution, and the Reconfiguration of the Victorian Body*. Ann Arbor: University of Michigan Press.

Castiglia, Christopher (2017). Hope for Critique? In Elizabeth S. Anker & Rita Felski (Eds.), *Critique and Postcritique* (pp. 211–229). Durham, NC & London: Duke University Press.

Cavallo, Guglielmo, & Chartier, Roger (Eds.) (2001). *Histoire de la lecture dans le monde occidental*. Paris: Points Histoire.

Charles Dickens: Man of Science (2018). [Museum exhibition]. London: Charles Dickens Museum. Retrieved from https://dickensmuseum.com/blogs/exhibitions/charles-dickens-man-of-science

Citton, Yves (2007). *Lire, interpréter, actualiser: Pourquoi les études littéraires?* Paris: Éditions Amsterdam.

Citton, Yves (2010). *L'avenir des humanités: Économie de la connaissance ou cultures de l'interprétation?* Paris: Éditions La Découverte.

Clayton, Jay (2003). *Charles Dickens in Cyberspace: The Afterlife of the Nineteenth Century in Postmodern Culture*. Oxford: Oxford University Press.

Collins, Jim (2010). *Bring on the Books for Everybody: How Literary Culture Became Popular Culture*. Durham, NC & London: Duke University Press.

Compagnon, Antoine (2007). *What is Literature for?* Trans. Liz Libbrecht. Marseille: OpenEdition. Retrieved from https://books.openedition.org/cdf/3314

Coover, Robert (1992, 21 June). The End of Books. *The New York Times*. Retrieved from http://movies2.nytimes.com/books/98/09/27/specials/coover-end.html

Dames, Nicholas (2007). *The Physiology of the Novel: Reading, Neural Science and the Form of Victorian Fiction*. Oxford: Oxford University Press.

Eco, Umberto (1979). *The Role of the Reader: Explorations in the Semiotics of Texts*. Bloomington: Indiana University Press.

Felski, Rita (2015). *The Limits of Critique*. Chicago: University of Chicago Press.

Felski, Rita (2016). Introduction. *New Literary History*, 47(2–3), 215–229.

Fish, Stanley (1980). *Is There a Text in this Class? The Authority of Interpretative Communities*. Cambridge, MA: Harvard University Press.

Forster, John (1872–1874). *The Life of Charles Dickens*. 3 vols. London: Chapman and Hall.

Global Dickens: For Every Nation on Earth (2019). [Museum exhibition]. London: Charles Dickens Museum. Retrieved from https://dickensmuseum.com/blogs/exhibitions/global-dickens-for-every-nation-upon-earth

Greenblatt, Stephen (1991). Resonance and Wonder. In Ivan Karp & Steven D. Lavine (Eds.), *Exhibiting Cultures: The Poetics and Politics of Museum Display* (pp. 42–56). Washington & London: Smithsonian Institution Press.

Hamilton, Nigel (2014). Foreword. In Hans Renders & Binne de Haan (Eds.), *Theoretical Discussions of Biography: Approaches from History, Microhistory, and Life Writing* (pp. ix–xi). Leiden & Boston: Brill.

Hayles, N. Katherine (1999). *How We Became Posthuman: Virtual Bodies in Cybernetics, Literature and Informatics*. Chicago: University of Chicago Press.

Hayles, N. Katherine (2012). *How We Think: Digital Media and Contemporary Technogenesis*. Chicago: University of Chicago Press.

Hillis Miller, J. (2002). *On Literature*. Abingdon: Routledge.

Holland, Norman N. (1975). *5 Readers Reading*. New Haven, CT: Yale University Press.

Iser, Wolfgang (1980). *The Act of Reading: A Theory of Aesthetic Response*. Baltimore, MD: Johns Hopkins University Press.

Jauss, Hans Robert (1982). *Toward an Aesthetic of Reception*. Trans. Timothy Bahti. Minneapolis: University of Minnesota Press.

Jockers, Matthew L. (2013). *Macroanalysis: Digital Methods & Literary Analysis*. Urbana, Chicago & Springfield: University of Illinois Press.

Jouve, Vincent (2010). *Pourquoi étudier la littérature?* Paris: Armand Colin.

Latour, Bruno (2004). Why Has Critique Run out of Steam? From Matters of Fact to Matters of Concern. *Critical Inquiry*, 30(2), 225–248.

Leenhardt, Jacques, & Jozsa, Pierre (1982). *Lire la lecture: Essai de sociologie de la lecture*. Paris: Éditions le Sycomore.

Lister, Martin, Dovey, John, Giddings, Seth, & Kelly, Kieran (2009). *New Media: A Critical Introduction*. 2nd ed. Abingdon: Routledge.

Macé, Marielle (2011). *Façons de lire, manières d'être*. Paris: Gallimard.

Macé, Marielle (2016). *Styles: Critique de nos formes de vie*. Paris: Gallimard.

Magnússon, Sigurður Gylfi (2017). The Life is Never Over: Biography as a Microhistorical Approach. In Hans Renders, Binne de Haan & Jonne Harmsma (Eds.), *The Biographical Turn: Lives in History* (pp. 42–52). London: Routledge.

Moore, Wendy (2018, 21 July). Exhibition: Charles Dickens' Scientific Network. *The Lancet*, 392(10143), 204.

Moretti, Franco (2013). *Distant Reading*. London: Verso.

Patoine, Pierre-Louis (2015). *Corps/Texte: Pour une théorie de la lecture empathique (Cooper, Danielewski, Frey, Palahniuk)*. Lyon: ENS Éditions.

Peltonen, Matti (2014). What is Micro in Microhistory? In Hans Renders & Binne de Haan (Eds.), *Theoretical Discussions of Biography: Approaches from History, Microhistory, and Life Writing* (pp. 105–118). Leiden & Boston: Brill.

Picard, Michel (1986). *La Littérature comme jeu*. Paris: Éditions de Minuit.

Renders, Hans, de Haan, Binne, & Harmsma, Jonne (2017). The Biographical Turn: Biography as Critical Method in the Humanities and in Society. In Hans Renders, Binne de Haan & Jonne Harmsma (Eds.), *The Biographical Turn: Lives in History* (pp. 3–11). London: Routledge.

Schaeffer, Jean-Marie (2012). *Petite écologie des études littéraires: Pourquoi et comment étudier la littérature?* Paris: Marchaisse.

Shepherd, Alison (2018, 16 May). Science and Literature: A Tale of Two Dickens. *British Medical Journal*, 361. doi: https://doi.org/10.1136/bmj.k2169

Shore, Daniel (2018). *Cyberformalism: Histories of Linguistic Forms in the Digital Archive*. Baltimore, MD: Johns Hopkins University Press.

Todorov, Tzvetan (2007). *La littérature en peril*. Paris: Flammarion.

Wardrip-Fruin, Noah, & Montfort, Nick (Eds.) (2003). *The New Media Reader*. Cambridge, MA: MIT Press.

Wall, John N. (2014). Transforming the Object of our Study: The Early Modern Sermon and the Virtual Paul's Cross Project. *Journal of Digital Humanities*, 3(1). Retrieved from http://journalofdigitalhumanities.org/3-1/transforming-the-object-of-our-study-by-john-n-wall/

Wall, John N. (Ed.) (n.d.). *Virtual St Paul's Cathedral Project*. Raleigh: North Carolina State University. Retrieved from https://vpcp.chass.ncsu.edu/

Warhol, Robyn (Ed.) (n.d.). *Victorian Serial Novels*. Columbus: Ohio State University. Retrieved from http://victorianserialnovels.org/

Part I

Reconfiguring Dickens

1

Dickens's Burial in Westminster Abbey

The Untold Story

Leon Litvack

While Dickens's life and work have been pored over by countless biographers, his death and burial are given far more cursory treatment (see Garnett 2008, p. 107) – partly because of the apparent scarcity of verifiable detail, and also on account of the deliberate attempt, by John Forster and others, to frame the narrative in such a way as to advance, as quickly as possible, towards Poets' Corner: that national pantheon, reserved for the country's literary élite, in the south transept of Westminster Abbey.

The full story of what happened at Gad's Hill in Dickens's final hours is difficult to reconstruct; however, one important contributing factor is that Forster (his closest friend) was at the time 250 miles away, at Launceston in Cornwall (Henderson 1979, p. 36). Dickens collapsed, while at dinner, on Wednesday 8 June 1870, in the company of his sister-in-law Georgina Hogarth; she initiated a flurry of activity, which included sending for medical assistance, alerting the family, informing Wilkie Collins (another of Dickens's intimate associates; see Baker et al. 2005, 2:292), and telling the author's lover, Ellen Ternan (Storey 1939, p. 137; Adrian 1957, p. 137; Tomalin 1990, p. 275). Forster briefly recounts in his authorised *Life of Charles Dickens* that Dickens's daughters, Mamie and Katey (who were visiting a friend; see Storey 1939, p. 136; Mamie Dickens 1897, p. 122), arrived that night, together with the author's physician, Frank Beard (Forster 25 November 1873). They were informed by telegram (the quickest possible means), as was Charley Dickens, who arrived the following morning (Forster 1928, p. 852). Other sources reveal that the local doctor at Strood, Stephen Steele, was also fetched, by the young page-boy Isaac Armatage (E[dwards] 1931, p. 234); Steele reached Gad's Hill at 6:30 (20 minutes after the stroke) and, by his own account, "found Dickens lying on the floor of the dining room in a fit." After having him moved to a couch he "applied clysters [enemas] and other remedies to the patient without effect" (Hughes 1891, p. 244). Beard relieved Steele, and stayed with Dickens through the night, together with Georgina, Katey, and Mamie, who remembers "keeping hot bricks to the feet which nothing could warm, hoping and praying

Reading Dickens Differently, First Edition. Edited by Leon Litvack and Nathalie Vanfasse.
© 2020 John Wiley & Sons Ltd. Published 2020 by John Wiley & Sons Ltd.

that [Dickens] might open his eyes and look at us" (Mamie Dickens 1897, p. 123). Steele returned in the morning (Thursday 9 June), and found that there was "no change in the symptoms, and stertorous [heavy] breathing, which had commenced before, now continued." While Georgina and the family were satisfied with the course of treatment, Steele thought otherwise:

> I said, 'That may be so ... but we have a duty to perform, not only to you, my dear madam, and the family of Mr. Dickens, but also to the public. What will the public say if we allow Charles Dickens to pass away without further medical assistance? Our advice is to send for Dr. Russell Reynolds.' (Hughes 1891, p. 244)

Thus Charley Dickens sent a telegram (Figure 1.1) from Higham (the nearest village) to George Holsworth, at the office of *All the Year Round* in London, to fetch,

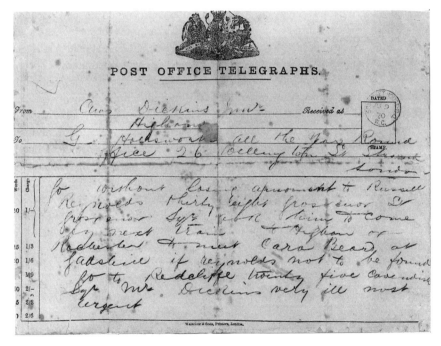

Figure 1.1 Telegram from Charley Dickens, Higham, to George Holsworth, *All the Year Round* Office, 26 Wellington St, Strand, London, 9 June 1870. The text (received at Somerset House) reads as follows: "Go without losing a moment to Russell Reynolds thirty eight Grosvenor St Grosvenor Sq^r tell him to come by next train to Higham or Rochester to meet Cara Beard [*sic*; that is, Dickens's physician, Francis Carr Beard], at Gadshill if Reynolds not to be found go to Redcliffe [*sic*] twenty five Cavendish Sq^r Mr Dickens very ill most urgent." "Redcliffe" is in fact Charles Bland Radcliffe (1822–1899), another eminent neurologist, who specialised in epilepsy and the electrical physiology of muscles and nerves. By kind permission of the Guildhall Museum, Rochester.

"without losing a moment," the eminent consultant neurologist John Russell Reynolds (see Obituary 1896; Eadie 2007), as his father was "very ill" (Dickens Jr 9 June 1870). It is interesting to follow the physicians' train of thought: they recognised not only the anxiety of those assembled – Dickens's devoted sister-in-law, his children, friends, including Mary Boyle (Boyle and Boyle 1902, p. 243), and, as noted above, Ellen Ternan – but also the distress of the nation at the prospect of losing so prominent a figure without employing what would now be termed "heroic measures" – that is, extraordinary life-sustaining treatment. Rescuing Dickens for "the public" therefore became a factor in his care; but even someone as skilled and knowledgeable as Reynolds, whose "personal interest" in his patients was his guiding principle (Obituary 1896, p. 1423) could not save the dying author. Steele recalls that on seeing the patient, the neurologist concluded, "He cannot live" (Hughes 1891, p. 244). The *Times* records Dickens's physical state at the end: "The pupil of the right eye was much dilated, that of the left contracted, the breathing stertorous, the limbs flaccid until half an hour before death, when some convulsion occurred" (The Late 1870, p. 9). Dickens expired at about 6:10 p.m.

It is important to note that medical cases like Dickens's should not be judged from a twenty-first-century perspective, where a range of effective treatments can be applied to victims of stroke. Pat Jalland usefully asserts that "Therapeutic medicine had a very limited power to cure disease" before the 1930s; nevertheless, she adds, "Upper- and middle-class Victorian families placed great reliance on their doctors while relatives were dying, despite their recognition of medicine's therapeutic weakness" (Jalland 1996, pp. 77, 81). When Reynolds submitted his fee note to Georgina, she sent it on to Dickens's solicitor, Frederic Ouvry, with a letter that began, "I enclose Dr. Reynolds' demand [of £20] for his fruitless visit" (Hogarth July 1870).

An exhaustive account of whom the family contacted first, in the hours following this momentous – though at that stage still private – event, is not discernible from existing evidence. Katey hurried to London to tell her mother (Storey 1939, p. 137), while Henry Dickens (who had been at Cambridge) arrived two hours too late, having been told the news by the porter at Higham railway station (Adrian 1957, p. 137; Curry 1988, p. 57). Letitia Austin (Dickens's surviving sister) also came. Thus by eight o'clock on the evening of 9 June word had begun to spread. The public, of course, had to be informed, though how this was effected, and by whom, is not recorded; what is now clear, though, is that one prominent person who did learn, on 9 June, of Dickens's death was the Dean of Westminster, Arthur Penrhyn Stanley.

Stanley (Figure 1.2) met Dickens on three occasions, very late on in the author's life (Adrian 1956, p. 152): at a dinner gathering in February 1870, at the Royal Academy Banquet in April (Banquet 1870, p. 10), and at the Deanery at Westminster Abbey in May. The introduction was made by Frederick Locker (later Locker-Lampson; Figure 1.3), whose first wife, Charlotte, was Stanley's sister-in-law. Locker was known as a poet and book collector; his literary friends included

Figure 1.2 Arthur Penrhyn Stanley, Dean of Westminster (1815–1881). Frontispiece to *The Life and Correspondence of Arthur Penrhyn Stanley*, vol. 1 (1893).

Thackeray, Bulwer Lytton, Wilkie Collins, George Cruikshank, Trollope and Tennyson (who was godfather to his eldest son). His reminiscences of Dickens were recorded in 1883, and published posthumously in a volume of memoirs, entitled *My Confidences* (1896). Locker's recollection of dates is somewhat imprecise: he writes that he first met the author in 1843 or 1844, at an Odd Fellows' club dinner; they encountered one another on several later occasions in succeeding years, including at the Athenaeum in 1848, and at the homes of Charles Knight and Richard Monckton Milnes, later Lord Houghton (Locker-Lampson 1896, pp. 319–321). Dickens and Locker corresponded in the 1850s and 1860s (*Letters* 6:566; 10:167) then met again after a long hiatus, in the summer of 1868, when they dined, together with Longfellow (who was visiting from America), at the home of the publisher George Routledge (*Letters* 12:133, 141, 143, 148).

The pair corresponded on at least a couple of occasions in 1869 (*Letters* 12:366, 374), and in January 1870 Dickens wrote to Locker about the possibility of gaining an introduction to Stanley; he said, "I have the greatest respect for, and interest in, the Dean of Westminster; and should be unusually grateful to [*sic*] any available opportunity of knowing him better. He is to my thinking foremost among the generous and wise spirits of this time" (*Letters* 12:468); the origins of this admiration date from the 1840s, in Dickens's reading a review, written by John Forster for

Figure 1.3 Frederick Locker (1821–1895; later Locker-Lampson). Frontispiece to *My Confidences* (1896).

the *Examiner*, of Stanley's *Life and Correspondence of Thomas Arnold, D.D.* (see Forster 1844; *Letters* 4:201). The pair's first encounter, on 2 February 1870, took place at the home of the Lockers (*Letters* 12:469). Dickens came with Mamie, and, in Locker's estimation, the dinner "went off excellently"; he added: "Arthur [Stanley] said he had had a delightful time, and had found Dickens 'most agreeable'." The last meeting between Dickens, Locker and Stanley occurred in late May 1870, at a dinner party at the Deanery, attended by clergy and politicians (Locker-Lampson 1896, pp. 323, 327).

Stanley's own comments on these events are recorded in a manuscript volume of *Recollections of Events Connected with Westminster Abbey*, composed between 1875 and 1880, and preserved in the Abbey Muniments (the institution's archives). A significant portion of the reminiscences relating to Dickens was transcribed in an article (riddled with errors) by Adrian (1956); but there are other passages which were not reproduced, and which throw further light on the Dean's impressions of the author. Stanley records that at the small dinner party given by the Lockers he was "much struck by [Dickens's] conversation, particularly by a story, which he related with keen appreciation, of the singular dreams of President Lincoln [see Forster 1928, pp. 783, 832], which has since been repeated at length in his biography" (Stanley 1875–1880, pp. 6–7). On the Royal Academy dinner Stanley recalls that Dickens "made one of the only three good speeches that I remember to have heard on the occasions [sic], much coveted and much thought-of, of the dinner" [sic] (Stanley 1875–1880, p. 7). The document conveys the impression that Stanley enjoyed Dickens's company, and appreciated the few opportunities he had to meet the author before he died.

To return to Locker's memoir, just before his comments on dining with Dickens in February, he recalled an interesting conversation he had with Stanley, which is relevant to the Dean's attitude towards the novelist, and to a reconsideration of Dickens's death and funeral. Locker writes:

> I had been talking to Arthur Stanley of the burials in the Abbey, and he told me that there were certain people who he sincerely hoped would survive him, as, if not, however much their friends would desire it, he should be obliged to refuse them burial in the Abbey. The names of one or two distinguished people were mentioned, such as Carlyle and Mill. Then Dickens's name came up, and the Dean said, 'Oddly enough, I have only once met Dickens. I do not know him; I have read hardly any of his writings; I should like to meet Dickens.' To gratify this pious wish, I asked Dickens and his daughter to dine. (Locker-Lampson 1896, pp. 322–323)

The prose in this passage is fascinating: according to Locker, the pair were talking about burials in the Abbey, and the Dean ruled out Carlyle and Mill (eventually buried in Ecclefechan and Avignon, respectively), on account of personal antipathies to both. The fact that, in the next sentence, "Dickens's name came up" would indicate that this was in the context of who should be buried in the Abbey, rather than who should come to dinner.

The Dean and Chapter had ultimate authority over burials and the erection of monuments in the Abbey. Rowland Prothero, in his biography of Stanley, outlines the arrangements that were made for some of the interments that occurred during the Dean's tenure (1864–1881); he gives the number of burials as 15 (Prothero 1893, 2:320), though in fact there were 26, including Lord Palmerston (Prime Minister, 1865); Sir John Herschel (mathematician and astronomer, 1871); Sir Edward Bulwer Lytton (1873); David Livingstone (missionary and explorer – died 1873, buried 1874); Lady Augusta Stanley (the Dean's wife, and formerly a member of the Royal Household, 1876); and Sir Rowland Hill (postal reformer, 1879) (*Westminster Abbey* 1811–1899, pp. 213–264). These individuals were buried in the Abbey under various circumstances and rubrics, and Stanley himself officiated at most of the funerals. Members of the Northumberland family, for example, had been buried by "prescriptive right" in their family vault in St. Nicholas's Chapel since 1745 (Prothero 1893, 2:320); members of the clergy were entitled to burial, without a fee; Lord Palmerston was interred at the government's request; the burial of Rowland Hill (who introduced the Penny Post) was, by Stanley's own admission, "reluctantly accepted in consequence of the persistent representation of the daily press," though he did not officiate, or preach the memorial sermon (Stanley 1875–1880, p. 52; see The Late Sir Rowland, p. 8). The Dean was, therefore, the key to the interment of most of the public figures – including Dickens – in the Abbey. While the details of the author's burial have been cursorily picked over by a few scholars, particularly Arthur Adrian, but also by Stanley's biographer, who relies on Prothero and Adrian, but not (surprisingly) Stanley's *Recollections* (Witheridge 2013, pp. 269–271), what is newly revealed here are the particulars of Stanley's meetings with Dickens in the months before his death, the Dean's sentiments about the author, and the role that Frederick Locker played in facilitating these encounters.

Locker occupied a key position in communications between Stanley and those closest to Dickens – especially his son Charley and his friend John Forster – in the hours following the author's death; but this role has not been heretofore recognised, on account of an absence of documentary evidence. In the archives of the Armstrong Browning Library in Texas, there are two key pieces of correspondence. The first is a letter from Stanley to Locker, dated 9 June 1870; the text is as follows:

Address: F. Locker | 91 Victoria St.

Private   June 9/70
             Deanery.
             Westminster.

My dear Fred,
Alas!– how soon we have been overtaken by the event which we were anticipating as so distant. I cannot amply thank you for having given me the opportunity of having met Charles Dickens while there was yet time.

You will gather from what I have already said that I am quite prepared to raise any proposals about the burial that may be made to me.

             Yours sincerely
             A P STANLEY (Stanley 9 June 1870)

While the text has never before been published, the document was mentioned by Stanley himself, in the *Recollections*: he recorded that this letter, in which he had "given it to be understood (privately) that I would consent to the interment if it was demanded," had "gone astray" (Stanley 1875–1880, p. 12; see also Adrian 1956, p. 153; a modified version of these later reminiscences appears in Prothero 1893, 2:322).

There are several significant aspects to this short note. The first, as intimated above, is the date: 9 June 1870 – that is, the day Dickens died. The envelope accompanying the letter carries no stamp or postmark, which strongly suggests that it was hand-delivered: the distance between the Deanery and 91 Victoria Street (Locker's residence) is about a third of a mile. Also, Stanley writes, "You will gather from what I have already said ..."; this would seem to refer to the discussion (analysed above) that he and Locker had about Carlyle, Mill and Dickens. Another important consideration rests on the final phrase, which refers to "any proposals about the burial that may be made to me"; this suggests that the Dean wished Locker to show this letter to relevant parties – in this case members of Dickens's family, and John Forster, who, as the author's most trusted friend and one of his executors (see Patten 2019, pp. 66, 88), took charge of arrangements for the funeral and burial. The regulations for interment in the Abbey stipulated that an individual could only be considered for burial there if an approach was made to the Dean and Chapter. In this vein it is significant to note Stanley's disappointment at not being able to bury Lord Stratford de Redcliffe in the Abbey in August 1880, owing to the absence of a formal request (Stanley 1875–1880, pp. 3B–4B).

Locker records that he heard of Dickens's death while staying with Tennyson at Aldworth House, near Haslemere. He says that he returned to London by train on Friday 10 June, and found the note from his brother-in-law waiting for him. In his written record, however, he fails to transcribe Stanley's words accurately; he writes: "I found a note waiting for me from Arthur Stanley, thanking me for having made him acquainted with Charles Dickens 'while there was yet time,' and adding that he was 'prepared to receive any communication from the family respecting the burial'." He "at once sent [the Dean's] note on to Charles Dickens, junior, then at Gad's Hill, whom up to that time I had never seen" (Locker-Lampson 1896, p. 327); Locker forwarded this important communication together with a covering note. That message does not survive; but Locker took the trouble to copy out its contents:

> Copy of my letter to Charles Dickens (Junr.)
>
> Private.
>
> I wrote, fearing that in your great sorrow any letter on almost any subject may appear an intrusion, but I wish to send you a copy of a letter that I have just received from Dean Stanley & I think it will explain itself. If I can be of any use pray tell me.
>
> I hope that hereafter you will assure Mrs Dickens your brothers & sisters & Miss Hogarth how sincerely we sympathize with them.
>
> I am going today to Mr. Tennyson's Blackdown Haslemere, but I shall be in London on Monday morning.
>
> F. LOCKER (Locker 10 June 1870)

There is some confusion on Locker's part about when he was at Aldworth (referred to in the note as "Blackdown Haslemere"): his 1883 reminiscences claim that he was with Tennyson at the time he heard about Dickens's death; but this letter from 1870 demonstrates that he was going to the poet's house on 10 June. This uncertain detail does not take away from the fact that Locker was apprehensive about making this approach, given the suddenness and import of what had just occurred; yet he clearly saw himself as the most appropriate intermediary between the Dickens family and Stanley, a prominent representative of the Established Church, though with a distinctly liberal outlook, as exemplified by the Dean's attitudes to Tractarianism; his tolerant approach towards the Prince of Wales on their excursion to Egypt and Palestine; and his views on Nonconformists (see Witheridge 2013, pp. 86–88, 122–123, 223–231, 272–273). The Dean would likewise have envisaged for Locker this role of intermediary, given that Stanley himself did not know Dickens well.

There also exists another new piece of evidence concerning Stanley's desire to have Dickens buried in the Abbey. On Saturday 11 June he wrote to his cousin Louisa about a number of matters of mutual interest, including the recent death of the author:

> Do you remember my being at Alderley [the Stanley family seat] – at the Park – when Pickwick was being read. [sic] That was my first acquaintance with Dickens – & indeed, I think, all that I ever read of Pickwick. I never met him till this year – when I dined with him for the first time at my brother in laws, F. Locker – & was much pleased with him – & then he dined with us. I also heard him make his speech at the Royal Academy dinner which was quite admirable. And now he is gone – & it is not improbable that I may bury him –. (Stanley 11 June 1870)

The final phrase is extremely telling: by this stage in the proceedings the Dean had already confirmed that he was ready to accept a proposal for burial, and presumably knew about Locker's conveying his message, together with a covering note, to Charley, who was at Gad's Hill. Forster arrived at Dickens's country house on the Saturday (11 June), but did not communicate with Stanley over the weekend about burial in the Abbey; instead, arrangements were apparently made to accede to Dickens's wishes, and inter him in the graveyard of one of the two churches near Gad's Hill: at St Nicholas Church, in Strood, or at the Church of St. Peter and St. Paul, in Shorne (see Hughes 1891 p. 87). These plans (for which no archival evidence exists) were abandoned, however, when a request came from the Vice-Dean and Chapter of Rochester Cathedral to bury him there.

While the Rochester interment initiative is mentioned in several standard sources (Storey 1939, p. 138; Mamie Dickens 1897 p. 126; Sala 1870, p. 114; Hughes 1891, p. 87), the evidence has not been heretofore examined. The executors left many of the practical arrangements for Dickens's funeral to Franklin George Homan, a partner in a firm of Thomas and Homan, auctioneers, cabinet-makers and upholsterers, based at 147 High Street, Rochester, to whom Dickens's estate paid £78.12.0 in November 1870 (*Executors* 1870–1896, 14 November 1870). Homan carried out joinery, upholstery and decorating work for Dickens at Gad's Hill (*Letters* 10:22; 11:263, 265; 12:48–50); after the author's death he conducted the valuation for probate, and sold the furniture and other domestic effects (*Gad's Hill* 1870). His involvement in the plan to bury Dickens in the Cathedral is confirmed in the Chapter minutes of 23 June, when a meeting was held between the Vice-Dean of Rochester, John Griffith, and two of the Canons, Thomas Robinson and Anthony Grant. Under the agenda item "Intended Grave for C. Dickens" there appear the following resolutions:

> Ordered that Mess[rs] Foord [John Foord & Sons, a firm of builders in Rochester] be instructed to forthwith send in their bill for the preparation of Grave in Saint Mary's Chapel originally intended for the late Mr. Charles Dickens and Ordered that upon the Treasurer being satisfied with the correctness of the charge he do pay the same.
>
> Ordered that the following Letter be written and sent to Mess[rs] Thomas & Homan
>
> The Precinct, Rochester
23rd June 1870
>
> Dear Sirs,
>
> In reference to the communication to the Vice Dean respecting the desire of the representatives of the late Mr. Charles Dickens to take upon themselves the cost of the Vault prepared for the burial of the distinguished Gentleman in the Cathedral, the Chapter desire me to inform you, and they beg you will communicate to the Executors, that while they highly appreciate the kindness and consideration which prompted the offer, they must be permitted to positively decline it. In proposing as they did to the family that the resting-place of their eminent relative should be within Rochester Cathedral, they desired to offer a tribute to his memory; and they believed, as they still believe, that no more fitting or honourable spot for his sepulture could be found than amidst scenes to which he was fondly attached, and among those by whom he was personally known as a neighbour and held in such honour.
>
> This feeling they believe was participated in by all the inhabitants of this neighbourhood. And although the wish of the Chapter could not be gratified and the burial finally took place at Westminster they cannot allow the slight expense that has been incurred to be borne by any but themselves.
>
> I am, Dear Sirs, Yours faithfully,
Geo. H. Knight   Joint Chapter Clerk
(*Rochester Cathedral* 1870, pp. 276–277)

This correspondence was sent in the wake of a letter written by Georgina Hogarth to Dickens's solicitor, Frederic Ouvry, on 18 June; she intimated that "there had been some expenses incurred by the Cathedral people at Rochester in preparing that grave, tolling the bell, etc.," and she wondered whether a reimbursement was required (because the interment was aborted) even though, she added, "no demand has been made" (Adrian 1956, p. 156). The letter from the Chapter quoted above not only instructs Homan to inform the author's executors that a reimbursement was unnecessary; it also confirms that the offer of burial in the Cathedral came from Vice-Dean Griffith and the Chapter. This then becomes a case of the ecclesiastical authorities' acting on what they described as the "wish" of "all the inhabitants of this neighbourhood" to offer an "honourable spot" for Dickens's "sepulture," regardless of the directions of the deceased. It is also useful to note that Georgina Hogarth intimated to Mary Howitt in a letter of September 1870 that the family would have preferred burial in the Cathedral:

> We should have preferred Rochester Cathedral, and it was a great disappointment to the people there that we had to give way to the *larger* demand. Rochester would have been a sort of shrine for him – he loved the place so much – it was the home of his boyhood – and close to the dear home of his last years – and the scenes of his first, and last, book are laid there. (Adrian 1956, p. 156; emphasis original)

Existing evidence does not clarify how the "*larger* demand" for burial in the Abbey was formulated or communicated. In his *Recollections* Stanley does not mention burial in a vault in Rochester Cathedral as a possibility; instead he only records that "apparently the funeral was to take place in Rochester," and adds, in a later note, "In the church yard [sic] of Rochester Cathedral where however burial was no longer legal" (Stanley 1875–1880, p. 11). It is curious that he does not mention the vault prepared by John Foord and Sons; instead he only alludes to the aborted plan to bury Dickens in the churchyard, which had in any case been closed by order of the Privy Council (Adrian 1956, p. 156). Yet on the Saturday (11 June) the Dean, as indicated above, told his cousin Louisa that it was "not improbable" that he would bury Dickens in the Abbey. Just as the officials at Rochester had imagined themselves as representing the interests of the public at large, Stanley too imagined himself as representing a "*larger* demand" – that of the national interest; thus the considerations at both Rochester and Westminster were similar to those of the physicians Frank Beard and Stephen Steele, in their desire to recruit John Russell Reynolds, and thus offer the most publicly appropriate and expected professional treatment to the dying man.

These newly discovered letters alter the accepted narrative concerning the path towards Dickens's burial in Westminster Abbey. It is clear that Stanley was aware of the Rochester plan; but it appears that he chose to disregard it – or even engineered to overrule it – so as to advance his own initiative to bury Dickens at Westminster. The evidence is clear concerning the extent of the preparations at Rochester; but Stanley's own pronouncements demonstrate that the offer to have the author's remains interred in the Abbey came from the Dean on the very day of Dickens's death, rather than in the wake of the leader that appeared in the *Times* on Monday 13 June 1870, which made this appeal:

> If his friends prefer it, let them have as quiet a funeral as they please; their wishes will be religiously respected. But let him lie in the Abbey. Where Englishmen gather to review the memorials of the great masters and teachers of their nation, the ashes and the name of the greatest instructor of the nineteenth century should not be absent. (Charles Dickens 1870, p. 11; see Litvack in press).

Thus when Forster asserts towards the close of his *Life* that "the *Times* took the lead in suggesting that the only fit resting-place for the remains of a man so dear to England was the Abbey" (Forster 1928, p. 855), he was shaping his narrative so as to offer a fitting conclusion, ostensibly bolstered by public support, to the exemplary life he was documenting. The reality, however, was rather different: in his authorised biography he did not – indeed could not – take into account Stanley's own feelings for Dickens, moulded through two recent personal encounters with the author; nor could he include any of the communications which passed between the interested parties in the days after Dickens's death. This is most telling, in terms of Forster's creating a narrative that has been accepted without question in historiography – up to now; what is beginning to emerge here, however, on account of new evidence, is a biographical "turn" that corrects and reshapes an established narrative (Renders et al. 2017, p. 10).

By daybreak on Monday 13 June there was still no approach from the family, or from any prominent associate of Dickens. Stanley records in his *Recollections* that

> On Monday Morning there appeared an elaborate leading article in the 'Times' newspaper, recommending strongly his burial in Westminster Abbey as the one place which alone could receive a person of such great distinction. Still, as I had received no application from any person in authority, I took no steps. (Stanley 1875–1880, p. 11)

But Stanley was determined to have his way. He therefore wrote to his friend Lord Houghton (formerly Richard Monckton Milnes), who was also a long-time intimate of both Dickens and Locker (Reid 1891, 1:110, 2:453–454), to reiterate his readiness to receive a request from those close to the author, and to emphasise that without such an approach he could not act unilaterally:

> June 13 '70
> Deanery.
> Westminster.
>
> My dear Lord Hougton,
>   On hearing of the news of the death of Charles Dickens, I communicated to his family, thr[ough] F. Locker that I should be ready to receive any proposal for his burial in the Abbey.
>   I have had no intimation of any kind – & it is possible that they have determined against it.
>   The usual course in these cases – (& the most suitable, for obvious reasons) – is that friends & distinguished persons should present the case to the Dean & ask for his approval. [sic] & I am unwilling to depart from this precedent, because, if the Dean were to take the initiative, a funeral of this kind would be regarded as an expression of his individual feeling, rather than of the public sentiment. But I am unwilling that a tribute of this nature, if desired by the public & the friends, should miscarry through any misunderstanding. Hence this note. Will you kindly act as you think best. [sic]
>
>   Yours siny,
>   A.P. STANLEY. (Stanley 13 June 1870)

Stanley's train of thought here merits closer examination: he feels that he cannot approach the Dickens family directly, on account of precedent, and because he does not wish to be seen as putting his individual interests forward; at the same time, however, he is strongly committed to seizing the opportunity to bury Dickens in the Abbey, and so is keen to find an intermediary to expedite his design. Houghton/Milnes had been a close friend of Dickens since 1840; the pair enjoyed a spirited correspondence, dined together on many occasions, and supported some of the same causes, including authors' copyright (*Letters* 2:54; 3:292; 4:135, 139, 331; 6:641). Because the peer was also a close associate of many friends of Dickens (including Forster), it seems clear that Stanley wished Houghton to appeal to those close to the recently deceased author, to make the necessary approach to the Dean.

It is not clear whether Houghton intervened; it is possible that Stanley also asked others to intercede. Nevertheless, very shortly after Stanley wrote the above letter – on the same morning, in fact – Forster, accompanied by Charley, appeared at the Deanery. The Dean recorded what transpired in his *Recollections*:

> At eleven o'clock there arrived Mr. Forster – his future biographer – and his son. When they entered Mr. Forster was at first, and also during several passages of the interview, so much overcome by the violence of his grief that he could hardly speak. Indeed, I have never seen any man so overcome by sorrow as he appeared to be on that occasion. When he had recovered his calmness he said, 'I imagine the article in the "Times" must have been

written with your concurrence.' I replied, 'No, I had no concern with it, but at the same time I had given it privately to be understood that I would consent to the interment if it was demanded.' The letter, it seems, had gone astray, and therefore it was only on this expression of public feeling in the 'Times' that they had ventured to apply. I said, 'After this expression in the "Times," of course all further application is unnecessary, and I at once consent.' (Stanley 1875–1880, pp. 11–12)

The particulars of Dickens's own wishes about his burial, the further negotiations between the family and Dean Stanley, the private funeral, the opening of the grave to the public (Figure 1.4), the presence of Ellen Ternan, and the memorial address delivered by Stanley, may be consulted elsewhere (Forster 1928, p. 859; Mamie Dickens 1897, p. 126; Storey 1939, p. 138; Stanley 1875–1880, pp. 12–18; Prothero 1893, pp. 322–324; Witheridge 2013, p. 270; Adrian 1956, p. 154; Adrian 1957, pp. 138–139; Funeral 1870; Garnett 2008; Dean Stanley 1870, p. 14). What is relevant to the present discussion, though, is the question of what went through the minds of Arthur Penrhyn Stanley, Frederick Locker, Lord Houghton, John Forster, Georgina Hogarth, Charley Dickens and perhaps others in the period leading up

Figure 1.4 "The Grave of Charles Dickens in Poets' Corner, Westminster Abbey," in *Illustrated London News*, 25 June 1870, p. 652.

to the meeting in the Deanery on 13 June, and especially what part Stanley's letter of 9 June played in this narrative.

The short answer is that Charley did not read the letter until the evening of 13 June; this is made clear in his reply, which has not heretofore been published:

Gadshill Place
14 June 1870

My dear Mr. Locker,

I regret extremely that your very kind letter of the 10th should remain without reply. But it was placed with some of my father's papers, and it only came into my hands last evening. All here desire me to thank you very sincerely for your kindness. As for Dean Stanley it is impossible for me to say how much we all owe him, or how deeply sensible we are of his thoughtful consideration. Without him we should have been quite unable to have complied with the public wish, and to have, at the same time, carried out in their integrity the wishes of my late beloved father.

Pray excuse the abruptness of this note, but I am well nigh worn out.

I am, dear Mr. Locker.

Very faithfully yours
CHARLES DICKENS JNR (Dickens Jr 14 June 1870)

This document is significant in several respects. It is clear from the text that Charley did not read the letter quoted above until after the meeting, on the morning of 13 June, that he and Forster had with Stanley. While the timing of the son's reading of Locker's letter did not affect the conduct of the funeral, Charley's reply reinforces the debt owed to the Dean personally, and points to just how significant the private contact with Dickens – as well as with Forster, Charley, Lord Houghton and perhaps others – was for Stanley. In his original note the Dean had emphasised his indebtedness to Locker for "the opportunity of having met Charles Dickens while there was yet time"; thus these complex circumstances coincided – either in a serendipitous fashion, or, as suggested here, through design – to secure this senior churchman's willing participation in this important event in the cultural history of the nation.

In the course of research for this study, other essential details have come to light – particularly concerning the conduct of Dickens's funeral. The Westminster Abbey Muniments possesses a funeral fee book stretching from 1811 to 1899, and featuring details and costs for the burials of many of the famous figures interred during Stanley's tenure and beyond, including Dickens (*Westminster Abbey* 1811–1899, pp. 233–234; Figures 1.5 and 1.6). A careful transcription reveals many previously unknown details:

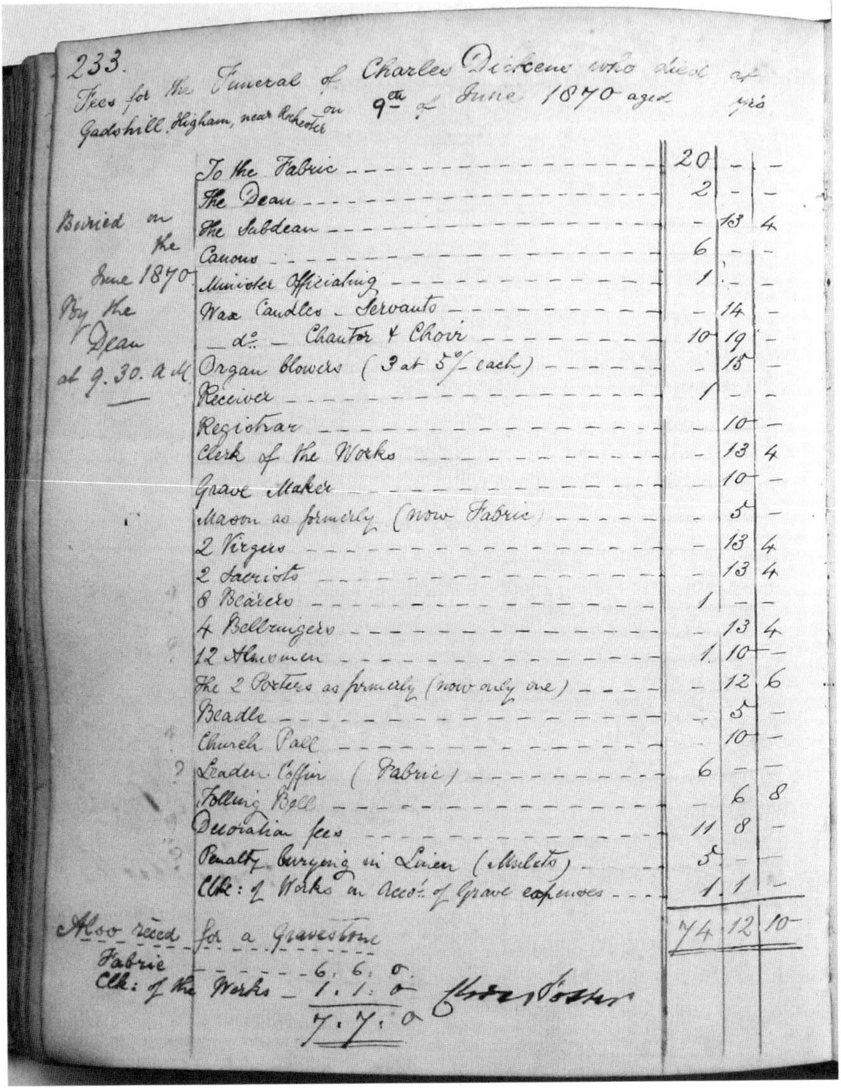

Figure 1.5 First page of Dickens's funeral fee account, Westminster Abbey Funeral Fee book, 1811–1899, folio 233. By kind permission of the Dean and Chapter of Westminster.

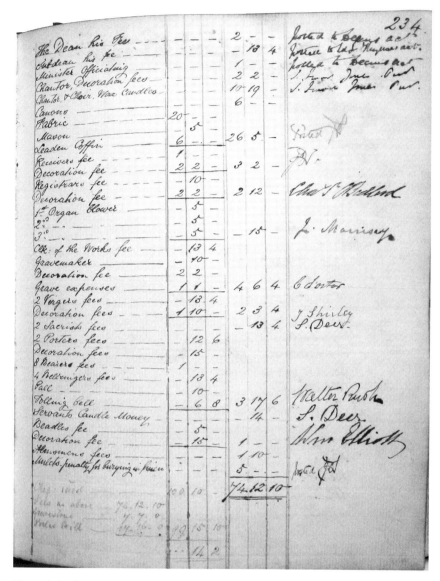

Figure 1.6 Second page of Dickens's funeral fee account, Westminster Abbey Funeral Fee book, 1811–1899, folio 234. By kind permission of the Dean and Chapter of Westminster.

Fees for the Funeral of Charles Dickens who died at Gadshill, Higham, near Rochester, on 9th of June 1870 aged   yrs [sic]

		To the Fabric	20		
		The Dean	2		
	Buried on	The Subdean		13	4
	the	Canons	6		
	June 1870 [sic]	Minister Officiating	1		
By the		Wax candles – Servants		14	
Dean		d⁰ Chantor & Choir	10	19	
at 9.30 am		Organ blowers (3 at 5 °/_ each)		15	
		Receiver	1		
		Registrar		10	
		Clerk of the Works		13	4
		Grave Maker		10	
		Mason as formerly (now Fabric)		5	
		2 Vergers		13	4
		2 Sacrists		13	4
	?	8 Bearers	1		
		4 Bellringers		13	4
	?	12 Almsmen	1	10	
		The 2 Porters as formerly (now only one)		12	6
		Beadle		5	
	?	Church Pall		10	
	?	Leaden Coffin (Fabric)	6		
		Following Bell		6	8
	?	Decoration Fees	11	8	
	?	Penalty burying in Linen (Mulcts)[1]	5		
		Clk: of Works on Acco´- of Grave expenses	1	1	
			74	12	10
	Also reced	for a Gravestone			
	Fabric	6.6.0			
	Clk: of the	Works 1.1.0 Chris Foster[2]			
		7.7.0			

The Dean his Fee				2			Posted to Deans act
Subdean his fee					13	4	posted to Ld J Thynnes[3] act.
Minister Officiating				1			posted to Deans Act
Chantor decoration fees				2	2		S. Flood Jones.[4] Paid
Chantor & Choir. Wax candles				10	19		S. Flood Jones Paid
Canons				6			
Fabric	20						
Mason		5					
Leaden Coffin	6			26	5		Posted JCT[5]
Receivers fee	1						
Decoration fee	2	2		3	2		JCT
Registrars fee		10					
Decoration fee	2	2		2	12		Chas S^t C Bedford[6]
1st Organ Blower		5					
2nd ,, ,,		5					
3rd ,, ,,		5			15		J. Morrisey[7]
Clk: of the Works fee		13	4				
Gravemaker		10					
Decoration fee	2	2					
Grave expenses	1	1		4	6	4	C Foster[8]
2 vergers fees		13	4				
Decoration fees	1	10		2	3	4	T Shirley[9]
2 Sacrists fees					13	4	S. Deer[10]
2 Porters fees		12	6				
Decoration fees		15					
8 bearers fees	1						
4 Bellringers fees		13	4				
Pall		10					
Tolling Bell		6	8	3	17	6	Walter Rush[11]
Servants Candle Money					14		S. Deer
Beadles fee		5					
Decoration fee		15		1			Wm. Elliott[12]
Almsmens fees				1	10		
Mulcts penalty for burying in Linen				5			posted JCT
				74	12	10	
Cheq reced	100	10					
Fees as above 74.12.10							
Gravestone 7.7.0							
Pooles Bill[13] 17.16.0	99	15	10				
	...	14	2				

The account (recorded on two facing pages) offers essential insight into this intensely private event, which was attended (officially) by the 14 mourners: Charley Dickens and his wife Bessie, Henry Dickens, Mamie Dickens, Katey and Charles Collins, Georgina Hogarth, Letitia Austin, Edmund Dickens, Frank Beard, Frederic Ouvry, Wilkie Collins, John Forster and Ellen Ternan (Garnett 2008, pp. 113–114); they were accompanied by the Dean, five members of the Abbey's clergy, and the Clerk of the Works, Christopher Foster (Funeral 1870, p. 12). The Abbey's fee for Dickens's funeral (£100.10s., recorded towards the bottom of Figure 1.6 in pencil), was forwarded by John Forster (Forster 22 July 1870), and compares favourably with the balance sheets for those buried in the church at around the same time (*Westminster Abbey* 1811–1899, pp. 225–226, 229–230, 231–232). Many of the costs are standard and self-explanatory; but it should be noted that in listing the names of various people entitled to fees, on the right-hand side of Figure 1.6 (such as the Sub-Dean Lord John Thynne, the Precentor Samuel Flood Jones, or the Dean's Verger Samuel Deer), it is not clear whether these individuals were present at the funeral: they were eligible for payment on account of their positions, rather than owing to their actual attendance at the event. It is also difficult to establish the precise total number of people in the Abbey on the morning of 14 June, because, according to leader-writer William Stebbing (who relied on information provided by Wilkie Collins, because Forster was overcome by grief; see Baker et al. 2005, 2:194), there were anonymous bystanders present, who joined the official party at the end of the service; he writes:

> The mourners – 14 in number, with perhaps as many more strangers who accidentally chanced to be present – gathered round the grave to take a last look at the coffin which held the great novelist's remains, and to place wreaths of *immortelles* and other flowers upon the coffin lid. (Funeral 1870, p. 12)

One detail from the fee breakdown that does require explanation is the "Penalty burying in Linen (Mulcts)"/"Mulcts penalty for burying in Linen," which appears towards the bottom in Figures 1.5 and 1.6, respectively (owing to the practice of double-entry accounting). This formulation relates to three Acts of Parliament instituted in the reign of Charles II: the Burial in Woollen Acts (passed between 1666 and 1680), which, in order to stimulate the domestic fabric trade, stipulated that the dead should be buried in "Shirt Shift Sheete [*sic*] or Shroud" made of English sheep's wool; if the corpse was interred in a winding sheet, burial garments, or coffin lining made of other materials, a penalty of £5 was payable (Raithby 1819, pp. 598, 885–886, 940). This option was often adopted by the well-to-do, to distinguish them from the general population (Litten 1991, p. 74). The law was repealed in 1814 (Puckle 1926, p. 88), but the tradition was maintained at Westminster Abbey, hence the penalty imposed on Dickens's executors, for burying the author in grave-clothes made of linen. His body was probably laid out and dressed by the women of the household, as was the custom of the time (Litten 1991, p. 124). The precise style of Dickens's shroud is unknown, but a partial idea may be gained from the detailed pencil sketch made by John Everett Millais on 10 June, the day after the author's death (Figure 1.7), for Katey (Storey 1939, p. 137; Millais 1899, pp. 30–33; Mamie Dickens 1897, p. 125). Dickens is depicted with a chin cloth (which served the practical purpose of keeping the mouth of the deceased closed), and with a fabric cravat around the throat; other details of the grave-clothes are concealed beneath the sheet that covers the body from the shoulders downward. With his head on a pillow, Dickens lies on a bed that was brought into the dining room after he died (Curry 1988, p. 57).

By the following day (11 June) Dickens had been placed in a plain, solid oak coffin (Funeral 1870, p. 12). A significant detail, derived from the fee book, is that the coffin was "Leaden" – that is, lead-lined. This feature was part of a series of processes designed both to preserve the body and to prevent seepage of noxious gases and bodily fluids; this was an important consideration, because of the length of time which passed between Dickens's death and the funeral: five days. The coffin was kept open for a time – at least long enough for Forster and others to say their farewells (Henderson 1979, p. 36) – and though it is impossible to tell from surviving details, it is probable that the bottom of the coffin was lined with a tailored mattress, and/or with a mixture of bran and sawdust (often infused with rosemary and balm; see Litten 1991, pp. 92, 114). Dickens's death certificate (which appears here for the first time) is held at Westminster Abbey (Figure 1.8); the event was registered at Strood on Sunday 12 June, by Charles Saunders, the

Figure 1.7 John Everett Millais, *Charles Dickens After Death*. This pencil drawing was executed at Gad's Hill on 10 June 1870. By kind permission of the Charles Dickens Museum.

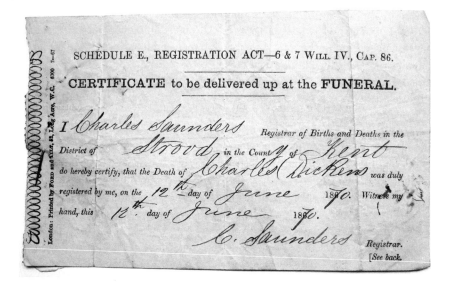

Figure 1.8 Death registration certificate for Charles Dickens, signed by Charles Saunders, Registrar of Births and Deaths for Strood, 12 June 1870, WAM58091. By kind permission of the Dean and Chapter of Westminster.

Registrar for Births and Deaths. On the morning of 14 June (according to the *Times*), the body was taken in a hearse from Gad's Hill to one of the stations on the North Kent Line (probably Higham); from there it was conveyed by special train to Charing Cross station, arriving "punctually at 9 o'clock" (Funeral 15 June 1870, p. 12); the fee paid to the South Eastern Railway was £15.4s. (*Executors* 1870–1896, 1 July 1870).

A second hearse conveyed Dickens's body down Whitehall to the Abbey. Its approach was witnessed by Frederick Locker, who did not attend the funeral, but was privy to the proceedings from without, on account of his intimacy with Dean Stanley:

> The morning of the funeral was very fine. Eleanor and I left 91 Victoria Street at twenty minutes past nine. As we reached the entrance to Dean's Yard, and as St. Stephen's clock chimed the half-hour, a hearse and mourning coaches swept round the Broad Sanctuary; they seemed to bring with them an unusual stillness; then, as they drove under the archway into Dean's Yard, the great bell began to toll. There was hardly a creature in the street or in the Abbey, that 'Temple of Silence and Reconciliation,' and no one but ourselves knew whose funeral had passed, or for whom the big bell was tolling. Later in the day we saw the coffin in the grave, covered with flowers, and then there was an immense crowd of excited and sympathetic mourners. (Locker-Lampson 1896, p. 328)

Locker's use of the phrase 'Temple of Silence and Reconciliation' is extraordinarily pertinent in relation to this study. The quotation comes from Thomas Babington Macaulay's essay *Warren Hastings* (1841), and is used in the context of where the former Governor-General of Bengal should have been buried. Hastings was impeached in 1787 for alleged misgovernment in India, then tried in Westminster Hall; he was acquitted in 1795, and lived the rest of his life at Daylesford, in Worcestershire. He was buried in the churchyard there, rather than in Westminster Abbey. Macaulay objects to this perceived mistreatment of Hastings:

> With all his faults, – and they were neither few nor small – only one cemetery was worthy to contain his remains. In that temple of silence and reconciliation where the enmities of twenty generations lie buried, in the Great Abbey which has during many ages afforded a quiet resting-place to those whose minds and bodies have been shattered by the contentions of the Great Hall, the dust of the illustrious accused should have mingled with the dust of the illustrious accusers. This was not to be. (Macaulay 1903, 3:173)

It is just possible that in evoking the words of Macaulay (who is buried very near Dickens), Locker was referring obliquely to the extraordinary sequence of events in which he and his brother-in-law played key roles, and which ensured that Dickens was laid to rest in Poets' Corner.

This corrective account of Dickens's death and funeral does not end here. Stanley's *Recollections* offer additional insight – particularly in relation to the funeral sermon he preached on 19 June:

> I was, as usual, to preach the funeral sermon on the next Sunday. I had a long conversation with Mr. Alwyne [*sic*], an intimate friend of Dickens and of Forster, who [and from him I learnt much of what was to be said, and what was not to be said, concerning the dead man. He][14] told me amongst other things of the extract from Dickens's will, – which accordingly I determined to read and thus for the first time to make public in the sermon – as to the funeral. (Stanley 1875–1880, p. 18)

The sermon was reported on in the *Times* of 20 June, and the text was published shortly afterwards, owing partly to the fact that Stanley lost his voice, and so could not be heard. The Dean quoted from the close of the will, where Dickens expressed his wish to be buried in an "inexpensive, unostentatious, and strictly private manner," spoke of his personal faith, and exhorted his children to "guide themselves by the teaching of the New Testament" (Stanley 1870, pp. 15–16). What is new here is the fact that the Dean consulted "Mr. Alwyne" – an erroneous rendering of the Rev. Whitwell Elwin, editor of the *Quarterly Review* from 1853 to 1860, a correspondent of Dickens, and one of John Forster's literary executors, thus responsible for "the examining, preservation, or destruction of a vast number of papers and letters" – including those from Dickens (Renton 1912, pp. 263–264; see also *Letters* 1:xix). He had met Forster in 1854, and officiated at his marriage in 1856 (Renton 1912, pp. 108–111); through Forster he was introduced to Dickens, whom he assisted in negotiations with the Royal Literary Fund in 1859–1860, over a large bequest from Forster (*Letters* 9:32, 561–563). After Dickens's death Forster communicated with Elwin, and asked him – in an effort, it seems, to affix the official biographer's seal onto proceedings – to deliver to Stanley the extract from the will, which the Dean used in his sermon. These details appear in the opening paragraph of a letter from Elwin to his friend, written just after the funeral:

> My dear Forster,
> I saw the Dean, & delivered your letter with the extract from the will, [*sic*] He is quite satisfied and much obliged. He took me to see the spot where poor Dickens lies. Many people where [*sic*] seated round looking at the dumb pavement, & the Dean says he hears from the Vergers that numbers come there & weep. (Elwin 15–18 June 1870)

Forster was incapacitated by overwhelming grief, which lasted for some time; yet he was sufficiently resilient at this stage to leak details of his friend's will – which was selectively quoted in the press in July 1870 after being proved at Doctors' Commons (see "Mr. Charles Dickens's Will" 1870, p. 9; Long 2019), and reproduced in full at the close of his *Life* – so that the image of Dickens conveyed by Stanley in the sermon (which prefigured the parting image communicated in the biography) was of someone who "lived and died" in a "simple but sufficient faith" (Stanley 1870, p. 16).

A few weeks later, on 8 July 1870, Elwin wrote to his friend to inquire after his emotional state:

> My Dear Forster,
> I hope I shall hear you are better in mind & body. I do not agree that it is wrong to be depressed. It is no more possible to be insensible to pain of mind than pain of body, but I shall be glad for your sake when cheerfulness returns. The affection happily never wanes, or grief itself would be worth cherishing for the sake of the affection. Your letter made me think, as I often do, what an old friendship ours is, & that not a single shadow has ever come across it from the first hour up to now. And certainly a more chivalrous, generous friend never existed in the world. How often and often have Dickens and myself exchanged this remark. I shall like to know that you meet no difficulties beyond the routine trouble which is inevitable. D. was to my thinking so loveable that I never associated him with his works. It was himself that I valued, & nothing more charming could be conceived. (Elwin 8 July 1870)

These letters attest to Elwin's depth of feeling for both Forster and Dickens, and also make him complicit in manufacturing an image of the author that accorded with what was envisaged for the authorised biography.

Stanley continued to have contact with Forster after Dickens's death – particularly in 1873, over the funeral of Edward Bulwer Lytton, who died in Torquay on 18 January. The first notice of Lytton's death in the *Times* indicated that he would be interred at Knebworth; but plans for burial could not be made straightaway, on account of Lytton's express instruction that his body should remain "untouched" for three days (The Late Lord Lytton 1873, 10). On 23 January a letter in the *Times*, from "F.N.B.," inquired whether Lytton's family had been asked about burial at Westminster. The writer joined the name of Lytton to those of Dickens and Thackeray (the latter was buried at Kensal Green), to form "a triumvirate of Caesars, each worthy of honourable burial." The letter concluded: "To the abbey, which is not only a treasure-house of English history, but which is itself at the very heart and centre of life in England, his body should now be carried" ("F.N.B." 1873, p. 9). Another letter, by "A.A.," published the following day, also associated Lytton with Dickens:

> It is for our sake, not for his, that [Lytton] should be buried with befitting honours in Westminster Abbey. Dickens wished to be buried in a quiet grave at Rochester, and had chosen the very spot for his last resting-place; but his feelings, likewise, were set aside at the bidding of a jealous and grateful people. ("A.A." 1873, p. 8)

Prothero is cautious in his biography about Dean Stanley's part in the proceedings: he simply notes that the burial of Lytton "seemed doubtful" (Prothero 1893, p. 321). A more accurate account of events reveals, however, that Stanley was initially resistant, but relented on account of a combination of public agitation and Forster's pressing the case for his close friend; the Dean records in his *Recollections*:

> Mr. Forster called upon me to request his interment. I think this was the first time I had met him since the affairs connected with Charles Dickens's funeral. He was not moved as he had been on that occasion, but he urged Lord Lytton's claims with great pertinacity. I maintained that I could hardly accept them unless I received a more general request, and suggested that he should endeavour to procure such a general declaration. He called later in the day without any such requisition, but still urged that if a man like Lord Lytton was not buried in the Abbey, He [*sic*] could not see on what ground any one else should be included.

Stanley added that he "thought that this was the funeral which was on the extremest verge of what ought to be allowed" (Stanley 1875–1880, pp. 32, 33), on account of Lytton's marital difficulties and indiscretions (Mitchell 2003, pp. 52–65).

The funeral (at which the Dean officiated) took place on Saturday 25 January; but rather than being buried in Poets' Corner, Lytton was laid in St. Edmund's Chapel, beside Sir Humphrey Bourchier (died 1471), ostensibly in allusion to the appearance of this figure in Lytton's *Last of the Barons* (1843). The *Times* reported this choice of burial plot in a conciliatory fashion:

> Though room for such a guest might, perhaps, have been found in the Corner itself, so that we should have been able to read on stones near together the names of 'Macaulay,' 'Dickens,' 'Lytton,' it was deemed advisable to make a new precedent in order to lessen the pressure upon one particular spot.

After providing clarification on how burials in the Abbey are considered and approved (noting that "The matter ultimately rests with the Dean"), the paper added a mollifying comment: "Considered quite apart from his position, there is no man in England by whom the power of admitting or rejecting any application is more certain to be wisely exercised than by Dean Stanley" (The Funeral of Lord Lytton 1873, p. 8).

Though there is little evidence on Forster's side concerning Lytton's funeral – or Dickens's burial, for that matter – he did show his appreciation to Stanley, by sending him a copy of the first volume of his *Life of Dickens*. Stanley wrote a letter of thanks:

> Jn 6. [72]
> Deanery.
> Westminster.
>
> My dear Sir,
> I have delayed to thank you for your kind remembrance of me & for your kind note till the book had arrived, & I had been able to make acquaintance with its contents.
> We have both [Stanley and his wife, Lady Augusta] been engaged upon it at all odd moments – & I think my foremost feeling is one of sympathy with the good fortune (if I may so call it) which enabled you under so great a personal loss to be touched by the erection of such a memorial – so full of unknown & herewith untold interest – to so dear & valued a friend.
> You are very good to speak so warmly of any assistance I may have rendered in carrying out your wishes & the desire of the country on the occasion of the funeral. The recollection of it will always be treasured amongst the most interesting of the various experiences which I have traversed in my official life.
>
> Yours very faithfully
> A.P. STANLEY. (Stanley 6 June 1872)

Thus the Dean acknowledged the significance in his career of overseeing the final journey of Dickens's remains, to what Forster called the "resting-place ... in which the most illustrious Englishmen are laid" (Forster 1928, p. 855).

The evidence presented in this study clearly confirms A.O.J. Cockshut's conclusion that there is often a necessary tension between "fact and interpretation" in rendering "sensitively-written death scenes" (Cockshut 1974, p. 104). Because of the care taken by Dickens's family and friends to keep the narrative "strictly private" (Forster 1928, p. 855), the task of recovering reliable details about Dickens's death and burial, and thus challenging the accepted myths, has proved particularly hazardous; but it is significant that the most fruitful sources of information have been those closely associated with Stanley himself – the man who was thankful for the opportunity of meeting the author "while there was yet time" (Stanley 9 June 1870). Without his range of influential contacts and determined pursuit of appropriate representation, there would have been no burial in the Abbey, and without his frank comments in correspondence and recollections, we would not now know of his depth of feeling, both as an individual and as a national representative, for the writer whose early demise came as such a shock to the public at large. Thus Stanley has made his own valuable contribution to Dickens biography, by facilitating a biographical "turn" that boldly confronts a canonical narrative and contests received opinion using methodologies that are essential to critical interpretive biography (Hamilton 2017, p. 21). This study in particular has approached events from below, through a microhistorical framework, and has shown how, by reducing the scale of observation, to allow intensive study of fresh documentary material, contradictions and gaps in our knowledge have emerged (Magnússon 2017, p. 45). We think we know Dickens so well – in large part owing to the account left to us by Forster, who diligently reproduced the texts of nearly nine hundred Dickens letters in his grand narrative, thus making it seem as if the novelist is narrating his own story; yet it is important not to trust implicitly this monumental three-volume account, but rather to invite in contradictory "voices," which "may offer competing explanations of specific aspects" of Dickens's life (Magnússon 2017, p. 49). As Renders poignantly observes, "Biography is not a selfie" (2017, p. 159).

Leon Edel (the biographer of Henry James, and an influential biography-theorist; see Walter 2014, pp. 45–47) observed in a *Paris Review* exchange, "In the writing of the life changes occur, discoveries are made. Realities emerge." He adds that critical acumen must be exercised over "the way the materials are melted down, the supreme art of summary, the delicate use of other persons' mail." He also acknowledges that "There is always an air of mystery – every box of letters you open, every attic in which you rummage, becomes filled with the emotions of the biographer's involvement"; but the effective biographer, "in touch with realities," must abandon his or her "love affair" with the subject, to become a more detached analyst (McCulloch 1985, pp. 160, 173, 174). The circumstances surrounding Dickens's death and burial have largely been taken for granted over the past 150 years, without critical reassessment. Now, however, by exposing ambivalences, paying heed to previously silenced voices, and abandoning expectations of a single, coherent narrative, a new, more detailed, but nonetheless sensitive and captivating account of this key moment is permitted to emerge.

Notes

1 "Mulcts" is a fine imposed for an offence (*Oxford English Dictionary*).
2 Christopher Foster, Clerk of the Works 1863–1871.
3 Lord John Thynne (1798–1881), Sub-Dean of Westminster.
4 Samuel Flood Jones (1826–1895), hymn writer and Secretary of the Religious Tract Society; Minor Canon 1859–1895, Precentor 1869–1895.
5 John Charles Thynne (1838–1918), son of Lord John Thynne, and Receiver General of the Abbey 1865–1902.
6 Charles St Clare Bedford (1810–1900), Chapter Clerk 1854–1900 and Coroner for the City of Westminster 1845–1888.
7 Unidentified.
8 Christopher Foster, Clerk of the Works 1863–1871.
9 Thomas Shirley, Verger 1868–1875.
10 Samuel Deer, Dean's Verger 1857–1894.
11 Walter Rush, Porter 1868–1890.
12 William Elliott, Verger 1868–1875.
13 Henry Poole & Sons, ornamental, ecclesiastical and monumental masonry, with premises at 47 Tufton Street and 14 Great Smith Street.
14 This passage in square brackets was marked for deletion in the manuscript.

References

"A.A." (1873, 24 January). Lord Lytton: To the Editor of the Times. The *Times*, 8.
Adrian, Arthur A. (1956). Charles Dickens and Dean Stanley. *Dickensian*, 52, 152–156.
Adrian, Arthur A. (1957). *Georgina Hogarth and the Dickens Circle*. London: Oxford University Press.
Baker, William, Gasson, Andrew, Law, Graham, et al. (Eds.) (2005). *The Public Face of Wilkie Collins: The Collected Letters*. 4 vols. London: Pickering & Chatto.
Banquet at the Royal Academy (1870, 2 May). The *Times*, 10–11.
Boyle, Courtenay, & Boyle, Muriel S. (Eds.) (1902). *Mary Boyle. Her Book*. London: John Murray.
Certificate to be delivered up at the Funeral (12 June 1870). [Dickens's death certificate]. Westminster Abbey Muniments (WAM58091). Westminster Abbey, London.

Charles Dickens and Westminster Abbey (1870, 13 June). The *Times*, 11.
Cockshut, A.O.J. (1974). *Truth to Life: The Art of Biography in the Nineteenth Century*. London: Collins.
Curry, George (1988). Charles Dickens and Annie Fields. *Huntington Library Quarterly*, 51(1), 1–71.
Dean Stanley on Charles Dickens (1870, 20 June). The *Times*, 14.
Dickens, Charles, Jr (1870, 9 June). [Telegram to George Holsworth]. Guildhall Museum (Item 314A [z]), Rochester, UK.
Dickens, Charles, Jr (1870, 14 June). [Letter to Frederick Locker]. The Locker Collection: A Volume of Bound Letters. Armstrong Browning Library, Baylor University, Waco, TX.
Dickens, Mamie (1897). *My Father as I Recall Him*. Westminster: Roxburghe Press.
Eadie, M.J. (2007). The neurological legacy of John Russell Reynolds (1828–1896). *Journal of Clinical Neuroscience*, 14(4), 309–316.
E[dwards], A.W. (1931). Sir Frederick Macmillan's Gift of Personal Relics of Dickens. *Dickensian*, 27, 234.
Elwin, Whitwell (1870, 15–18 June). [Letter to John Forster]. In possession of Tom Wingate.
Elwin, Whitwell (1870, 8 July). [Letter to John Forster]. In possession of Tom Wingate.
Executors of Charles Dickens Esq. Decd. with Messrs. Coutts & Co. (1870–1896). [MS account book]. Charles Dickens Museum, London.
"F.N.B." (1873, 23 January). The Late Lord Lytton: To the Editor of the Times. The *Times*, 9.
Forster, John (1844). The Literary Examiner. *Examiner*, 12 October, 644–646.
Forster, John (1870, 22 July). [Fee remittance note for Dickens's burial]. (WAM58091*). Westminster Abbey Muniments. Westminster Abbey, London.
Forster, John (1873, 25 November). [Letter to Francis Carr Beard]. In possession of Tom Wingate.
Forster, John (1928). *The Life of Charles Dickens*. Ed. J.W.T. Ley. London: Cecil Palmer.
The Funeral of Lord Lytton (1873, 27 January). The *Times*, 8.
Funeral of Mr. Charles Dickens (1870, 15 June). The *Times*, 12.
Gad's Hill Place, Higham, by Rochester. Catalogue of the Household Furniture, Linen, about 200 Dozen of Superior Wines and Liquors, China, Glass, Horse, Carriages, Green-House plants, and Other Effects, of the Late Charles Dickens. Which Will Be Sold by Auction, by Messrs. Thomas & Homan on Wednesday, August 10th and Three Succeeding Days (1870). Rochester: W.T. Wildish.
Garnett, Robert (2008). The Mysterious Mourner: Dickens's Funeral and Ellen Ternan. *Dickens Quarterly*, 25(2), 107–117.
Hamilton, Nigel (2017). Biography as Corrective. In Hans Renders, Binne de Haan & Jonne Harmsma (Eds.), *The Biographical Turn: Lives in History* (pp. 15–30). London: Routledge.

Henderson, Heather (1979). "To You Only ..." : Forster to C.E. Norton on Dickens's Death. *John Forster Newsletter*, 1(2), 32–40.

Hogarth, Georgina (1870, July). [Letter to Frederic Ouvry]. Farrer Ouvry Papers (Envelope 17/34). Charles Dickens Museum, London.

Hughes, William R. (1891). *A Week's Tramp in Dickens Land*. London: Chapman and Hall.

Jalland, Pat (1996). *Death in the Victorian Family*. Oxford: Oxford University Press.

The Late Lord Lytton (1873, 20 January). The *Times*, 9–10.

The Late Mr. Charles Dickens (1870, 11 June). The *Times*, 9.

The Late Sir Rowland Hill (1879, 5 September). The *Times*, 8.

Litten, Julian (1991). *The English Way of Death: The Common Funeral Since 1450*. London: Robert Hale.

Litvack, Leon (in press). Charles Dickens and Westminster Abbey: The Elusive *Times* Leader of 13 June 1870. *Dickensian*.

Locker, Frederick (1870, 10 June). [Copy of letter sent to Charles Dickens, Jr, accompanying letter of A.P. Stanley of 9 June 1870; written on the verso of letter from Dickens's son to Locker, 14 June 1870]. The Locker Collection: A Volume of Bound Letters. Armstrong Browning Library, Baylor University, Waco, TX.

Locker-Lampson, Frederick (1896). *My Confidences: An Autobiographical Sketch Addressed to My Descendants*. Ed. Augustine Birrell. 2nd ed. London: Smith, Elder & Co.

Long, William F. (2019). "Surely This is Not Right:" Contemporary Reaction to Dickens's Will. *Dickens Quarterly*, 36(1), 105–114.

Macaulay, Thomas Babington (1903). *Critical and Historical Essays Contributed to the Edinburgh Review*. Ed. F.C. Montague. 3 vols. London: Methuen.

Magnússon, Sigurður Gylfi (2017). The Life is Never Over: Biography as a Microhistorical Approach. In Hans Renders, Binne de Haan & Jonne Harmsma (Eds.), *The Biographical Turn: Lives in History* (pp. 42–52). London: Routledge.

McCulloch, Jeanne (1985). The Art of Biography I: Leon Edel. *Paris Review*, 98(1), 157–207.

Millais, John Guille (1899). *The Life and Letters of Sir John Everett Millais, President of the Royal Academy*. London: Methuen & Co.

Mitchell, Leslie (2003). *Bulwer Lytton: The Rise and Fall of a Victorian Man of Letters*. London & New York: Hambledon Continuum.

Mr. Charles Dickens (1870, 10 June). The *Times*, 9.

Mr. Charles Dickens's Will (1870, 22 July). The *Times*, 9.

Obituary: Sir J. Russell Reynolds, M.D., F.R.C.P., F.R.S. (1896, 6 June). *British Medical Journal*, 1422–1425.

Oxford English Dictionary. Retrieved from www.oed.com

Patten, Robert L. (2019). Dickens Wills. *Dickens Quarterly*, 36(1), 60–94.

Prothero, Rowland (1893). *Life and Correspondence of Arthur Penrhyn Stanley, D.D., Late Dean of Westminster*. 2 vols. London: John Murray.

Puckle, Bertram S. (1926). *Funeral Customs: Their Origin and Development*. London: T. Werner Laurie.

Raithby, John (Ed.) (1819). *Statutes of the Realm: Volume 5, 1628–80*. London: Record Commission.

Reid, T. Wemyss (1891). *The Life, Letters and Friendships of Richard Monckton Milnes, First Lord Houghton*. 2 vols. New York: Cassell Publishing Co.

Renders, Hans (2017). Biography Is Not a Selfie: Authorisation as the Creeping Transition from Autobiography to Biography. In Hans Renders, Binne de Haan & Jonne Harmsma (Eds.), *The Biographical Turn: Lives in History* (pp. 159–164). London: Routledge.

Renders, Hans, de Haan, Binne, & Harmsma, Jonne (2017). The biographical turn: Biography as critical method in the humanities and in society. In Hans Renders, Binne de Haan & Jonne Harmsma (Eds.), *The Biographical Turn: Lives in History* (pp. 3–11). London: Routledge.

Renton, Richard (1912). *John Forster and His Friendships*. London: Chapman and Hall.

Rochester Cathedral Chapter Minutes (1870). (DRc/Ac14). Medway Archives Centre, Strood, Kent.

Sala, G.A. (1870). *Charles Dickens*. London: George Routledge and Sons.

Stanley, Arthur Penrhyn (1870, 9 June). [Letter to Frederick Locker]. The Locker Collection: A Volume of Bound Letters. Armstrong Browning Library, Baylor University, Waco, TX.

Stanley, Arthur Penrhyn (1870, 11 June). [Letter to Louisa Stanley]. Westminster Abbey Muniments (WAM63525). Westminster Abbey, London.

Stanley, Arthur Penrhyn (1870, 13 June). [Letter to Lord Houghton (Richard Monckton Milnes)]. Trinity College Cambridge Archives (Houghton 23/148). Cambridge, UK.

Stanley, Arthur Penrhyn (1870). *Sermon Preached by Arthur Penrhyn Stanley, D.D. Dean of Westminster. In Westminster Abbey, 19 June 1870 (the First Sunday After Trinity) being the Sunday following the Funeral of Charles Dickens*. London: Macmillan and Co.

Stanley, Arthur Penrhyn (1872, 6 June). [Letter to John Forster]. Forster Collection, National Art Library (MSL/1970/2993/59). Victoria & Albert Museum, London.

Stanley, Arthur Penrhyn (1875–1880). *Recollections of Events Connected with Westminster Abbey*. [Transcription of manuscript reminiscences]. Westminster Abbey Muniments, Westminster Abbey, London.

Storey, Gladys (1939). *Dickens and Daughter*. London: Frederick Muller.

Tomalin, Claire (1990). *The Invisible Woman: The Story of Nelly Ternan and Charles Dickens*. London: Penguin.

Walter, James (2014). The Solace of Doubt? Biographical Methodology after the Short Twentieth Century. In Hans Renders & Binne de Haan (Eds.), *Theoretical Discussions of Biography: Approaches from History, Microhistory, and Life Writing* (pp. 43–58). Leiden & Boston: Brill.

Westminster Abbey Funeral Fee Book 1811–1899 (1811–1899). [Manuscript fee book]. Westminster Abbey Muniments. Westminster Abbey, London.

Witheridge, John (2013). *Excellent Dr Stanley: The Life of Dean Stanley of Westminster*. Norwich: Michael Russell.

2

A Tale of Two Brothers

Reading Differently Dickens's French Revolution
Lillian Nayder

In a memorable scene from *Great Expectations*, the protagonist Pip overhears a conversation between his guardian – the solicitor Mr Jaggers – and the character Mike, who has found a witness to provide an alibi for one of Jaggers's clients. "What is he prepared to swear?" the lawyer asks; Mike replies: "Well, Mas'r Jaggers ... in a general way, anythink." This reply leaves Jaggers "most irate," and leads Wemmick, his clerk, to reprimand the "spooney": "Need you say it face to face?" Wemmick asks (*GE* 2:1).

Dickens was a writer drawn to the workings of the law, and he considered the behaviour of the witness, and what a witness will or will not say, from the start of his career. "Lawyers hold that there are two kinds of particularly bad witnesses," he writes in his first novel, *The Pickwick Papers* – "a reluctant witness and a too willing witness" (*PP* 34). He illustrates this point, to comic effect, when Pickwick stands trial for breach of promise, and his friend Winkle takes the stand, proving too willing and reluctant by turns. Testifying on Pickwick's behalf, Winkle readily reveals that, before Pickwick was charged with breach of promise in the present case, his friend had been found in a compromising position: in a strange lady's bedroom at midnight, though "no doubt" the incident "might be easily explained." Winkle further aids the prosecution by trying to withhold the necessary details from the court. Asked to "describe the occasion," he replies that he'd "rather not"; "Perhaps so," the judge tells him, "but you must" (*PP* 34).

Like *The Pickwick Papers*, *A Tale of Two Cities* centres on a trial – more precisely, on four trials, each involving Charles Darnay. Although Dickens wrote the 1859 novel in a very different tone to *Pickwick*, and at a very different stage of his career, it too has its fair share of "particularly bad" witnesses; the reluctant ones are the concerns of this study. Dickens introduces the motif when Jerry Cruncher admits to his employer that he knows the Old Bailey, where he serves as a messenger during Darnay's first trial. Cruncher sounds "not unlike a reluctant witness at the establishment in question" (*TTC* 1:2), the narrator explains; the double negative ("not unlike") helps to convey Cruncher's reticence to speak the truth. Called on by the judge shortly thereafter, Lucie Manette dramatises this reticence; when she refers to "the prisoner" as "the gentleman" and "unhappily" confirms that she met Darnay on his channel crossing from France, "the plaintive tone of her compassion" meets with a strong reproof: "Answer the questions put to you, and make no remark upon them," the judge commands. He assures her that "If the prisoner does not perfectly understand that you give the evidence which it is your duty to give – which you must give – and which you cannot escape from giving – with great unwillingness, he is the only person present in that condition" (*TTC* 1:3).

In *A Tale of Two Cities* the reluctant witness is embodied, most strikingly, in Lucie's father, Doctor Manette, when, during Darnay's fourth and final trial, the Doctor is forced to testify against his own family member by means of a manuscript he penned decades before, as a prisoner in the Bastille. Ernest Defarge has discovered the manuscript and, when read at the trial, it ensures Darnay's death sentence; Manette's manuscript concludes thus:

> If it had pleased God to put it in the hard heart of either of the [Evrémonde] brothers, in all these frightful years, to grant me any tidings of my dearest wife ... I might have thought that He had not quite abandoned them. But, now I believe ... that they have no part in His mercies. And them and their descendants, to the last of their race, I Alexandre Manette, unhappy prisoner, do this last night of the year 1767, in my unbearable agony, denounce to the times when all these things shall be answered for. (*TTC* 3:10)

Because Charles Darnay is Charles Evrémonde, the son of the eldest brother whom Manette denounces, the Doctor's testimony effectively condemns his son-in-law to death, although the anguished Manette would save him if he could.

Sources for Manette's prison narrative – and for Darnay's four trials – are legion in Dickens's scholarship. Andrew Sanders and Richard Maxwell identify several Bastille prisoners whose accounts inform Manette's; both critics cite Francis de la Motte's 1781 state trial as a prototype for Darnay's at the Old Bailey (Sanders 1988, p. 50; Maxwell 2003, p. 423). So too does Sally Ledger, who broadly traces Dickens's historical and literary sources, citing the "political trials of ... radical Regency activists" as well as the set-piece trial scenes in popular melodramas that "held ... a central place in the popular cultural imagination" (2009, p. 77).

Yet one crucial source for the trials in *A Tale of Two Cities*, for the telling reluctance to testify that characterises some of its witnesses, and for the very crime that lies at the heart of the novel, has gone unnoticed by critics. This source has not been recognised, even though – or perhaps because – it lies much closer to home than the histories usually cited in discussions of Dickens's 1859 work. This unidentified source is the 1859 trial of the novelist's brother Frederick (1820–1868), which was held before a common jury in the newly established Court for Divorce and Matrimonial Causes. The motions and proceedings of the case were reported in the London *Times* in several instalments, as *A Tale of Two Cities* was first appearing weekly in *All the Year Round*; Dickens was drawn into the failed negotiations that preceded Fred's trial shortly before he began writing his novel.

In recognising the importance to Dickens's work of this source material, and of the novelist's fraternal dynamics more generally, this study contributes to the broadening of literary critique through the biographical "turn" – that is, the transformation of biography from a commemorative activity into a critical one (Renders & de Haan 2014, p. 2), and the "methodological and theoretical" changes that have ensued (Renders et al. 2017, pp. 3–4). Biographers who are engaged in a scholarly and "corrective" enterprise (Hamilton 2017, p. 18) prove wary of the self-representations of their famous subjects, and are eager to consider those on the margins, and indeed to acknowledge as significant "the many" or minor as well as "the one" (Woloch 2003). Although *A Tale of Two Cities* is a canonical novel written by a highly celebrated author, the approach here is decentred: it considers Fred Dickens, in part, from the perspective of a "discredited" younger sibling, a figure generally dismissed by the novelist and by scholars following Dickens's lead. Using Fred's perspective and experience to illuminate his famous brother's novel, this study calls into question those deeply entrenched ideas of the literary genius, his autonomy and control.

Fred was the novelist's next-youngest brother: the fourth of six surviving siblings, and the second of the four Dickens brothers who lived to adulthood (see Nayder 2013; Moss & Moss 1994; Paroissien 1972; Wedgewood 1967; Grubb 1954). Born in 1820, eight years after Charles, Fred was four years old when their father was arrested for debt, and when the family moved into the Marshalsea, at which point Charles began his work at Warren's Blacking. Fred attended day school in the early 1830s, and left in 1834, when John Dickens again faced a serious financial crisis. Family members separated as a result, and Charles took Fred in to live with him at Furnival's Inn. He found work for Fred with his publisher, John Macrone, in 1837; when Macrone died the same year, Dickens helped Fred obtain a Treasury clerkship. Fred took up residence with his four young nieces and nephews when Charles and Catherine left the country for six months in 1842 on their American tour. Over the next few years, Fred spent time with the family at their London home, on the coast and abroad, acted in several of the amateur theatricals managed by his older brother, and at times served as Dickens's secretary.

In the 1840s, friends and acquaintances often noted the camaraderie between the two eldest Dickens brothers; yet their close relations came under significant strain as a result of Fred's mounting debts, and relentless borrowings, as well as his marriage – against the novelist's advice and objections – to Anna Weller in

1848. Unable or unwilling to live within his means, Fred had accrued debts of at least £600 by 1850, after which Dickens refused to give him money to pay them off.

Towards the end of 1856, Dickens was "force[d] ... to write a very plain answer" to Fred's most recent request, and told his brother that the expenses he had already assumed for him were "little else than monstrous. The possibility of your having any further assistance from me," Dickens curtly noted, "is absolutely and finally past" (*Letters* 8:236). In January 1857 the novelist refused to make an appointment with Fred, and in the following month he declined yet another request for money: "Firstly because I cannot trust you ... Secondly because if this were otherwise it would do you no real good and would not in the least save you against creditors who have already power of taking you in execution" (*Letters* 8:275). Fred's angry reply to this last refusal so irritated Dickens that he forwarded it to W.H. Wills, his subeditor, and one of Fred's creditors; Fred's letter brought communications between the brothers to an end for nearly two years.

They broke this silence in October 1858, when Fred, faced with the threat of a trial for judicial separation from Anna, wrote to his older brother, asking to see him; Dickens agreed, and met Fred on 8 November. The novelist had separated from his own wife, Catherine, just a few months earlier, after 22 years of marriage and the birth of 10 children; the split was effected by a deed of separation rather than a trial – that is, by negotiating a contract that was handled through the law of equity rather than under English common law. Yet Dickens's persistent efforts at self-justification, with the publication of his "Personal" statement in *Household Words* in June 1858 and, in August, the appearance of the so-called "violated letter" in newspapers both in England and abroad (*Letters* 8:740–741), created the very publicity and scandal that the deed of separation was intended to avoid (see Nayder 2011). Thus the novelist had his own reasons for allowing Fred to reestablish contact: he hoped to keep his brother's marital woes – and his sexual misconduct – as private as he could. Dickens learned of Fred's adultery from Thomas James Thompson, who in 1845 had married Christiana Weller, the elder sister of Fred's wife (Thompson was trying to mediate discreetly between the two parties). Writing to Thompson shortly before he met with Fred, Dickens professed ignorance of "the details of the relations between [Fred] and his wife," and explained that, "for some time past," he had "known nothing of [his brother]" – that "no one in the world was stranger to me than he" – and that "thus severed from him ... [Fred's affairs] have been so entirely unknown to me that I do not now know what you mean when you mention 'that astonishing Dorking business'" (*Letters* 8:690).

Before Dickens met with his brother in early November, Thompson had written back to explain what he meant by "that astonishing ... business" – an explanation that Anna would later provide to a judge and jury; the general public also learned of it through a report in the *Times* of 27 July 1859. Anna testified that while she was preparing for a charity concert at the Red Lion Inn in Dorking in October 1857,

> Her suspicions were roused by some expressions that fell from one of the servants, to the effect that she and her husband had been there before, and they were strengthened by the conduct of her husband when he joined her at Dorking. She taxed her husband in the following November ... with having committed adultery during her absence at Jersey, and in consequence of the communication he then made to her she left him and went to live with her family. Inquiries were made, and it was ascertained that on the 25th of April Mr. Dickens, during his wife's absence at Jersey, took a woman to the Red Lion, at Dorking, and passed a Saturday and Sunday night with her there, returning to town on the Monday. A long correspondence took place, in which Mr. Dickens expressed his deep and heartfelt regret for the wrong he had done to his wife, and implored her to forgive him and return to him. She refused, and presented this petition.
>
> The adultery was proved by the landlady of the hotel, and by a gentleman who accompanied Mr. Dickens and the lady with whom it was committed. It appeared that there was a party of four – Mr. Dickens and a friend and two ladies. (Dickens v. Dickens 1859c, p. 12)

Hoping to avoid the publication of just such details, Dickens focused on "the Dorking matter" when he met with Fred on 8 November, and on Fred's refusal "to make his wife any allowance," which Dickens hoped to overcome; in their lengthy negotiations five months earlier, the novelist himself had agreed to give his estranged wife Catherine an annual allowance of £600. He urged Fred to negotiate with Anna, but felt that he had failed to convince his brother (*Letters* 8:699).

Their next meeting, on 21 November, gave Dickens more hope. Fred had considered his brother's advice and agreed to "make any reasonable terms" with Anna. Writing to Thompson the next morning, Dickens asked him to use his influence "to stay the legal proceedings," to determine what Anna expected for an allowance and what Fred's "burdened means" could afford, and hence bring "this wretched business ... to a quiet end" (*Letters* 8:706). By January 1859, however, negotiations had fallen through; he wrote to Thompson:

> I am much of your mind as to the ... annual allowance ... But my dear fellow, it is mere beating the air for you and I to discuss the question. If Mr. Weller [Anna's father] will make no proposal on the one hand, and Frederick will make none on the other, any proposal from us will only draw us into difficulty – will only be twisted into a proposal from the fountain head – and will necessitate our personal explanation and disclaimer in the Witness Box. They must go on. We can do nothing. (*Letters* 9:6).

Dickens, who was wary of creating further complications by offering his own proposal for a settlement, and unwilling to appear in the witness box to provide explanations or disclaimers should further negotiations fail, imagined himself a reluctant witness at Fred's trial – as reluctant as any of the characters he would soon invent for *A Tale of Two Cities*. His aversion was due to the publicity that his appearance at such a trial would create, especially given his own recent, spectacular separation from Catherine; it also marks his (at best) equivocal feelings about Fred – a "stranger" to him, as he noted to Thompson. Unlike their brother Alfred, who appeared at the 1859 trial in Fred's defence (in an attempt to prove that Anna had condoned Fred's adultery), Dickens seems to have found Fred indefensible.

The author's own experience of how best to handle a marital separation must have raised uncomfortable questions for him about his tie to Fred – even putting aside the obvious difference between his success in life and his financial support of his estranged wife on the one hand, and Fred's failure, irresponsibility and insolvency on the other. Two years after Fred's trial, Dickens rebuffed the suggestion, made by Thompson, that his brother's "disgrace" reflected on him: "An implication conveyed in your letter renders it necessary for me to observe that I know no one can disgrace me but myself, and that the name I have made is in my keeping, and in no other man's" (*Letters* 9:485). Yet faced with allegations of adultery himself in 1858 – with reports that paired him with his sister-in-law Georgina Hogarth on the one hand, and with the young actress Ellen Ternan on the other – Dickens could not neatly or completely distance himself from Fred and Fred's marital misconduct, even if his relationship with Nelly had not yet become a sexual one (though it did later: according to some sources and critics, she gave birth to a son in France; see Garnett 2006; Tomalin 1991, p. 140). Dickens sought to remain detached and neutral, claiming that, in trying to mediate between Fred and Anna, he had "no interest but in doing right" (*Letters* 8:706); but Dickens may well have seen himself reflected in Fred, albeit in a distorted form: a mirror image of sorts, both identical and inverted. In offering his advice to Fred about how best to manage his separation (for instance in his comments about determining an apt allowance for Anna), Dickens clearly compared his situation, behaviour and desires to those of his brother. These comparisons were not lost on members of the author's extended family; as Catherine Dickens's aunt Helen wrote disparagingly of the novelist to a friend in the summer of 1858, "he is the third Dickens brother who has deserted his wife, and I understand a fourth Dickens is about to be separated from his wife by the desire of her parents" (*Letters* 8:749). Although Alfred Dickens (one of the four brothers) remained married until his death, and although Fred was not yet separated from Anna, Helen Thompson's point about the fraternal pattern emerging in the late 1850s seems well made.

Magnifying the uncanny echo of the older brother in the younger was the fact that Fred had only met Anna, in the mid-1840s, because of Dickens's infatuation with her sister Christiana, a young concert pianist. The novelist, who continually praised Christiana (an ethereal being who reminded him of Mary Hogarth) and fantasised about how best to court her, gave Fred the impression that the Weller sisters were highly desirable creatures to be pursued and won. In effect, Dickens triggered what Bodenheimer describes as "a mirroring sub-plot" to his own fantasy courtship of Christiana Weller, with his "younger brother ... grasp[ing] what [he himself] could not" (2007, p. 104).

During the very years in which Dickens grew apart from Fred, identifying him as a "stranger" and disavowing their connection, he also signalled, in various ways, their inescapable link; he suggested, for example, that he recognised himself in his younger sibling, and bore some responsibility for what Fred had become. Not only was Dickens's pursuit of one Weller sister reflected in Fred's pursuit (and ill-fated conquest) of another, and not only did Fred's separation from Anna replay (albeit with differences) that of his older brother from Catherine, there was also a recognition on the novelist's part that if Fred and his borrowings were "monstrous," Dickens was the Frankenstein-like creator to whom Fred was indebted. So Dickens implied in his indictment of Fred: "I have already done more for you than most dispassionate persons would consider right or reasonable in itself. But, considered with any fair reference to the great expences [sic] I have sustained for other relations, it becomes little else than monstrous" (*Letters* 8:236). According to the wording here, Dickens's continued and unreasonable support of Fred – what he has "already done" for him – is in fact the monstrous thing, not simply Fred's endless requests and "borrowings."

In *A Tale of Two Cities* Dickens draws on these fraternal dynamics: on his efforts to set himself apart from Fred; the impossibility of his doing so; and his desire to reform his brother and halt the misconduct he felt he had enabled. Considering how closely interwoven his composition of the novel was with his strained dealings with his brother, these connections are not surprising. *A Tale of Two Cities* appeared in *All the Year Round* from 30 April to 26 November 1859, and the impact of Dickens's fraternal dynamics on the novel was no doubt enhanced by the immediacy of his writing. On 9 July he told Forster that he could "do no more than hold his ground" in writing the story ahead of its publication; his "old month's advance" was all that he had been able to achieve (*Letters* 9:32).

According to Andrew Sanders, Dickens began to think about his new book in late January 1859 (1988, p. 3; *Letters* 8:510), shortly after he told Thompson that negotiations between Fred and Anna had failed, and after he had expressed his unwillingness to appear in court. On 7 January Anna's solicitors filed her case for motion, and on 29 January they submitted a petition for financial support in advance of judgement. On 21 February Dickens wrote to Forster of his dissatisfaction "with the opening of [his] story" and his inability to "settle at it or take to it" (*Letters* 9:30); three days later the *Times* reported that the judge in the pending case was ruling on pretrial motions, including the question of Fred's responsibility for Anna's legal fees (Dickens v. Dickens 1859a, p. 11). The first instalment of Dickens's novel appeared at the end of April, and on 5 May the *Times* reported that Fred had not paid alimony of £60 as ordered (Dickens v. Dickens 1859b, p. 11). Hence Anna's solicitor requested that Fred's salary be attached; the judge, Sir Cresswell Cresswell, agreed. By mid-July Dickens had published slightly more than the first third of his novel, taking the story through "The Fellow of No

Delicacy" (*TTC* 2:12), four chapters beyond the assassination of the Marquis, with Carton's telling Lucie of his love; Dickens asked Wills to post the revised proofs for the 16 July installment "to Miss Ellen Ternan, 2 Houghton Place, Ampthill Square, N.W." (*Letters* 9:87), the home where he had installed Nelly. By 23 July, the Pilgrim editors conjecture, Dickens was working on "Still Knitting" (*TTC* 2:16), which appeared on 9 August, in the fifteenth weekly installment (*Letters* 9:90n). On 26 July, Anna was granted her judicial separation, and the history of the unhappy marriage and the sordid details of Fred's adultery were reported the following day: the *Times* noted that "The jury returned a verdict for the petitioner on both issues" – that is, on Fred's adultery and Anna's refusal to condone it – and Cresswell "decreed a judicial separation" (Dickens v. Dickens 1859c, p. 12).

Two days after the divorce was finalised, Dickens hosted Anna's sister Christiana, and her husband T.J. Thompson, at Gad's Hill. The couple had been in court with Anna, along with their parents, to lend moral support to the petitioner. Christiana, perhaps owing to her perception of the resemblance between the Dickens brothers, was reluctant to join the novelist at his home, despite what she saw as Anna's victory over Fred. After all, it was Charles Dickens who had encouraged Fred to prohibit Anna from taking on music pupils five years earlier, when Fred proved unable to extricate himself from debt and adequately support his wife. At the time, Dickens offered what was, to Anna, his most unwelcome advice against her objections and those of her family. Indeed her father wrote a letter of reproof to the novelist, facetiously telling him that they would all be "quite content" if he would "allow [them] to pass out of [his] mind altogether" – and beyond the reach of his meddling (Weller 1854). Although Christiana was persuaded by her husband to conquer her reservations and go to Gad's Hill after the trial, her objections seem to have manifested themselves in bodily form while in transit: "Not fit to go but Tom wished to ... I with hysterics in train – a novelty" (Thompson 1859, p. 73).

In his *Companion to A Tale of Two Cities* Sanders describes the novel as "very personal," and a well-researched work of historical fiction; he cites Dickens's "affection for France" and his intimate knowledge of the country (1988, p. 9). Yet the concurrence of the novel's composition and Fred's trial and judicial separation – and more specifically, Dickens's use of Fred's trial as a source – reveals the novel to be "very personal" in another sense. Dickens's fraught experience of brotherhood may be traced in his tale about French Revolution and "fraternité" by considering, in particular, the novel's male doubles and identical twins, and the romantic interests and sexual transgressions that link the figures in each of these male pairings.

Critics have labelled *A Tale of Two Cities* a novel "about" adultery, though not in connection with Fred's trial, the charges levelled against him by Anna, or the novelist's own involvement in the case. Tamar Heller, who focuses on the love triangle formed by Lucie, her husband Charles Darnay and Sydney Carton (Lucie's admirer and would-be seducer, who is also her husband's double), identifies Carton's love for Lucie, "chaste and sublimated as it is," as "potentially adulterous," though that possibility is averted by Carton's sacrifice "for the good of domesticity" (1992, p. 123). Hilary Schor reads the novel in terms of "the daughter's … perilous trek through the adultery plot"; she compares Lucie to other Dickens heroines who are tempted to fall, while also emphasising their ultimate vindication (2000, p. 83). Schor notes that Carton "imagin[es] himself as adulterous father to Lucie's children"; his "paternity" is suggested in his final vision of Lucie (2000, p. 95) with (as Carton puts it) "a child upon her bosom, who bears my name" (*TTC* 3:15). Schor also argues that the adultery plot "works itself out," in part, through Carton's heroic self-sacrifice, as he substitutes himself for Lucie's condemned husband; she emphasises what she refers to as Dickens's "intense overidentification" with that figure (2000, p. 96). Other critics concur, particularly those who see Ellen Ternan as the prototype for Lucie Manette – among them, Michael Slater (1983, pp. 210–211) and Claire Tomalin (1991, pp. 125–126, 264).

Yet Carton – who is, according to Schor, "a wastrel, a drunkard, a ne'er-do-well … probably a rake" (2000, p. 84) – bears a much more obvious resemblance to Fred Dickens than he does to the novelist. The narrator's view of Carton as "the man of good abilities and good emotions, incapable of their directed exercise, incapable of his own help and his own happiness" (*TTC* 2:5), reflects what Dickens saw as Fred's ultimate failure to show "independent spirit" and to achieve the "self-extrication" that lay "in [his] own power" (*Letters* 5:424). Such connections suggest that Dickens's novel not only follows "the daughter's … perilous trek through the adultery plot" (Schor 2000, p. 83), but that it also traces, less triumphantly, the brother's trek through that plot. In fact, the adultery frame was one that Fred helped the novelist to construct in the late 1850s, and through which, in Dickens's fictional rendering, both brothers pick their perilous way.

In *A Tale of Two Cities*, Dickens most obviously plays Charles Darnay to Fred's Sydney Carton, with Darnay's determination to succeed in life, through his own merits and effort, acting as the counter to Carton's dissipation, self-destruction and wasted strengths. The uncanny physical doubling of these two characters – captured in Dickens's text as well as in Hablot Browne's illustrations for the later monthly numbers published by Chapman and Hall – recalls the physical doubling of Dickens and Fred as the elder brother comically conceived it in the 1840s, when claiming that Fred so closely resembled him that he "feel[s] (as the Stage Villains say) that Either [*sic*] he or I must fall. Earth will not hold us both" (*Letters* 4:192). Dickens's ability to see himself in Carton as well as in Darnay only underscores the point that, whatever his efforts to set himself apart from and above his fallen brother, he found their resemblance inescapable.

In his 1859 work, Dickens captures this fraternal resemblance in a more explicit and disturbing way than in the doubling of Darnay and Carton – that is, in his portrait of Darnay's father and uncle: identical twins whose sex crime lies at the heart of the narrative. As revealed in Doctor Manette's manuscript, Darnay's uncle – the younger of these twins and, at the novel's start, the Marquis St Evrémonde – had, as a young man, abducted and raped the older sister of Madame

Defarge, and had tortured to death the woman's husband when he resisted the nobleman's "right" to his wife (the so-called *droit du seigneur*), thus breaking her father's heart, and murdering her brother when the latter followed in pursuit. Critics such as Schor define the adultery plot of *A Tale of Two Cities* against this story of aristocratic sexual violence, which Dickens claimed to have drawn from historical sources depicting "feudal privileges ... used to the frightful oppression of the [French] peasant, quite as near to the time of the Revolution as the doctor's narrative" (*Letters* 9:258–259). In citing such sources, Dickens places distance between his own experience of brotherhood in the years 1858–1859 and the story of the Evrémonde twins.

Yet if either Evrémonde twin is paired with the third brother in this innermost narrative – the peasant who challenges the aristocrats, forces the younger to duel, and thus receives his mortal wound – we see the Dickens fraternity as Fred himself conceived of it in the late 1850s, in the letter that so angered the novelist that he sent it on to Wills to read and that may have served, consciously or not, as a source for Dickens here. In Fred's version of their relationship, he plays the part of a slave to Dickens's master, who has "the world at [his] foot"; Fred imagines his older brother standing on a "Pinnacle," whip in hand, himself below. "The world fancy from your writings that you are the most Tolerant of Men," Fred writes; "let them individually come under your lash — (if one is to judge from your behaviour to your own flesh & blood) & God help them!" (F. Dickens 1857). In *A Tale of Two Cities*, the Marquis strikes at the peasant brother "with a whip" before the latter forces him to draw his sword and, on the night of his assassination, tells his nephew Darnay that "repression is the only lasting philosophy. The dark deference of fear and slavery ... will keep the dogs obedient to the whip, as long as this roof ... shuts out the sky." A display of family weaponry at the château includes "certain heavy riding-rods and riding-whips, of which many a peasant ... had felt the weight when his lord was angry" (*TTC* 2:9).

Another factor that ties the text's innermost narrative to Dickens's relations with Fred at the time is the author's original conception of the story of the Evrémonde twins as a story of adultery – not rape; thus it becomes a tale more plausibly indebted to Fred's trial and to the workings of England's new divorce court than to the eighteenth-century French histories cited by Dickens after the novel appeared (*Letters* 9:258–259). In the first version of the manuscript (in the Victoria & Albert Museum), pasted over with the novelist's revision and only revealed more than a century later, the younger twin seduces the peasant woman, stages a false wedding with her and then – as "the honour of the great family demand[s]" – reveals their tie to be adulterous: "She was a good girl not long ago," her brother tells Manette in this first draft, "and had a good lover. She deceived him for this man's brother ... [and] met him every night" (Sanders 1988, pp. 156–157; Tucker 1979, pp. 453–454). In the published text Dickens retained elements of the adultery theme – most obviously in a way that emphasises the wrongs done to the woman's husband. As the peasant brother indignantly puts it, pointing to the older of the Evrémonde twins then present, "that man's brother saw and admired her, and asked that man to lend her to him – for what are husbands among us!" (*TTC* 3:10).

In the 1859 case of "Dickens v. Dickens," the husband was the adulterer and not the petitioner. Nonetheless, we hear elements of the case – and of Anna's testimony against Fred – through the Marquis's wife, who is "not happy in her marriage," appalled by her husband's behaviour, and who visits Doctor Manette because she has failed to discover the name of "the other woman," Madame Defarge's sister (*TTC* 3:10), just as Anna had failed in her own quest for such information, testifying that her husband had "committed Adultery with a woman whose name is to your petitioner wholly unknown" (Divorce Court File D16 1858, p. 2). As Manette explains concerning the Marquis's wife, "her inducement to come to me ... had been the hope that I could tell her the name" (*TTC* 3:10). Ostensibly, she seeks this knowledge in order to assist the victimised peasant woman: "to show her, in secret, a woman's sympathy" (*TTC* 3:10) and to right a wrong. Yet the "great agitation" and "great distress" that Manette observes in the wife herself, like her "suspicions" and partial "discoveries" of "the main facts of the cruel story," with "her husband's share in it" (*TTC* 3:10) suggest that she, too, is a wronged party. The importance she places on uncovering the peasant woman's name ties her to those wives who, like Anna Dickens, were wronged by adulterous husbands and petitioned the court for separation or divorce under the 1857 Matrimonial Causes Act, which stipulated that "every petition presented by a wife for dissolution of marriage" name as a respondent "the person with whom the husband is alleged to have committed adultery" if "the Court ... see[s] fit" to so direct her (Nelson 1889, p. 114). Under the 1857 Act, this was mandatory for husbands who petitioned the court, but judges had discretion in cases where wives requested dissolution of their marriages.

Dickens may also be using elements of Fred's troubled marriage when he reveals that the woman seized or seduced by the younger twin actually "belongs" to his older brother, who stands at her sickbed, "looking down at her with some curiosity" (*TTC* 3:10). These details convey the novelist's understanding of the *droit du seigneur*, but also reflect the triangulated dynamics that were at work among Dickens, Fred and Anna for more than a decade, when Dickens often counselled Fred on how best to keep Anna in line, and even attended at her bedside, as mesmerist, when she was ailing. Christiana, who was present at such a treatment of Anna in April 1850, noted in her journal that, in mesmerising her sister, Dickens "did it completely" (Thompson 1850).

In *A Tale of Two Cities*, the issue of marital separation serves as a focal point in a way that allows the novelist both to acknowledge and to disavow his story's connection to "Dickens v. Dickens." In the marital history of Doctor Manette, Dickens reimagines separation as a condition enforced on a loving couple, rather than the result of one partner's adultery or betrayal – a mode of punishment inflicted on a political prisoner and the woman who loves him – a source of "unbearable agony," as Manette terms it: "O my wife, beloved of my heart! My fair young English wife!" (*TTC* 3:10). In forcing apart husband and wife and treating them as if they were dead to each other, the Evrémondes, Manettte asserts, prove themselves "abandoned" by God (*TTC* 3:10), thus echoing the language of those who objected on spiritual grounds to the 1857 Act, which made possible civil divorce and transformed a sacrament into a matter for non-ecclesiastical courts. The insistence on the part of some Victorians that marriage should remain sacred and indissoluble helps to explain the shock that Lucie endures at the outset of the novel, at the revelation that her mother was not, in fact, a widow who survived her husband by "only two years" but a woman who lost him by means of a separation (*TTC* 1:4). The idea that the complexities of marriage law could make a "widow of a living husband" is one that is conveyed elsewhere in *All the Year Round*, in an essay entitled "Happy and Unhappy Couples" ([Dixon] 1860, p. 156).

One of the more troubling details of the Evrémonde story is the older brother's complicity in the crimes of the younger. In Dickens's draft, the Marquis smiles when the peasant brother recounts details of the sham marriage, amused by the adulterous "trick" played on the peasant woman by his own younger brother (Tucker 1979, p. 454); in the published version, the elder brother helps to torture the woman's husband before giving his twin "permission and even aid" when the latter abducts her (*TTC* 3:10). Although the younger brother is described as "the worst of a bad race" (*TTC* 3:10) – the one guilty of adultery or rape – critics consistently mistake this plot detail; they write of "the older … brother's desire for and taking of" the woman (Tucker 1979, p. 453), or claim that Darnay's "father and uncle raped the sister" (Schor 2000, p. 91), or refer to "a peasant girl raped by the evil lords of the manor" (Ledger 2009, p. 83). In so doing, they blur the distinction that Dickens draws between the two men, but simultaneously invites us to question. So some of his contemporaries queried the distinction between what he insisted was his "fair" treatment of Catherine and what seemed Fred's more obvious mistreatment of Anna – just as Dickens himself may have questioned it when advising his brother.

In transforming a story of seduction and adultery into one of violence and rape, Dickens develops the political theme of his novel; he connects class exploitation with gender oppression, "better fusing the personal and public levels of the novel" and highlighting "the abuses of the *ancien régime*" (Tucker 1979, pp. 456–457). But in making this revision, Dickens also pushes out to arm's length his autobiographical sources. Moving from the hidden past revealed by Manette's manuscript to the novel's present – from a tale of identical twin brothers to one of uncanny male doubles with no blood tie – Dickens distances himself from the wayward Fred, redefines his very idea (or ideal) of brotherhood, and obscures the life experiences that informed his novel. At the same time, he recuperates Fred in the self-sacrificing Carton, reforming him in fiction if not in fact, and redefining as heroic what it means to be "taken in execution," as Fred, an imprisoned debtor, so often was, his goods or person seized in default of payment (*Letters* 8:275). In this fictional recreation of Fred and his fall, the seizure for execution – while still reflecting the judgement of a court – becomes a form of martyrdom, not a mark of dependence and debt. In these ways, Dickens wishfully reimagines the personal experiences that informed his novel.

His eagerness to interweave fact and fiction in this way is evident in a letter Dickens wrote to John Forster in January 1859, shortly after voicing his reluctance to appear at Fred's trial, and as he was considering titles for what soon became *All the Year Round*. When Dickens suggested *Household Harmony* as a title for the periodical, Forster objected, noting that it "might hardly be accepted as a happy comment" on recent "occurrences" in his life (*Letters* 9:15, n.5). The novelist testily replied: "I am afraid we must not be too particular about the possibility of personal references and applications; otherwise it is manifest that I can never write another book" (*Letters* 9:15–16). Seeking to avoid the personal in writing his new novel, yet aware that "one's family ... write[s] one's story" (Schor 2000, p. 93), as Charles Darnay tragically discovers, Dickens told his own "tale of two brothers" in *A Tale of Two Cities* but in displaced form; the novel thus served as a reluctant witness to his own life story.

References

Bodenheimer, Rosemarie (2007). *Knowing Dickens*. Ithaca, NY: Cornell University Press.
Dickens, Frederick (1857, 7 February). [Autograph Letter to Charles Dickens]. Henry E. Huntington Library, Art Collections, and Botanical Gardens (HM18484). Los Angeles, CA.
Dickens v. Dickens (1859a, 24 February). The *Times*, 11.
Dickens v. Dickens (1859b, 5 May). The *Times*, 11.
Dickens v. Dickens (1859c, 27 July). The *Times*, 12.
Divorce Court File: D16. Appellant: Anna Delancey Dickens. Respondent: Frederick William Dickens. Type: Wife's Petition. (1858, 30 October). National Archives, Kew. (J 77/13/D16). London.
[Dixon, Edmund Saul] (1860, 24 November). Happy and Unhappy Couples. *All the Year Round*, 4, 156–161.
Garnett, Robert R. (2006). The Crisis of 1863. *Dickens Quarterly*, 23(3), 181–191.
Grubb, Gerald (1954). Charles Dickens and His Brother Fred. *Dickensian*, 50, 123–131.
Hamilton, Nigel (2017). Biography as Corrective. In Hans Renders, Binn de Haan & Jonne Harmsma (Eds.), *The Biographical Turn: Lives in History* (pp. 15–30). London: Routledge.
Heller, Tamar (1992). *Dead Secrets: Wilkie Collins and the Female Gothic*. New Haven, CT: Yale University Press.
Ledger, Sally (2009). From the Old Bailey to Revolutionary France: The Trials of Charles Darnay. In Colin Jones, Josephine McDonagh & Jon Mee (Eds.), *Charles*

Dickens, A Tale of Two Cities and the French Revolution (pp. 75–86). Basingstoke: Palgrave Macmillan.

Maxwell, Richard (2003). Appendix III: Dickens and His Sources. *A Tale of Two Cities* by Charles Dickens (pp. 399–443). London: Penguin.

Moss, Sidney P., & Moss, Carolyn J. (1994). Frederick Dickens: From Courtship to Courtroom. *Dickensian*, 90, 102–112.

Nayder, Lillian (2011). *The Other Dickens: A Life of Catherine Hogarth*. Ithaca, NY: Cornell University Press.

Nayder, Lillian (2013). "He has a Mustache"; or, "Earth Will Not Hold Us Both": Charles Dickens and the Problem of Fred. *Dickens Quarterly*, 30(2), 141–153.

Nelson, Horace (1889). *Selected Cases, Statutes and Orders Illustrative of the Private International Law as Administered in England*. London: Stevens and Sons.

Paroissien, David H. (1972). Charles Dickens and the Weller Family. *Dickens Studies Annual*, 2, 1–38.

Renders, Hans, & de Haan, Binne (2014). Introduction: The Challenges of Biography Studies. In Hans Renders & Binne de Haan (Eds.), *Theoretical Discussions of Biography: Approaches from History, Microhistory, and Life Writing* (pp. 1–8). Leiden & Boston: Brill.

Renders, Hans, de Haan, Binne, & Harmsma, Jonne (2017). The Biographical Turn: Biography as Critical Method in the Humanities and in Society. In Hans Renders, Binn de Haan & Jonne Harmsma (Eds.), *The Biographical Turn: Lives in History* (pp. 3–11). London: Routledge.

Sanders, Andrew (1988). *The Companion to A Tale of Two Cities*. London: Unwin Hyman.

Schor, Hilary (2000). *Dickens and the Daughter of the House*. Cambridge: Cambridge University Press.

Slater, Michael (1983). *Dickens and Women*. London: J. M. Dent.

Thompson, Christiana (Weller) (1850). [MS Journal]. Meynell Family Papers, Greatham, Sussex.

Thompson, Christiana (Weller) (1859). [Journal (typescript)]. Meynell Family Papers, Greatham, Sussex.

Tomalin, Claire (1991). *The Invisible Woman: The Story of Nelly Ternan and Charles Dickens*. New York: Knopf.

Tucker, David (1979). Dickens at Work on the MS of *A Tale of Two Cities*. *Études Anglaises*, 32, 449–457.

Wedgewood, Maurice (1967). The Quest for Frederick Dickens. *Dickensian*, 63, 32–35.

Weller, Thomas E. (1854, 23 March). [Autograph Letter to Charles Dickens (copy)]. Meynell Family Papers, Greatham, Sussex.

Woloch, Alex (2003). *The One vs. the Many: Minor Characters and the Space of the Protagonist in the Novel*. Princeton, NJ: Princeton University Press.

3

Parallel Lives, Converging Destinies

Charles Dickens and Thomas Babington Macaulay

David Paroissien

Of the under-researched areas of Dickens's childhood and youth, inattention to the influence of Thomas Babington Macaulay stands out: Dickens biographies by Slater (2009), Tomalin (2011), Douglas-Fairhurst (2011) and Patten (2012) treat this historian, essayist and Whig politician as no more than a spear-carrier. Prominent social and familial differences between the novelist and the historian suggest one reason why biographers and literary critics may have overlooked ideas and practices which connect the two writers. Accordingly, this essay addresses what Peter Rowland terms "a complete and utter silence" about their relationship (2011, p. 53), by confining attention to two overlooked topics: the failure by scholars to acknowledge Dickens's debt to Macaulay for his early political education, and the reluctance of critics to read *Barnaby Rudge* (1841) in the context of the historiographical landscape invoked by Macaulay when he urged MPs to support a change in England's system of Parliamentary representation in 1831–1832. Attention to history and the way it was recorded, declares Claire Tomalin, was not one of Dickens's strengths (2011, p. 122); this comment typifies a perception of Dickens as ill-informed about the discipline, and indifferent to methodological questions raised by historians in the early decades of the nineteenth century. Central to the debate – to be explored below – were competing notions about the importance of individual agency, the role of external forces and the historian's choice of focus: all pertinent considerations when Dickens made a bid for literary recognition by announcing his intention to write a three-volume novel based on events in the recent past.

Without question, the way each writer "began the world" presents a dramatic contrast between their respective fortunes and careers, and so perhaps accounts for a refusal to consider the two together. In the year Dickens turned 11, and started his "business life" in a "tumble-down old house" by the Thames (Allen 2011, p. 94), Macaulay (1800–1859) was admitted to Lincoln's Inn, one of London's four prestigious Inns of Court: the professional associations for barristers. Versed in Latin and Greek, fluent in French and Italian (Thomas 2010, pp. 43–44), his expectations of advancement as a barrister inadvertently mock the "evil hour" when it was proposed that young Charles should become "useful" and contribute to the family's domestic circumstances by earning six shillings a week. Writing in an autobiography he later abandoned, Dickens characterised the reaction of his parents to his becoming a "labouring hind" at Warren's Blacking. It was as if at 20, he wrote, with bitter detachment, "and distinguished at a grammar-school" he had been going to the very university Macaulay had recently left (Forster 1969, pp. 23–25). Yet despite the noticeable distance between them – 12 years chronologically, light years socially and educationally – Dickens and Macaulay, like "the Mercury in powder" and the "outlaw with a broom" in *Bleak House*, were curiously drawn together "from opposite sides of great gulfs" (*BH* 16).

The notion of individuals from different walks of life unified by an aggregate of social and cultural bonds that they failed to recognise, remains fundamental to the six pro-reform speeches Macaulay delivered in the House of Commons between 2 March 1831 and 28 February 1832. Insistence on the same trope of a web of complex and multiple relationships also characterises the social reality Dickens exposes in the passage above. "What connexion can there be," asks the anonymous narrator (*BH* 16), only to answer 30 chapters later, when the "infection and contagion" propagated by the "corrupted blood" of a London slum works "its retribution, through every order of society, up to the proudest of the proud, and to the highest of the high" (*BH* 46). Earlier, in a rejoinder to John Forster's observations that "two leading incidents" in Dickens's life had brought the two of them together in "some shadowy association," he elaborates how it was on "the coincidences, resemblances and surprises of life" that Dickens liked especially to dwell. Few things moved his fancy "so pleasantly. The world, he would say, was so much smaller than we thought it; [and] people supposed to be far apart were so constantly elbowing each other" (Forster 1969, p. 59). When rephrased, this homily about connectedness resembles the more rigorous theorising that Macaulay expressed when he urged MPs to recognise the interdependence of "the young energy of one class and the ancient privileges of another" (Macaulay 1898, p. 415), both of whom had a common stake in supporting parliamentary reform to preserve tranquility and promote the well-being of English society.

Six years after Dickens's introduction to work at Warren's Blacking, a succession of events combined to cement the biographical and intellectual "connexions" that this essay explores. In March 1830 Macaulay began his parliamentary career; he took his seat in the old Westminster Hall as a member for Calne, a village in Wiltshire and a "rotten" or "pocket" borough controlled by Lord Lansdowne, whose prerogative under the old system of parliamentary representation enabled him to nominate candidates. Once elected, Macaulay made his maiden speech in support of a bill to remove Jewish civic disabilities (see Henriques 1968; the bill finally received assent in 1860); however, he remained silent for the rest of the

Parliamentary session. After a visit to the Continent in July 1830 for a first-hand view of the July Revolution in Paris, he returned to London, a city alive with expectations of reform, which had already been triggered by the death of George IV in June, and further intensified when William IV opened the new Parliament on 26 October, amidst speculation that electoral reform would finally begin.

Meanwhile, the circumstances of Dickens's early life improved during the same interval. After release from industrial labour, a brief resumption of formal schooling and employment as a solicitor's clerk, he took two decisive steps: he enhanced his opportunities for employment, and restored his fractured education. Thus with assistance from John Henry Barrow (a maternal uncle who had founded *The Mirror of Parliament* in 1828), he obtained work as a freelance reporter (*Letters* 1:10, n.4), and simultaneously put to good use the reader's ticket to the British Museum that he had acquired on 8 February 1812, one day after he turned 18 (see Litvack 2018, p. 30). Casting a wide net, he extended his knowledge of English history and politics at a formative period of his intellectual development, against a political background enlivened by a sense of accelerated national change. Later, Dickens looked back on days passed in the Reading Room "as decidedly the usefullest to himself he had ever passed" (Forster 1969, p. 48). Seated there among copies of Britain's leading quarterlies and other journals – not unlike Pip inspired by his tutor – Dickens educated himself well enough to "hold [his] own" discussing the interesting topics of the day, "with the average of young men in prosperous circumstances" (*GE* 2:5). "No man who knew him in later years," Forster observed in his *Life*, would have suspected "his education in boyhood, almost entirely self-acquired as it was, to have been so rambling or hap-hazard" (1969, p. 48).

Thus equipped, and with his shorthand skills honed by a period of freelance reporting at Doctors' Commons (whose courts handled such matters as parochial business, divorce, marriage and probate), Dickens soon found himself assuming his place in the "old back row of the old [reporters'] gallery of the old House of Commons" (Fielding 1960, p. 347). In a sketch recalling his experiences and speaking in the persona of Boz, Dickens describes the reaction of "a county member" (that is, one who represented the interests of landowners and members of the aristocracy) to Macaulay, the eloquent and youthful MP for Calne. With a taste for long stories about brilliant figures of the past like Fox, Pitt, Sheridan and Canning, this "old hard-featured man" confessed to doubts about the disruptive contribution of newcomers. "He has a great contempt for all young Members of Parliament," Boz recounts. He "thinks it quite impossible that a man can say anything worth hearing, unless he has sat in the house for fifteen years at least, without saying anything at all. He is of opinion," he added, "that 'that young Macaulay' was a regular impostor," at one with "the throng of Exquisites" standing around in the old House, whom he regarded "with most profound contempt" ([Dickens] 1835).

Whatever autobiographical or class-conscious sentiments inflect the fictional voice of the elderly county member, the fact remains that Macaulay had had much to say. In the interval between his maiden speech and the publication of Dickens's sketch in the *Evening Chronicle* on 7 March 1835, he had made an indelible contribution to the national debate on Parliamentary reform: a fact that Dickens was well positioned to appreciate, given his exposure to the debates that followed, and his personal experiences.

The 18-year-old who perched on a bench in the reporters' gallery with colleagues – who were equally youthful but better educated than he – looked down on the nation's leaders from an unusual perspective. In contrast to his peers, and to adapt the words of Mr Weller, speaking of his son's "eddication," Dickens, like Sam, had been left to "run in the streets when he was wery young, and shift for hisself" (*PP* 20). Understandably, Dickens put this less humorously when he began an autobiographical account of his early days. In the section he contemplated in Geneva in 1846, while working on chapters 9 and 10 of *Dombey and Son* (where Paul Dombey is installed at Mrs Pipchin's establishment), he recalled a "passage in [his] own small life" (*Letters* 4:653), when, "so young and childish, and so little qualified," he had been left to undertake "the whole charge of [his] own existence" when fate assigned him to daily work at Warren's Blacking factory (Forster 1969, p. 479). "It's the only way to make a boy sharp, Sir," Mr Weller explained, reflecting on his unusual theory of childrearing: a sentiment to which Dickens assented but never recommended (*PP* 20). Pitching children "neck and crop into the world, to play at leap-frog with its troubles" (*PP* 16) might just as easily produce "a little robber or a little vagabond," he warned. Fortunately, in his own case "all these things worked together" to make him the disciplined and ambitious man he was (Forster 1969, pp. 28, 35).

With an outlook informed by hardship and misery, intimately experienced and keenly observed in the wretched lives of others, Dickens took in the spectacle before him. Below, in a packed House of Commons, MPs reassembled amidst bustle and excitement to debate the country's fate at a critical moment in its history. On one side stood advocates of reform; on the other, their opponents, High Tory upholders of privilege, committed to defending the status quo. Thus on the afternoon of 2 November 1830, the Duke of Wellington rose to his feet in this confrontational atmosphere to declare his own implacable resistance to reform. Britain, he stated, "possessed at the present moment a Legislature which answered all the good purposes of legislation, and this to a greater degree than any Legislature ever had answered in any country whatever" (*Hansard* 1830). Historians consider Wellington's response to be "one of the great parliamentary blunders of all time" (Hilton 2006, p. 418). Riots broke out, and London experienced seven days of violence; a week later, Wellington resigned. On 16 November, Charles Grey took over as the Whig Prime Minister, and five months later, the Parliamentary stage stood clear for Macaulay. Of the six pro-reform speeches he delivered between 2 March 1831 and 28 February 1832, it was the first that proved a "turning point" in the debates (Hilton 2006, p. 432); this development warrants further attention.

Nine days after Macaulay had spoken in support of a motion by Lord John Russell to bring forward a bill to amend the representation of the people in

England and Wales, the motion was carried without a division. There is no conclusive proof of Dickens's presence throughout the entire proceedings, but circumstantial evidence suggests that he participated in reporting the speeches that followed (see *Letters* 1:2, n.3), and that much of what Macaulay had to say fell upon receptive ears. Interesting questions arise concerning what Dickens heard first-hand; what he later digested on reflection from the pages of *The Mirror of Parliament*; and how the "lessons" Macaulay delivered to MPs might have appealed to a young reporter, committed to his role in taking down the first draft of English history at a unique moment; and what a young man – with a notebook on his knees, a pencil in hand and a nascent desire for literary recognition – might have made of Macaulay's words.

For someone eager to understand the political challenge England faced in the 1830s, the clarity of Macaulay's analysis had much to recommend it. "On his legs," in the jargon favoured by reporters, Macaulay began on 2 March 1831 by affirming his distrust "in all general theories of government," a tactic well suited to the enemies of change; he added that nothing would induce him to support "Universal Suffrage, because I think it would produce a destructive revolution." Accordingly, the case he put was both modest and pragmatic: he made it clear that reform of the franchise promised no panacea, and that the relief of social distress, particularly among the labouring classes, lay "beyond the control of the Government" (Macaulay 1898, pp. 409–410). The bill, he added on a later date, "will not give the people more work, or higher wages, or cheaper bread" (1898, p. 446); yet at the same time, he believed that government did have a role to play, most crucially to extend representation to its "natural allies." In Macaulay's eyes they constituted the "great masses of property and intelligence," a significant portion of the population who, he argued, "are most interested in preserving tranquility, and who know best how to preserve it" (1898, p. 411). Therefore the case for action, he believed, was self-evident and of benefit to the whole of society. "I hold it to be clearly expedient," Macaulay continued, that "in a country whose capital was superior in size and in population to the capitals of many kingdoms" and superior in "opulence, intelligence, and general respectability," we broaden the representation of the people in England and Wales (1898, pp. 410, 412).

Caution on this scale proved necessary in order to convince his target audience: the High Tory opponents of reform; among them were the four MPs who represented Oxford and Cambridge, together with others staunch in their allegiance to God, King and the Established Church. Such individuals, whom Dickens later scorned in *Bleak House* for their "Dandyism – in Religion, for instance" (*BH* 12), Macaulay handled with circumspection. Avoiding the ridicule employed by the anonymous narrator of Dickens's novel to mock those eager to cancel "a few hundred years of history" and put back "the hands upon the Clock of Time" (*BH* 12), Macaulay allowed that "in one respect at least [our ancestors] were wiser than we. They legislated for their own times" by framing a representative system, which, while not without defects, "was well adapted to the state of England in their own time" (1898, p. 414). But now, with the new wine bursting in "the old bottles," the appropriate recourse, he claimed, was to pay "a decent, a *rational*" reverence to the past rather than remain bound to the system for representation devised by superstitious adherence to the laws once framed centuries ago (1898, p. 415; emphasis added).

Macaulay's juxtaposition of the superstitious with the rational characterises the stance he assumes throughout his six speeches in favour of reform – that of the philosophic historian, whose role was to make secular sense of current events, and to draw inferences and assign responsibility for social change to a human rather than a divine agency. Societies, he understood, never remained static; rather, they evolved over centuries. Old corporations, formerly granted the right to choose representatives and send MPs to Westminster, change from one century to the next. Thus as new forms of property came into existence, new portions of society rose into prominence, with towns shrinking into villages, and villages "[swelling] into cities larger than the London of the Plantagenets." But while this natural growth continued, "Unhappily ... the artificial polity continued unchanged. The ancient form of representation remained; and precisely because the form remained, the spirit departed," only to be replaced by new pressure. Citing examples from European history and North America, Macaulay drew this conclusion: at the heart of the drive to extend the electoral franchise lay a democratic determination to curtail the power of landowners and the aristocracy. "All history," he continued,

> is full of revolutions, produced by causes similar to those which are now operating in England. A portion of the community which had been of no account expands and becomes strong. It demands a place in the system, suited, not to its former weakness, but to its present power. If this is granted, all is well. If this is refused, then comes the struggle between the young energy of one class and the ancient privileges of another. (Macaulay 1898, p. 415)

Macaulay drove home the implications of his analysis by way of a clear warning against inaction, delivered to Sir John Walsh (Tory MP for Sudbury), who had opposed Russell's bill as an "abortive" measure poised between leaving the existing representative system "as it is" and a failed effort "to make it perfectly symmetrical" (1898, p. 408). "I, Sir," Macaulay retorted, "do entertain great apprehension for the fate of my country. I do in my conscience believe that, unless the plan proposed, or some similar plan, be speedily adopted, great and terrible calamities will befall us" (1898, p. 411). These words, in fact, anticipate the keynote of the famous peroration in which Macaulay sounded the tocsin for all MPs: "Turn where we may, within, around, the voice of great events is proclaiming to us, Reform, that you may preserve." He urged:

> Save the greatest, and fairest, and most highly civilised community that ever existed, from calamities which may in a few days sweep away all the

rich heritage of so many ages of wisdom and glory. The danger is terrible. The time is short. If this bill should be rejected, I pray to God that none of those who concur in rejecting it may ever remember their votes with unavailing remorse, amidst the wreck of laws, the confusion of ranks, the spoliation of property, and the dissolution of the social order. (1898, pp. 425–426)

Macaulay returned to this sombre warning about "the state of the public mind" nine months later, when Lord Porchester (MP for Wooton Bassett) moved an amendment designed to delay the second reading of Russell's bill. Speaking in the Commons on 16 December 1831, he emphasised how from the beginning of these discussions, he had "supported Reform on two grounds; first, because I believe it to be in itself a good thing; and secondly, because" with the kingdom "convulsed by the question of Reform" from one end to the other, the dangers arising from delay have "greatly increased" (1898, pp. 486, 482, 486). All that he knew of the history of past times, he added, has "convinced me that the time has arrived when a great concession must be made to the democracy of England." Questions about whether the change "be in itself good or bad" have become irrelevant. The "thing" must now be done: "a law as strong as the laws of attraction and motion has decreed it" (1898, p. 489). These words may be compared with those Dickens later placed in the mouth of the Goblin of the Great Bell in *The Chimes*: "The voice of Time ... cries to man, Advance! ... Who seeks to turn him back, or stay him on his course, arrests a mighty engine which will strike the meddler dead" (*C* 3).

Macaulay's penultimate reform speech in December 1831 illustrates a second overriding contribution to the debates: the importance of assuming a calmer tone when the voice of Cassandra no longer served. Thus in a shift of tactics, he assumed the role of the philosophic historian anxious to encourage calm reflection, as he urged MPs to read "signs, of which it is impossible to misconceive the import" (Macaulay 1898, p. 424). Amplifying what he meant by "signs," Macaulay cautioned that history, looked at "in small portions, may be so constructed as to mean any thing, that it may be interpreted in as many ways as a Delphic oracle." Such easy explanations that the French Revolution "was the effect of concession" to popular rage, or, alternatively, that it was "produced by the obstinacy of an arbitrary government" remain "controversies [that] can never be brought to any decisive test, or to any satisfactory conclusion." However, to be "full of useful and precious instruction," he continued, we must contemplate history "in large portions," assessing, in one view, "the whole lifetime of great societies" (1898, pp. 489–490). To achieve that sweep, as he had argued earlier, MPs needed to approach the call for Parliamentary reform with an eye to the panorama of English history. He also noted that it was important to remember recent legislation. Just four years had elapsed since the repeal, in 1828 and 1829, of the oppressive Test and Corporation Acts (which made the holding of public office conditional on being a practising member of the Church of England); thus with the removal of Catholic disabilities, "The question of Parliamentary Reform" loomed ominously. "Is it possible," Macaulay reflected, "that gentlemen long versed in high political affairs cannot see the significance of such obvious developments? Let us therefore profit by experience and learn to see "the folly of delaying inevitable changes" (1898, pp. 424, 423).

By viewing the arguments Macaulay expressed during the Parliamentary debates as part of a context in which Dickens's political education developed in the 1830s, it is possible to compensate for what Humphry House identified as "One of the most irritating things about Dickens's biography"; the problem, in House's view, was that we "know so little about his work as a reporter in the House of Commons." He concedes that Dickens "must, in fact, have attended many of the chief debates between 1832 and 1836"; but he also admits the impossibility of saying "exactly which." Besides the Reform Bill and other significant acts such as the 1834 Poor Law Amendment Act and the Municipal Corporations Act of 1835, Dickens "must have been familiar with the details of argument on both sides of all the questions this legislation involved: they are in fact reflected in his work" (House 1941, p. 37). Nevertheless, House admitted, significant gaps persist; this is a source of annoyance to scholars, because it frustrates efforts to discern what Dickens knew.

Two rejoinders might be proposed to alleviate such frustration. First, as suggested above, a case exists for recognising Dickens's indebtedness to Macaulay. As one of a team of reporters on the staff of *The Mirror of Parliament*, the young Dickens took advantage of a unique opening: engaged by his uncle, he exploited this opportunity to make up for the formal schooling he had missed. Although evidence of his attendance at the reform debates remains partial, grounds exist to support the suggestion that Macaulay served as a worthy tutor, an able instructor versed in the central political issues of the time. In the course of six speeches delivered over nine months, he ranged widely over a variety of topics. On some occasions he addressed specifics such as the cost of elections, the problem of "outvoters" (those without a domicile in the constituency) or the need to double the number of candidates for large constituencies like Lambeth. On others, he spoke more professionally; for example, he raised questions about the instructional use of history, about the reliability of evidence, about how one should (and should not) read significance into past events and how facts about the past depend on contingencies that change over time and place. In short, besides speaking directly to the matter at hand – Lord John Russell's Bill to amend the representation of the people of England and Wales – he also explored issues fundamental to the practice and craft of history and to the theoretical concerns of the profession. It is therefore to these issues that this essay should turn, in order to assess a second lasting debt: the relevance of Macaulay's ideas about history to *Barnaby Rudge*, originally a three-volume historical novel promised for delivery in November 1836, but in fact not started and completed until 1841 (*Letters* 1:150).

Dickens's first historical novel benefited from its long postponement. With time for his thoughts to mature, he had an opportunity to reflect on what he had learned about historiography from Macaulay. That same interval also allowed him to absorb ideas from a second influential source: Thomas Carlyle, whose pronouncements in *Fraser's Magazine* in 1830 and elsewhere had the effect of echoing Macaulay's demand for historians to listen to a range of voices. Both urged a broadening of the discipline of history beyond the stiff and archaic limitations of their predecessors. Macaulay suggested that London be perceived through the eyes of a foreigner, in order to acquire a fresh perspective. He recommended taking in the view from "opulent seaports," "gigantic suburbs" and "manufacturing towns" – a call for expanded perspectives that Carlyle heartily endorsed. Historiography, the Scottish sage argued, had lost much of its vitality, in part because professionals had restricted their attention. He believed that a "disproportionate fondness" for "Senate-houses," "Battle-fields" and even "Kings' Antechambers" had marginalised other voices, and ignored past scenes and lives worthy of recognition. "Which was the greater innovator, which was the more important personage in man's history?" Carlyle asked. "[H]e who first led armies over Alps, and gained the victories of Cannae and Thrasymene; or the nameless boor who first hammered out for himself an iron spade?" In the course of time, he continued, "much of this must be amended; and he who sees no world but that of courts and camps; ... will pass for a more or less instructive Gazetteer, but will no long be called a Historian" (Carlyle 2002, pp. 10, 6, 10). The question, in essence, was, to whom does history belong?

Elsewhere, Macaulay voiced similar concerns. Like Carlyle, he complained that history had become ossified and conventional; it was, he believed, a discipline borne down by a self-imposed "code of conventional decencies, as absurd as that which has been the bane of the French Drama" (Macaulay 1828, p. 362). Improved history, therefore, would not necessarily omit "the court, the camp, the senate"; rather "[t]he perfect historian," he argued, would look below "the surface of affairs," where "noiseless revolutions" occur. Urged thus to explore "even the retreats of misery," historians committed to a new agenda could "reclaim those materials which the novelist had appropriated." By judiciously selecting, rejecting, and arranging, they could also show us "the nation," could "elucidate the condition of society," and illustrate "the operation of laws, of religion, and of education" (Macaulay 1828, pp. 363–364, 362).

If *Barnaby Rudge* is read in this context, fascinating connections between the novel and the agenda advocated by Macaulay and Carlyle begin to emerge. Macaulay argued in his influential review of Henry Neele's *The Romance of History: England* that since no history in its current form "approaches our notion of what history ought to be," historians should reflect on what Macaulay considered its inadequacies. Among these he singled out a narrowness of scope and a preoccupation with government papers, archives and official documents. An interesting example cited by Macaulay is Lord Clarendon's tendency, in his six-volume *History of the Rebellion and Civil Wars in England* (1702–1704), to fill hundreds of folio pages "with copies of state papers, in which the same assertions and contradictions are repeated" until the reader "is overpowered with weariness." He asks his readers to suppose, instead, that Clarendon had "condescended" to be "Boswell of the Long Parliament." In that capacity, the reviewer notes, he could have drawn on a wealth of other material: anecdotes, gossip, ribaldry, cant, letters, memoirs and biographies. He summarises: "Let us suppose that he had made his Cavaliers and Roundheads talk in their own style ... Would not his work in that case have been more interesting? Would it not have been more accurate?" (Macaulay 1828, p. 362).

This affirmation of the suitability of such materials for serious history conveyed an important directive. Past historians, Macaulay cautioned, have been too preoccupied with "the dignity of history" and artificial rules. They narrowed the field of inquiry by being rigorously enforced, thereby excluding voices from "below" – that is, the rebellious inhabitants of squalid courts and alleys later so powerfully figured and given voice in *A Tale of Two Cities*. As a corrective, therefore, he recommended that writers should open their eyes "to ordinary men." Historians need to see men "as they appear in their ordinary business and in their ordinary pleasures." They must mingle with them "in crowds of the exchange and the coffee house"; they must gain admittance "to the convivial table," "the domestic hearth," and "even bear with vulgar expressions." Working by judicious selection, rejection and arrangement, the "perfect historian," Macaulay concluded, "is he who gives to truth those attractions" which in practice "have been usurped by fiction" (Macaulay 1828, pp. 362, 364). Two years later, Carlyle made much the same point. He maintained in his essay "On History" that while a talent for history "may be said to be born with us, as our chief inheritance," we must retain our vigilance and adopt a "reverent humility in our inquiries into History ... Let us search more and more into the Past," he urged, and explore it "as the true fountain of knowledge; by whose light alone ... can the Present and the Future be interpreted or guessed at" (Carlyle 2002, pp. 3, 8).

Although *Barnaby Rudge* falls short of the achievement of Dickens's later novels, his panoramic "Tale of the Riots of 'Eighty" comes close to providing an anatomy of society compatible with strictures like these. For example, the two halves of the novel combine to produce a five-year sweep of history, opening "In the year 1775," then falling silent, before resuming "One wintry evening" five years later, recommencing the narrative in preparation for a description of eight days of rioting in June 1780. The first half concentrates on private and domestic scenes, tensions at home and generational conflicts between family members occasioned by changing values. In the second, historical figures and verifiable public events predominate, as Dickens provides a slowly unravelled account of the attack on Newgate prison and the destruction unleashed by drunken rioters. A comparable commitment to covering a cross-section of society characterises both halves: the action moves from humble domestic interiors and blind courts "reeking with stagnant odours" to a genteel residence off the Strand, or to the estate of a landed Catholic gentleman. On one occasion the narrator asserts: "Chroniclers are privileged to enter where they list, to come and go through keyholes, to ride upon the wind, to overcome, in their soarings up and down, all obstacles of distance, time, and place" (*BR* 9). The language lacks eloquence and verges on the bathetic; but the sentiment affirms the historian's freedom to move where he will, while spinning a central thread.

Dickens anchored the text's action around Gabriel Varden, an artisan hero in the democratic mode recommended by Macaulay and Carlyle. Humble yet brave, his conception of "the sturdy blacksmith" offers an alternative model of heroic conduct: a craftsman with courage and dignity ignored by those historians anxious to write history in an "elevated" tone and to treat only public men and public ceremonies. Dickens's Varden had the additional advantage of authenticity: he was grounded in recorded history. The original source remains to be identified, but the "Vardon" [*sic*] of the original title (*Letters* 1:150) took shape owing to the bravery of a Moravian blacksmith who, under threat, refused to strike off the irons of prisoners released from Newgate prison during the Gordon riots. Such a figure bears a resemblance to individuals now sought by microhistorians committed to the historiological goal of finding representatives whose personal qualities extend to a whole class (Loriga 2014).

Dickens's "respectable tradesman" also does service as a surrogate historian, given the task of solving some of the story's mysteries; an early description of Varden outside his shop in Clerkenwell hints at this agenda. He is portrayed as "gazing disconsolately at a great wooden emblem of a key" dangling from the house-front. The key swings to and fro "with a mournful creaking noise, as if complaining that it had nothing to unlock"; inside, the shop appears dark and dingy, full of tools of "uncouth make and shape," whose purpose or function remains unclear (*BR* 4). Later, with the business of the day behind him, Varden sets off on his first assignment: an outing to ascertain the progress of a "wounded gentleman" (*BR* 5) he had helped to a friend's house the night before.

The action that follows unfolds with all the familiar Gothic trappings; but to admit that is not to deny the sophistication with which the novel examines the role of the historian. The hinted mismatch between signs and things, and the challenge of reading the past, suggest the seriousness of the novel's engagement with the task of history, further underlined by the role of the raven in the story. Ironically named Grip, his name and hoarse croak mock the combined efforts of both the locksmith and Mr Haredale to comprehend the actions of Mary Rudge. On the occasion of her evasive explanation for giving up the annuity she receives, the raven hops onto a table in the chamber where her meeting with Mr Haredale takes place. Assuming "the air of some old necromancer" intent on "a great folio volume that lay open on a desk," the bird kept his eye on the book throughout the whole interview, "listening to everything" under the mask "of pretending to read hard," and with the air "of a very sly human rascal" (*BR* 25).

The raven's "highly reflective state" continues. When taken by Barnaby to a churchyard, he is later described as walking up and down with an eye on the nearby tombstones. As he studies these markers of past lives "with a very critical taste," he would cry in hoarse tones, "after a long inspection of an epitaph," "'I'm a devil, I'm a devil, I'm a devil!' but whether he addressed his observations to any supposed person below, or merely threw them off as a general remark, is a matter of uncertainty" (*BR* 25). David Copperfield has a comparable moment of doubt, prompted by Mr Dick's questioning the date he had supplied for the execution of Charles I. In response to Mr Dick, wondering whether or not history ever lied, David quickly assures him that it does not. David later explains that he was "ingenuous and young" at the time, and full of the confidence that deeper introspection would have undermined, in order to produce a less decisive response (*DC* 17). The preferred stance of the chronicler, one is left to conclude, is that of the historian willing to stand back and take a look at "The World as it rolled" by, one of the novel's trial titles Dickens briefly contemplated (Stone 1987, p. 106).

The "connexions" this essay has proposed took root shortly after Dickens's own eyes became used "to the mist" of the old House and looked down from the reporters' gallery on its Members below, conscious of having passed through scenes of which they could have had no knowledge. Amidst a hum of voices and confusion, and beyond "the glare of the chandeliers," he was able to fix on the voice and gestures of a single figure: "that young Macaulay" might have aroused the contempt of those who belonged to a class of men "now nearly extinct"; but to a novice reporter eager for news about the world to which he was heir, that young "imposter" had wisdom to impart (Dickens 1854, p. 94). What Dickens appears to have learned he was quick to absorb in the course of his evolution from sketch writer to novelist. In both capacities, he developed a voice no less distinctive than Macaulay's. Each writer, in fact, acquired an equally impressive public following, Macaulay as the author of four volumes of his unfinished *History of England* (1848–1856) and Dickens as a novelist whose reputation increased with every publication.

From their respective heights, the two authors viewed each other's achievements with wary respect. Macaulay regarded Dickens as "both a man of genius and a good-hearted man" whose "faults of taste" he acknowledged in private but refused to air in public. Given the opportunity to review *American Notes* (1842) and finding he could not praise it, he refused to cut it up. He declared in a letter to Macvey Napier of 19 October 1842 that the book had "some gleams of genius" but too frequently appeared "vulgar and flippant" (*Letters* 3:289, n.2). Dickens, for his part, was not averse to venting reservations; he wrote, in his article "Insularities":

> The accomplished Mr. Macaulay, in the third volume of his brilliant History, writes loftily about 'the thousands of clerks and milliners who are now thrown into raptures by the sight of Loch Katrine and Loch Lomond.'

No such responsible gentleman, in France or Germany, writing history – writing anything – would think it fine to sneer at any inoffensive and useful class of his fellow subjects. If the clerks and milliners – who pair off arm in arm, by thousands, for Loch Katrine and Loch Lomond, to celebrate the Early Closing Movement, we presume – will only imagine their presence poisoning those waters to the majestic historian as he roves along the banks, looking for Whig Members of Parliament to sympathise with him in admiration of the beauties of Nature, we think they will be amply avenged in the absurdity of the picture. ([Dickens] 1856, p. 3)

Shortly before the appearance of these comments in *Household Words*, Dickens treated the volume under review with more respect. In an incident recorded by George Augustus Sala, he describes calling on Dickens, then resident in Paris; the meeting occurred on 8 January 1856 and was not without awkwardness. Sala had come to borrow money and arrived, Dickens later recalled, with "a strong flavour of the wine shop and the billiard table" on him (*Letters* 8:20). He found Dickens, "slightly fatigued," seated in a big armchair, intent on the book before him: Macaulay's *History of England*. The novelist, Sala explains, had "dug" himself into the text, "determined to master Macaulay." With his head between his hands "and pored into the pages," Dickens conveyed "the attitude of the man of indomitably Strong Will, who had addressed himself to a task … which he had inflexibly made up his mind to accomplish" (Sala 1894, 1:124–125). Evidently mute to Sala, the voice of "that young Macaulay," first heard 45 years before, seems to have played on in Dickens's ear. Three years later, Dickens began a second historical novel, this time focusing on the French Revolution. *A Tale of Two Cities* was openly indebted to Carlyle; but if the text is read attentively, traces of Thomas Babington Macaulay's counsel about the historian's critical reflections subtly and persistently declare their presence.

References

Allen, Michael (2011). *Charles Dickens and the Blacking Factory*. St Leonard's: Oxford-Stuckley Publications.
Carlyle, Thomas (2002). On History. In Chris R. Vanden Bossche (Ed.), *Historical Essays* (pp. 3–13). Berkeley: University of California Press.
[Dickens, Charles] (1835, 7 March/in press). The House, 7 March, *Evening Chronicle*. [from forthcoming *Sketches by Boz*, ed. Paul Schlicke, Oxford University Press].
Dickens, Charles (1854). *Sketches by Boz. Illustrative of Every-Day Life and Every-Day People*. London: Chapman and Hall.
[Dickens, Charles] (1856, 19 January). Insularities. *Household Words*, 13, 1–4.
Douglas-Fairhurst, Robert (2011). *Becoming Dickens: The Invention of a Novelist*. Cambridge, MA: Harvard University Press.

Fielding, K.J. (Ed.) (1960). *The Speeches of Charles Dickens*. Oxford: Clarendon Press.
Forster, John (1969). *The Life of Charles Dickens*. New ed., with notes & index by A.J. Hoppé. 2 vols. London: Dent.
Hilton, Boyd. (2006). *A Mad, Bad, & Dangerous People? England 1783–1846*. Oxford: Clarendon Press.
Hansard Parliamentary Debates (1830, 2 November). 3rd series, vol. 1, 52.
Henriques, U.R.Q. (1968, July). The Jewish Emancipation Controversy in Nineteenth-Century Britain. *Past and Present*, 40, 126–146.
House, Humphry (1941). *The Dickens World*. 2nd ed. London: Oxford University Press.
Litvack, Leon (2018). "Dickens's Lifetime Reading," In Robert L. Patten, John O. Jordan & Catherine Waters (Eds.), *The Oxford Handbook of Charles Dickens* (pp. 25–42). Oxford: Oxford University Press.
Loriga, Sabina (2014). The Role of the Individual in History: Biographical and Historical Writing in the Nineteenth and Twentieth Century. In Hans Renders & Binne de Haan (Eds.), *Theoretical Discussions of Biography: Approaches from History, Microhistory, and Life Writing* (pp. 75–93). Leiden & Boston: Brill.
Macaulay, Thomas Babington (1828, May). Art III: *The Romance of History. England*. By Henry Neele. *Edinburgh Review*, 47, 331–367.
Macaulay, Thomas Babington (1898). *The Works of Lord Macaulay, Speeches, Poems and Miscellaneous Writing*. Albany Edition. Vol. 1. London: Longmans, Green.
Patten, Robert L. (2012). *Charles Dickens and "Boz": The Birth of an Industrial-Age Author*. Cambridge: Cambridge University Press.
Rowland, Peter (2011). Bout No. 2: Boz v. Bab. In *Dickensian Digressions: The Hunter, the Haunter and the Haunted* (pp. 51–119). Palo Alto: Academica Press.
Sala, G[eorge] A[ugustus] (1894). *Things I Have Seen and People I Have Known*. 2 vols. London: Cassell.
Slater, Michael (2009). *Charles Dickens*. New Haven, CT & London: Yale University Press.
Stone, Harry (1987). *Dickens' Working Notes for His Novels*. Chicago, IL: University of Chicago Press.
Thomas, William (2010). Thomas Babington Macaulay, Childhood and Education. *Oxford Dictionary of National of Biography* (Vol. 35, pp. 43–44). Oxford: Oxford University Press.
Tomalin, Claire (2011). *Charles Dickens: A Life*. London: Viking.

4

Decent Restraint Spurned

Dickens, Penal Policy and Conflict at Cold Bath Fields Prison, 1846–1850

Neil Davie

The subject of Dickens's relationship with London's Cold Bath Fields Prison, and its governor George Laval Chesterton in the second half of the 1840s, was first explored over 50 years ago by Philip Collins in his *Dickens and Crime* (1962), a work which, as Jeremy Tambling has noted, remains, despite its limitations, "indispensable for anyone interested in prisons, the police, capital punishment and the treatment of crime in Dickens" (2009, p. 48). This essay draws on current understandings of penal policy of the period, and of Dickens's complex and often paradoxical penology, which is "hard to pin down" (Paroissien 2009, p. 27); it also benefits from new evidence from the prison's archives, to suggest that the conflict between governor Chesterton and a section of the Middlesex justices had wider implications than hitherto suspected, both for Dickens's attitudes towards penal reform, and for his involvement (along with the prison governor and Angela Burdett Coutts) in the Urania Cottage project. These events shed fresh light on the background to Dickens's article entitled "Pet Prisoners," with its reference to those who "spurn every sort of decent restraint and reasonable consideration" and who "hold the dangerous principle that the end justifies any means, and to whom no means, truth and fair dealing usually excepted, come amiss" ([Dickens] 1850, p. 97).

During the 1840s, the fate of four central London prisons, along with that of their 2,500 inmates, was caught up in a maelstrom of debate, controversy and conflict. Two of the four prisons in question – Cold Bath Fields in Clerkenwell and Tothill Fields in Westminster, both houses of correction for the county of Middlesex – were financed by local ratepayers and supervised by the county magistrates. They catered for a heterogeneous population of petty criminals of both sexes and all ages: debtors, inmates awaiting trial and a smaller group of prisoners earmarked for the gallows or for one of the transport ships bound for the Antipodes. Pentonville and Millbank, by contrast, were convict prisons; financed and run by central government, their inmates were serving sentences for crimes

Reading Dickens Differently, First Edition. Edited by Leon Litvack and Nathalie Vanfasse.
© 2020 John Wiley & Sons Ltd. Published 2020 by John Wiley & Sons Ltd.

that had formerly carried the death penalty, but which now involved terms of two or three years' imprisonment in the case of Millbank, or a short "probationary" period of incarceration followed by transportation for those being held at Pentonville.

The existence of two parallel systems of penal discipline was not in itself a recipe for controversy and conflict; so-called "local" prisons like Cold Bath Fields and Tothill Fields had existed side by side with the convict system for more than a century; however, a number of other aspects of the situation on the ground need to be recognised. First is the fact that since the mid-1830s, the Middlesex magistrates and the Home Office had opted for diametrically opposed systems of prison management. This would not have been a problem in itself, but for the fact that the Home Office and its newly appointed team of national prison inspectors considered such magisterial independence a wholly unacceptable state of affairs; they used every means at their disposal to steer the wayward county bench back onto the penal straight and narrow. Another complicating factor was that while generally the Middlesex magistrates of this period presented a united front in the face of what they saw as unwarranted meddling in their affairs by central government, there was one brief period at the end of the 1840s when internal dissention on the bench resulted in the county's penal policy taking a radically different direction, much closer to that favoured by the Whig government of the day. This had dramatic consequences for Cold Bath Fields and for its governor George Laval Chesterton (1801–1868), a former army captain in charge at the prison since 1829; there would also be significant consequences for Dickens.

In "Pet Prisoners," the leading article for *Household Words* in the issue of 27 April 1850, Dickens would make clear his position in the great penological debate of his day. "There is a hot class of riders of hobby-horses in the field, in this century," he wrote,

> who think they do nothing unless they make a steeple-chase of their object, throw a vast quantity of mud about, and spurn every sort of decent restraint and reasonable consideration under their horses' heels. This question has not escaped such championship. It has its own steeple-chase riders, who hold the dangerous principle that the end justifies any means, and to whom no means, truth and fair dealing usually excepted, come amiss. (1850, p. 97)

This was no mere abstract question for Dickens; he had chosen his colours in the penal steeplechase at the beginning of the 1840s and had indeed taken to the saddle himself. In his acerbic travelogue, *American Notes for General Circulation* (1842), he had condemned unequivocally the system of cellular isolation he had seen on a visit to Philadelphia's Eastern Penitentiary in March 1842, describing one of its solitary inmates as "a man buried alive; to be dug out in the slow round of years; and in the meantime dead to everything but torturing anxieties and horrible despair." In contrast, Dickens had nothing but praise for the rival system of supervised daytime "association" in operation at Boston's House of Correction, where, he stated, "keen and vigilant superintendence" meant that "five hundred men may pick oakum in the same room, without a sound" or walk the treadwheel "with little or no noise." As a result, he declared, "even a word of personal communication among the prisoners" was "almost impossible" (*AN* 3; see also Grass 2000, pp. 50–70; Paroissien 2009, pp. 34–38). In the same work, Dickens had publicly commended the regimes in place at the two London prisons operating the same associated or "silent" system: Cold Bath Fields and Tothill Fields (*AN* 3). A laudatory footnote (not found in modern reprints of *American Notes*) named Cold Bath Fields' governor George Chesterton and his Tothill Fields colleague, former Royal Navy Lieutenant Augustus Frederick Tracey, as "enlightened and superior men." He added that "it would be as difficult to find persons better qualified for the functions they discharge with firmness, zeal, intelligence, and humanity, as it would be to exceed the perfect order and arrangement of the institutions they govern" (Dickens 1842, pp. 121–122; see also Dickens 1846).

The silent system had been running at Cold Bath Fields since the end of 1834 and at Tothill Fields since June 1835 – that is, less than a year into Tracey's governorship (House of Lords 1835, pp. 89–90; Westminster Bridewell 1834–1835). Dickens had first visited Cold Bath Fields in 1835, while preparing *Sketches by Boz*, and had observed operations at Tothill Fields in 1841; as his letters demonstrate, he followed closely the affairs of both institutions during the 1840s (Collins 1962, p. 67; *Letters* 2:270). The tone and content of those communications tend to confirm Collins's assertion that "Tracey was a closer friend ... while Chesterton was the man whose prison Dickens knew better, and whom he consulted more on penal matters" (1962, p. 65). With such connections, Dickens was well-placed to observe the repeated efforts made during that decade by Home Office officials, notably inspectors William Crawford and Whitworth Russell, to force upon the Middlesex prisons the rival separate system. The latter had become official British government policy after Crawford had returned from a tour of the United States in 1833–1834, full of admiration for the regime in place at Philadelphia's Eastern State Penitentiary. His subsequent report for the Home Office noted that he had been "particularly struck by the mild and subdued spirit which seemed to pervade the temper of the [Philadelphia] convicts, and which is essentially promoted by reflection, solitude and the absence of corporal punishment" (House of Commons 1834, p. 12; see also Davie 2017, pp. 371–450; Johnston 2006).

The report was, however, highly critical of the associated or silent system, which its author had witnessed in operation at New York's Auburn Prison; his conclusions were diametrically opposed to those that Dickens reached in the following decade. Crawford claimed that plentiful opportunities for illicit communication remained, and that punishment for breaches of discipline was frequent, swift and brutal. The British visitor was deeply shocked by both the severity and the arbitrariness of punishment at Auburn: prison staff seemed to be empowered to flog at will. Crawford cited an official report of 1827, in which the institution's physician, Dr Tuttle, stated that "cases of punishment, so severe as to require hospital treatment, were very common, perhaps every month" (House of Commons 1834, pp. 17–18).

Crawford's report was ready by July 1834; by the summer of the following year the separate system was government policy, and in October 1835 Crawford himself was named as one of a team of five Home Office inspectors charged with implementing the programme. Along with Whitworth Russell (a former Millbank prison chaplain), Crawford was nominally responsible for inspecting the houses of correction in the "Home District" – that is, the counties of Middlesex, Kent, Essex, Hertfordshire, Surrey, Berkshire, Buckinghamshire, Sussex, Dorset, Wiltshire, Hampshire and Oxfordshire; in practice the two men wielded considerable influence over both the direction and the pace of penal reform throughout the country in the late 1830s and 1840s (Forsythe 1991, pp. 321–324).

Cold Bath Fields attracted particular attention from the government inspectors (Davie 2017, pp. 291–369). There were several reasons for this. First was the prison's sheer size: with close on 1,000 inmates packed into its 500 cells, its prison population was twice that of the "model" Pentonville prison (opened in 1842, run on strictly separate lines), or that of Millbank (the other government-run penitentiary-style prison, opened in 1816) (House of Commons 1843b, p. 119; 1847a, p. 152). The regime at Cold Bath Fields was, moreover, closely linked with the Society for the Improvement of Prison Discipline, an influential penal pressure group founded in 1816. The Society's longstanding chairman, Samuel Hoare Jr, was a Middlesex magistrate, who had played a leading role on the prison's committee of visiting magistrates since Chesterton's appointment in 1829, and may well have been instrumental in the decision to appoint the former army captain to the governorship at Cold Bath Fields. Hoare was a late convert to the silent system, but in the years leading up to his death in 1847 he proved a resourceful and articulate advocate for the regime in place in the Middlesex prisons, and thus represented a very public challenge to orthodox penal expertise as represented by the prison inspectorate (Davie 2017, pp. 291–369).

Finally, mention should be made of the Cold Bath Fields governor himself. Whereas Augustus Tracey might complain in private of the opprobrium heaped on Tothill Fields and its management by the Home Office inspectors (Westminster Bridewell 1843; House of Commons 1842) – though the latter were careful to make clear that the governor himself was beyond reproach – Chesterton's opposition was of a more public kind. Working together with Hoare, Chesterton authored a number of reports and letters in the late 1830s and early 1840s, in which he defended Cold Bath Fields' silent regime. Some of them were openly critical of what he considered the shoddy treatment that he and his prison had received at the hands of Crawford and Russell; all were widely reported in the press (Middlesex Sessions 1837; Prison Discipline 1838). Chesterton was even more forthright in a pair of anonymously authored articles published in the *Monthly Law Magazine and Political Review* in October and November 1838 ([Chesterton]

1838a, 1838b). Referring to the inspectors' *Third Report* of the previous year (House of Commons 1838), he castigated its authors both for the report's content and for the method adopted:

> The Report is remarkable for contrasts exhibited to disparage the opponent cause, and to exalt the one which it adopts. We find every term of reproach and depreciation which polite language supplies levelled at the silent system, and the choicest encomiums bestowed on the happy contrast afforded by its rival ... [T]his Third Report hazards assertions of so positive and dogmatical a kind, and indulges in such sanguine anticipations and fanciful hopes, that we must a fortiori conclude either that its authors are so blinded by zeal as to behold every thing on this subject through a false medium; or that they are unequal to the just appreciation of human character; or that they are woefully incompetent to draw plain logical deductions. If the subject were one demanding less gravity, we should ourselves be induced to smile. (1838a, p. 6; 1838b, p. 165)

Particularly galling to Chesterton was a section of the *Third Report* (House of Commons 1838, p. 111) devoted to "Effects of imprisonment in the Metropolitan gaols," in which Cold Bath Fields and Tothill Fields found themselves included among what Chesterton regarded as some of the worst examples of penal practice in the capital, while separate prisons like Pentonville and Millbank were wholly omitted from censure:

> Can these gentlemen adduce any sound reason why their praise and censure (if, indeed, either is to be at all esteemed) are not more justly distributed, or why, in the face of such testimony, the obloquy cast upon other prisons is to be withheld from the General Penitentiary [at Millbank]? And do they not perceive how inevitably they must sink in public estimation, while their course is marked by such wayward partiality? ... We warn these gentlemen that to class the prison at Cold-Bath Fields, with its careful discipline, and the Westminster Bridewell [at Tothill Fields], no less respectably conducted ... with gaols where sound discipline is from various considerations unattempted, is to perpetrate a crying injustice, calculated to arouse reproachful sentiments, nearly allied to indignation. ([Chesterton] 1838b, pp. 172–173)

That Chesterton felt confident enough to take the unusual step for a public servant of voicing – albeit anonymously – his opposition to the plans of the government inspectorate says much for his combative personality; it also reflects his confidence in backing the Middlesex bench on this issue. This state of affairs must be understood in the context of broader policy debates and political divisions in the 1840s. Such contextualisation is crucial for the argument to be developed here.

It relies on an approach that involves what historical sociologist Philip Abrams calls "the meshing of life-history and social history in a singular fate" (1982, p. 297), which constantly juxtaposes microhistory and biography on the one hand, with broader historical narratives and structures on the other, to the benefit of both (Renders & De Haan 2014; Magnússon 2017). In short, as historian John Lewis Gaddis has observed, "It's a little like riding a unicycle; you need to be aware all the time of a wider horizon, even as you concentrate on the single problematic point at which the rubber meets the road" (2002, p. 116).

The death of Samuel Hoare in December 1847 seems to have triggered a power struggle on the Middlesex bench for control of the county's prisons, with lawyer and former Whig MP Benjamin Rotch leading a faction that was keen to see the county give up its longstanding opposition to government penal policy. Rotch was a convinced separator; he had told a meeting of the Middlesex bench in October 1846 that "the congregated system of prison discipline was not one which ought to be tolerated in any Christian country, in consequence of the odious contamination which was necessary to it" (Meeting 1846, p. 6). He made no secret of his ambition to see Cold Bath Fields prison demolished and replaced by "another which would be far more applicable to an improved system of prison discipline"; indeed he was in discussion with a Tottenham-based railway company – seemingly without the sanction of his fellow magistrates – with a view to selling the site for the construction of a new railway terminus (Meeting 1846, p. 6).

Alongside these plans for the medium term, however, Rotch was also keen to bring immediate changes to the regime at the Middlesex House of Correction; it was no doubt with this objective in mind that he successfully lobbied for the chairmanship of the prison's visiting justices' committee (Samuel Hoare's old power base) at the beginning of 1848. Despite the impression given in Chesterton's memoirs (Chesterton 1856, 2:196), and indeed in Collins's work on the subject (1962, pp. 68–70), it is clear that Rotch was not the only member of the county bench to challenge the support given to the silent system by Hoare and other leading silentists like Sir Peter Laurie, and his nephew Peter Northall Laurie (see Northall Laurie 1837; Laurie 1846).

That Rotch's was not a lone voice among his fellow magistrates is confirmed by the result of an election for the chairmanship of the Middlesex Quarter Sessions in December 1844, in which he gained a respectable 25% of the vote (Meeting 1844, p. 2) and again took up the post he had previously held in 1833–1835 (*Letters* 5:184). Indeed, on several occasions in the following period, Rotch was able to gain backing from his fellow magistrates for policy changes at Cold Bath Fields, though admittedly not without difficulty. A good example of this is a meeting of the county bench in May 1847, when he supported a successful motion calling for the abolition of treadwheel labour for female inmates at the prison; Rotch's subsequent motion proposing that a committee be set up to consider alternatives to the treadwheel – which he termed a "disgrace" (Meeting 1847a, p. 7) – was also carried (Meeting 1847b, p. 7). It is worth noting that when the subject had first been raised the previous autumn, the magistrates had been presented with letters from the governor, the chaplains and the prison surgeon, all opposing any change of policy on the treadwheel (Meeting 1846, p. 6); the motion had failed on that and on a subsequent occasion, but would ultimately be carried, with a comfortable majority of 18 to 4. Although Rotch would no doubt have been gratified by such advances, his lack of an effective power base had limited his ability to effect root-and-branch reform at the Middlesex prisons. That was about to change.

Like other advocates of the separate system, Rotch was keen to challenge publicly the arguments Dickens had advanced in *American Notes*. It is clear, moreover, as Collins's pioneering research demonstrated (1962, p. 68), that Rotch considered an attack on Cold Bath Fields and an attack on Dickens's penology to represent two sides of the same coin. Rotch's priorities can be explained in part by the fact that by 1848 both Chesterton and Dickens were well-known public advocates of the silent system. Rotch's initiative also needs to be seen though in the context of the close relationships which had been established by this date between Dickens and the governors at Cold Bath Fields and Tothill Fields, and to a lesser extent with the chaplains of the two prisons, Edward Illingworth and George Henry Hine, in the joint enterprise the novelist had conceived with Angela Burdett Coutts: Urania Cottage (Hartley 2008; Collins 1962, pp. 94–116).

Chesterton's memoirs, *Revelations of Prison Life* (1856), published shortly after his retirement, record an undated meeting of the Middlesex bench, in which Rotch

> attempted with much asperity, to depreciate the writings of Mr. Dickens, and quoted a work on prisons, by a *Mr. Adshead* [1845, 1847], a rabid separatist, and making that citation, Mr. Rotch caustically exclaimed, 'Mr Dickens, whose statements on the prisons of America have been blown to the four winds of heaven, by the work of Mr. Adshead!' (1856, 2:186–187)

New evidence from the archives of the Middlesex prisons and from contemporary press accounts indicate that this declaration (which referenced Joseph Adshead, who was very critical of Cold Bath Fields, and of Dickens) was part of a broader attack by Rotch and his supporters on the county's silent-system prisons. As noted above, Rotch's party had been calling for some time for the demolition of Cold Bath Fields and Tothill Fields, and for the construction in their place of one or more new prisons on the Pentonville model; but it was only in 1848 that were they in a position to take concrete action. Thus in September of that year, Rotch, along with fellow justice Hector Rose, set in motion a new inspection of Cold Bath Fields, alleging, in a presentment to the Quarter Sessions, that the prison was "insufficient, inconvenient and inadequate to give effect to the several rules and regulations relating thereto prescribed by law." A series of inspections did indeed take place over the next few months; but despite a damning report by a committee of the visiting justices in December 1848 – presumably at the initiative of Rotch – which spoke of the need for "great alterations" involving "a considerable outlay" in order to achieve "the profitable employment of the prisoners" and "effect reformation and moral employment," nothing came of the initiative (Meeting 1848b; Cold Bath 1848c; Chesterton 1856, 2:201–202).

Rotch never entirely succeeded in quashing the opposition to his plans for the county prisons. The obstruction sprang from principled hostility among Conservatives and radicals to the perceived cruelty of the Pentonville-style separate system favoured by Russell's Whig government (see Laurie 1846); it also arose out of concerns about government function creep in the criminal justice field, and from what one Middlesex magistrate described as the "monstrous and unnecessary expenditure" involved in the proposed changes (Marylebone 1848, p. 6). In this sense, as Davie has observed (2017), the politics of penal reform in this period was never simply "about" the arguments for or against the separate and silent systems, as both Collins and McKnight imply (Collins 1962, pp. 52–93, 117–139; McKnight 1993, pp. 18–25). Indeed for some, both within and without Parliament, discussions of the finer points of the silent and separate systems paled into insignificance when compared with the urgent need to pursue other priorities such as restraining spending on prisons, imposing longer sentences, or scaling up transportation to Australia.

Despite opposition to his plans on such grounds, for much of 1848 and the early months of 1849 Rotch maintained a tight grip over the management of Cold Bath Fields. One consequence of his new influence in the prison was a campaign to urge both prisoners and warders to commit themselves to teetotalism, a cause clearly close to his heart; indeed Rotch chaired the first meeting of the National Temperance Society in 1843 (Couling 1862, p. 168). Chesterton was no impartial observer of course; but his later description of the mood in the prison during this period gives a vivid sense of the enmity which developed between the two men:

> [D]isorganization prevailed, espionage was encouraged, and idle rumours, baseless charges, and mock abuses, constituted grounds for vexatious investigations, until that enormous establishment was rent by complicated intrigues, by internal broils, and by a state of anarchy which threatened to derange the whole machinery of its discipline.
>
> In the midst of all this turmoil, one would scarcely fail to marvel at Mr. Rotch's rare indefatigability (worthy, indeed, of a better cause), for he was at the prison gate, day after day, shortly after six in the morning, and would continue taking notes and administering pledges for successive hours. No sooner had a prisoner subscribed to teetotalism, than he easily convinced Mr. Rotch of his 'innocence.' (Chesterton 1856, 2:197)

Writing anonymously in *The Examiner* in October 1849 (see Brice and Fielding 1981; Drew 2003, pp. 91–104), Dickens had condemned Rotch's temperance initiative in equally forthright terms. He introduced "[o]ne Mr Rotch – we had almost written Mr Botch," and continued:

the monstrous absurdity and impropriety of an indiscriminate administration of this pledge to common London thieves and vagabonds *in prison* – to such of them, in short, as chose to take it from the hands of Mr Rotch, in the palmy days of his superseded visitation. Any one in the least degree acquainted with the habits of these persons, knows that there is nothing the generality of them would not profess, when at that disadvantage, to curry favour with a man in power ... We contend that a prison-yard is not fit pasturage for Mr Rotch's hobby, or Mr anybody else's; and we believe that the last state of those men was worse than the first. ([Dickens] 1849, p. 164)

Chesterton's *Revelations* provides some further clues as to the nature of the "baseless charges" and "vexatious investigations" referred to in the passage from his book quoted above, including the undated order that it was no longer "to be tolerated that Mr. Charles Dickens should walk into the prison whenever he pleased" (1856, 2:186). Evidence from the London Metropolitan Archives indicates that this decree probably dates from the early months of 1848, when a special meeting of the visiting justices was held at Cold Bath Fields to consider alterations to the prison rules. The minutes of the meeting, held on 15 February of that year, record that Chesterton was formally instructed to break off his connection with "Miss Coutts' establishment," because it was considered "not desirable that he should be a member of any Institution requiring his personal attendance" (Cold Bath 1848a). This was but one of a number of orders issued that month, and aimed at bringing the Cold Bath Fields governor to heel; thus Chesterton was reprimanded for failing to attend prison chapel regularly, and for organising an allegedly lavish dinner party which had attracted unfavourable publicity in the press (Grand Ball 1848, p. 3). The following spring, he was taken to task – this time for taking part in a fox hunt; the activity was judged "incompatible with the situation of governor," and he was requested to desist (Cold Bath 1849).

Full details of the modified prisoners' rule book drawn up in this period do not appear to have survived, though details about regulations concerning, for example, communication are found in official documents (Cold Bath 1848b). Nevertheless there is evidence of a directive to keep detailed records, for weekly presentation to the visiting justices, of "all persons entering the prison to visit any of the officers or servants." The rule was aimed at preventing the two chaplains at Cold Bath Fields from receiving unauthorised private visits from representatives of charitable institutions catering for ex-offenders. Supporters of the new regulation – whose number included Rotch – claimed that "unless such a rule were brought into operation, the discipline of the prison would become more lax than it already seemed to have been" (Meeting 1848a, p. 7). Despite vigorous opposition from some of the justices present, and a written complaint from the chaplains, the motion was carried by a two-thirds majority.

Urania Cottage was not mentioned by name during the meeting; but given the existence of the order of the previous month aimed at severing Chesterton's ties with the establishment, it is not unreasonable to surmise that the new directive was motivated, at least in part, by a desire to take further steps to limit contact between prison staff and the "Home for Homeless Women" at Shepherd's Bush ([Dickens] 1853). This new order may well be the origin of the Chesterton's undated claim that, on Rotch's instructions, "Miss Coutts had no right to confer with prisoners within those walls" (Chesterton 1856, 2:186). It should be remembered, though, that one of the prison chaplains targeted by the new rule, Edward Illingworth, had been co-opted by Dickens, along with Chesterton and Tracey, onto Urania Cottage's management committee (Hartley 2008, p. 77; Collins 1962, pp. 63, 100). The plausibility of this interpretation of events is further suggested by the content of a letter written by Illingworth to Angela Burdett Coutts that August, in which he urged her to postpone a visit to the prison to see a potential candidate for the Home, Mary Ann Stonnell. "At the present time," the churchman wrote, "we are exposed to such annoyance ... from a factious and tyrannical member of our Visiting Committee, that we are anxious to avoid any thing which might bring us into Collision with him" (*Letters* 5:403, n.1). Dickens had also urged caution on his patron in a letter written that May, again concerning a planned visit of the latter to see Stonnell:

> In case you should, by any evil chance, in visiting Stonnell, encounter a magistrate of the name of Rotch ... say nothing to him, either about her, or about the Home. For whatever is said to him, he is as certain to pervert, if it should suit his purpose, as the Sun is to rise tomorrow morning. (*Letters* 5:313)

Whether Rotch's initiatives at Cold Bath Fields had any practical impact on the Urania Cottage project is uncertain. What is clear, though, is that they failed to end the involvement of Chesterton and Illingworth in the project, or indeed cut off the supply of former Cold Bath Fields inmates to the Home: in 1849 and 1850 the prison supplied (respectively) nine and eight of the Home's 13 residents (Collins 1962, p. 326; [Pownall] 1849, p. 39).

By the time "Pet Prisoners" was published on 27 April 1850 the "collisions" to which Illingworth had referred were a thing of the past. In November 1849 Dickens had been able to joke in a letter to Tracey about "going over to the Rotch faction" (*Letters* 5:636) if Chesterton proved to be boring company at his correspondent's wedding – an indication, perhaps, that the issue had lost its gravity by that point. Earlier that year, however, Rotch had been ousted from the committee of the visiting justices at Cold Bath Fields, and his ambitious rebuilding programme for the county prisons was abandoned in favour of a smaller-scale (and considerably cheaper) refurbishment plan that was more in keeping with the new mood abroad in the country (shared by Dickens): that prisons needed to combine greater punitive severity and lower running costs. Magistrate Peter Northall Laurie captured this new mood in facetious style in a speech made before the

Middlesex justices in March 1849. In commenting on the recent increase in the prison population at Cold Bath Fields, Northall Laurie stated:

> The truth was that that which was termed the House of Correction was not a house of correction; it was a place very far more attractive to, than it was abhorred by the thief. So strong indeed were the attractions of that prison to the evil-disposed, that he was inclined to hope that the entrance gates would be doubly fortified on the outside, for his fear was that they were more likely to have an attempt at breaking into the prison by those who wished to participate in its comforts rather than a breaking out to obtain a release ... Such had become the hospitable treatment of the inmates of their two prisons at Cold Bath-fields and Westminster, that whilst he anticipated the one would be denominated by the title of the 'Chesterton Arms', so the other would revel in the designation of the 'Tracey Hotel.' (Meeting 1849, p. 8; see also [Northall] Laurie 1849, p. 5)

An article on "Prison and Convict Discipline," published the following week in *The Examiner* (1849), and possibly a collaborative piece with input from Dickens (Brice and Fielding 1981; Newlin 1995, p. 402; Slater 1996, p. 160), made many of the same points, and blamed directly "Mr Rotch's absurdities" for making Cold Bath Fields more popular than ever among the members of London's criminal classes (Prison 1849, pp. 146–147). This was a reference to the fact that in November 1848 Rotch had organised a demonstration of sheep-shearing in the prison, as part of a plan to provide the inmates with useful skills that might facilitate their emigration to the Antipodes once released. The initiative provoked much criticism, and some mockery in the press when the initiative was publicised in March – complete, on one occasion, with a letter purporting to be from "Bo Peep" (1849, p. 8; see also The Sheep-Shearing 1849, p. 4; Chesterton 1856, 2:199). The *Examiner* piece declared that, owing to Rotch's various initiatives in the prison,

> Cold Bath Fields becomes popular. The average of its occupants had been little more than a thousand, and suddenly they are more than fourteen hundred. The competition for admission grows alarming. The annual cost to the country, which had been some 13,000*l*., threatens to run up to as much as half as much again. New rooms must be built. The old accommodation is exhausted. Already the tailors' shops are made sleeping rooms for increasing crowds of soup-loving, sheep-shearing applicants. (Prison 1849, p. 146)

By March 1849, it seems that the tide was beginning to turn against Rotch and his supporters, thus marking the return of what the *Examiner* article called "magisterial good sense to the county meetings at Clerkenwell" (Prison 1849, p. 146). By

September that year, the new chairman of the visiting justices was able to announce that the diet had been cut at Cold Bath Fields, and shot-drill, judged "only nominally '*hard*'" (Collins 1962, p. 70), introduced as a replacement for other forms of labour. Rotch subsequently complained of "a wicked crusade ... against all the warders and sub-warders who had signed the temperance pledge"; he alleged that "the governor [had] insulted them, [and] the subordinates designated them as '*Rotch's saints*'." He also claimed that the new-look visiting justices' committee had raised the beer allowance in the prison (Beggs 1849, p. 179).

Given this background, it is reasonable to assume that the recent events at the prison were still fresh in Dickens's mind when he was preparing "Pet Prisoners" the following spring – particularly when it is recalled, as demonstrated above, that those events had prompted the author to take up his pen once, and possibly twice, for *The Examiner* in 1849, and that the Rotch episode also inspired the depiction of Mr Creakle (initially the headmaster of Salem House; *DC* 5) as a Middlesex magistrate (Collins 1961), who invites David Copperfield to visit a model prison closely resembling Pentonville (*DC* 61). Thus it seems plausible that events at Cold Bath Fields in 1848–1849 played a significant role in Dickens's decision to rejoin the penal steeplechase in 1850, eight years after *American Notes* – though the publication of Thomas Carlyle's pamphlet "Model Prisons" in March 1850 may well have been the immediate impetus (Carlyle 1850; see Collins 1962, p. 155; McKnight 1993, pp. 23–24; Slater 1996, p. 51; Hansen 2009, p. 105). It is significant in this context that it was during Rotch's ascendancy at Cold Bath Fields, in April 1848, that Dickens obtained official permission from Pentonville's management committee to see for himself the much-lauded separate system in action in the capital (Minute Book 1847–1848, f. 232, 13 May 1848). It is unclear, however, whether the author ever made the intended visit (Collins 1962, p. 132; Grass 2003, p. 51), and instead relied on secondary sources like William Hepworth Dixon's *London Prisons* (1850) for his piece in *Household Words* ([Dickens] 1850, p. 98; see *Letters* 6:62, n.8).

It is clear that by the time "Pet Prisoners" was published, Dickens's position on penal reform had shifted significantly. It is not simply, as McKnight has argued, that the novelist, like Carlyle, "turned increasingly harsh and conservative in his [journalistic] writings" after the "liberalism" of *American Notes* (1993, p. 24), for, as has been demonstrated above, Dickens's travelogue had included both a robust defence of the silent system, and praise for its leading British practitioners. Indeed, on this particular point, "Pet Prisoners" largely reprises its author's previous advocacy of the silent regime, though there is a significant new focus on the advantages of association in terms of low cost and a creditable tendency not to "pet and pamper the mind of the prisoner and swell his sense of his own importance" ([Dickens] 1850, p. 97). What had most clearly changed by 1850 was the basis of Dickens's rejection of the separate system. As Adam Hansen has pointed out (2009, p. 89), and indeed as Dickens's title hints, he was less concerned than before to condemn the "torturing anxieties and horrible despair" caused by cellular isolation (*AN* 7), than with the "strange absorbing selfishness" shown by inmates of the model prison, where "spiritual egotism and vanity, real or assumed" are the order of the day ([Dickens] 1850, pp. 101, 99). The term "pattern penitence" was new (1850, p. 101), but its substance was not: as demonstrated above, Dickens had already roundly denounced such formulaic piety in his discussion of Cold Bath Fields' teetotalling inmates for *The Examiner* the previous October ([Dickens] 1849, pp. 673–674). In other words, by 1850 Dickens had evidently reached the conclusion that Pentonville was Rotch's Cold Bath Fields writ large; in this respect, events at Pentonville in 1848–1849 (and the reactions of the various actors involved to those events) provide vital context for understanding the subsequent development of Dickens's thinking on penal matters; the analysis is further evidence of that "meshing of life-history and social history" referred to earlier (Abrams 1982, p. 297).

In the space of six months in 1854–1855, governors Chesterton and Tracey both retired, and Benjamin Rotch died. By that point, the unalloyed separatism favoured by Rotch and by other leading advocates like John Burt, John Field and Joseph Adshead had fallen from favour; their efforts were undermined by the failure of prisons like Pentonville and Millbank to live up to the great reformatory expectations predicted for them (Henriques 1972, p. 84). Indeed, by the time "Pet Prisoners" was published, Millbank had been converted into a humble staging-post for convicts on their way to Australia. As for Pentonville, it had been stripped of its "model prison" status, and the hope that its inmates could be cured of their criminal tendencies by a short sharp shock of rigorous isolation had been abandoned. In the years that followed, under the leadership of Colonel Joshua Jebb, Britain's convict prisons would adopt a hybrid regime, combining elements of the silent and separate systems. Local prisons like Cold Bath Fields and Tothill Fields would ultimately follow the same path (Davie 2017, pp. 223–535; Johnston 2006, pp. 116–118).

Philip Collins has described Dickens's interest in prisons and prison reform as "spasmodic and unsystematic" (1962, p. 132). Concerning the period after "Pet Prisoners," it would be more accurate to say that with the controversies and conflicts over penal policy, which had marked the previous decade and a half, now effectively resolved – though they would return with a vengeance at the end of the 1850s (McConville 1981, p. 349) – Dickens's interest in the issue did not so much diminish as shift focus. As Sean Grass has argued, Dickens's mature fiction would be characterised by "a hovering obsession with the prison … [and a] growing artistic concern with the relation between the prison, the novel, and the private self" (2009, p. 173). Dickens's relationship with London's prisons had entered a new phase.

References

Abrams, Peter (1982). *Historical Sociology*. Shepton Mallet: Open Books.
Adshead, Joseph (1845). *Prisons and Prisoners*. London: Longman, Brown, Green & Longman.

Adshead, Joseph (1847). *Our Present Gaol System Deeply Depraving to the Prisoner and a Positive Evil to the Community: Some Remedies Proposed.* London: Falkner.

Beggs, Thomas (1849). *An Inquiry into the Extent and Causes of Juvenile Depravity.* London: Charles Gilpin.

"Bo Peep" (1849, 12 March). Sheepshearing in Cold Bath Fields: To the Editor of the Times. The *Times,* 8.

Brice, Alec W., & Fielding, K.J. (1981). A New Article by Dickens: "Demoralisation and Total Abstinence." *Dickens Studies Annual,* 9, 1–19.

Carlyle, Thomas (1850). Model Prisons. In *Latter Day Pamphlets* (pp. 41–73). London: Chapman & Hall.

[Chesterton, George Laval] (1838a, October). Third Report of Inspectors of Prisons – Home District, dated 1st May 1838. *Monthly Law Magazine and Political Review,* 1–17.

[Chesterton, George Laval] (1838b, November). Third Report of Inspectors of Prisons – Home District, dated 1st May 1838. *Monthly Law Magazine and Political Review,* 157–173.

Chesterton, George Laval (1856). *Revelations of Prison Life, with an Enquiry into Prison Discipline and Secondary Punishments.* 2nd ed. 2 vols. London: Hurst & Blackett.

Cold Bath Fields. Visiting Justices Draft Minutes, 1848–1849 (1848a, 15 February). London Metropolitan Archives (MA/G/CBF/018). London.

Cold Bath Fields. Visiting Justices Draft Minutes, 1848–1849 (1848b, 14 July). London Metropolitan Archives (MA/G/CBF/018). London.

Cold Bath Fields. Visiting Justices Draft Minutes, 1848–1849 (1848c, 20 October; 31 October; 7 December). London Metropolitan Archives (MA/G/CBF/018). London.

Cold Bath Fields. Visiting Justices Draft Minutes, 1848–1849 (1849, 13 April). London Metropolitan Archives (MA/G/CBF/018). London.

Collins, Philip (1961). The Middlesex Magistrate in *David Copperfield. Notes and Queries,* N.S. 8, 86–91.

Collins, Philip (1962). *Dickens and Crime.* London: Macmillan.

Couling, Samuel (1862). *History of the Temperance Movement in Great Britain and Ireland; From the Earliest Date to the Present Time.* London: William Tweedie.

Davie, Neil (2017). *The Penitentiary Ten: The Transformation of the English Prison, 1770–1850.* Oxford: Bardwell Press.

Dickens, Charles (1842). *American Notes for General Circulation.* 2 vols. London: Chapman and Hall.

Dickens, Charles (1846, 4 February). Crime and Education: To the Editors of "The Daily News." *Daily News,* 4.

[Dickens, Charles] (1849, 27 October). Demoralisation and Total Abstinence. *The Examiner,* 673–674.

[Dickens, Charles] (1850, 27 April). Pet Prisoners. *Household Words,* 1, 97–103.

[Dickens, Charles] (1853, 23 April). Home for Homeless Women. *Household Words*, 7, 169–175.

Dixon, [William] Hepworth (1850). *The London Prisons; with an Account of the More Distinguished Persons who have been Confined in Them. To which is added, a Description of the Chief Provincial Prisons.* London: Jackson and Walford.

Drew, John M.L. (2003). *Dickens the Journalist.* Basingstoke: Palgrave.

Forsythe, William J. (1991). Centralisation and Local Autonomy: The Experience of English Prisons 1820–1877. *Journal of Historical Sociology*, 4(3), 317–345.

Gaddis, John Lewis (2002). *The Landscape of History: How Historians Map the Past.* Oxford: Oxford University Press.

Grand Ball at Cold Bath Fields Prison (1848, 11 February). *Daily News*, 3.

Grass, Sean C. (2000). Narrating the Cell: Dickens on the American Prisons. *Journal of English and Germanic Philology*, 99(1), 50–70.

Grass, Sean C. (2003). *The Self in the Cell: Narrating the Victorian Prisoner.* London & New York: Routledge.

Grass, Sean C. (2009). *Great Expectations*, Self-Narration, and the Power of the Prison. In Jan Alber & Frank Lauterbach (Eds.), *Stones of Law, Bricks of Shame: Narrating Imprisonment in the Victorian Age* (pp. 171–190). Toronto: University of Toronto Press.

Hansen, Adam (2009). "Now, Now, the Door was Down": Dickens and Excarceration, 1841–2. In Jan Alber & Frank Lauterbach (Eds.), *Stones of Law, Bricks of Shame: Narrating Imprisonment in the Victorian Age* (pp. 89–111). Toronto: University of Toronto Press.

Hartley, Jenny (2008). *Charles Dickens and the House of Fallen Women.* London: Methuen.

Henriques, U.Q.R. (1972). The Rise and Decline of the Separate System of Prison Discipline. *Past and Present*, 54, 61–93.

House of Commons (1834). *Report of William Crawford, Esq., on the Penitentiaries of the United States, Addressed to His Majesty's Principal Secretary of State for the Home Department.*

House of Commons (1838). *Third Report of the Inspectors Appointed Under the Provisions of the Act 5 & 6 Will. IV. c. 38. to Visit the Different Prisons of Great Britain. I. Home District.*

House of Commons (1842). *Seventh Report of the Inspectors Appointed under the Provisions of the Act 5 & 6 Will. IV. c. 38, to Visit the Different Prisons of Great Britain. I. Home District.*

House of Commons (1843, March). *Penitentiary (Milbank). Report of the Superintending Committee, for the year 1842.*

House of Commons (1847, February). *Gaols. Copies of all reports, and of schedules (B.) transmitted to the Secretary of State pursuant to the 24th section of the 4th Geo. IV. cap. 64, and 14th section of the 5th Geo. IV. cap. 12.*

House of Lords (1835, July). *First Report from the Select Committee of the House of Lords appointed to inquire into the present state of the several gaols and houses of correction in England and Wales*.

Johnston, Helen (2006). "Buried Alive": Representations of the Separate System in Victorian England. In Paul Mason (Ed.), *Captured by the Media: Prison Discourse in Popular Culture* (pp. 103–121). Cullompton: Willan.

Laurie, Sir Peter (1846). *"Killing no Murder"; or, the Effects of Separate Confinement on the Bodily and Mental Condition of Prisoners in the Government Prisons and Other Gaols in Great Britain and America*. London: John Murray.

Magnússon, Sigurður Gylfi (2017). The Life is Never Over: Biography as a Microhistorical Approach. In Hans Renders, Binne de Haan & Jonne Harmsma (Eds.) *The Biographical Turn: Lives in History* (pp. 42–52). London: Routledge.

Marylebone Vestry (1848, 19 November). *Observer*, 6.

McConville, Seán (1981). *A History of English Prison Administration: Volume I, 1750–1877*. London: Routledge.

McKnight, Natalie (1993). *Idiots, Madmen and Other Prisoners in Dickens*. London: Palgrave Macmillan.

Meeting of Middlesex Magistrates (1844, 20 December). *Morning Post*, 2.

Meeting of Middlesex Magistrates (1846, 23 October). The *Times*, 6.

Meeting of Middlesex Magistrates (1847a, 18 April). *Observer*, 7.

Meeting of Middlesex Magistrates (1847b, 28 May). The *Times*, 7.

Meeting of Middlesex Magistrates (1848a, 24 March). The *Times*, 7.

Meeting of Middlesex Magistrates (1848b, 9 September). The *Times*, 8.

Meeting of the Middlesex Magistrates (1849, 2 March). The *Times*, 8.

Middlesex Sessions – Prison Discipline (1837, 16 September). *Champion*, 594–595.

Minute Book, Pentonville Prison (1847–1848). The National Archives, Kew (PCOM 2/84). London.

Newlin, George (Ed.) (1995). *Everyone in Dickens, Volume 1: Plots, People and Publishing Particulars in the Complete Works, 1833–1849*. Westport & London: Greenwood Press.

Northall Laurie, Peter (1837). *Prison Discipline and Secondary Punishments: Remarks on the First Report of the Inspectors of Prisons: With Some Observations on the Reformation of Criminals*. London: Whittaker & Co.

[Northall] Laurie, P[eter] (1849, 1 January). The Middlesex House of Detention. [Letter]. The *Times*, 5.

Paroissien, David (2009). Victims or Vermin? Contradictions in Dickens's Penal Philosophy. In Jan Alber & Frank Lauterbach (Eds.), *Stones of Law, Bricks of Shame: Narrating Imprisonment in the Victorian Age* (pp. 25–45). Toronto: University of Toronto Press.

[Pownall, Henry] (1849). *Observations on the Expenses of the County of Middlesex, the Prisons and Management, by a Magistrate of the County*. London: Warr & Low.

Prison and Convict Discipline (1849, 10 March). The *Examiner*, 146–147.

Prison Discipline – The Silence and Separation Systems – Special Report of the Visiting Justices of the House of Correction, Cold-Bath Fields, Middlesex (1838, 24 February, 3 March). *Justice of the Peace and County, Borough, Poor Law Union and Parish Law Recorder*, 2(7), 102–103; 2(8), 117–118.

Renders, Hans, & de Haan, Binne (Eds.) (2014). *Theoretical Discussions of Biography: Approaches from History, Microhistory, and Life Writing*. Leiden & Boston: Brill.

Slater, Michael (Ed.) (1996). *Dickens' Journalism Volume 2: The Amusements of the People and Other Papers: Reports, Essays, and Reviews, 1834–51*. London: Dent, 1996.

The Sheep-Shearing Magistrate (1849, 18 March). *The Sunday Times*, 4.

Tambling, Jeremy (2009). New Prisons, New Criminals, New Masculinity: Dickens and Reade. In Jan Alber & Frank Lauterbach (Eds.), *Stones of Law, Bricks of Shame: Narrating Imprisonment in the Victorian Age* (pp. 46–69). Toronto: University of Toronto Press.

Westminster Bridewell, Tothill Fields. Visiting Justices Reports, 1834–1843 (1834, 22 August; 1835, 20 June). London Metropolitan Archives (WA/G/001). London.

Westminster Bridewell, Tothill Fields. Visiting Justices Reports, 1840–1845 (1843, 6 May). London Metropolitan Archives (WA/G/002). London.

Part II

Reincorporating Dickens

5

A Somatic Experience of Dickens's Fiction
Georges Letissier

The term "somatic reading" refers to all the bodily effects induced on a subject by the activity of reading – that is, all the physiological responses elicited by printed words on a page. This approach is by no means new in the field of Victorian studies, where reading has often warranted attention for its own sake, essentially in two ways. First, by focusing on women readers, it has been investigated through ideological debates which presented reading in terms of addiction, poison or disease. It was argued in particular that female readers could not resist the allure of fiction, and proved unequal to the task of mustering the necessary physiological resources to withstand the somatic pull of the text, especially where sensational fiction or romance were concerned (Leckie 1999, pp. 8–9). The second manifestation of somatic reading involved the deployment of physiological novel theory, defined as "a set of what one might call 'microsciences' ... such as acoustic natural science (or scientific musicology), 'psychophysics' (the attempt to arrive at a unit measurement for consciousness), ocular or ophthalmological physiology (the study of eye movements), and 'psychometrics' (the attempt to time the speed of neural operations)" (Dames 2007, p. 14).

Contemporary criticism acknowledges the epistemological potential afforded by somatic reading to enlarge and enrich the field of reader-response theory. Indeed, whilst Hans Robert Jauss (1982) focused his attention on the history-bound, collective reception of texts, and Wolfgang Iser (1980) highlighted the phenomenological aspect of the individual act of reading, both prioritised a rational, logical approach, resting on cognition and the intellect at the expense of emotions, sensations and subjective affects. The latter were even seen as dangerously interfering with the production of meaning, which implies intellectual control and mastery.

A renewed interest in corporeal responses to reading, severed from both moral concerns and quantitative empirical science, has been kindled by what is known as "body genres" in the cinema industry – that is, the kind of films most likely to

Reading Dickens Differently, First Edition. Edited by Leon Litvack and Nathalie Vanfasse.
© 2020 John Wiley & Sons Ltd. Published 2020 by John Wiley & Sons Ltd.

arouse peaks of sensations in spectators through the display of bodies in extreme situations, either of pain or pleasure, including gore or snuff movies, hardcore pornography and also horror or melodrama. The grid of analysis devised to study this cinematic output has subsequently proven relevant to tackling contemporary American novels by Dennis Cooper, James Frey, Chuck Palahniuk or Mark Z. Danielewski. This is precisely the approach that Pierre-Louis Patoine has taken in his recent, groundbreaking work entitled *Corps/texte* (Patoine 2015). What follows is indebted to this study.

The fact that Dickens might be eligible for somatic (also known as embodied) reading should not, on principle, raise any major objections. After all, the author was the first to point out the physiological effects of his fiction, both on himself and on his readers. Peter Ackroyd quotes Dickens's opening address to a Bradford audience during his first reading tour: "If you feel disposed as we go along to give expression to any emotion, whether grave or gay, you will do so with perfect freedom from restraint, and without the apprehension of disturbing me" (Ackroyd 1991, p. 754). Claire Tomalin alludes to the "almost hypnotic power" which passages from *Pickwick*, *Nickleby*, *Dombey*, *Chuzzlewit* and *Copperfield* exerted on audiences during the Inimitable's American reading tour in 1867–1868. Of course, it might be claimed that it was all as a result of Dickens's impersonation: 'the power of the great actor" (Tomalin 2011, p. 355) and that the passages had been meticulously selected and transcribed into shortened scripts, granting pride of place to the more salient characters and keeping only the highlights of the narratives. Indeed, if empathetic, embodied reading, as a method furthering already existent reader-response approaches, is critically effective, it must apply to the text *per se*, independently of its performance, with a view to establishing the tight bond between the somatic and the semiotic.

In *Corps/texte*, Patoine purports to investigate the somaesthetic impact (concerned with bodily sensations) of text-reading on those indulging in this activity (2015). This presupposes that the active construction of meaning – what Roland Barthes calls the "writerly stance" (1974, p. 5) – should be complemented, shadowed, or in some cases, undermined, by bodily stimuli which, in the last resort, also partake of the overall experience of reading. Thus somatic or empathetic reading must be construed as an umbrella term encompassing a whole range of situations, from hallucinatory reading in which the reader is fully immersed or submerged in the fictitious realm, to more transitory proxy, phantom sensations caused at given moments by the experience of reading. Because there is no longer the possibility to attend Dickens's public readings, it must be agreed that sensory motor simulations may only be triggered by the text. In this sense, they have to be correlated with style: the voice of the text, its rhythm, pace and intonation. The connection between these compositional effects and their physiological counterparts – heartbeats and respiratory rhythm for instance – has long been established. For example, Miall has argued that the foregrounded, syntactic, semantic and unusual rhetorical forms of a text do not immediately register with the reader's consciousness (which is initially concerned with working out meaning), but that they do affect him or her deeply in the long run (Miall 2009). Thus things like the vocal flow or stylistic expressiveness resonate with the reader's more unconscious reception, and inform his/her corporeal relation to the text; therefore stylistic features hold readers in their sway; ultimately they, to a greater or lesser degree, find themselves in thrall to them. Within the limited scope of this essay, the best that can be attempted is to propound a form of close reading, relying on somatic parameters, which will be inferred from close attention to style.

In the case of *Little Dorrit*, prison is a central feature, and the novel tropes the motif of imprisonment in all its guises. An investigation of the somatic reading of this novel demonstrates that there is a shift from intellectual understanding to a physical, possibly physiological, take on the text. In other words, the reader's emotions and sensations, triggered by a fictive universe, and extensively relying upon embodied responses and sensory-motor stimuli, both intensify and enrich the reading activity. Interestingly, the springs of the intricate plot converge on a confined space, arousing poignant sensations: apprehension, confusion, repulsion. The slowly collapsing, dilapidated Clennam house is indeed the linchpin of the plot, with the Marshalsea Prison as the metaphoric hub. Right from the start, the hermeneutic act of disentangling the plot's mystery is clearly bound up with overwhelming physical sensations. The somatic somehow screens the semantic – a fact that is repeatedly signalled by Affery Flintwinch's throwing her apron over her head, "lest she should see something" (*LD* 15). It could be said that the novel displaces the hermeneutic quest for the secret in order to dwell upon the pathological side/after-effects of some hindered, embodied knowledge. This is achieved by underscoring the physical apprehension (in the double sense of fear or misgiving and mental grasp) of the truth.

First the reader is invited to occupy bodily Mrs Clennam's and Mrs Flintwinch's spaces; this is crucial to the embodied reading experience. The reader is beckoned, as it were, to sit in the invalid's wheelchair and to slip into her body in order to figure out, from a phenomenological perspective, the way in which she physically and sensorily relates to the world: "The wheeled chair has its associated remembrances and reveries, one may suppose ... to be unable to measure the changes beyond our view by any larger standard than the shrunken one of our own uniform and contracted existence, is the infirmity of many invalids, and the mental unhealthiness of almost all recluses" (*LD* 29). "Contracted" is of course seminal because it affords an incarnated variant of the overarching imprisonment metaphor. Yet even more striking is Affery Flintwinch's example. The wife of Jeremiah Flintwinch (Mrs Clennam's retainer) turns out to be the somatic beacon of this hindered – or at least deferred – access to a truth to which, paradoxically, she finds herself exposed from the beginning to the end of the novel. Dickens plays on the metaleptic gap (involving the deliberate transgression of the framing threshold of diegetic or ontological levels; see Genette 2004, pp. 14, 354) between the oneiric world of surreal visions and the plain and hard facts occurring in the reality represented in the fiction. In other words, Affery is the eyewitness to all the shady dealings going on at the widow Clennam's house, all carried out to defraud Little Dorrit of her inheritance, complicated by a taxing codicil. Affery does see, but she experiences her seeing as dreaming, either through what might be described as an unconscious mechanism of self-protection, or as a result of a permanent near-hypnotic condition, induced by a frightening environment and Jeremiah's manipulative control. By making the dreaming Affery the focal point of the plot's entanglement, Dickens stresses the physical outcome of being unknowingly confronted by decisive facts, and he goes so far as to pathologise access to knowledge. Described by her husband as demented, the flustered, flurried Affery comes to doubt her own sanity. Besides, on account of her status as both outsider and insider (being exposed to facts whilst not being privy to them), Affery may act as a stand-in for the reader. In this capacity, she is a conduit for a somatic perception of the plot. Indeed, her physiological reactions are invariably foregrounded: her "palpitating heart," her "trembling," her "dreadful turns," and her gnawing sensation of being crushed out of existence by the pressures of her surroundings: "I am frightened out of one half of my life, and dreamed out of the other" (*LD* 15). Significantly, she is so overpowered by events that her uncontrolled bodily reactions may at times provoke phantom responses, "as if she had been touched by some awful hand" (*LD* 15). Drawing on William James's writings, the neurobiologist Antonio Damasio conceived of what he calls "as-if body loops" (1994, p. 100) to describe these neural or hormonal reactions sparked off by seeing someone else being touched, or by imaginary contact with a fancied presence. These sensations are simulated rather than actual: the brain puts in place a certain body state as if an emotional change were occurring in reality, even if nothing tangible is taking place. The potential that such situations constitute for empathetic reading should not be downplayed. When the narrator remarks that Affery felt "a rustle and a sort of trembling behind [her]" (*LD* 15), under certain conditions it may be conjectured that the same spooky sensation may be shared by the reader at this stage of the story.

Somatic reading relinquishes any claim to master and control the text, to channel the sensorial, emotional disorder induced by the aesthetic experience by means of constructive reason. In many respects, *Dombey and Son* is about loss of control and surrendering one's hold on events by force of circumstances: loss of kin, the ruthless law of a new market economy and, as it is a Dickens novel, a moral flaw – that is, pride. The main driving force is, of course, the train: "The power that forced itself upon its iron way – its own – defiant of all paths and roads ... a type of the triumphant monster, Death" (*DS* 20). Stylistic studies have been dedicated to Dickens's use of the historical present in this novel, showing that it marks a crisis of the action through a suspension of the linear chronology by means of stasis – Dombey's house plunged into a benumbed state in the wake of young Paul's death or an exhilarating acceleration entailing the severance from any temporal, clockwork landmarks (Pettit 2013). This second modality is exemplified by two journeys at breakneck speed: the first in chapter 20, with Dombey aboard a train, and the second in chapter 55, with Carker's escaping from Dijon to return to London, first in a horse-drawn carriage and then by train. In each case there is a surrender of voluntary consciousness and a sensory intensity of experience, which is conducive to a fully immersive, near hypnotic form of reading. The sensation of automaticity prevails: "Through the hollow, on the height, by the heath, by the orchard, by the park, by the garden, over the canal, across the river, where the sheep are feeding, where the mill is going, where the barge is floating, where the dead are lying" (*DS* 20). Fleeting visual images force themselves in unrelenting, serial succession to the point of erasing the focaliser's consciousness. It is as if both Dombey and the reader are swept along, irrespective of their willpower. The effect is obtained by means of well-honed stylistic tricks: clipped clauses, anaphoras, a mix of regularities and irregularities ("by ... by ... where ... where" but "over" and "across") and unexpected juxtapositions, like "where the barge is floating, where the dead are lying." Another characteristic of this trance-like state is the obsession with one detail, as when Carker pointlessly repeats the question "whither":

> Hallo! Hi! Away at a gallop over the black landscape; dust and dirt flying like spray, the smoking horses snorting and plunging as if each of them were ridden by a demon, away in a frantic triumph on the dark road – whither?
>
> Again the nameless shock comes speeding up, and as it passes, the bells ring in his ears 'whither?' The wheels roar in his ears 'whither?' (*DS* 55)

Such a hypnotic state implies a mental split between the to-the-moment perception of fleeting images as the landscape flies past, and the persistent consciousness of the character who stays anchored in his permanent identity amidst this kaleidoscopic flow. Thus, for example, while Dombey travels at an unprecedented speed (*DS* 20), the intoxicating progress of the train does not in any way efface the memory of young Paul's loss. So the accelerated pace of the syntax conveys both the exaltation of the railway journey and the grievous recollection of the lost son who is swallowed by the infernal machine, annihilating any distinction between past and future as a result of being tensed up in the here and now of its indomitable impetus, defying any spatial or temporal limitations: "The very speed at which the train was whirled along, mocked the swift course of the young life that had been borne away so steadily and so inexorably to its foredoomed end" (*DS* 20). Meanwhile, time passes and miles are indeed crossed so that these perfectly controlled stylistic purple patches afford illustrations of what the psychiatrist Greg Mahr labels "highway hypnosis" (2003, p. 261).

Dickens provides an experiential narrative that allows his readers to feel for themselves a dissociative psychological state; this is what happens when the subject's attention is temporarily captivated by passing images, to the point of seeming to lose his/her bearings, whilst in actual fact there persists deep down the foundational sense of his/her own identity, to quote *Dombey* yet again: "So, pursuing the one course of thought, he had the one relentless monster still before him" (*DS* 20). This dissociation of consciousness can be transposed onto the reader's experience, since reading involves both an absorption in fictitious situations and the sustaining throughout of a more or less acute awareness of the real world to which the reader belongs. Of course, the level of involvement in fiction constantly varies, through a combination of personal interest in the story being told, and outer circumstances from everyday life's sundry commitments potentially impinging upon a privileged moment of isolation.

The shift of emphasis between nineteenth-century physiological theory and contemporary somatic or empathetic theory would probably lie in the latter's concern with borderline aesthetics: transgressive fiction, dirty realism, blank fiction or splatterpunk (a subgenre of horror fiction, characterised by graphic descriptions of grisly violence). What is striking is the fact that, though this might sound anachronistic, Dickens's *œuvre* does occasionally provide textual fragments which are perfectly amenable to the critical apparatus of empathetic reading. The confrontation scene between Pip and Orlick at the sluice-house by the limekiln in *Great Expectations* (*GE* 3:14) enacts psychological defence mechanisms and hallucinatory states that call for interpretive paths, going beyond the realm of the rational, to address drives and impulses entailing the reader's somaesthetic involvement – that is, to his/her bodily sensations, such as touch, pressure, heat, cold and pain.

The encounter between Pip and Orlick at night, in an isolated house, is imbued with an hallucinatory aspect which evokes a nightmare. Adopting a psychoanalytical perspective, critics like Julian Moynahan see in Orlick Pip's nocturnal double: a distorted, darkened mirror image (Moynahan 1960). William A. Cohen construes the corporeal proximity between the two protagonists in homoerotic terms, thus underlining what he sees as blatant tokens of sado-masochism (1993). The scenery is perfectly suited to somatic interpretation: somaesthetic effects are palpable, notably through the close sensory blending of chiaroscuro and voice. Pip, who is the focaliser, has no clear optic perception of the place; his vision is haptic: it depends upon the sense of touch and kinaesthetic experiences. He cannot conceive of the place as a whole, and cannot stare from a distance to occupy a vantage point of optic control and intellectual grasp. His eye acts like a substitute for a groping hand, and fulfils a tactile function: "As the sparks fell thick, and bright about him, I could see his hands, and touches of his face" (*GE* 3:14). Haptic visuality, unlike optic visuality, is vulnerable: here the sparks may die out or Pip may be strangled at any moment. The haptic also entails a tight bond with other sensory perceptions – touch obviously, but also hearing, as Orlick's menacing presence is at first signaled by his suppressed voice and repeated oaths: "I've got you" (*GE* 3:14). The critical distance between the reader and the characters is reduced due to this haptic proximity, and a corporeal experience is induced through the diegetic tension which is liable to quicken the reader's heartbeats at this juncture. Pip's utter submission to Orlick's goodwill also places the reader in a position of passive surrender. Literary texts stimulate motor representation when dramatic tension escalates.

A study by the neuroscientists Hauk et al. (2004) has shown that on hearing some phonemes like "lick," "pick," or "kick," the senses in the motor system are likely to be stimulated. In the Dickens passage under consideration, the syllable "-lick" in "Orlick" defines an isotopy that ties in with lisps: "blue lips" and "licked up," which extends to include references to the buccal organ: "mouth snarling like a tiger's" and "mouth watered for me" (*GE* 3:14). It has often been argued that this emphasis on the mouth calls to mind the novel's opening churchyard scene and Magwitch's well-remembered cue: "Give it mouth!" (*GE* 1:1). However, in this extract, this buccal tropism rebounds on Pip, who is several times addressed as "wolf" (*GE* 1:11, 3:14). There is therefore a regression towards a primitive consciousness, which effaces the separation between the two characters, between the internal and the external, and between the text and its addressees. This blurring of contours is conducive to empathetic simulation. Neuropsychology establishes the subject's propensity to feel pain even when the nociceptors (the sensory receptors of pain) – whether they be cutaneous, muscular or articular – are not primed; this well-known phenomenon is illustrated by patients' behaviour after the amputation of limbs. There is every reason to believe that the same holds true when neural simulation operates in the case of readers' experiencing phantom pains through fiction, especially when these proxy pains revive traumatic incidents from earlier in their lives. Scientists like Vilayanur Ramachandran have established that mirror neurons respond to a situation that is perceived and not experienced first-hand by reactivating mechanisms that have been encoded from previous actions (Ramachandran 2000; Rizzolatti et al. 2000). This leads to a sort of epistemological revolution, whereby biology advances the idea of an imitative relation to the world. Thus represented reality in fiction may spark off responses in the reading subject, who unwittingly taps into his/her somatic memory, evolved through the succession of actions and movements in the course of life. Neuronal activities may therefore be triggered by witnessing someone else's pain, or through the act of empathetic reading. Viewed in this light, the novel ceases to be the Stendhalian mirror reflecting in turn the blue of the skies and the mud puddles underfoot – that is, a graphic image of the theory of mimesis; it becomes instead a simulator, an incubator of proxy experiences.

It is of course difficult to extrapolate a model of the empathetic reader along the lines of Iser's implied reader (1980), if only because each individual's somatic memory is by definition unique. Dickens's text, however, dramatizes a somatic response to words in the famous sluice-house scene; this in itself may be programmatic of what happens on the larger scale of a whole novel. Language is indeed shown in different instances to elicit a response more corporeal than cognitive. Firstly, Pip has been burnt shortly before, as he strove to rescue Miss Havisham from self-immolation: "[I] tried to ease my arm ... but it was bound too tight ... I felt as if, having burnt before, it were now being boiled" (*GE* 3:14). The "as if," whilst envisioning a possible analogy to injuries caused by searing hot water in the present case, also points to the impossibility of finding the right words to bring home to the reader an untranslatable sensation of physical pain. In doing so, "as if" calls forth each and every reader's memory of a similar experience, or at least one approximating it. But this is not all: under duress, with his mouth gagged by Orlick's heavy hand, Pip is forced to heed every word uttered by his tormentor, who says, "I won't have a rag of you, I won't have a bone of you, left on earth. I'll put your body in the kiln" (*GE* 3:14). Given that Pip still suffers shooting pains from his burns, this threat is most likely to prime his nociceptors. Subjected as he is to both physical and moral torture, Pip still finds it in himself – or maybe it is his older double, Mr Philip Pirrip the extradiegetic narrator – to analyse the power of words as harmful stimuli and how they are mentally processed: "It was not only that I could have summed up years and years and years while he said a dozen words, but that what he did say presented pictures to me, and not mere words" (*GE* 3:14). In this hyperalgesic condition, when Pip's pains are at their most unbearable, the linguistic "words" turn into iconic "pictures," as if iconicity could transcend physicality at this crucial juncture. Pip emphatically declares, "It is impossible to over-state the vividness of these images" (*GE* 3:14).

Dickens shows that at death's door, when the crouching tiger (that is, Orlick) is about to spring, Pip unwittingly practises what is known today as pain management. He forces himself to direct all his mental energy towards looking ahead in time, by searching beyond the immediate prospect of his impending death: "the death close before me was terrible, but far more terrible than death was the dread of being misremembered after death" (*GE* 3:14). He therefore substitutes psychological suffering (which is only virtual at this stage, as he is not dead yet) for the more tangible aches to which he is prey, in order to put up with them and betray no signs of weakness in the presence of his captor. Thus he indulges in a succession of visions, conveyed in long-winded sentences conducive to a trance-like state. The surge of this hypnotic string of pictures serves as an antidote to the Damocles sword hanging over his head, and works as a balm for the physical pain: "Wild as my inward hurry was, and wonderful the force of the pictures that rushed by me instead of thoughts" (*GE* 3:14). Through this psychological insight into the consciousness of his young protagonist in the throes of mental and physical torture, Dickens leads his readers vicariously through a paroxysmal, life-threatening situation. To flesh out what amounts to a case study, fiction needs to rely upon the sensorial and experiential more than on cognitive understanding.

The limekiln scene dramatises an intimate, physical confrontation between two antagonistic characters; indeed they might represent the delirious fantasy of a split personality. *A Tale of Two Cities*, for its part, represents mostly crowds; it stages large numbers of anonymous individuals and records a historical collapse on the scale of a whole blinded nation. The "Grindstone" scene (*TTC* 3:2) is paradigmatic, as it gathers together all the symptoms of this collective tragedy.

Its insistence upon all forms of excess sets a challenge to the usual Dickensian rhetoric, and initiates transgressive reading by breaking into the unrepresentable. To preclude the risk of prurient voyeurism inherent in the spectacle of the horrific, Dickens can only count on the text's capacity to cause nausea and revulsion; in doing so, he elicits somatic responses.

As an historical fiction, the *Tale* conjures up the darkest episodes of the French Terror by emphasising suffering, torture and martyred bodies. In this respect, it is an embodied novel playing up the corporeal transcription of the past; hence the omnipresence of sacrilege – that is, the reverse side of the religious – in a story set in France, a predominantly Catholic country, which, to an English mind, is striking on account of the part played by blood and incarnation in the Roman Church's liturgy. Even if this may sound trivialising, it is, to all intents and purposes, a blood-and-guts tale that is more likely to trigger somaesthetic responses in the reader than to inspire deep intellectual reflection.

In the famous "Grindstone" chapter, the large sharpening instrument has been set up in the inner courtyard of Tellson's Bank, in the Saint Germain Quarter of Paris. It is to this spot that bloodthirsty revolutionaries converge to hone their knives, swords or pilfered bayonets. The grindstone keeps rotating as two inebriated men with "the visages of the wildest savages" (*TTC* 3:2) madly turn at its two handles. Dickens chose this blood-curdling backdrop as the staging area for the dramatic encounter between Doctor Manette and Lucie and her daughter (also called Lucie) on the one hand, and Jarvis Lorry, their guide and protector, on the other. The tension is heightened when the news breaks of Charles Darnay's arrest. It has often been claimed that the scene works symbolically through the looming presence of the grindstone which, together with the guillotine, emblematise all the atrocities associated with the French Revolution. This most horrendous episode has also been studied as an example of regressive entertainment, with intoxicated ruffians' grovelling in the "*jouissance* of the obscene" (Letissier 2013, p. 90). Such a despicable manifestation would herald the collapse of civilisation through a Bacchanalian release from the ideology of blood-guilt, imposed by the Christian doctrine of Original Sin (Michelet 1974). Without disclaiming these interpretations, it could be argued that the Grindstone passage affords a rare occasion for empathetic reading because, as a consequence of the sheer excesses it graphically depicts, it challenges the very possibility of any exclusively rational, logical apprehension.

In this short chapter in the third person, the emphasis is on visual perception; however, the focalisation precludes any voyeuristic sensationalism. Indeed, sensationalism would rest on a clear dichotomy between an observer and the degrading sight of men on the rampage, who might unwittingly, and in some perverse sort of way, appeal to this viewer's basest instincts. As the one who perceives the scene and controls it, Lorry makes it crystal clear that the demeaning spectacle of the grindstone can only be received as a potential intrusion, threatening to undermine the observer's human integrity; this perspective avoids any potentially lurid tendencies. The impression of malaise is achieved by depriving the witnesses – Lorry and Doctor Manette – of any intellectual distance, and by placing the reader in a condition of physical nausea towards all that the purposefully neutral description calls up. Thus the text produces effects pertaining to somatic discomfort, eschewing both semiotic control and voyeuristic consummation.

It is no intentional fallacy to surmise that Dickens took great care in anticipating how a scene mixing retrogressive instincts, predatory impulses, sexual drives and self-destructive, collective behaviour could affect his readers. The fact that the novelist's concern with human nature far exceeded what can be explained by science is confirmed by his conception of Doctor Manette. He suffers from catatonia as a result of having been exposed to a traumatic shock; but until the end, the riddle of his disease, and the no less enigmatic circumstances of his recovery, are never fully elucidated. The character's muteness induced by stupor pushes the reader to understand Manette's comportment not so much through linguistic signs (which would open direct access to the mind) but rather through words referring to facial expression and body movements, which may maintain their indecipherable mystery till the end. Paradoxically, Dickens, who may at times be blamed for his incorrigible garrulousness, can also display genuine interest in acts of communication that bypass language. This is the case, for example, when Lucie testifies at the Old Bailey: "Any strongly marked expression of face on the part of a chief actor in a scene of great interest to whom many eyes are directed, will be unconsciously imitated by the spectators" (*TTC* 2:3). What the novelist intuitively diagnoses is a kind of telepathic contagion through facial and physical mimicry; this might extend to scenes in which bodies exert their influence on spectators – sometimes without a word being spoken.

The grindstone episode is a gross, barbaric performance that must not be attended by everyone. It is only once Lucie has been safely sent to Lorry's room and the key properly turned in the lock, that Lorry, the employee of Tellson's Bank, half-reluctantly consents to open the blind a crack. It is as if the sight about to be seen had to be kept within a controllable frame. The account of what is espied, whilst defying the action of seeing through its sheer atrocity, purports to be clinically factual, but rapidly stumbles upon the impossibility of discriminating and, as a result, provokes nausea and revulsion. Thus the long hair of the two men, who keep turning the grindstone handles, is indistinguishable from the fake eyebrows and moustaches that they sport and which are, in all likelihood, the pubic hair of female aristocrats' dismembered and mutilated bodies. Blood has been spilled all over the place, and there is no distinction between the dripping wine that is held out to the men turning the grindstone and the blood drops trickling down. To underscore the mounting physical unease caused by a sight that unsettles visibility, the narrator momentarily loses control of the syntax. Sentences fail to proceed smoothly to their logical endings, by stumbling on halting, stuttering false starts: "their hideous countenances were all bloody and sweaty, and all awry with howling, and all staring and glaring" (*TTC* 3:2). Breathing plays a significant part in the shift from the semantic to the somatic and the breaks and repetitions: the construction "all ... and all ... and all ..." in this passage foregrounds the respiratory tension generated by the act of reading, even when the latter is silent and internalised.

Visual perception is crucial throughout the text under discussion. Interestingly, in the absence of noise and vociferous outbursts, chaos is chromatically rendered through the hyperbolic, tautological red: "the same red hue was red in their frenzied eyes" (*TTC* 3:2). Moreover, observation may be perilous; this is a fact that has been amply discussed in the wake of Darwinian epistemology (Levine 1991, pp. 218–219). The observer is indeed in a position of vulnerability because he/she is always inadequate, and is confronted by the infinity of incommensurable reality; as Levine notes, "It is the power of reality, not the scientist, that determines the conclusion." This entails that all acts of observation presuppose the self-awareness of the observer assessing the scope and limitations of his/her activity: "all observation is ultimately observation of the self ... all truth is ultimately about the self formulating it" (Levine 1991, pp. 214, 218). To put it another way, observation, because it is correlated with self-observation, is the foundation of the rational, logical self. However, the grindstone episode defeats and excludes the rational self, predicated on the act of seeing, by showing how the repetition of callous, beastly action can only touch off somaesthetic reactions in the viewer. Overwhelmed by an unbearable succession of unbearable sights, Lorry, the focaliser, can no longer sustain the visual perception that would also shape his identity. Notwithstanding this major hindrance, the text continues to list all the dreadful deeds that are going on in the bank's courtyard. Under extreme duress, the visual becomes depersonalised and, to bring this idea home to the reader, Dickens imagines a virtual, prosthetic ocular organ that would be like an interface between the repulsed reader and the visually incapacitated Lorry. Indeed the latter, before closing the lattice, as if he were closing his eyelids, is no longer equal to the daunting task of registering the revolutionaries who are running amok. He is in a way no longer cognitively responsible for what is reported: "all their wicked atmosphere seemed gore and fire. *The eye* could not detect one creature in the group free from the smear of blood" (*TTC* 3:2; emphasis added). At this critical juncture, and as an outcome of the perception of cumulative acts of horror, Lorry's stare and mind have ceased to focalise the insufferable. In such indiscriminate confusion of bodies' surrendering to their basest instincts, there is no longer room for an embodied eye/I, representing a consciousness; hence the inclusion of this impersonal, disembodied "the eye." This phantom ocular organ is a narrative proxy, as it were, that keeps on recording the self-annihilating urge of a hell-bent mob brought down to its biological functions. The somatic crushes the semantic, and the horrific description concludes on a phenomenological allusion to the viewer's extreme stress: "All this was seen in a moment, as the vision of a drowning man, or any human creature at any very great pass, could see a world if it was there" (*TTC* 3:2). Seeing may have lethal consequences, and the choking sensation that is likely to grip the reader at this stage is conveyed by the predictive, deterministic syntax. The somatic ultimately ushers in the physical sensation of personal extinction.

As is well known, it is in *Our Mutual Friend* that Dickens addresses in the most thorough fashion the issue of reading. A number of articles dedicated to the author's last completed novel tackle this topic; yet these studies have largely confined themselves to the structural function of reading in the novel's economy. Even if passing allusions are made to the reader's emotional involvement in the plot (Mundhenk 1979, p. 50), the emphasis is clearly put on the intellectual implication. Stanley Friedman considers the three ways in which reading informs the novel: by advancing the plot, developing characterisation and reflecting the Victorians' growing dedication to print (1973). Mundhenk adopts a reader-response perspective to show how the novel's intradiegetic readers (Silas Wegg, Nicodemus Boffin [a reader by proxy] and Bella Wilfer) are caught up in a game of manipulation which, in the end, contributes to the reader's education; she observes: "the reader of *Our Mutual Friend* is not always *told*, but often offered clues which lead him to unravel for himself the complexities of plot and character" (1979, p. 43; emphasis original). All in all, scant attention is paid to the body – be it the body of the represented characters in diverse reading activities within the fiction, or the body of the actual reader, fully engrossed in this loose, baggy monster of a novel. Adopting a body-centered approach in connection with reading has three elements: first, *Our Mutual Friend* shows an awareness of the bond between reading and physiology; second, it exposes maverick attitudes towards reading which go beyond rational, logical considerations; third, it engages the real reader in an immersive relation to the text which is most likely to induce temporary suspension of cognitive vigilance.

Our Mutual Friend explores the whole gamut of reading practices, from the most physically incarnated ones to the most abstracted and ethereal. Long before the introduction of digital literature, this text forcefully acknowledges the tangibility of the indispensable artefact: "the needful implement – a book" (*OMF* 1:5). Because of his insatiable appetite for fiction, Boffin, the Golden Dustman, goes for huge quantities: the "Eight wollumes [sic]" of Gibbon's *Decline and Fall of the Roman Empire* (*OMF* 1:5), and later in the novel, whole cartloads of notorious misers' biographies (*OMF* 3:5, 3:6). Dickens is not sparing of details concerning the ways in which the body is affected by books, but also by paper and writing utensils. As a rule, the Golden Dustman is prone to let himself be swamped in paper, and is generally at a loss with all types of documentation. Through metonymic chains of associations, Dickens draws unexpected parallels between secretarial activities and physiology. Thus Wemmick's "post-office of a mouth" in *Great Expectations* (*GE* 2:2) would correspond to Boffin's "exceedingly distrustful and corrective thumb" (*OMF* 1:15), which has the aggravating habit of smearing its master's notes. Moreover, ink is like an infectious disease spreading to all parts of the body, from the roots of the hair to the calves of one's legs, without leaving a single line on paper. In fact, not everyone is innately adept at reading and writing, since physical limitations may set obstacles. In the "confoundingly perplexing jumble of a school" where Charlie Hexam receives his early education (*OMF* 2:1), adult learners do not even reach the stage of literal comprehension, as the formation of syllables constitutes an impediment they are unable to overcome. The novelist establishes a proprioceptive diagnosis of Boffin before he finds himself in a suitable condition to receive the story Wegg starts reading out to him. In other words, a physiological assessment of the character's condition momentarily becomes the text's focus, independently of any external textual input: "Mr. Boffin was in such severe literary difficulties that his eyes were prominent and fixed, and his breathing was stertorous" (*OMF* 1:15). Conversely, once the telling of *Decline and Fall* is set on track and Wegg has found the right reading pace, the gap between the text and the characters' movements is erased: Boffin and Wegg become consubstantial with the book. Wegg signals the beginning of the reading session by proclaiming Gibbon's title: "And now, Mr. Boffin, sir, we'll decline and we'll fall ... Is it your pleasure, sir, that we decline and we fall?" (*OMF* 1:15). This endows Gibbon's phrase with an iconic function, as it is performed bodily – or at least the intention to suit the letter to the gesture is expressed blatantly. The notion of declining and falling is also translated kinetically, if only because both characters have to shift from their standing position to take their respective seats. In this sense, the fictional experience stimulates corporeal movements. The same is true of Wegg the versemonger, each time Boffin jocularly asserts that he "*drops* into poetry" (*OMF* 1:9; emphasis added). A more cerebral analysis would probably point to the symbolic acceptation of the decline, fall and drop motif, as the literary activities subsequently turn out to be a cover-up for more manipulative strategies. This being said, the physical, corporeal shifts, counterpointing the more abstract occupation of reading, also need to be underscored.

Dickens often depicts cranks in his novels. Eccentric reading habits may be seen as an equivalent to this well-known tendency, and in *Our Mutual Friend* they frequently affect the body in one way or another – at times with comic effects in a predominantly gloomy novel. The chapters in which Boffin turns into a tight-fisted miser, supposedly to enhance Bella Wilfer's moral edification, have been variously interpreted by critics. Some of them claim that the Golden Dustman's avaricious deportment is too authentic to be merely a pose; others subscribe to the role-playing theory. In either case, the striking fact remains that Boffin's sudden passion for all types of books recording the life of misers throughout the ages pushes him to purchase books extravagantly, while he pointedly emulates these models of miserliness. Reading sessions conflate the somatic and the semiotic, with Silas Wegg, the wooden-legged reader, stumping his way leisurely into a whole array of publications. Some of them are cited in Dickens's text; they include R.S. Kirby's *Wonderful and Scientific Museum* and F.S. Merryweather's *Lives and Anecdotes of Misers* (*OMF* 3:6). The sordid narratives arouse both glee and covetousness in the circle formed by Boffin, Wegg and Mr. Venus, the taxidermist. The promise of money, hoarded in the most unpredictable spots, excites their curiosity and greed. The thrill that the delayed revelation provokes in this small company is manifested by somatic or, more to the point, prosthetic, gestures. As this storyline builds up to its climax, Wegg's wooden leg rises up in what amounts to a tumescent elevation, which is delicately hinted at in a parenthetical aside: "(Here Mr. Wegg's wooden leg started forward under the table, and slowly elevated itself as he read on)" (*OMF* 3:6). The near paronomasia between "read on" and "hard-on" is too prominent to be missed. As a matter of fact, when the story's crisis becomes too much to bear, "the literary man" (*OMF* 1:5) loses his balance, pulling Boffin down with him, until both end up "in a kind of pecuniary swoon" (*OMF* 3:6).

Dickens alternates opposed ambiences and genres in quick succession. The tragic and the comic are to be found in close proximity like "the layers of red and white in a side of streaky, well-cured bacon" (*OT* 17). What is true of staged melodrama may be equally relevant to modes of reading in *Our Mutual Friend*. Alongside the concern for the tangible materiality of books, in various allusions to bodily functions confronted by the physical challenge of reading, or the duty of storing up knowledge as if it were accumulated wealth (for example, Bradley Headstone "had acquired mechanically a great store of teacher's knowledge", *OMF* 2:1), Dickens envisages reading like a mirage – that is, an activity unshackled from the corporeal, that can dispense with books altogether, though not the visionary imagination, which is the correlative of reading. In a sterile world, the writer points to alternative ways of reading by doing away with books: a most unexpected proposal, no doubt. Lizzie Hexam is shown reading in and into the flames, and her younger brother Charley perceptively remarks, "You said you couldn't read a book, Lizzie. Your library of books is the hollow down by the flare, I think" (*OMF* 2:1). It might be said that Dickens is going beyond a mere romantic idealisation of a much-praised activity, to focus primarily on the bodily effects of the act of reading, even in the absence of books. This would give a further turn of the screw to the idea of simulation that has been encountered in several instances in this essay. Here, indeed, it is reversed, as it is no longer the book which affords vicarious experiences, but rather an illiterate subject (Lizzie), who builds up a relation to the outside world through the mediation of reading protocols to which she never ever had access. There remains a phenomenology of reading with books *in absentia*, so to speak, placing the somatic and the empathetic in the foreground; Charley says, "I used to call the fire at home, her books, for she was always full of fancies, – some quite wise fancies, considering – when she was looking at it" (*OMF* 2:1).

Our Mutual Friend inscribes within its diegesis the type of reader which it creates through its many pages. In addition to Wayne Booth's "postulated reader" (1983), Walker Gibson's "mock reader" (1950), Wolfgang Iser's "implied reader" (1980) and Umberto Eco's "model reader" (1979), it is possible to add an "immersed reader" in *Our Mutual Friend*. Immersion is a more committed involvement than empathetic reading, which relies essentially upon somaesthetic responses. Indeed, immersion entails a prolonged change in the state of consciousness that is coterminous with the duration of the reading. This altered condition implies the sensation of being severed from one's immediate surroundings, of being thrown into a kind of reverie and of being temporarily transported into a biosemiotic *Umwelt* (Uexküll 2010), in which the reader, having consented to a willing suspension of disbelief, is affected by secondary beliefs. A long novel, conjuring up different layers of represented reality, is of course liable to induce such a condition. Admittedly, *Our Mutual Friend* affords the holistic experience of an imitated England, even if the fictitious copy is somewhat askew: a jarring juxtaposition of the different worlds of Thames watermen, West End upstarts, corrupt, self-serving politicians, moneylenders and jobbers and, since it is Dickens, the occasional surreal flights from mundane reality.

The novelist in fact imagines two characters who are often depicted in altered states of consciousness, which approximate the reader's probable mindset as he or she is immersed in the alternative world of the novel. Mortimer Lightwood, the solicitor, and Eugene Wrayburn, the barrister, are often shown as being at one remove from their milieu, mentally split, as it were, between a deferred perception of their surroundings and their absorption in imaginary representations. This trance-like condition is rendered palpable through an intensification of sensory perceptions, which are transformed into visons fed by the lingering persistence of textual memory. Thus when the two lawyers are searching for Gaffer Hexam and waiting in an uncomfortable position causing pins and needles in their arms and legs, the pain becomes an incubator of literary recollections triggering surreal images:

> 'Invisible insects of diabolical activity swarm in this place. I [Eugene Wrayburn] am tickled and twitched all over. Mentally, I have now committed a burglary under the meanest circumstances, and the myrmidons of justice are at my heels.'
>
> 'I am quite as bad,' said Lightwood … 'This restlessness started, with me, long ago. All the time you were out, I felt like Gulliver with the Lilliputians firing upon him.' (*OMF* 1:13)

It seems that the two characters evolve simultaneously in the tangible world of London and in a mental scenario which is constantly secreted. When they progress through the London docks, both the proximity of water and the looming ships are conducive to frightful hallucinations: "Not a sluice gate, or a painted scale upon a post or wall, showing the depth of water, but seemed a hint, like the dreadfully facetious Wolf in bed in Grandmamma's cottage, 'That's to drown *you* in, my dears!'" (*OMF* 1:14; emphasis original). For both men, each wrapped up in his own fantastic reconfiguration of his purlieu, there is no longer any ontological gradient between the factual and the mental; as Dickens writes, "everything so vaunted the spoiling influences of water … that the after-consequences of being crushed, sucked under, and drawn down, looked as ugly to the imagination as the main event" (*OMF* 1:14). Even if this is not the main purpose of this passage (which is intent on building up narrative tension), the description implicitly delineates the conditions of immersive reading, by eschewing rational control to heighten subjective sensations.

The near-hallucinatory state provoked by prolonged bouts of reading generates a form of automaticity, whereby the process of decision-making is surrendered to an external agency. This is what happens when the real reader is carried along by the impetus of succeeding events in a plotline. Dickens vividly conveys a loss of control, when a character recaps a whole list of occurrences, in which he has played some part, without being totally committed to them. The extract in which Mortimer Lightwood finds himself mentally going over the day's events, whilst seated in front of the fire in an unspecified "public-house kitchen" (*OMF* 1:14), is illustrative of this liminal condition resulting from being simultaneously in and out of the action. This passage exemplifies the process of immersive reading. The latter consists in mental and physical relaxation, the fluid flow of thoughts, a light spatial and temporal dislocation and the attendant loss of awareness of the immediate presence of others:

> As Mortimer Lightwood sat before the blazing fire, conscious of drinking brandy and water then and there in his sleep, and yet at one and the same time drinking burnt sherry at the Six Jolly Fellowships, and lying under the boat on the river shore, and sitting in the old boat that Riderhood rowed, and listening to the lecture recently concluded, and having to dine in the Temple with an unknown man, who described himself as M.R.F. Eugene Gaffer Harmon, and said he lived at Hailstorm, – as he passed through these curious vicissitudes of fatigue and slumber, arranged upon the scale of a dozen hours to the second he became aware of answering aloud a communication of pressing importance. (*OMF* 1:14)

A stream of images files past in the mind of a character, who has but a distant awareness of what is going on, to the extent that he only realises in hindsight that he has mechanically replied to an urgent query without specifying any further what is the matter at hand.

This essay establishes the relevance of a somatic approach to Dickens's fiction, and propounds a method of close reading. The difficulty consists in treading the thin dividing line between, on the one hand, the characters' bodily functions, and the way they affect meaning, and on the other, the reader's own somaesthetic responses to the texts under consideration. In the absence of any performance of texts, style and punctuation become paramount in the extrapolation of the reader's physical and emotional reactions. The range of novels treated above is sufficiently wide to tackle the topic over a large spectrum, with easily identifiable physiological manifestations at one end, and more elusive phenomena such as reverie and trance-like or near-hallucinatory states resulting from immersive reading at the other. The final issue that could be raised is the ethical repercussions of this emphasis on the corporeal over the intellectual. Is there not, in the final analysis, some hermeneutic bias in foregrounding what is beyond, below or beside the reader's rational control and creative potential? Could it not be claimed that it somehow leads to curtailing the reader's freedom, since automatic, body responses are not triggered by any wilful decision? For obvious reasons, such as the immediacy of their effects on readers – or for that matter, spectators – somatic responses partake of genres which are rightly or wrongly labelled as popular, such as melodrama. So this would contribute to relegating Dickens to the camp of popular sentiment: a dismissive taunt which does not do justice to the multiple facets of his unputdownable *oeuvre*. His fiction continues to inspire new connections between the humanities and the sciences. This versatility is abundantly evident in the prolific writer's DNA, and in his predilection for what Clayton calls "undisciplined cultures" (2003, pp. 81–104).

References

Ackroyd, Peter (1991). *Dickens*. London: Minerva.
Barthes, Roland (1974). *S/Z*. Trans. Richard Miller. Oxford: Blackwell.
Booth, Wayne C. (1983). *The Rhetoric of Fiction*. Chicago, IL: University of Chicago Press.
Clayton, Jay (2003). *Charles Dickens in Cyberspace. The Afterlife of the Nineteenth Century in Postmodern Culture*. Oxford: Oxford University Press.
Cohen, William A. (1993). Manual Conduct in Great Expectations. *ELH*, 60(1), 217–259.
Damasio, Antonio R. (1994). *Descartes' Error: Emotion, Reason, and the Human Brain*. New York: G.P. Putnam.
Dames, Nicholas (2007). *The Physiology of the Novel: Reading, Neural Science & the Form of Victorian Fiction*. Oxford: Oxford University Press.
Eco, Umberto (1979). *The Role of the Reader: Explorations in the Semiotics of Texts*. Bloomington: Indiana University Press.
Friedman, Stanley (1973). The Motif of Reading in *Our Mutual Friend*. *Nineteenth-Century Fiction*, 28(1), 38–61.
Genette, Gérard (2004). *Métalepse: De la figure à la fiction*. Paris: Seuil.
Gibson, Walker (1950). Authors, Speakers, Readers, and Mock Readers. *College English*, 11(5), 265–269.
Hauk, Olaf, Johnsrude, Ingrid, & Pulvermüller, Friedemann (2004). Somatopic Representation of Action Words in Human Motor and Premotor Cortex. *Neuron*, 41(2), 301–307.
Iser, Wolfgang (1980). *The Implied Reader: Patterns of Communication in Prose Fiction from Bunyan to Beckett*. Baltimore, MD: Johns Hopkins University Press.

Jauss, Hans Robert (1982). *Toward an Aesthetic of Reception*. Minneapolis: University of Minnesota Press.

Leckie, Barbara (1999). *Culture and Adultery: The Novel, The Newspaper and the Law, 1857–1914*. Philadelphia: University of Pennsylvania Press.

Letissier, Georges (2013). A Tale of Two Cities as Entertainment. *Cercles*, 31, 80–93.

Levine, George (1991). *Darwin and the Novelists: Patterns of Science in Victorian Fiction*. Chicago, IL & London: University of Chicago Press.

Mahr, Greg (2003). Was St. Anthony Crazy? Visionary Experiences and the Desert Fathers. In James Philips & James Morley (Eds.), *Imagination and its Pathologies* (pp. 253–262). Cambridge, MA: MIT Press.

Miall, David S. (2009). Neuroaesthetics of Literary Reading. In M. Skov & O. Vartanian (Eds.), *Neuroaesthetics* (pp. 233–248). Amityville, NY: Baywood Publishing.

Michelet, Jules (1974). *Le Peuple*. Ed. Paul Viallaneix. Paris: Flammarion.

Moynahan, Julian (1960). The Hero's Guilt: The Case of *Great Expectations*. *Essays in Criticism*, 10(1), 60–79.

Mundhenk, Rosemary (1979). The Education of the Reader in *Our Mutual Friend*. *Nineteenth-Century Fiction*, 34(1), 41–58.

Patoine, Pierre-Louis (2015). *Corps/texte. Pour une théorie de la lecture empathique: Cooper, Danielewski, Frey, Palahniuk*. Lyon: ENS Éditions.

Pettitt, Clare (2013). Dickens and the Form of the Historical Present. In Daniel Tyler (Ed.), *Dickens's Style* (pp. 110–136). Cambridge: Cambridge University Press.

Ramachandran, Vilayanur S. (2000). Mirror Neurons and Imitation Learning as the Driving Force Behind 'The Great Leap Forward' in Human Evolution. *Edge*, 69. Retrieved from https://www.edge.org/documents/archive/edge69.html

Rizzolatti, Giacomo, Fogassi, Leonardo, & Gallese, Vittorio (2000). Cortical Mechanisms Subversing Objects Grasping and Action Recognition: A New View on the Cortical Motor Functions. In M.S. Gazzaniga (Ed.), *The Cognitive Neurosciences* (pp. 539–552). Cambridge, MA: MIT Press.

Tomalin, Claire (2011). *Charles Dickens: A Life*. London: Viking.

Von Uexküll, Jakob (2010). *Milieu animal et milieu marin*. Paris: Payot & Rivages.

6

Dickens and Lawrence

Mimicry, Totemism, Animism

Michael Hollington

As a young man, D.H. Lawrence certainly read Dickens in a passionate manner, in the company of his first flame, Jessie Chambers (the "Miriam" of *Sons and Lovers*) – that is to say, reading him "as if for life," to borrow a phrase from the novel the two of them most admired at that time, *David Copperfield* (*DC* 4). He was 16 or 17 when, according to Chambers's account in *D. H. Lawrence: A Personal Record*, she and he embarked on "a kind of orgy of reading," first devouring Walter Scott until he "was succeeded in our affections by Dickens, with *David Copperfield* pre-eminent" (Chambers 1935, p. 95). Growing up as Lawrence did in the Midlands in the late nineteenth century, with the range of books at his disposal limited by and large to what was available in the local Eastwood library, it is hardly surprising that this should be the case.

But Chambers also describes how they read: "the characters interested us most, and there was usually a more or less unconscious identification of them with ourselves, so that reading became a kind of personal experience" (1935, p. 94). Thus, in the case of *David Copperfield*, it seems Lawrence tried to become a version of his hero – just like David himself, who describes his metamorphosis into "Tom Jones (a child's Tom Jones, a harmless creature) for a week together" or "my own idea of Roderick Random for a month at a stretch" (*DC* 4). Chambers writes: "I was aware even then that Lawrence felt an affinity with the hero of that story – 'the nicest young man in the world,' he would quote mischievously"; she adds in conclusion that "to say that we *read* the books gives no adequate idea of what really happened. It was the entering into possession of a new world, a widening and enlargement of life" (1935, pp. 95–96; emphasis original).

The apparent intensity of this encounter with Dickens as a young man accounts in general for the frequency of reference to the novelist in the corpus of Lawrence's work: novels, stories, poems, plays, critical writings, letters. Yet the earliest Dickens

Reading Dickens Differently, First Edition. Edited by Leon Litvack and Nathalie Vanfasse.
© 2020 John Wiley & Sons Ltd. Published 2020 by John Wiley & Sons Ltd.

reference – to *David Copperfield* of course – in *The White Peacock* (1911; his first published novel) points to another aspect of Lawrence's absorption of the elder novelist:

> When I went down to Eberwich in the March succeeding the election, I found several people staying with my sister. She had under her wing a young literary fellow who affected the 'Doady' style – Dora Copperfield's 'Doady.' He had bunches of half-curly hair, and a romantic black cravat; he played the impulsive part, but was really as calculating as any man on the stock-exchange. It delighted Lettie to 'mother' him. He was so shrewd as to be less than harmless. His fellow guests, a woman much experienced in music and an elderly man who was in the artistic world without being of it, were interesting for a time. Bubble after bubble of floating fancy and wit we blew with our breath in the evenings. I rose in the morning loathing the idea of more bubble-blowing. (Lawrence 1987b, p. 304)

This is obviously a satirical passage, specifically aimed at the flamboyant appearance and manners of Ezra Pound, whom Lawrence had recently met. It sets the tone for many Dickens references in his work, for it is clear that Dickens the caricaturist and satirist was a major influence on Lawrence's own satires and caricatures. Thus it is no surprise that the unforgettable Mrs Skewton in *Dombey and Son* – together with *Bleak House*, Jessie Chambers remembers, one of our "great favourites" (1935, p. 96) – is remembered in the essay "The Future of the Novel" as "the loony Cleopatra in *Dombey and Son* murmuring 'rose-coloured curtains,' with her dying breath – old hag" (Squires 1990, p. 51), in a passage where Lawrence seems to share T.S. Eliot's admiration, later in the 1920s, for Dickens's ability to create character through a single phrase. Eliot's example was young Bailey in *Martin Chuzzlewit* (*MC* 9; see Eliot 1991, p. 462); thus Dickens is placed in the exalted company of Dante and Shakespeare as one of the very few writers able to employ this technique successfully. In the short story "Smile," Lawrence uses a reference to Jerry Cruncher's constant irritation at his pious wife's "flopping" onto her knees in prayer (*TTC* 2.1) in the blackly humorous context of Mathias's visit to the corpse of his "infinitely provoking" wife laid out in a convent: "'At it again!' – he wanted to say to her, like the man in Dickens" (Lawrence 1961, 2:585). In *The Lost Girl*, the 1920 novel which is particularly noteworthy for its Dickensian elements, there is an obvious satiric comparison of the inept, dandified linen merchant James Houghton to the Marquis de St Evrémonde in *A Tale of Two Cities*: "No marquis in a Dickens novel could be as elegant and *raffiné* and heartless" (Lawrence 1981, p. 4).

As Lawrence's attitude towards Dickens evolved beyond his early infatuation, his satiric bent began to go into reverse – that is to say, to train its fire on its *fons et origo* as a representative of Victorian England. At a certain stage of his career, even novels that he admired, like *David Copperfield*, furnished Lawrence with risible or indeed pernicious instances of past attitudes against which he, like many of his contemporaries, rebelled. A representative statement of the attitude of mind that later infected him is made in Leonard Woolf's *Autobiography*: "Thackeray and Dickens meant nothing to us or rather they stood for a way of life, a system of morals against which we were in revolt" (Woolf 1980, p. 105). Thus, like many present-day readers, Lawrence balked at the figure of Agnes Wickfield in his favourite novel, regarding her as a prototype of the "angel in the house" ideal which he may have seen partly reflected in his own mother:

> Dickens invented the child-wife, so child-wives have swarmed ever since. He also fished out his version of the chaste Beatrice, a chaste but marriageable Agnes. George Eliot imitated this pattern, and it became confirmed. The noble woman, the pure spouse, the devoted mother took the field, and was simply worked to death. Our own poor mothers were this sort.

Lawrence was a good deal more attracted to Dora, a type on which he felt the young men of his day had turned their backs, because they were "definitely frightened of the real female. She's too risky a quantity. She is too untidy, like David's Dora" (Lawrence 2004, p. 162).

Lawrence's strongest satiric critique of Dickens is contained in a letter written from Lerici, near La Spezia, to Henry Savage in August 1913:

> I retract what I say against Dickens characters – I am jealous of them. But there is something fundamental about *him* that I dislike. He is mid-Victorian, he is so governessy towards life, as if it were a naughty child. His God is a Sunday-School Superintendent, on the prize-giving day, and he is the mistress of the top class. Curse him. (Zytaruk & Boulton 1981, p. 94; emphasis original)

However, Lawrence's attitude towards Dickens, and much besides, is never one-sided. Even here there is praise for Dickens's characters, who incite a jealousy that is reflected in *The Lost Girl*, in attempts to create characters using what are recognisably Dickensian techniques. Elsewhere in his work there is praise for Dickens in strikingly un-Victorian terms; in *Mr Noon*, for instance, he is found among a company of "truly sensual" writers, including Milton and Wordsworth; Lawrence observes: "These are the truly sensual poets [*sic*] [...]: great men they are, perhaps the greatest" (Lawrence 1987a, p. 193). In a remarkable late reference – one that at first sight vies in its apparent wildness with Edmund Wilson's acceptance of the claim that John Jasper is a member of the Thuggee cult (Wilson 1941, p. 85) – in an early draft of *Apocalypse* (Lawrence's last book), Dickens is thoroughly assimilated to Lawrentian paganism: "the religious experience one gets from Dickens comes from Baal or Ashtaroth, but still is religious" (Lawrence 2002a, p. 156).

It would seem, then, that the later Lawrence has once more moved on, away from his middle-period reading of Dickens as a great novelist limited by the Victorianness of his attitudes, to a view of him in alignment with very anti-Victorian values and emphases, for in *Kangaroo* Baal and Ashtaroth signify "the dark God, the Unknown" that blasts open the door that "the wondrous Victorian age managed to fasten … so tight" (Lawrence 2002b, p. 285). If that were so, it would in some sense reproduce the way in which *The Lost Girl* – by common consent the most Dickensian of Lawrence's novels (see Gurko 1963) – moves on as it progresses from the Midlands of England and what Virginia Woolf describes, in her 1920 review of the book, as "the laborious process … of building up a model of life from saying how d'you do, and cutting the loaf, and knocking the cigarette ash into the ash tray, and standing the yellow bicycle against the wall" (Woolf 1920; see also Lawrence 1981, pp. xlv–xlvii), to writing of a quite different kind about Italy: "how unspeakably lovely it was, no one could ever tell, the grand, pagan twilight of the valleys, savage, cold, with a sense of ancient gods who knew the right for human sacrifice. It stole away the soul of Alvina" (Lawrence 1981, p. 315)

From realism to Modernism – this is how, in very crude terms, the linear trajectory of *The Lost Girl* might be described; but it is possible that the structure of the text itself is at some level a Dickensian one, derived principally from *Great Expectations*, which, it has been suggested, Lawrence must have read as a young man, but which is in fact not mentioned in his letters until 1917 (Game 2016, p. 54). "Expectations Well Lost" – the title of Stange's famous article (1954) – is as relevant to *The Lost Girl* as it is to Dickens's first-person masterpiece. Lawrence's novel can be seen as an ironic, Modernist reading of its prototype: the expectations are much more humdrum and commonplace, and belong essentially to the community, which assumes that Alvina Houghton must not end up "on the shelf" as an old maid, but should marry someone suitable, from her own set of comfortable middle-class tradespeople. Here too her own disdain for the offers that come her way is a far from negligible cause of their failure to materialise. But the central paradox is the same: that Alvina is "found" when she is "lost" by becoming aligned with the despised "common folk," through meeting an itinerant peasant Italian in a troop of performers that she herself joins. The chief structural difference is the much more extended coda in *The Lost Girl* about her life after being "lost," when she has married her peasant, decamped with him to the desolate mountains of the Abruzzi, and, in an atmosphere of ambiguity not dissimilar to that of the ending of *Great Expectations*, is about to bear his child.

There are three strands in *The Lost Girl* of Lawrence's distinctive reading of Dickens. It was Lawrence's Scottish friend Catherine Carswell who identified the first of these:

> Nobody who ever heard him describe the scenes and persons of his boyhood, or watched him recreate with uncanny mimicry the talk, the movements and the eccentricities of the men and women among whom he grew

up, can doubt but that Lawrence, if he had liked, might have been a new kind of Dickens of the Midlands. (Carswell 1981, p. 64)

These remarks are amplified by John Worthen in his essay entitled "Drama and Mimicry in Lawrence":

> [Lawrence] resembled, in fact, no one so much as Charles Dickens in his capacity for mimicry, in his fascination with the dramatic, in the frenzied energy he would pour into performances, in his natural tendency to act out in his fiction performances of the human grotesque and in his manipulation, as a fictional narrator, of his comic characters. Just as Lawrence struck David Garnett as the best mimic he had ever known – so Dickens, too, struck everyone who knew him as the most accomplished mimic they had ever known. (Worthen 1996, p. 30)

This capacity for mimicry is very much in evidence in *The Lost Girl*, where a preoccupation with "voice" is prominent in the creation and differentiation of character. But there is a further possible contextual perspective: the novel's date of publication is 1920, a year in which Lawrence was friendly for a time on Capri with another noted writer and mimic, the former actor Compton Mackenzie – with whose work, incidentally, *The Lost Girl* was compared by contemporary reviewers. It is possible that Mackenzie had done some Dickensian mimicry and/or reading aloud for Lawrence during that period. He certainly did so in later life: the writer Eric Linklater provides a wonderful illustration of this in his autobiography *The Man on My Back*; he depicts Mackenzie deploring the disappearance of "genuine" Cockney speech as it appears in Dickens, and proceeds to give a demonstration of the genuine article:

> 'I listened the other night to a young man in the BBC trying to impersonate Sam Weller. He was no more like Sam Weller than a marmoset's like a two-toed sloth. You remember the trial, Bardell versus Pickwick? Well, this is how it ought to be done.'
> He got up, and after a false start recited with astonishing virtuosity the exchanges between Mr Justice Stareleigh and Sam Weller, the anonymous interruptions, the questions of Mr Buzfuz, and Sam's response. He made Sam speak a husky constricted voice that was like a London fog.
> 'But it's meant to be a fog!' he exclaimed. 'Not the shallow fog of today, but a regular pea-soup London particular. Fog in the throat. That's how Dickens used to read the trial scene.'
> 'How do you know that?'
> 'Because my father heard him, and imitated him, and I learnt from my father. My father was a first-class mimic, and I'm a good one. So what you've just heard was practically the voice of Charles Dickens himself. As well as a piece of authentic Cockney.' (Linklater 1992, pp. 265–266)

Likewise, from the very beginning of *The Lost Girl*, Lawrence shows his capacity to "do the police in different voices" (*OMF* 1:16). For instance, there is James Houghton in the first chapter, "raising his musical voice, which the work-girls hated, against one or other of the work-girls"; he is differentiated immediately from the village blacksmith, who teaches in Sunday School and is an essential peacemaker, "gripping any recalcitrant boy just above the knee, and jesting with him in a jocular manner, in the dialect," or from Miss Pinnegar (with a Dickensian name, rhyming with "vinegar"), who comes to work for him, and is able to get the better of him, establishing an ascendancy through her "soft, near, sure voice, which seemed almost like a secret touch upon her hearer" (Lawrence 1981, pp. 8, 9, 12).

Houghton's daughter Alvina, at the beginning of chapter 2, is at first assimilated to him, identified by her "quiet, refined, almost convent voice ... Like her father's, flexible and curiously attractive" (Lawrence 1981, pp. 20–21). It is clear that there are hidden depths to her personality that will emerge as the novel progresses; this is signified through her capacity to move into quite a different register – that of the "half-hilarious clang ... in her voice, taunting," when she undertakes her first flight from the stifling world of Manchester House, or when she is in the process of "losing" the various suitable bachelors in the community: "her voice had a curious bronze-like resonance that acted straight on the nerves of her hearers; unpleasantly on most English nerves, but like fire on the different susceptibilities of the young man" (Lawrence 1981, pp. 30, 23)

Voice, in Lawrence as in Dickens, regularly signifies class, and if the focus is reversed, to look for voices that stir Alvina, it is apparent that they commonly speak in Midlands dialect. The man who shows her down her father's mine is a strong example, speaking in vivid metaphor: "no, you dunna get th' puddin' stones i' this pit – 's not deep enough, Eh, they come down on you plumb, as if th' roof had laid an egg on you." It is not just that he utters the "authentic" speech of the working class; he stands, in fact, for something beyond the human altogether, for he is represented as a totemic bat dwelling in the dark, cave-like underground recesses of the mine:

> and still his voice went on clapping in her ear, and still his presence edged near her, and seemed to impinge on her – a smallish, semi-grotesque, grey-obscure figure with a naked brandished fore-arm: not human: a creature of the subterranean world, melted out like a bat, fluid. (Lawrence 1981, p. 47)

The second distinctive aspect of Lawrence's reading of Dickens in this novel is their shared appreciation of the resemblances between human physiognomies and the facial contours of animals (it is also interesting to note how there has been a recent turn towards interpreting Dickensian characters by means of their hands; see Capuano 2015, pp. 127–151, 185–213; Briefel 2015, pp. 52, 168). In *The Lost Girl* the anthropological anchorage is achieved by means of foregrounding of North American Indian totems in the Natcha-Kee-Tawara chapters, where the matriarchal Madame Rochard and her small band of male subalterns act out Wild West fantasies involving animals and humans, white and Indian. In Dickens the composite intellectual background is made up of such things as the animal masks of the *commedia dell'arte*; the tradition of Lavater's physiognomical pseudo-science, and the adoption of its principles in work by the caricaturists William Hogarth and Thomas Rowlandson; and the moralising correspondences between humans and animals favoured by contemporary Fourierists such as Toussenel about whom Dickens published articles, authored by E.S. Dixon, in *Household Words* (*Letters* 7:125). The flavour of these is glimpsed in a passage in *Martin Chuzzlewit*, where Mark Tapley runs through a gamut of possible totems for the United States that would fit that country, in his view, more suitably than the official national Eagle: "I should want to draw it like a Bat for its short-sightedness; like a Bantam, for its bragging; like a Magpie, for its honesty; like a Peacock, for its vanity; like an ostrich, for its putting its head in the mud, and thinking nobody sees it" (*MC* 34).

Such thinking leaves profound traces on Dickens's habit of differentiating character on the basis of resemblance to differing animals and birds. To take only the genus *Corvidae* (a bird family that includes crows and ravens, who are noted for their mimicry) in his work, the totem of the evil toymaker Tackleton in *The Cricket on the Hearth* is the raven, for his "whole sarcastic ill-conditioned self" is seen "peering out of one little corner of one little eye, like the concentrated essence of any number of ravens" (*CH* 1). Dickens imagines Grandfather Smallweed in *Bleak House* as a crow, whom Phil Squod has to restrain himself from shooting:

> Phil, who has never beheld the apparition in the black-velvet cap before, has stopped short with a gun in his hand with much of the air of a dead shot intent on picking Mr. Smallweed off as an ugly old bird of the crow species. (*BH* 26)

Another rookish example is Zephaniah Scadder in *Martin Chuzzlewit*, who sports "rumpled tufts ... on the arches of his eyes, as if the crow whose foot was deeply printed in the corners had pecked and torn them in a savage recognition of his kindred nature as a bird of prey" (*MC* 21). Perhaps on the basis of childhood memories of their prominence as inhabitants of Rochester Cathedral tower and precincts, they are associated with peace and tranquillity, and seem to recognise Doctor Strong as one of their own; when he retires from Canterbury to Highgate, and is seen by David "walking in the garden at the side, gaiters and all" – as much like a rook as ever – he

> had his old companions about him, too; for there were plenty of high trees in the neighbourhood, and two or three rooks were on the grass, looking after him, as if they had been written to about him by the Canterbury rooks, and were observing him closely in consequence. (*DC* 36)

Lawrence's reading of Dickens clearly noted these techniques of differentiating character. He employs them himself in *The Lost Girl* in the superbly Dickensian character Mr May, who is based on Maurice Magnus, whom Lawrence also met on Capri via Norman Douglas. He is first introduced as "one of those men who carry themselves in birdie fashion, so that their tail sticks out a little behind, jauntily" (Lawrence 1981, p. 90), and as with Dickens, the motif, once introduced, is repeated at every suitable moment. Thus he is seen shortly thereafter in conversation with Miss Pinnegar "with his chest perkily stuck out like a robin," and then again in the company of James Houghton, "like a perky, pink-faced grey bird standing cocking his head in attention" (Lawrence 1981, p. 95); he resembles Mr Chillip, the mild-mannered doctor who delivers the baby boy in the opening chapter of *David Copperfield*, timidly looking at the formidable Aunt Betsy and offering remarks "like an amiable bird" (*DC* 1).

The body language of Mr May in Lawrence's novel manifestly reflects Magnus's homosexuality: he establishes a "curious … intimacy" with Alvina, but, the narrator observes, makes "no physical advances"; rather, "he was like a dove-grey, disconsolate bird pecking the crumbs of Alvina's sympathy, and cocking his eye all the time to watch that she did not advance one step towards him" (Lawrence 1981, p. 104). He is obviously scared stiff of women, and the language of Lawrence's critical account of *David Copperfield* is very much in evidence here. May wants women in general, and Alvina in particular, to behave like angel-mothers and not like sexually alive women – that is to say, to be Agnes Wickfields rather than Dora Spenlows. He regards the latter as "horrific two-legged cats without whiskers. If he had been a bird, his innate horror of a cat would have been such. He liked the *angel*, and particularly the angel-mother in woman. Oh! – that he worshipped. – But coming-on-ness!" (1981, p. 104).

The third stylistic trait that Lawrence clearly adopted from his reading of Dickens is that "animistic" treatment of things noted in a classic essay by Dorothy Van Ghent (1950). This device, hugely prominent in *The Lost Girl*, was something that Lawrence was equally aware of in the work of Katherine Mansfield, who was herself greatly indebted to Dickens (Hollington 2015). Frieda Lawrence, in a letter written after Katherine's death to her lover John Middleton Murry (who had been Mansfield's husband), observed that "Lawrence said Katherine had a lot in common with Dickens, you know when the kettle is so alive on the fire and things seem to take on such significance" (Tedlock 1961, p. 347). It should be noted that Mansfield may have more to do with *The Lost Girl* than initially meets the eye: Darroch argues that the character of Alvina Houghton is based on the New Zealand writer's own career as a "lost girl" (Darroch 2012, pp. 5–7).

It should be stressed that the relationship between people and things, in both authors, is very much a two-way process: things can be seen as alive and people can be seen as if they were things. The latter principle is one of the most prominent features of the thoroughly Dickensian humorous impulse of Lawrence's novel. The reification of other people – treating them as things rather than as live human beings – comes in for frequent satiric treatment here. Thus Arthur Witham, the brother of Albert (one of the deadly series of middle-class suitors whom Alvina roundly rejects) takes a tradesman's eye to her at church, "as if she were a chimney that needed repairing, and he must estimate the cost, and whether it was worth it." One of the artistes whom Mr May hires to do an accompanying "turn" at Houghton's film shows is Miss Poppy, a kind of downmarket Loie Fuller (a groundbreaking pioneer of modern dance), able to transmogrify herself into a Dickensian miscellany of shapes and things; she "could whirl herself into anything you like, from an arum lily in green stockings to a rainbow and a Catherine wheel and a cup and saucer." She treats Mr Houghton with appropriate disdain, "as if he were a cuckoo-clock, and she had to wait till he'd finished cuckooing" (Lawrence 1981, p. 107); this is classic Dickensian phrasing!

Of course such characters are themselves directly handled as things. Albert and Arthur Witham, whose "mechanical, overbearing way was something ... [Alvina] was unaccustomed to" are compared to "the jaws of a pair of insentient iron pincers"; and Albert seems to move as if his body were a machine-like collection of separate parts, in the manner of Samuel Beckett's Murphy or Watt (the protagonists of two of his novels): "He always seemed to be advancing from the head and shoulders, in a flat kind of advance, horizontal. He did not seem to be walking with his whole body" (Lawrence 1981, p. 66). Madame Rochard's eyes – alive enough though they are, compared to "twin swift extraneous creatures: oddly like two bright little dark animals in the snow" (Lawrence 1981, p. 144) – follow a regular principle in Dickens (Zephaniah Scadder in chapter 21 of *Martin Chuzzlewit* is an example), of separating eyes out from the rest of the face, and indeed from each other.

Two similar passages in *The Lost Girl* come closest to Lawrence's account of Katherine Mansfield's Dickensian imagination, because they employ a culinary metaphor to express that essential vitalism, embracing humans as well as things, in both writers. The first concerns the audience at Houghton's film shows, "on its feet and not very quiet, hissing like doughnuts in the pan even when the pan is taken off the fire" (Lawrence 1981, p. 111). The second stands as a comprehensive culminating instance of the Dickens-inspired comic genius on display in *The Lost Girl*; it is a mimic scene that contains a number of layers. Madame Rochard has been ill, and Mr May has of course been only too happy to indulge his appetite for cross-dressing by appearing in drag in her place; but now she reappears, and is treated to a performance welcoming her back from one of her troupe, the Suisse Romande Louis, described as "a good satiric mimic," who gives her a glimpse of the fun she has missed:

> Louis glanced round, laid his head a little on one side and drew in his chin, with Mr May's smirk exactly, and wagging his tail slightly, he commenced to play the false Kishwégin. He sidled and bridled and ejaculated with raised hands, and in the dumb show the tall Frenchman made such a

ludicrous caricature of Mr Houghton's manager that Madame wept with laughter, whilst Max leaned back against the wall and giggled continuously like some pot involuntarily boiling. (Lawrence 1981, p. 147)

Mimicry, totemism, wholesale imbrication of persons and things – all three are on display here. Steeped in his work, Lawrence indeed read Dickens in a memorably distinctive way.

References

Briefel, Aviva (2015). *The Racial Hand in the Victorian Imagination*. Cambridge: Cambridge University Press.

Capuano, Peter J. (2015). *Changing Hands: Industry, Evolution, and the Reconfiguration of the Victorian Body*. Ann Arbor: University of Michigan Press.

Carswell, Catherine (1981). *The Savage Pilgrimage: A Narrative of D. H. Lawrence*. Cambridge: Cambridge University Press.

[Chambers, Jessie] ("E.T.") (1935). *D. H. Lawrence: A Personal Record*. London: Jonathan Cape.

Darroch, Sandra Jobson (2012, October). Katherine Mansfield: Lawrence's Real Lost Girl. *Rananim*, 19(2), 2–7.

Eliot, T.S. (1991). *Selected Essays*. London: Faber and Faber.

Game, David (2016). *D. H. Lawrence's Australia: Anxiety at the Edge of Empire*. London: Routledge.

Gurko, Leo (1963). *The Lost Girl*: D. H. Lawrence as a "Dickens of the Midlands." *PMLA*, 78(5), 601 605.

Hollington, Michael (2015). Mansfield Eats Dickens. In Sarah Ailwood & Melinda Harvey (Eds.), *Katherine Mansfield and Literary Influence* (pp. 155–167). Edinburgh: Edinburgh University Press.

Lawrence, D.H. (1961). *The Complete Short Stories*. 3 vols. London and New York: Viking Press.

Lawrence, D.H. (1981). *The Lost Girl*. Ed. John Worthen. Cambridge: Cambridge University Press.

Lawrence, D.H. (1987a). *Mr. Noon*. Ed. Lindeth Vasey. Cambridge: Cambridge University Press.

Lawrence, D.H. (1987b). *The White Peacock*. Ed. Andrew Robertson. Cambridge: Cambridge University Press.

Lawrence, D.H. (2002a). *Apocalypse and the Writings on Revelation*. Ed. Maria Kalnins. Cambridge: Cambridge University Press.

Lawrence, D.H. (2002b). *Kangaroo*. Ed. Bruce Steele. Cambridge: Cambridge University Press.

Lawrence, D.H. (2004). *Late Essays and Articles*. Ed. James T. Boulton. Cambridge: Cambridge University Press.

Linklater, Andro (1992). *Compton Mackenzie: A Life*. London: Hogarth Press.

Squires, Michael (1990). Lawrence, Dickens, and the English Novel. In Michael Squires & Keith Cushman (Eds.), *The Challenge of D. H. Lawrence* (pp. 42–61). Madison: University of Wisconsin Press.

Stange, G. Robert (1954). Expectations Well Lost. *College English*, 16, 9–17.

Tedlock, E.W. (Ed.) (1961). *Frieda Lawrence: The Memoirs and Correspondence*. London: Heinemann.

Van Ghent, Dorothy (1950). The Dickens World: The View from Todgers's. *Sewanee Review*, 58(3), 419–438.

Wilson, Edmund (1941). Dickens: The Two Scrooges. In *The Wound and the Bow: Seven Studies in Literature* (pp. 1–104). Cambridge, MA: Houghton Mifflin Co.

Woolf, Leonard (1980). *An Autobiography I: 1880–1911*. Oxford: Oxford University Press.

Woolf, Virginia (1920, 2 December). Postscript or Prelude? [review of *The Lost Girl*]. *Times Literary Supplement*, 705.

Worthen, John (1996). Drama and Mimicry in Lawrence. In Paul Eggert & John Worthen (Eds.), *Lawrence and Comedy* (pp. 19–31). Cambridge: Cambridge University Press.

Zytaruk, George J., & Boulton, James T. (Eds.) (1981). *The Letters of D. H. Lawrence Volume II, June 1913–October 1916*. Cambridge: Cambridge University Press.

7

Wreckage and Ruin

Turner, Dickens, Ruskin

Jeremy Tambling

After Dickens's death on 9 June 1870, Charles Eliot Norton, who had known the novelist since at least 1855, and supported his second American journey in 1867–1868, wrote to John Ruskin, noting that Dickens "took the most serious view of the conditions of society in England"; he continued:

> I thought of him as almost certain to come to the fore in case of any terrible overflow of the ignorance, misery & recklessness which the selfishness of the upper classes has fostered, & which now … are far more threatening to those classes than they seem to have the power of conceiving … He would have read your Inaugural with the deepest interest. (Bradley & Ousby 1987, pp. 191–192; see also Hilton 2002, p. 151).

This "Inaugural" was Ruskin's oration as Slade Professor of Fine Art, on 8 February 1870 (Hunt 1982, p. 332; Ruskin 1909–1912, 20:18–44). Ruskin replied to Norton:

> The literary loss is infinite – the political one I care less for than you do. Dickens was a pure modernist – a leader of the steam-whistle party *par excellence* – and he had no understanding of any power of antiquity except a sort of jackdaw sentiment for cathedral towers. He knew nothing of the nobler power of superstition – was essentially a stage manager, and used everything for effect on the pit. His Christmas meant mistletoe and pudding – neither resurrection from dead, not rising of new stars, nor teaching of wise men, not shepherds. His hero is essentially the ironmaster [Mr Rouncewell in *Bleak House*]; in spite of *Hard Times*, he has advanced by his influence every principle that makes them harder – the love of excitement, in all classes, and the fury of business competition, and the distrust both of nobility and clergy which, wide enough and fatal enough, and too justly

Reading Dickens Differently, First Edition. Edited by Leon Litvack and Nathalie Vanfasse.
© 2020 John Wiley & Sons Ltd. Published 2020 by John Wiley & Sons Ltd.

founded, needed no apostle to the mob but a grave teacher of priests and nobles themselves, for whom Dickens had essentially no word. (Ruskin 1909–1912, 37:7; Bradley & Ousby 1987, pp. 194–195)

Ruskin (who met Dickens around 1851) here provides an early use of the term "modernist," which for him implies that Dickens rejected "antiquity." Yet this criticism may be an inconsistency, thus prompting the question of what he really thought of Dickens, since the critic's five-volume *Modern Painters* (1843–1860) sympathised with the "modern."

Norton convinced Ruskin to alter his views of Dickens, whose writing was superior to that of the art critic in every way but one: "the desire of truth without exaggeration"; rather than "the pure facts," Dickens's delight in "grotesque and rich exaggeration" had, according to Ruskin, made him "nearly useless in the present"; he wrote to Norton in July 1870:

> I quite feel all that you say of Dickens ... I do not believe he has made *any-one* more good-natured – I think all his finest touches of sympathy are absolutely undiscerned by the British public – but his mere caricature – his liberalism – and his calling the Crystal Palace 'Fairyland' – have had fatal effects – and profound.
>
> I heard him read the death of Nancy – and pursuit of Sykes [sic] – Nothing that he has done is more truly tender and deep in pity.
>
> After it was over – a respectable bald headed gentleman got up on his seat – and begged to protest in the name of the audience against 'such an utter piece of abomination'. There was a titter on the part of the Audience – but I believe that nearly every soul of them liked it ... only for the 'sensation', and were at heart of the old gentleman's opinion – I believe Dickens to be as little understood as Cervantes, and almost as mischievous. (Bradley & Ousby 1987, pp. 197–198)

The article referred to above, concerning the Crystal Palace, was not actually by Dickens, though as editor Dickens approved it; he was negative about the Great Exhibition, which he considered "modernist" in its use of iron for construction: the title *Bleak House* (published 1852–1853) contrasts with the optimism of the Crystal Palace. Although a Dickens letter of 18 April 1852 speaks of knowing Yorkshire "iron-masters" who "have done wonders with their workpeople" (*Letters* 6:645), Dickens's admiration for Mr Rouncewell is ambiguous. The alignment Ruskin makes with Cervantes is strange as well: the novelist could not have shared the critic's negativity about Cervantes, on account of the Spanish writer's ironic approach to chivalry – Ruskin prefers Scott – and because of Cervantes's sense that madness shadows utopian thought.

The index to the Library Edition of Ruskin's works (1909–1912) references nothing of Dickens after *Little Dorrit* (1855–1857); none of the novels parallels

Ruskin's evolution of mind around 1860, when he lost his faith, finished *Modern Painters*, and wrote the socially and politically direct *Unto This Last* (1860). His essay "Fiction, Fair and Foul" (1880) labels *Oliver Twist* Dickens's "greatest work" (Ruskin 1909–1912, 34:277); this text and *The Old Curiosity Shop* are most often mentioned, followed by *David Copperfield* and *Bleak House* (see Ruskin 1909–1912, 11:175, 1:xlix, 9:200, 9:429). Ruskin's praise of *Hard Times* (1854), a text he must have found interesting for comparing the childhoods of Louisa and Tom Gradgrind with his own, appears in *Unto This Last* (1860), concerning the relations between employers and servants. Here Ruskin defends Dickens by conceding what he considers a fault:

> I wish that he could think it right to limit his brilliant exaggeration to works written only for public amusement; and when he takes up a subject of high national importance, such as that which he handled in *Hard Times*, that he would use severer and more accurate analysis. The usefulness of that work (to my mind, in several respects the greatest he has written) is with many persons seriously diminished because Mr Bounderby [the novel's Ironmaster] is a dramatic monster, instead of being a characteristic example of a worldly master; and Stephen Blackpool a dramatic perfection, instead of a characteristic example of an honest workman. But let us not lose the use of Dickens's wit and insight, because he chooses to speak in a circle of stage fire. He is entirely right in his main drift and purpose in every book he has written, and all of them, but especially *Hard Times*, should be studied with close and earnest care by persons interested in social questions. (1909–1912, 17:31)

He fails to praise Dickens's exaggeration and excess, which contemporaries found in Turner, who, in the spirit of "WE NEVER SEE ANYTHING CLEARLY" (Ruskin 1909–1912, 6:75), had seen beyond the conventions of pictorial art, exposing deficiencies of perception in his critics. It is curious that he did not praise in Dickens what he lauded in Turner, whom he identifies as "the father of modern art" (Ruskin 1909–1912, 3:258; see also Herrmann 1968; Birch 1990); indeed, he cut the novelist less slack than he did the painter. Dickens is not often thought of as interested in the visual arts, and Melville is the novelist with whom Turner has been compared (Wallace 1992); but because Ruskin was steeped in Turner and Dickens, he notices a Turneresque Dickens, encouraging – as here – a reading that finds Turner inside Dickens, though Ruskin never aligns the two.

Dickens knew that Turner had been a "barber's boy" (*Letters* 8:729), and they shared lower-middle-class origins. Dickens's introduction to the artist was perhaps via Samuel Rogers, whose *Italy, A Poem* had led Ruskin to Turner (Hewison et al. 2000; see also *Letters* 2:103, 5:12, 5:43); Turner was also present at a dinner for Dickens before the author's Italian journey in 1844 (*Letters* 4:147). Dickens's familiarity with Turner's paintings is evident in his writing to Daniel Maclise from the Mediterranean, alluding to the painting *War: The Exile and the Rock-Limpet* (1842; see *Letters* 4:159), noting the sky and the green and the blue (Ruskin 1909–1912, 3:285–289; 13:160–161; see Butlin & Joll 1984, p. 400). Another letter, to Forster, speaks of the impossibility of capturing Venice in description: "Canaletti and Stanny [Dickens's friend Clarkson Stanfield], miraculous in their truth. Turner, very noble" (*Letters* 4:217; see also Sulkin 2009, pp. 178–181, 200–201; Warrell 2003, pp. 18–19, 105–107). This Stanfield-Turner pairing cannot be accidental, for Stanfield, Dickens's friend since 1837, had exhibited *Venice from the Dogana* at the Royal Academy in 1833. In the same exhibition Turner (who was in Venice in 1819, 1833 and 1840) had shown *Bridge of Sighs, Ducal Palace and Custom-House, Venice: Canaletti Painting*, which includes Canaletto painting at an easel in the left foreground (Figure 7.1). Though the painting is centered by the St Mark's Campanile, the basilica is not visible, save for two domes glimpsed behind the Ducal Palace, while the pillar of the Lion of St Mark is almost invisible. Dickens's calling it "noble" alludes to Turner's freedom, perhaps because, unlike Stanfield, he doubles the buildings seen across the water by reflection; this aura contrasts with the unsorted wreckage of wood, sails and detritus in the painting's left foreground, where Canaletto paints, almost invisible and indistinguishable (see Trotter 2000, pp. 33–59). Yet this is not an "historical" painting: Dickens, describing the paintings from memory, adds: "but the reality itself [of Venice], beyond all pen or pencil, I never saw the thing before that I should be afraid to describe" (*Letters* 4:217); thus it goes beyond what he feels he, as a writer, can do.

Figure 7.1 Joseph Mallord William Turner, *Bridge of Sighs, Ducal Palace and Custom-House, Venice: Canaletti Painting*, 1833; © Tate, London 2019.

Dickens's seeing Niagara Falls in 1868 prompts his observation to Forster about "this most affecting and sublime sight"; the comment demonstrates what he learned from Turner:

> All away to the horizon on our right was a wonderful confusion of bright green and white water. As we stood watching it with our faces to the top of the Falls, our backs were towards the sun. The majestic valley below the Falls, so seen through the vast cloud of spray, was made of rainbow. The high banks, the riven rocks, the forests, the bridge, the buildings, the air, the sky, were all made of rainbow. Nothing in Turner's finest water-colour drawings, done in his greatest day, is so ethereal, so imaginative, so gorgeous in colour, as what I then beheld. I seemed to be lifted off the earth and to be looking into Heaven. (*Letters* 12.75)

Dickens matches Turner's interest in water (and watercolours), in his vortices, and energy. Perhaps the novelist owes something to Ruskin, whose *Modern Painters I* (1843) recalls *American Notes* (1842), noting how Dickens on a barge deck looks upwards, not at, but through the sky (Ruskin 1909–1912, 3:347). Ruskin appreciates that Dickens responds to natural phenomena, though a letter of 1841 considers Dickens urban; he declares the last chapters of *The Old Curiosity Shop* (though "what no one else could do") a falling off, demonstrating "a diseased extravagance, a violence of delineation." Ruskin's Dickens is "a thorough cockney" in regard to country life, though incomparable with the "London life" of *Sketches by Boz* (1909–1912, 36:25–26). Yet in a letter of 1863, on Dickens as a comic novelist, he adds, generously:

> his powers of description have never been enough esteemed. The storm in which Steerforth is wrecked, in *Copperfield*; the sunset before Tigg is murdered by Jonas Chuzzlewit; and the French road from Dijon in *Dombey and Son*, and numbers of other such bits, are quite unrivalled in their way. (Ruskin 1909–1912, 36:432)

There is, he claims, "nothing in sea-description, detailed, like Dickens's storm at the death of Ham" (Ruskin 1909–1912, 3:570; see also Tambling 2014, pp. 197–203; Konishima 2017). Ruskin links three Dickens passages where death comes on; they are all anticipated, violent and subtending the land- or seascape. The second Ruskinian example, the sunset in *Martin Chuzzlewit* (1844), opens conventionally, as Montague Tigg, who is about to be murdered, enters a wood; but it becomes complex:

> The last rays of the sun were shining in, aslant, making a path of golden light along the stems and branches in its range, which even as he looked began to die away; yielding gently to the twilight that came creeping on. It was so very

quiet that the soft and stealthy moss about the trunks of some old trees, seemed to have grown out of the silence, and to be its proper offspring. Those other trees which were subdued by blasts of wind in winter time, had not quite tumbled down, but being caught by others, lay all bare and scathed across their leafy arms, as if unwilling to disturb the general repose by the crash of their fall. Vistas of silence opened everywhere, into the heart and inmost recesses of the wood: beginning with the likeness of an aisle, a cloister, or a ruin open to the sky; then tangling off into a deep green rustling mystery, through which gnarled trunks, and twisted boughs, and ivy-covered stems, and trembling leaves, and bark-stripped bodies of old trees stretched out at length, were faintly seen in beautiful confusion. (*MC* 47)

This wood and sunset also presage a "creeping" or "stealthy" death, as in the synaesthesia of "vistas of silence." "Vistas," recalling how Dickens looks through the skies in *American Notes*, derives from the language of the picturesque, like "scathed," for which *Oxford English Dictionary* gives a first example from William Gilpin's *Remarks on Forest Scenery* (1791), relating mainly to descriptions of the New Forest. Behind Gilpin, and Dickens, is the description in *Paradise Lost* Book 1: "Heaven's Fire / Hath scath'd the Forest Oaks" (Milton 1957, p. 227). "Vistas" parallels Turner paintings in which a vortex of light leads away from the immediate foreground; the passage is full of such intricacies.

The "French road" chapter from *Dombey and Son* (1846–1848) ends with Dickens's version of *Rain, Steam and Speed* (1844; Figure 7.2): the train which kills Carker, fleeing from Dijon to Kent. It was a death foretold, since, on those French roads, Carker was attracted towards and possessed by death, and the climactic "fiery devil, thundering along so smoothly, tracked through the distant valley by a glare of light and lurid smoke, and gone!" (*DS* 55). The train is less seen than its "trace," so that when it comes again, in the night, it is

a trembling of the ground, and quick vibration in his ears; a distant shriek; a dull light advancing, quickly changed to two red eyes, and a fierce fire, dropping glowing coals; an irresistible bearing on of a great roaring and dilating mass; a high wind, and a rattle – another come and gone … (*DS* 55)

The object, neither animal nor machinic, but rather more indefinable, has indeed gone, but is known by what is in its wake: that, like the red appearing out of gloom, is Turneresque.

In *Fors Clavigera* (Ruskin's series of letters to workmen, 1871–1884) the critic recalls Dickens's description of rain in Glencoe, via a letter reproduced in Forster's *Life*:

Through the whole glen, which is ten miles long, torrents were boiling and foaming, and sending up in every direction spray like the smoke of great fires. They were rushing down every hill and mountain side, and tearing

Figure 7.2 Robert Brandard, engraving of Turner's *Rain, Steam and Speed*, 1844; in *The Turner Gallery: A Series of One Hundred and Twenty Engravings from the Works of the Late J.M.W. Turner, R.A.* 2 vols; New York: D. Appleton & Co., 1880, vol. 1, n.p.

like devils across the path, and down into the depths of the rocks. Some of the hills looked as if they were full of silver, and had cracked in a hundred places. Others looked as if they were frightened and had broken out into a deadly sweat. In others there was no compromise or division of streams, but one great torrent came roaring down with a deafening noise, and a rushing of water that was quite appalling. (*Letters* 2:326–327; see also Forster 1969, 1:159)

This sense of an explosion of water pairs with the violence of rain in Turner, and suggests a connection between the two in Ruskin's mind. This appears in the context of Ruskin's saying something palpably untrue: that he cannot write description, his forte being political economy (Ruskin 1909–1912, 27:324–325). The account of the rain's irresistible force is not different from a sense of the train, as when Dickens compares the water's flow with diabolic elements, the train of *Dombey and Son* is a "fiery devil." The comparison of the water gushing to the smoke of great fires industrialises the landscape, like Turner.

To those hints of Turneresque weather in Dickens may be added fog in *Bleak House*, the "London Particular" (*BH* 3): a Dickens phrase taken into Ruskin's "The

Storm-Cloud of the Nineteenth Century" (1884; Ruskin 1909–1912, 34:15), for his reading of modernity; a lack of colour in dull skies (which Ruskin calls the contamination of the late nineteenth century) forms the city's "monotony" (Ruskin 1909–1912, 34:270). Here, Dickens's influence is as pervasive as Turner's, manifesting itself as "a loathsome mass of sultry and foul fog, like smoke" (Ruskin 1909–1912, 34:37). Rain in chapter 2 of *Bleak House* negates colour, like fog: "all men … enjoy colour," Ruskin writes in *Modern Painters 4*, even giving colour a precedence over form (1909–1912, 6:71–72). The negativity of dulling rain in *Little Dorrit* increases throughout the novel; there rain is associated with equinoctial gales, for the novel starts in August, and progresses through September (*LD* 1:3, 1:8, 1:9, 1:17, 1:29; 2:29). One London passage in Dickens, when Pip is helping Magwitch to escape down the Thames, seems to be derived from Turner:

> The winking lights upon the bridges were already pale, the coming sun was like a marsh of fire on the horizon. The river, still dark and mysterious, was spanned by bridges that were turning coldly grey, with here and there at top a warm touch from the burning in the sky. As I looked along the clustered roofs, with Church towers and spires shooting into the unusually clear air, the sun rose up, and a veil seemed to be drawn from the river, and millions of sparkles burst out upon its waters. From me, too, a veil seemed to be drawn, and I felt strong and well. (*GE* 3:14; see Carlisle 2004, p. 66)

The move is from gas lamps to the sun and its reflections, with the pun on "coldly grey" on a March morning, to the "warm touch" from the colour of the rising sun. Water and fire are both here, anticipated in "marsh of fire," which suggests the undifferentiated wet light low on the horizon like a marsh (with the idea of "marshlight" present as well). The passage moves from the loosely patterned to the sharply distinguished separate points of light, with shootings upwards (like shooting stars) and light rising up in the image of the veil; also notable are the sparkles from the water, where light comes from above and below simultaneously, showing itself in colour. The extract closes with a sense of personal investment. If Ruskin had read this on the "veil," he might have taken it as evidence of a tortured frame of mind for the novelist: one familiar with both psychic and social storm clouds.

Ruskin implicitly connects Turner and Dickens by writing about Covent Garden (on Turner and London see Rodner 1997; Butlin & Joll 1984, p. 525; Hill 1993, pp. 1–23; Hamilton 2003, pp. 172–177). "The Two Boyhoods," from *Modern Painters 5* (1860) recalls Giorgione's Venice, but then comes Turner's boyhood, and his studio in Hand Court, adjacent to 26 Maiden Lane:

> [At] the south-west corner of Covent Garden, a square brick pit or well is formed by a close-set block of houses, to the back windows of which it admits a few rays of light. Access to the bottom of it is obtained out of Maiden Lane, through a narrow archway and an iron gate; and if you stand

long enough under the archway to accustom your eyes to the darkness you may see on the left hand a narrow door, which formerly gave quiet access to a respectable barber's shop ... (Ruskin 1909–1912, 7:375)

This setting may be compared with Nemo's graveyard in *Bleak House*, on the other side of Covent Garden (*BH* 11). Maiden Lane was north of the Strand, and the Thames, which, prior to the completion of the Embankment in 1869, was in closer proximity. "Never certainly a cheerful" area, according to Ruskin (1909–1912, 7:36), Covent Garden had been awarded to the Earl of Bedford after the dissolution of the Abbey (Convent) of St Peter at Westminster. Its piazza and St Paul's Church (completed in 1633, restored 1795), were commissioned from Inigo Jones (see Thorne 1980, p. 7). Turner's parents were married there, and it was the site of the artist's baptism (Lindsay 1966, pp. 12–15; Bailey 1997, pp. 21, 35). A fruit and vegetable market on the site dates from 1670, and in 1830 Charles Fowler constructed a market building, thus filling the square. Ruskin thinks of Turner's context, and of "deep furrowed cabbage-leaves at the greengrocers's, magnificence of orange in wheelbarrows round the corner; and Thames' shore within three minutes' race." Turner's foregrounds, observes Ruskin,

> had always ... greengrocery at the corners. Enchanted oranges gleam in Covent Gardens of the Hesperides; and great ships go to pieces in order to scatter chests of them on the waves. (1909–1912, 7:376)

This wittily allusive writing recalls Turner's *Entrance of the Meuse: Orange Merchantman on the Bar, Going to Pieces; Brill Church bearing S.E. by S., Masenluys E. by S.* (1819). The merchant-ship is Dutch (of the House of Orange; Turner had toured Holland in 1817); its cargo consists of oranges, and it goes to pieces on a sandbank where the Meuse reaches the sea at Rotterdam. Turner's painting is topographically precise, with the two towns seen on the horizon; the fishermen scavenge for oranges, as if they were boys in Covent Garden. Bachrach interprets the painting as an allegory of Holland's shipwrecked economy; he records that a schooner was wrecked off Whitehaven (reported in the *Times*, 16 January 1819), carrying oranges, making this "another illustration of the amazing combination of memory, association of thought, and urge to communicate topical feeling" characterising Turner (Bachrach 1994, pp. 44–45; see also Butlin & Joll 1984, p. 57). Ruskin's wordplay, with his fantasies about the Hesperides, continues in what follows: "The Nereids' Guard," discussing Turner's *The Goddess of Discord Choosing the Apple of Contention in the Garden of the Hesperides* (1806; see Hewison et al., pp. 28–29; Birch 1988, pp. 45–47). It is a version of the Fall: the Garden of the Hesperides replaces the Garden of Eden, but both recur in Covent Garden. If the first garden symbolises England, the ambiguity of what the Hesperides represent – that is, wealth, yet discord, for two apples imply division – is capped by the dragon who guards the garden. The creature is volcanic, evoking industrial power, creating a "paradise of smoke" (Ruskin 1909–1912, 7:408). Eden is already ruined, yet Covent Garden gives hope: unlike the Hesperides, it yields oranges, not apples, yet if these are "enchanted," they may also embody deceptiveness.

So Ruskin associates Turner with London, and its river, thus recalling Turner's death by the river, in Chelsea, looking westwards (Ruskin 1909–1912, 12:133). London takes precedence over Venice in grotesque ugliness, and Ruskin's description is clearly Dickensian:

> No matter how ugly it is – has it anything about it like Maiden Lane or like Thames' shore? If so, it shall be painted ... Turner could endure ugliness ... Dead brick walls, blank square windows, old clothes, market-womanly types of humanity – anything fishy or muddy, like Billingsgate or Hungerford Market, had great attraction for him; black barges, patched sails, and every possible condition of fog.

After noting that the "noblest" of his endurances was dirt, the critic continues:

> no Venetian ever draws anything foul, but Turner devoted picture after picture to the illustration of effects of dinginess, smoke, soot, dust, and dusty texture; old sides of boats, weedy roadside vegetation, dung-hills, straw-yards, and all the soilings and stains of every common labour ... he not only could endure, but enjoyed and looked for *litter*, like Covent Garden wreck after the market ... He delights in shingle, debris, and heaps of fallen stones. (Ruskin 1909–1912, 7:377–378)

In the space of two pages, Ruskin twice evokes wreckage: the sea's, and the market's, like that wreckage in the foreground of the "noble" picture of *Bridge of Sighs, Ducal Palace and Custom-House, Venice*. The word "foul," which shows Venetian artists' limitations, since they do not paint it, is significant; it recalls the "foul fog" of the "Storm-Cloud" essay (Ruskin 1909–1912, 34:37). "Foul" makes Ruskin say how much Turner regarded the poor; he then returns to city commerce, focused on warehouses on the Thames, and on

> that mysterious forest below London Bridge on one side; and, on the other, with these masses of human power and national wealth which weigh upon us, at Covent Garden here, with strange compression, and crush us into narrow Hand Court. (Ruskin 1909–1912, 7:379)

Hand Court, opposite Maiden Lane, housed Turner's studio in the 1790s. Ruskin takes the forest image from *The Harbours of England* (1856), which speaks admiringly of fishing boats, colliers, ships of the line and the "'new Forest' of mast and yard that follows the winding of the Thames" (Ruskin 1909–1912, 12:28). Covent

Garden is the "other" to the sea, connected to it by the river (its mouth so often painted), by trade (the oranges) and by litter (a lighter form of wreckage; see Butlin & Wilton 1974, pp. 73–74; Selborne 2008, pp. 132–133). Ruskin asks what Turner saw between Covent Garden and Wapping, and specifically in Maiden Lane; he replies:

> religion maintained ... at point of constable's staff; but, at other times, placed under the custody of the beadle, within certain black and unstately iron railings of St Paul's, Covent Garden. Among the wheelbarrows and over the vegetables, no perceptible dominance of religion ... [only] high pews, heavy elocution, and cold grimness of behaviour. (1909–1912, 7:382)

Ruskin notes that only once did Turner depict a clergyman (see Shanes 1990, pp. 295–338). He compares St Mark's, as related to Venice's lagoon, with the other St Paul's, with its dome, ruling over death, over St Paul's Churchyard (Ruskin 1909–1912, 7:383). Turner did not see Venetian life, but rather "in the present work of men, meanness, aimlessness, unsightliness; thin-walled, lath-divided, narrow-garreted houses of clay; booths of a darksome Vanity Fair, busily base" (Ruskin 1909–1912, 7:385).

The young Dickens's love of Covent Garden was nurtured partly through observation, but also through being lent George Colman's comic verse, *Broad Grins*, which opens thus:

> Centrick, in London noise, and London follies,
> Proud Covent Garden blooms, in smoky glory;
> For chairmen, coffee-rooms, piazzas, dollies,
> Cabbages, and comedians, fam'd in story!
> *(Colman 1819, p. 109; see also Brown 2012)*

According to John Forster, Colman

> seized [Dickens's] fancy very much; and he was so impressed by its description of Covent Garden, in the piece called the 'Elder Brother' that he stole down to the market by himself to compare it with the book. He remembered, as he said in telling me this, snuffing up the flavor of the faded cabbage leaves as if they were the very breath of comic fiction. (Forster 1969, 1:14).

It was at that time that Dickens's uncle, Thomas Barrow, was shaved by "a very odd old barber out of Dean Street, Soho, who was never tired of reviewing the events of the last war, and especially of detecting Napoleon's mistakes, and rearranging his whole life for him on a plan of his own" (Forster 1969, 1:15). Slater speculates that the barber may have been Turner's father, who provided then the substance of a lost description by the child Dickens, perhaps like *Tristram Shandy*'s Uncle Toby (Slater 2011, p. 19). Covent Garden was central to Dickens's writing: his office in Wellington Street is the location of his "rooms in Covent-garden [sic]" in "The Uncommercial Traveller" ([Dickens] 1860, 28 January, p. 321; see also Dexter 1924, pp. 81–90; Chancellor 1930). It is associated with squalor, and the little boy lost (*OT* 13): Bill Sikes wants to know why Fagin is so concerned with corrupting Oliver Twist when "there are fifty boys snoozing about Common Garden [sic] every night" (*OT* 19). Dickens's later "Uncommercial Traveller" essay (subsequently retitled "Night Walks") depicts "one of the worst night sights I know in London ... in the children who prowl about [Covent Garden], who sleep in the baskets, fight for the offal, dart at any object they think they can lay their thieving hands on, dive under the carts and barrows, dodge the constables, and are perpetually making a blunt pattering on the pavement of the Piazza with the rain of their naked feet" ([Dickens] 1860, 21 July, p. 351). In *Little Dorrit*, Covent Garden features "miserable children in rags ... like young rats" (*LD* 1:14), while in *Great Expectations* the location is mentioned when Pip is in his most alienated state, yearning for Estella: the club with which he associates, the Finches of the Grove, meets in a hotel near Covent Garden (*GE* 2:15). Later, when Pip is unable to go home, because his chambers are being watched, he spends a miserable night in the "Hummums," which is also in the vicinity (*GE* 3:6). Covent Garden is also a place to observe from, and go from, as when David Copperfield travels from rooms there to Yarmouth, where he observes the tempest and shipwreck, which causes the deaths of Ham and Steerforth (*DC* 55).

Ruskin sees such wreckage, or its likelihood, as pervasive in Turner, as in the painting *The Snowstorm: Steamboat off a Harbour's Mouth Making Signals in Shallow Water and Going by the Lead* (1842). He also sees it in *The Slave Ship* (*Slavers throwing overboard the dead and dying – Typhon coming on*, 1840; Figure 7.3), with its Atlantic sunset (see Costello 2012, pp. 203–232). Ruskin describes Turner's sea before reaching

> the mist of night, which gathers cold and low, advancing like the shadow of death upon the guilty ship as it labours amidst the lightning of the sea, its thin masts written upon the sky in lines of blood, girded with condemnation in that fearful hue which signs the sky with horror, and mixes its flaming flood with the sunlight, and, cast far along the desolate heave of the sepulchral waves, incarnadines the multitudinous sea. (1909–1912, 3:572)

Ruskin addresses what he sees as the ship's guilt: "she is a slaver, throwing her slaves overboard. The near sea is encumbered with corpses," and the dying bodies are prey to monsters of the deep; it would be over-naturalistic to call them sharks: they partake of the mythical, like the word "Typhon," the name for the monstrous serpentine giant of Greek mythology (see Hamilton 2004, pp. 92–113, who notes that both Dickens and Turner were friends of Captain E.E. Morgan; see also Litvack 2014). Everything shows "the power, majesty, and deathfulness of the open, deep, illimitable sea" (Ruskin 1909–1912, 3:573), where "deathfulness"

Figure 7.3 Joseph Mallord William Turner, *Slavers throwing overboard the Dead and Dying – Typhon coming on* ("*The Slave Ship*"), 1840; by kind permission of the Museum of Fine Arts, Boston, MA.

gives "depth" as an unspoken pun on death, as if the sea conjures up an image of something else: an anonymous power of destruction which piles "wreckage upon wreckage"; this is to quote Walter Benjamin on the "angel of history," who, in a later, more developed modernity, sees only such wreckage at work in European history (Benjamin 2003, p. 392). In "The Harbours of England," recalling his word "deathfulness," Ruskin evokes a "true" Atlantic sea wave:

> its green mountainous giddiness of wrath, its overwhelming crest – heavy as iron, fitful as flame, clashing against the sky in long cloven edge, – its furrowed flanks, all ghastly clear, deep in transparent death, but all laced across with lurid nets of spume, and tearing open into meshed interstices their churned veil of silver fury, showing still the calm grey abyss below; that has no fury and no voice, but is as a grave always open, which the green sighing mounds do but hide for an instant as they pass. (1909–12, 13:37–38)

Green mountains recall Ham Peggotty's swimming out to the wreck in *David Copperfield* and facing "a high, green, vast hill-side of water, moving on shoreward, from beyond the ship," which takes both him and the stranded vessel (*DC* 55). Ruskin observes that Turner knew "that both ships and sea were things that broke to pieces" (1909–1912, 13:42). The verb is ambiguous: ships break up, intransitively (and are broken up, as with the Fighting Téméraire, Figure 7.5, which, as a fighting vessel, took on the task of "breaking up"), while the sea breaks up what breaks up – that is, the ship – to "pieces." There is fascination with the ruin, which Turner and Ruskin appreciate in different ways. There is a Ruskinian anxiety about madness, as if the wave was an image of that, and of the abyssal, as in the phrase quoted above, "the calm grey abyss." Ruskin adds that Turner, after 1818, in portraying a shipwreck off the coast at Ilfracombe, "*never afterwards painted a ship quite in fair order*"; the critic concludes, judging from the artist's last marine picture, *The Wreck Buoy* (Figure 7.4), that after 1818, "when first he saw a ship rent asunder, he never beheld one at sea, without, in his mind's eye, at the same time, seeing her skeleton" (Ruskin 1909–1912, 13:42, 43; see Boase 1959; Brown et al. 2014, pp. 174–175). The painting depicts shipping, probably in the Thames estuary, beneath a double rainbow, which almost spectrally transforms it. In the left foreground of the picture is the trace of wreckage (on Turner and the sea see Riding & Johns 2013).

Turner's intimations of death in the image may be associated with the connections Ruskin implied about Dickens's landscapes. All three figures seem fascinated by ruins. What Ruskin says of *The Wreck Buoy* makes Turner an allegorist, in Walter Benjamin's sense, where every aspect of modernity becomes a *memento*

Figure 7.4 Joseph Mallord William Turner, *The Wreck Buoy*, c. 1807, reworked 1849; by kind permission of National Museums Liverpool.

mori. Benjamin says that Balzac shows "the monuments of the bourgeoisie as ruins even before they have crumbled" (Benjamin 1999, p. 13). Turner's Covent Garden, his ships and sea, all feature wreckage. The sense of death-in-life compares with what Ruskin writes in *Fors Clavigera*, and quotes in "The Storm-Cloud of the Nineteenth-Century": that the bitter wind, like Mr Jarndyce's East Wind in *Bleak House* (*BH* 15, 23), and the dull atmosphere under which the country exists, may be associated with the "poisonous smoke" made from "dead men's souls" (Ruskin 1909–1912, 34:33). Violence marking wreckage is associated with violence in the painting, which dissolves form and outline. *The Wreck of a Transport Ship* (1810) renders a moment of intense detail, with people in the boats; their sliding downwards into abyssal emptiness is represented by the central U-shaped valley of water. What is happening to the lifeboats decentres attention from the ship high above on the left, a wreck on its side; these are representations of alternative destructions (see Riding & Johns 2013, pp. 196–201).

Dickens too, describing the imminent breaking to pieces of Pip's fortunes, connects London and the Thames flowing eastwards towards the sea, and emphasises the dissolution of all solid forms and structures:

> It was wretched weather; stormy and wet, stormy and wet; and mud, mud, mud, deep in all the streets. Day after day, a vast heavy veil had been driving over London from the East, and it drove still, as if in the East there were an Eternity of cloud and wind. So furious had been the gusts, that high buildings in town had had the lead stripped off their roofs; and in the country, trees had been torn up, and sails of windmills carried away; and gloomy accounts had come in from the coast, of shipwreck and death. Violent blasts of rain had accompanied these rages of wind. (*GE* 2:20)

Ruskin, in his comments on *The Slave Ship* (Figure 7.3), speaks of the "*multitudinous* sea," quoting *Macbeth*, and Aeschylus, who uses a phrase Ruskin translated as "innumerable smile" (Ruskin 1909–1912, 2:36; here he is quoting the Greek tragedian's *Prometheus Bound*). The sea exists as neither singular nor plural, nor as an entity; rather, as William Hazlitt hints, it is a negation:

> the artist delights to go back to the first chaos of the world, or to that state of things when the waters were separated from the dry land and light from darkness, but as yet no living thing nor tree was seen upon the face of the earth. All is 'without form and void'. Some one said of his landscapes that they were *pictures of nothing, and very like*. (Hazlitt 1951, p. 76)

Dickens's fog, rain and mud imply shapeless primaeval landscapes. Hazlitt's sense of a negative in Turner praises what is modern in him: the sea as neither formed nor unformed, not one thing, reality as unrepresentable because it is not "there" as a definable presence. These are indeed pictures of nothing that emphasise the negative (see Riding & Johns 2013, pp. 66–67; Richter-Musso 2011). Starting with the primal nothing, there is, Turner claims, a progress to decay within history. What fascinates is the sense of an event which has, or might have, happened, leaving behind only a trace. The watercolour *Dawn after the Wreck* (c. 1841) has only a dog on the sands to recollect what has happened at sea (see Selborne 2008, p. 30). Wreckage indicates the catastrophic; here the artwork focuses on disappearance, as if all is going, leaving only the faintest of impressions behind.

Wreckage is the allegorical image inside *The Fighting Téméraire, tugged to her last berth to be broken up* (1839; Figure 7.5), which Ruskin considered an allegory of Turner's "returning to die by the shores of the Thames" (making this a London picture); he added that "no *ruin* was ever so affecting as this gliding of the vessel to her grave" (1909–1912, 13:169, 171; emphasis added); the artist gives the ship phantasmatic masts, which it then lacked historically; indeed, it had been at Plymouth, serving as a prison ship, like the "hulks." Already a ruin, it is conducted to further ruin by the tug, appearing here in a reverse structure, black funnel to the fore, as the sunset is seen in reverse, as if in the east (see Butlin & Joll 1984, p. 377; Egerton 1995). Red and yellow smoke drifts back from the funnel, as if connecting to the ship, and linking both to death. The tug's blackness resembles that found in Turner's *Peace – Burial at Sea* (1842), which commemorates David Wilkie's funeral off Gibraltar, from the deck of an East Indiaman. Ruskin criticised the

Figure 7.5 James Tibbits Willmore, engraving of Turner's *The Fighting Téméraire*, 1839; in *The Turner Gallery*, vol. 1, n.p.

blackness of *Peace – Burial at Sea*, as though anxious about this negativity, which may be associated with nineteenth-century factory processes (Ruskin 1909–1912, 13:159–160). Even *Rain, Steam and Speed* (Figure 7.2) – hardly discussed by Ruskin, as if it implied a modernism he feared – is allegorical: this real historical event lacks place: it comes to go (thus recalling the Biblical formulation "it came to pass"), meaning that nothing stays. The abstract term "Speed" draws out something else from the painting: speed is an absolute, with nothing of its older sense of abundance, or prosperity (as in "God send you speed"; see *Oxford English Dictionary*; Bailey 1997, p. 364). The title anticipates Benjamin's writing of the "angel of history": "this storm is what we call progress." Progress, equated with "the catastrophe" in Benjamin, is represented by the train (Benjamin 2003, pp. 392–393). All passes with the evanescence of steam which, like Dickens's "green wave," connotes power; steam and smoke double the force of cloud and mist in Turner's *Staffa, Fingal's Cave* (1832; see Butlin & Joll 1984, p. 347; Rodner 1997, pp. 66–71): another painting on which Ruskin passes no comment.

Rain, Steam and Speed implies a Romantic, nineteenth-century, pre-Impressionistic history (see Gage 1972; Ruskin 1909–1912, 35:601, n.1). Dickens, of the "steam-whistle party" (Ruskin 1909–1912, 37:7), may be drawing on it when he describes the warm baths where Mr Merdle, the fraudulent financier in *Little Dorrit*, cuts his throat and is found by the physician in the drained-off bath:

> A sky-light had been opened to release the steam with which the room had been filled; but it hung, condensed into water-drops, heavily upon the walls, and heavily upon the face and figure in the bath. The room was still hot, and the marble of the bath still warm; but the face and figure were clammy to the touch. The white marble at the bottom of the bath was veined with a dreadful red.
>
> 'Separation of jugular vein – death rapid – been dead at least half an hour.' This echo of the physician's words ran through the passages and little rooms, and through the house while he was yet straightening himself from having bent down to reach to the bottom of the bath, and while he was yet dabbling his hands in water; redly veining it as the marble was veined, before it mingled into one tint. (*LD* 2:25)

Like Ruskin on *The Slave Ship* (Figure 7.3), Dickens here evokes *Macbeth*, putting redness, steam and dissolution into elemental, cloud-like nothingness and undifferentiated matter (through, for instance, the repeated "heavily") to Turner-like use. Rain becomes apocalyptic redness and water drops, with puns on the word "vein," as the blood's "tint" becomes a colour in a work of art. The horror follows an interest in death and the funereal and disaster which is Turneresque: fire, including fire at sea; storms; warfare; snowstorms; the eruption of Vesuvius. Ruskin poignantly notes: "there is no form of violent death which [Turner] has not painted" (1909–1912, 7:437).

Ruskin appreciates this trend in both Turner and Dickens; but the strangeness of his selective reactions – especially against Dickens – proves challenging. His essay "Fiction, Fair and Foul" deprecates "*modern* fiction" (Ruskin 1909–1912, 34:268; emphasis added). Such works are typically set, the critic believes, in the "hot fermentation and unwholesome secrecy of the population crowded into large cities"; he cites Balzac's *Le Père Goriot* (1834/1835) as being typical. He notes that "the mere trampling pressure and electric friction of town life" and the city's "monotony of life" produce a taste among authors for the varied horrors of death. The city for Ruskin is death, and he categorises *Bleak House* – elsewhere admired for its analysis of the law (*BH* 28) – as "foul" (thus recalling Act 1 Scene 1 of *Macbeth*), and, unlike what he says in his critique of Turner, here renders "foul" a negative. He notes the novel's nine deaths – adding in Miss Flite, who fascinates him, and Sir Leicester Dedlock, and equating their madness, and paralysis, with death. Elsewhere, Richard Carstone's "pathetic death" is adjudged "mere blue fire of the stage … no real tragedy" (Ruskin 1909–1912, 28:196). "And all this [mortality]," Ruskin concludes, is "not in a tragic, adventurous, or military story, but merely as the further enlivenment of a narrative intended to be amusing; and as a properly representative average of the statistics of civilian mortality in the centre of London." He calls this piling up of corpses "grotesquely either violent or miserable" (1909–1912, 34:272). Such death was Turner's subject too, but it is astonishing that Ruskin should be so reductive – or self-protective – as to say the novel was written for amusement. He compares Dickens with Walter Scott, who, though "tainted" and "destroyed by modern conditions of commercial excitement" and by "mercilessly demanded brain toil," did favour the "funereal excitement" which characterised Dickens. Little Nell, in *The Old Curiosity Shop*, was, Ruskin believes, "simply killed for the market, as a butcher kills a lamb … and Paul [Dombey] was written under the same conditions of illness which affected Scott – part of the ominous palsies, gripping alike author and subject both in *Dombey and Son* and *Little Dorrit*" (Ruskin 1909–1912, 34:276, 275). Dickens is here seen as mentally disturbed, while modern fiction becomes literature "of the prison-house" because

> the thwarted habits of body and mind, which are the punishment of reckless crowding in cities, become, in the issue of that punishment, frightful subjects of exclusive interest to themselves; and the art of fiction in which they finally delight is only the more studied arrangement and illustration … of the daily bulletins of their own wretchedness, in the prison calendar, the police news, and the hospital report. (Ruskin 1909–1912, 34:276)

Ruskin's "Fiction, Fair and Foul" renders Lady Dedlock's death excessive, in relation to what the critic calls Scott's "old-fashioned morality" (1909–1912, 34:273). Elsewhere, Tom-all-Alone's is criticised as "got up, like the darkness in a theatre, to increase the horror of the extremely improbable death of Lady

Dedlock," which is deemed a "vulgar exaggeration" (Ruskin 1909–1912, 30:155). Ruskin also links Dickens, modern novelists and delirium; he notes that the creation of Quilp in *The Old Curiosity Shop* indicates a madness in the author's *oeuvre*. *Barnaby Rudge* "runs entirely wild," conjoining psychic craziness with physical mutilation (Ruskin 1909–1912, 34:279); Ruskin's aversion to this novel is extreme, possibly because he contrasts it with the historical fiction of Scott. The essay "Ariadne Florentina" (1872) attacks everything in *Barnaby Rudge* save the raven, which, "like all Dickens' animals, is perfect, and I am the more angry with the rest because I have every now and then to open the book to look for him" (Ruskin 1909–1912, 22:467). Ruskin's tribute to how Dickens renders the non-human is acute; in a comic Freudian disavowal, he declares that the book is bad, but that he must re-read it! His use of the term "angry" suggests his personal investment in Dickens, whose urbanism and possible delirium threaten him, making him unable to separate art from life. He believes that Dickens's "corrupted language" disturbs (Ruskin 1909–1912, 34:294), and cites examples from *Martin Chuzzlewit*, *Pickwick Papers*, *Bleak House*, *Nicholas Nickleby* and *Oliver Twist*: works he had earlier admired as the best, not least for Cruikshank's renderings of Noah Claypole, whom he called "the intensest rendering of vulgarity" (1909–1912, 7:349; see also 6:471, 7:350, 13:504 and 36:512). Perhaps the admiration stems from the fact that Oliver lives, whereas the other children die.

The examples cited above point to Dickens's vividness for Ruskin, and highlight what is "grotesque" in the novelist's work (this is Ruskin's word, writing to Norton; see Sprinker 1979). Yet in *Modern Painters 3* Ruskin writes:

> A fine grotesque is the expression, in a moment, by a series of symbols thrown together in bold and fearless connection, of truths which it would have taken a long time to express in any verbal way, and of which the connection is left for the beholder to work out for himself the gaps, left or overleaped by the haste of the imagination, forming the grotesque character. (1909–1912, 5:132)

These double images, "inconsistencies of the human capacity," render as grotesque the truth seen by the imagination; Ruskin notes, "it would seem to be rare that any very exalted truth should be impressed on the imagination without some grotesqueness." It is linked with "distortion" and with dreams, which the critic takes seriously (1909–1912, 11.181, 178). The essay "Of Imagination Penetrative" (in *Modern Painters 2*) connects the imagination not to outward perception, but to unconscious thought, since, Ruskin claims,

> there is in every word set down by the imaginative mind an awful undercurrent of meaning, and evidence and shadow upon it of the deep places out of which it has come. It is often obscure, often half-told … but if we choose to dwell upon it and trace it, it will lead us always securely back to

> that metropolis of the soul's dominion from which we may follow out all the ways and tracks to its farthest coasts. (1909–1912, 4:252)

The words "undercurrent" and "deep places" evoke the sea; what that means to Turner, and the image for the unconscious, is the city: the metropolis, from which Ruskin cannot withdraw.

In a defence of Turner's realism in seeing, Ruskin notes its phantasmatic character. Dreams and their grotesque elements, he believes, contrast with the "picturesque" quality within other landscape painters. They belong to "that mode of symbolical expression which appeals altogether to thought and in nowise trusts to realization" (Ruskin 1909–1912, 11:212). In "The Lamp of Truth" in *The Seven Lamps of Architecture* (1849), which Dickens read, imagination calls up that which is not; it has gaps in its thinking:

> When the imagination deceives, it becomes madness. It is a noble faculty so long as it confesses its own ideality; when it ceases to confess this, it is insanity. All the difference lies in the fact of the confession, in there being *no* deception. It is necessary to our rank as spiritual creatures, that we should be able to invent and to behold what is not; and to our rank as moral creatures, that we should know and confess at the same time that it is not. (Ruskin 1909–1912, 8:58)

"No art is noble which in any wise depends upon direct imitation," writes Ruskin (1909–1912, 11:212). Imaginative work is indeed "noble"; perhaps that sheds light on Dickens's intention in calling Turner "noble" (*Letters* 4:217).

If imputations of madness, threatened or real, haunted Ruskin, Turner and Dickens – each a victim of the "storm cloud of the nineteenth century" – they threaten the division that Ruskin requires between spiritual and moral states. Hazlitt's pronouncements on Turner help Ruskin's characterisation of the imagination: he produced pictures of nothing – that is, works characterised by negation. Ruskin knew that what the imagination grasps, and produces as grotesque, lacks a basis in perceived reality. That hypothesis provides another reason for considering Turner and Dickens in terms of allegory, in a sense that Ruskin means, when he says that the imagination, "depriving the subject of material and bodily shape,"

> forges these qualities together in such groups and forms as it desires, and gives to their abstract being consistency and reality, by striking them as it were with the die of an image belonging to other matter, which stroke having once received, they pass current at once in the peculiar conjunction and for the peculiar value desired. (1909–1912, 4:291)

In other words, one thing appears as something else: what circulates as valuable is not how it appears. Much of what was then considered modern positivist thought implied a deficiency in "the modern contemplative mind ... inability to comprehend that these phenomena of true imagination are yet no less real, and often more vivid than phenomena of matter" (Ruskin 1909–1912, 34:163–164). No one seems better equipped than Ruskin for reading Turner or Dickens, and seeing that they speak of something else, expressible only in another mode, beyond appearances. Ruskin wrote of his interpretation of *The Slave Ship* (Figure 7.3):

> the question is, not whether all that you see is indeed there, but whether your imagination has worked as it was intended to do, and whether you have indeed felt as the artist did himself and wished to make you ... many of the passages respecting Turner are not actual descriptions of the pictures, but of that which the pictures were intended to suggest, and *do* suggest to me. I do not say that much of my conjecturing may not be wrong but ... the superiority of Turner ... consists in great measure in this very suggestiveness; it is one of the results of his own great imaginative power. (1909–1912, 36:81–82)

Such a view impels Ruskin to a theory of the grotesque: the power which makes it the unconscious of the painting. It is strange that he finds no allegorical reality in the negativity of those *Bleak House* deaths; but it constitutes a fear he could hardly acknowledge. Perhaps he found something of the sublime in Turner to protect him from the insight of the modern as catastrophic, whereas Dickens offered no such shield, though his comedy increased the obvious power of the grotesque. While responding to it, Ruskin denies the grotesque in "Fiction, Fair and Foul." Perhaps the cost of Dickens was too high, demanding too much response to the modern city. It made him in criticism recall only what he wanted to remember: the conventional purveyor of Christmas. But he allows Turner and Dickens to be put together, in mutual illumination: they speak together, and particularly to Ruskin, who wants and needs them both.

References

Bachrach, Fred G.H. (1994). *Turner's Holland*. London: Tate.
Bailey, Anthony (1997). *Standing in the Sun: A Life of J. M. W. Turner*. London: Sinclair-Stevenson.
Benjamin, Walter (1999). *The Arcades Project*. Trans. Howard Eiland & Kevin McLoughlin. Cambridge, MA: Harvard University Press.
Benjamin, Walter (2003). On the Concept of History. In *Selected Writings Volume 4: 1938–1940*. (pp. 389–400). Trans. Harry Zohn. Eds. Howard Eiland & Michael W. Jennings. Cambridge, MA: Belknap Press of Harvard University Press.
Birch, Dinah (1988). *Ruskin's Myths*. Oxford: Clarendon Press.
Birch, Dinah (1990). *Ruskin on Turner*. London: Cassell.

Boase, T.S.R. (1959). Shipwreck in English Romantic Painting. *Journal of the Warburg and Courtauld Institutes*, 22(3/4), 332–346.

Bradley, John Lewis, & Ousby, Ian (Eds.) (1987). *The Correspondence of John Ruskin and Charles Eliot Norton*. Cambridge: Cambridge University Press.

Brown, David Blayney (Ed.) (2012). *J. M. W. Turner: Sketchbooks, Drawings and Watercolours*. Retrieved from https://www.tate.org.uk/about-us/projects/jmw-turner-sketchbooks-drawings-watercolours

Brown, David Blayney, Concannon, Amy, & Smiles, Sam (2014). *Late Turner: Painting Set Free*. London: Tate.

Butlin, Martin, & Wilton, Andrew (1974). *Turner: 1775–1851*. London: Tate.

Butlin, Martin, & Joll, Evelyn (Eds.) (1984). *The Paintings of J.M.W. Turner*. 2 vols. New Haven, CT: Yale University Press.

Carlisle, Janice (2004). *Common Scents: Comparative Encounters in High Victorian Fiction*. Oxford: Oxford University Press.

Chancellor, E. Beresford (1930). *The Annals of Covent Garden and its Neighbourhood*. London: Hutchinson.

Colman, George, the Younger (1819). *Broad grins, Comprising, with New Additional Tales in Verse, Those Formerly Publish'd Under the Title: My Night-Gown and Slippers*. London: T. Cadell and W. Davies.

Costello, Leo (2012). *J. M. W. Turner and the Subject of History*. Farnham: Ashgate.

Dexter, Walter (1924). *The London of Dickens*. New York: E.P. Dutton.

[Dickens, Charles] (1860, 28 January). The Uncommercial Traveller. *All the Year Round*, 2, 321–326.

[Dickens, Charles] (1860, 21 July). The Uncommercial Traveller. *All the Year Round*, 3, 348–352.

Egerton, Judy (1995). *Turner: The Fighting Temeraire*. London: National Gallery Publications.

Forster, John (1969). *The Life of Charles Dickens*. Ed. A.J. Hoppé. 2 vols. London: Everyman.

Gage, John (1972). *Rain, Steam and Speed*. London: Penguin Press.

Hamilton, James (2003). *Turner's Britain*. London: Merrell.

Hamilton, James (2004). *Turner: The Late Seascapes*. New Haven, CT: Yale University Press.

Hazlitt, William (1951). *The Round Table and Characters of Shakespeare's Plays*. London: Everyman.

Herrmann, Luke (1968). *Ruskin and Turner*. New York: Frederick A. Praeger.

Hewison, Robert, Warrell, Ian, & Wildman, Stephen (2000). *Ruskin, Turner and the Pre-Raphaelites*. London: Tate.

Hill, David (1993). *Turner on the Thames: River Journeys in the Year 1805*. New Haven, CT: Yale University Press.

Hilton, Tim (2002). *John Ruskin*. New Haven, CT: Yale University Press.

Hunt, John Dixon (1982). *The Wider Sea: A Life of John Ruskin*. London: Dent.

Konishima, Nanako (2017). Storm and Sunset: Turnerian Seascapes in *David Copperfield*. *Dickensian*, 113, 150–159.

Lindsay, Jack (1966). *J. M. W. Turner: His Life and Work*. London: Cory, Adams and Mackay.

Litvack, Leon (2014). Messages from the Sea: New Dickens Letters to E.E. and W.D. Morgan. *Dickensian*, 110, 242–254.

Milton, John (1957). *John Milton: Complete Poems and Major Prose*. Ed. Merritt Y. Hughes. Indianapolis, IN: Odyssey Press.

Oxford English Dictionary. Retrieved from www.oed.com

Richter-Musso, Inés (2011). Fire, Water, Air and Earth: Turner as a Painter of the Elements. In Inés Richter-Musso & Ortrud Westheider (Eds.), *Turner and the Elements* (pp. 41–51). Munich: Himer Verlag.

Riding, Christine, & Johns, Richard (2013). *Turner & the Sea*. London: Thames and Hudson.

Rodner, William S. (1997). *J. M. W. Turner: Romantic Painter of the Industrial Revolution*. Berkeley: University of California Press.

Ruskin, John (1909–1912). *The Works of John Ruskin*. Eds. E.T. Cook & Alexander Wedderburn. Library Edition. 39 vols. London: George Allen.

Selborne, Joanna (2008). *Paths to Fame: Turner Watercolours from the Courtauld Gallery*. London: Courtauld Gallery and the Wordsworth Trust.

Shanes, Eric (1990). *Turner's Human Landscape*. London: Heinemann.

Slater, Michael (2011). *Charles Dickens*. New Haven, CT: Yale University Press.

Sprinker, Michael (1979). Ruskin on the Imagination. *Studies in Romanticism*, 18, 115–139.

Sulkin, David (Ed.) (2009). *Turner and the Masters*. London: Tate.

Tambling, Jeremy (2014). *Dickens' Novels as Poetry: Allegory and the Literature of the City*. London: Routledge.

Thorne, Robert (1980). *Covent Garden Market: Its History and Restoration*. London: Architectural Press.

Trotter, David (2000). *Cooking with Mud: The Idea of Mess in Nineteenth-Century Art and Fiction*. Oxford: Oxford University Press.

The Turner Gallery: A Series of One Hundred and Twenty Engravings from the Works of the Late J.M.W. Turner, R.A. The Descriptive Text by W. Cosmo Monkhouse (1880). 2 vols. New York: D. Appleton and Co.

Wallace, Robert K. (1992). *Turner and Melville: Spheres of Love and Fright*. Athens: University of Georgia Press.

Warrell, Ian (Ed.) (2003). *Turner and Venice*. London: Tate.

8

Boz without Phiz

Reading Dickens with Different Illustrations

Chris Louttit

In his essay "Publishing in Parts," Robert L. Patten recalls that there have been no "comprehensive assessments of the illustrations … to reprints or editions published after Dickens's death" (2006, p. 47); since this point was made, very little has changed. Scattered articles and essays dealing with such "reprints" or later "editions" have appeared, including work by Allingham (2012) and Louttit (2014) on the 1870s Household Edition. Scholars still await that comprehensive discussion of the posthumous illustration of Dickens. While it is not possible to provide such a conclusive account here, what follows aims to draw further critical attention to this neglected terrain of illustrated editions completed after Dickens's death. Since the field of Dickens illustration from 1870 to the present is such a capacious one, this essay does so by expanding upon Louttit's existing research on the Household Edition (2014), focusing especially on the edition's reframing of *Bleak House* (1852–1853). The significance of this analysis, however, extends beyond this case study: it casts light on the factors that brought about the neglect of the edition in the first place, and explains why knowing more about the posthumous illustration of Dickens makes us read the work of the Inimitable differently.

It has become a critical commonplace to note the importance of understanding Dickens's novels as serial, illustrated texts. As Malcolm Andrews has claimed, Dickens's "novels, more than any of his contemporaries, have come to seem incomplete without their original illustrations" (2008, p. 97). In other words, reading Boz alongside the work of the original illustrators such as Phiz has come to seem entirely natural, in part thanks to the efforts of critics like Cohen (1980) and Patten (2002), who have attuned readers to the inseparability of the words of the one from the pictures of the other. As these and other scholars have demonstrated, Dickens and contemporary illustrators of his work including Hablot Knight Browne and George Cruikshank were influenced strongly by the same cultural

Reading Dickens Differently, First Edition. Edited by Leon Litvack and Nathalie Vanfasse.
© 2020 John Wiley & Sons Ltd. Published 2020 by John Wiley & Sons Ltd.

and visual milieu of the 1830s and 1840s. They also collaborated to produce texts that were not only verbal, but also visual, artefacts; as Patten succinctly states, "the majority of Dickens's serials are resonant dialogues between pictures and text" (2002, p. 123).

These well-established readings are convincing ones; but what can easily be forgotten is that the centrality of the work of illustrators like Browne and Cruikshank to a complete understanding of Dickens's fiction has not always been taken for granted. Indeed critics like Patten had to work hard to bring artists like Phiz back into the critical spotlight. Before the 1970s, the study of illustration was a rather minor pursuit for Dickens scholars. Even earlier than that, at the start of the twentieth century, Browne's drawings were thought to have contributed to the maligning of Dickens as caricaturist and merely an entertainer for the masses. As the socialist novelist and critic Edwin Pugh claimed of the original illustrations, they "are as unlike the creations of the Master's brain as a painted, stuffed wax effigy is unlike the warm, breathing body of a beautiful woman or man" (1908, p. 98). He believed, like many other Dickensians of his time, that "they damaged Dickens's reputation almost irremediably" (1908, p. 98). Those writing on visual Dickens in this period preferred instead the more realistic and less emblematic productions of the generation of artists including Fred Barnard, Charles Green and James Mahoney, all of whom worked on the Household Edition of the 1870s. Many contemporary Dickens scholars would likely disagree with Pugh's strongly worded dismissal of Browne and Cruikshank, in part thanks to the excellent recovery work of later critics such as Cohen and Patten. This should not mean, however, that the work of these artists, who came after such significant forbears, should be neglected.

The Household Edition illustrations provide, in the first instance, an historical insight into the popular reception of Dickens in the period roughly between 1870 and the outbreak of World War I. For those Victorian readers who came of age in the last third of the nineteenth century, this was their particular edition of Dickens. As Edwin Pugh (born in 1874) put it of his generation: "many of us first read Dickens in the green-covered, large-paper *Household* edition, as the present writer did" (1908, p. 97). For Pugh, and, it may be assumed, many others in the late nineteenth century, the Household artists' "illustrations of Dickens seemed as inevitably right and fitting as brown crust to a white loaf of bread. I had a feeling of finality about them. I could conceive of no other presentment of Dickens's characters as being even possible" (1908, p. 97). Pugh's claim that "many" of his contemporaries must have read Dickens for the first time in this edition with new illustrations is certainly borne out by the bare facts of the great popular success of the edition. Its sales likely exceeded those of the cheap editions published in Dickens's lifetime, and the new illustrations appeared in later cheap reprints, sometimes even alongside those by the original artists (Louttit 2014, pp. 324–325). What the edition succeeded in doing, in short, was to adapt and update Dickens for a later generation of readers more familiar with the sober, realistic style of the

1860s and 1870s than with the satirical and finely detailed approach of artists like Browne and Cruikshank.

Later sets of illustrations like those completed for the Household Edition usefully illuminate how perceptions of Dickens were shifting through the decades after his death. What is perhaps of greater significance for the field of illustration studies, however, is how these posthumous Dickens illustrations provide a pertinent case study, through which new theoretical approaches may be applied to illustrated texts. As critics like Leighton and Surridge (2008) have noted, older studies of Victorian illustration tended to approach it from a particular standpoint; these accounts were frequently interested in considering how faithfully a particular illustration reflected the novelistic scene to which it was related. As a result, earlier work in illustration studies saw its subject "through the lenses of authorial intention or chronology of artistic creation" (2008, p. 66). One of the dangers of such an approach is that the illustration always remains "supplemental" to the verbal text (2008, p. 97) and the illustrator is relegated to a position beneath that of co-creator. More recently critics of illustration have tended to conceptualise it differently; as Julia Thomas argues, "Illustration exposes the fact that texts are never in the author's control, nor are their meanings singular or fixed: illustration is an interpretation or 'reading' of the text, and, as such, can conflict with other readings" (2004, p. 14). While the connection between an illustration and the verbal text remains significant, this take on "illustration" as "interpretation" acknowledges the varied, complex function of illustration in the literary text and in the broader culture. A number of critics have now adopted this more theoretically sophisticated view of image-word relations and have begun to take illustration more seriously as a field of Victorian cultural endeavour. In their focus on the illustration of Victorian serial texts, for instance, Leighton and Surridge warn against paying "mere lip service to serial illustration, page layout, and serial breaks" and "treating them as supplemental – rather than intrinsic – to these complex texts," since a particular edition's illustrations are really "constitutive of plot ... rather than supplemental to it" (2008, p. 97). David Skilton has been keen to stress the intertextual and interpictorial life of illustrations beyond just the relationship with the illustrated text and its author. As textual objects, illustrations have a relationship, Skilton stresses, not only with the verbal text they illustrate, but also with a web of other textual and visual forms, "be they verbal or visual, 'high' art or 'popular' art, literary, factual or journalistic" (2007, n.p.).

While these new approaches to illustration studies apply well to the work of Dickens's original illustrators, they provide particular justification for paying more attention to the Household Edition and other posthumous illustrated editions. If all illustration is best understood as a reading of a verbal text, with the search for the author's influence in shaping the pictorial text no longer being a central preoccupation for critics, then posthumous illustrations can be appreciated as meaningful interpretations of Dickens rather than as secondary, inferior productions. These new illustrations are, to adopt the phrasing of Leighton and

Surridge, far from "supplemental" to the texts in which they appear; instead they function as an "intrinsic" part of them (2008, p. 97). This analysis can be extended, to argue that they are essential parts of new texts which can be placed within a network of other visual, literary and cultural forms. This might seem a rather generalised point; but close study of one particular volume of the Household Edition – *Bleak House*, published in 1873 with illustrations by Fred Barnard – provides a specific example of this process of intertextual and interpictorial exchange at work.

For the viewer who is familiar with the illustrated serial parts of Dickens's fiction, whether Victorian reader or twenty-first-century Victorianist scholar, the Household Edition of *Bleak House* certainly looks different to the original release of the novel. Like the first instalments of the novel, the Household *Bleak House* did appear serially, in weekly numbers, monthly parts and a final volume issue. Its visual appearance, though, had altered: instead of the initial small, octavo paper-covered parts in which two illustrations preceded each 32-page monthly number, illustrations were dropped into every eighth double-columned, quarto-sized page, and three full-page illustrations were included in the final volume. In basic structural terms, then, this means that the experience of reading Dickens in the Household Edition was rather unlike its consumption in the original format.

This structural dissimilarity is also evident, in various ways, at the level of content and style. There is certainly a shift in the frequency of scenes and characters illustrated, since Fred Barnard completed 61 illustrations, as opposed to the 36 that appeared during *Bleak House*'s first serial run. Indeed, this enhanced representation results in a steep rise in the creation of what Kamilla Elliott has aptly labelled "frozen moments for visual and spatial contemplation" (2003, p. 18). Paul Goldman has described the particular "'moment' chosen by [the] illustrator" as a significant "matter of interest and point of discussion" for readers of an illustrated text (2012, p. 25); the increased number of these moments in Barnard's *Bleak House*, in turn, opens up the possibility of new emphases and visual readings of Dickens's text. As tended to be the case with the 10 other volumes of the edition to which he contributed, Barnard also seems purposefully to have avoided illustrating the same scenes as those represented by the original illustrator, Hablot Browne. Only three draw direct inspiration from Phiz's pictures, even if many choose moments a paragraph or two before or after Browne. Barnard's illustrations provide a tonal and stylistic reinterpretation of Dickens's novel; displacing the caricatural, emblematic and architectural emphases of the original images by Browne and Cruikshank, Barnard and the other illustrators who worked on the edition favoured the new realist graphic style, which was increasingly popular by the 1860s and 1870s through its dissemination in the popular press in key periodicals of these decades, such as *Once a Week*, *Good Words* and *London Society* (Cooke 2010).

Delving further into neglected materials that tell us more about Barnard's own response to Dickens and his motivations in taking on the work of the edition, provides further context for reconsidering the meaning of his *Bleak House* illustrations as a sequence. Existing accounts of Barnard as a man and artist stress his humour, and thus his similarity in outlook to Dickens himself. He was, according to the Dalziel brothers, "a delightful companion, amusing, and full of bright repartee" (1901, p. 339), and in the words of the Dickensian F.G. Kitton, Barnard "has been not inaptly termed 'the Charles Dickens among black-and-white artists'. Like Dickens himself, he was essentially a humourist" (1899, p. 222). Yet this romanticised alignment of the skills of different artists is made problematic in the light of archival evidence that reveals a rather less idealised relationship between illustrator and writer. In an intriguing comment from a letter to Harold Faraday in the late 1860s, just a few years before the Household Edition commission, Barnard told his friend and future brother-in-law about his recent reading of works by William Makepeace Thackeray:

> I've just been reading Vanity Fair and Philip. They are both magnificent! I think that on the whole he takes a much higher standing than Dickens – Thackeray to Dickens is as Roast Beef to devilled whitebait – Both delicious in their ways. But one has more *body* than t'other – and t'other has more 'go' & piquancy than the one. (Barnard ?1866–1869; emphasis original)

This may seem merely a stray remark in a letter to a close friend, but it is a revealing one. Barnard remains positive about Dickens's fiction, but in comparing it to "white-bait" and claiming it has more "go" than "body," he deprecates its aesthetic value when viewed alongside the work of Thackeray. This evidence suggests a more critical engagement with Dickens than the one proposed by Joseph Grego, who observed Barnard's "congenial spirit of humorous appreciation," which meant that the Household illustrations commission was "happily suited to his tastes and inclinations" (1899, 2:469). Indeed, other contemporary sources confirm Barnard's pragmatic attitude to his work on the edition. While he was illustrating the *Dombey and Son* parts and volume in 1876, for instance, he evoked the fatigue brought on by his efforts in a humorous illustration showing himself pinned down to a woodblock, unable to enjoy himself by following the sign pointing "This way to Brighton" (Figure 8.1; Broadley 1910, p. 281). In July of the same year, he was demanding more money for his work in a letter to the Dalziel Brothers, justifying his claim with reference to his successful illustration of seven of the preceding Household volumes (Barnard 1876, n.p.).

Taken together, these examples reveal that Barnard was more than just a "humorist" deeply sympathetic to the writings of the Inimitable; he was working, rather, at more of a distance, and as a young illustrator in a crowded market who saw the still-popular Dickens as a vehicle through which to make his name; this reading is confirmed by the evidence of his *Bleak House* illustrations. If these are viewed as a coherent whole, it is clear that Barnard decided to depart from one of

Figure 8.1 Fred Barnard, drawing in undated letter, depicting the artist, and communicating his fatigued state while working on the plates for the Household Edition of *Dombey and Son* (1876). In A.M. Broadley, *Chats on Autographs* (1910), p. 281. Brighton (on the signpost) was the location of Dr Blimber's school.

the most striking elements of Browne's original illustration of the novel: his innovative use of the so-called dark plates. These 10 illustrations focus on the architectural rather than the human, and, as Cohen has aptly put it, serve as a way of foregrounding tonal and thematic issues in the novel, functioning both to embody "the suggestively sinister atmosphere of *Bleak House*" and as an "effective graphic means with which to reinforce Dickens's sober portrayal of society" (1980, p. 109). Barnard's images do not entirely neglect the dark, sombre atmospherics of the novel: in his visual rendering of the meeting between a disguised Lady Dedlock and Jo in chapter 16, for instance, he uses visual effects to convey convincingly the drab dampness of a rainy city street. Yet it is noticeable how little the well-known, external environments of Tom-all-Alone's and Chesney Wold feature in Barnard's *Bleak House*. Instead, he favours domestic and frequently melodramatic compositions. In his original illustrations to Dickens, Hablot Browne did, of course, utilise theatrically posed tableaux; the *Bleak House* images of this type focus often on female characters like Esther Summerson, Caddy Jellyby and Lady Dedlock. In Barnard's later interpretation, he adopts an even more full-blooded theatrical style: the numerous posed scenes range from frozen moments of dramatic tension, such as Jo's identification of "the lady" in chapter 22, to the use of mirroring melodramatic gestures to represent overflowing pain and suffering in the consecutive illustrations to scenes in chapters 23 and 24 (Figures 8.2 and 8.3).

"O, YOU RIDICULOUS CHILD!" OBSERVED MRS. JELLYBY, WITH AN ABSTRACTED AIR, AS SHE LOOKED OVER THE DESPATCH LAST OPENED; "WHAT A GOOSE YOU ARE!"

Figure 8.2 Fred Barnard, plate depicting (L to R) Esther, Caddy Jellyby and Mrs Jellyby, to accompany chapter 23 of the Household Edition of *Bleak House* (1873).

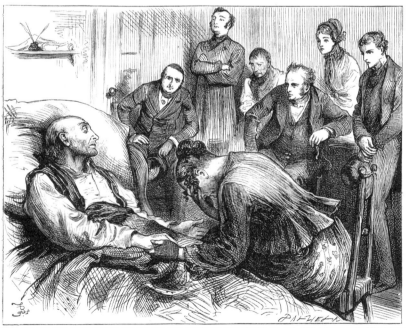

"OF ALL MY OLD ASSOCIATIONS, OF ALL MY OLD PURSUITS AND HOPES, OF ALL THE LIVING AND THE DEAD WORLD, THIS ONE POOR SOUL ALONE COMES NATURAL TO ME, AND I AM FIT FOR."

Figure 8.3 Fred Barnard, plate depicting (foreground L to R) Mr Gridley, Miss Flite; (background L to R): Inspector Bucket (seated), George Rouncewell, Phil Squod, Mr Jarndyce (seated), Esther Summerson, Richard Carstone. The image accompanies chapter 24 of the Household Edition of *Bleak House* (1873).

"O MY CHILD, O MY CHILD!"

Figure 8.4 Fred Barnard, plate depicting Lady Dedlock, to accompany chapter 29 of the Household Edition of *Bleak House* (1873).

This melodramatic impulse culminates in one of Barnard's full-page, vignette illustrations for the edition: his depiction of Lady Dedlock's secret outburst of agony after she has found out, at the end of chapter 29, that her child survived after all (Figure 8.4). Here, with the desperation of Lady Dedlock's gesture enclosed within the deadening, curtained staging of her domestic setting, Barnard brings great theatrical power to the character's quiet but intense suffering. Given its emotional and theatrical excess, it is tempting to read Barnard's picture as one indebted to the affective extremes of the (frequently illustrated) sensation fiction craze of the 1860s, which arose a few years after the first appearance of Dickens's novel. With the way in which the image heightens and externalises the emotional effect of the scene, it might playfully be claimed that Lady Dedlock is being seen through the lens of sensational heroines like Braddon's Lady Audley. This is to neglect, however, the fact that Barnard's full-page illustration merely foregrounds the intensely melodramatic elements of *Bleak House*, and Lady Dedlock's narrative in particular. The common critical view of the novel might well emphasise its satirical bite and formal and thematic patternings; but as Mary Saunders points out, Dickens's melodramatic scenes, even in a seemingly weighty state-of-the-nation novel like *Bleak House*, "should be taken seriously as essential to Dickens's characterizations" (1989, p. 70).

The frequent recourse to theatrical compositions in Barnard's series of *Bleak House* illustrations demonstrates a keen understanding of how the dynamics of the novel might appeal to the popular audience for which Chapman and Hall were aiming with the Household illustrations. His popular touch is also evident in another key aspect of his work for the edition: his seeming fascination with Jo. While Browne's original plates only depict Jo twice beyond the title-page vignette, in "Consecrated Ground" and "Mr Chadband 'improving' a tough subject" (to accompany chapters 16 and 25 respectively), Barnard includes nine illustrations that feature the crossing sweeper. The artist's frequent portrayal of Jo may relate in part to his interest in street life as an aesthetic subject generally, and the figures of crossing sweepers and urchins in particular. There is, for instance, a crossing sweep who looks much like Jo in the foreground of his contribution to 1867's *The Savage Club Papers*, "The Lost Child" (Halliday 1867, p. 65). Immediately before the serial appearance of the Household Edition of *Bleak House* in March 1873, Barnard had completed a few illustrations for *Lost Gip*, Hesba Stretton's children's story dealing with slum life. That story includes a spirited street urchin named Sandy who, very much like Dickens's Jo, is always being asked to "move on." It is possible that Sandy's pathetic situation remained in Barnard's mind as he worked on his *Bleak House* illustrations. What also seems likely, especially given the melodramatic approach of the commission as a whole, is that the edition's repeated representation of Jo further underlines Barnard's responsiveness to the ways in which Dickens was already being appropriated by his popular audience. As Jane Lydon has argued, much of *Bleak House*'s popular cultural appeal resided with Jo, who was transformed "from a minor character in Dickens's ... novel" into "a popular figure in his own right, escaping from the original plot, to feature in stage performances, photographs, and art, and becoming an emblem of the homeless waif" (2015, p. 308).

Barnard's enthusiastic response to Jo both reflects and participates in this rich multimedia afterlife. One of the other full-page vignette illustrations, simply labelled "Jo," certainly brings the character to the attention of readers, since the image was placed opposite the title page in volume editions (Figure 8.5). Hablot Browne, of course, had also put Jo at the centre of his volume frontispiece in 1853. Twenty years later, Barnard reinterprets Jo for a new generation so that, rather than taking up the playful, satirical style of Phiz, he responds to what Lydon calls "the popular interest in street urchins" that flourished slightly later in realist painting and photography (2015, p. 310). This "popular interest" is evident in images such as William Powell Frith's painting *The Crossing Sweeper* (1858) and the Swedish-born photographer Oscar Rejlander's 1860 image *Night in Town*. With his "Jo," Barnard does not mimic the compositional structure of Frith or

Figure 8.5 Fred Barnard, "Jo"; full-page vignette illustration for the Household Edition of *Bleak House* (1873).

Rejlander; but, like these other visual artists, he depicts the character as a strikingly human, sympathetic figure, rather than a grovelling, animalistic one.

There was a similar humanising of Jo on the Victorian popular stage. Indeed, playwrights like George Dibdin Pitt, who catered for largely working-class East-End audiences, did something even more radical; as Julianne Smith explains, Pitt "performs a critical revision of class stereotypes in *Bleak House* that is most evident in the way he represents the poor. His play enlarges on working-class heroes, notably challenging Dickens's portrayal of Jo the crossing sweeper as a dumb animal" (2014, p. 5). Given that there is little direct evidence about Barnard's political views beyond his membership of radical Bohemian clubs such as the Savage and Hogarth, and his brief spell as lead editorial cartoonist at *Fun* immediately before he started work on the Household Edition, it is perhaps overhasty to classify his revisioning of Jo straightforwardly alongside Pitt's politicised theatrical transformation of the character into a "working-class hero" who "is a knowing linguist whose speeches feature frequent wordplay" (Smith 2014, p. 8). Unlike a play, of course, Barnard's visual interpretation of the crossing sweeper cannot give voice to the experiences of the working poor. Yet it is undeniable that both Barnard's illustrations and the various theatrical productions arose out of the "Jo-mania" that pursued Dickens's novel in the popular culture of the nineteenth century and beyond, and transformed a supporting, symbolic character into a more human and significant one (Bolton 1983, p. 86). By way of a postscript, Barnard himself ended up contributing again to "Jo-mania" after he had completed work on the edition. He was the illustrator tasked with creating an image of Jennie Lee, an American actress who first realised Jo on the London stage in 1876, and went on to build a career out of representing the street waif; the illustration was later used in at least one theatrical poster to advertise a subsequent production (Figure 8.6). As Smith notes, there was something curious in the fact that, at this point in the 1870s, "after more than twenty years on the shelf, *Bleak House* suddenly became a

Figure 8.6 Fred Barnard, Miss Jennie Lee as "Jo"; Theatre Royal Edinburgh poster 1885. By kind permission of the National Library of Scotland.

hot theatrical property" (2014, p. 8). Seen alongside the intrinsic popular appeal of pathetic street urchin and waif figures, Jo's prominent position in Barnard's illustrations for the widely circulated Household Edition may well have contributed to this revival of interest in the character into the 1870s and beyond.

Kamilla Elliott has argued that the subsequent reception of sixties-style realist illustration has suffered due to critical interest in the "narrative, semantic, and commenting aspects" of illustrations that come to the fore in the style of the 1830s and 1840s, rather than the "pictorial dimensions" that are most obvious in the later, more naturalistic style favoured by artists like Fred Barnard (Elliott 2003, p. 42). It has been the aim here to offer an alternative to this limiting position, by reading Barnard's productions for *Bleak House* not only as commentary on Dickens's verbal text, but also in the context of the wider range of other cultural, visual and verbal networks that influenced the creation of them. It would therefore be useful to examine how such dense, labour-intensive forms of intertextual, interpictorial analysis might be facilitated by a new, digital Dickens illustration resource.

The sequence of illustrations Barnard completed for *Bleak House* undoubtedly changes the experience of reading Dickens, and emphasises different structural, tonal and thematic elements of the novel to appeal to a broad audience. It is only in recent years, however, that scholars have been able more easily to access posthumous editions of Dickens with fresh illustrations like those in the Household Edition. Mass digitisation projects such as Google Books and the Internet Archive have made various miscellaneous scans of different illustrated editions freely available. On the *Victorian Web* (n.d.), Philip Allingham has begun to digitise materials related to illustrated books and periodicals, including an impressive collection of Dickensian images. These developments are, of course, positive ones in terms of basic accessibility; yet challenges remain concerning the status of illustrations as digital artefacts, and in relation to the sheer intimidating bulk of resources represented by such treasure troves as the Internet Archive. Dino Felluga suggests that most discussions of the digital humanities "either present some already completed digital project … or they consider the larger theoretical implications of the move to digital platforms" (2015). It is therefore an opportune moment to contemplate a project that does not yet exist: a scholarly and more developed digital archive of Dickensian illustration. This endeavour would be timely, in broadening out the existing Dickensian digital ecology formed by sites such as *Dickens Journals Online* (n.d.) and *Project Boz* (n.d.). It could also provide new materials to expand discussions about Dickens's relationship with popular (visual) culture and illustration studies more broadly.

An imagined Dickens Visual Archive project would certainly be able to draw upon some of the pioneering research that has been done in the past 10–15 years in considering the relationship between illustrated texts and the digital environment. As Julia Thomas notes, illustrations "are often nowhere to be seen" in the twentieth- and twenty-first-century conceptions of the Victorian era, since modern reprints of novels leave out (some of) the illustrations, and "scholarly engagement with them" tends to "go against the grain" (2017, pp. 17–18). Digital archives go some way towards bringing these neglected images to light; but a number of scholarly challenges remain. One of the most significant of these is the fact that, as Thomas eloquently puts it, "There are aspects of a visual image ... that cannot easily be fitted into a linguistic structure: its surface, marks, lines, its very status as a visual object" (2007, p. 199). The "pictorial features of the image" are problematic in the digital archive as searching and information retrieval operate linguistically (Thomas 2007, p. 199); as a result, adequate methods must be found for describing and therefore "tagging" visual images to make them discoverable at the level of a deep search. Scholars have already worked through some of these theoretical conundrums; therefore the creation of a Dickensian illustration digital resource would be able to build on these advances in the tagging and keywording of digital images. It could also take as its starting point some existing projects, as models of how to create this sort of site, especially those that focus on a single-author or genre corpus, such as Kate Holterhoff's *Visual Haggard* and Michael John Goodman's *Victorian Illustrated Shakespeare Archive*. *Visual Haggard* in particular, with its scholarly short essays on textual histories and biographies of Haggard's illustrators, provides an excellent example of how a single-author resource can successfully draw attention to neglected visual materials.

It would be useful to speculate about what a potential Dickens Visual Archive could do to build on the achievements of existing sites such as these, and what it would need to do to benefit Dickens scholars and satisfy (or even advance) models in the digital archiving of illustrated texts. From the vantage point of the present moment, three issues of particular importance arise, in thinking through the creation of this digital visual Dickens resource: its scope in terms of what illustrations should be included; its connectivity with other, related resources; and the extent to which it will reflect print technologies or embrace some of the potentialities of digital reading and searching. In the first instance, it would be appropriate to begin with the Household Edition illustrations. Its 866 images are, in fact, fewer in number than the 911 gathered together for the *Visual Haggard* resource. This may well be a sensible starting point, but it would seem rather unadventurous to stop there; it would make sense to include the original illustrations, and to move selectively through other illustrated editions, such as those by Harry Furniss and Frank Reynolds. In an ideal – if most likely unrealisable – form, the archive could strive to include every Anglophone illustrated edition of Dickens up to the present day, and might even range to illustrated texts produced for other literary cultures in Europe and beyond. The inclusion of contextual materials, such as drafts, working drawings and other miscellaneous visual Dickensian ephemera such as advertisements and political cartoons would, moreover, give a sense of the rich interpictoriality of Dickensian cultures, and would prompt scholars to think about the limits of the term "illustration." Some of these visual artefacts may, of course, already be available in existing digital archives. For this reason, it would be important to consider how a potential Dickensian resource could interact with and depend upon others, rather than functioning in isolation. A current digital project that may well be pertinent to a hypothetical Dickens one is Bethan Stevens's *Woodpeckings* (2016), which aims to make the British Museum's Dalziel Collection more accessible; since the Dalziels were the engravers for the Household Edition, their own archive might hold pertinent materials for the study of Dickens. A final, major consideration facing a project team would be the extent to which such a digital archive should attempt to reflect or mimic printed sources. It is true that access to accurate reproductions of the original physical texts might be desirable for scholarly purposes, and that editorial standards would ideally be high. As Julia Thomas has recently noted, however, "attempts to reproduce the format of the book in a digital environment can be problematic" since "they erase the specificity of the digital" (Calè et al. 2015, n.p.). Any attempt at a Dickens Visual Archive should, then, embrace the potential of the digital, which, after all, is a format that is particularly flexible in its ability to display and facilitate interaction with images.

Beyond the obvious benefits of preservation and improved access, this final point underlines why such a resource would ultimately be of value to Dickensians. As Thomas has claimed, unlike one or two printed volumes consulted at home or in a library, a "digital display" is particularly useful for students of illustration as it "allows the user to see many [images] simultaneously and to trace the connections between them" (Calè et al. 2015). Particular tools, moreover, allow digital reproductions of illustrations to be manipulated and studied in unusual ways. Thomas has explained how her *Database of Mid-Victorian Illustration* (2011) used "Zoomify, a tool that magnifies the picture, showing it in the detail in which the engraver might have seen it with his magnifying glass," demonstrating, as a result, that "in the digital archive we can often see more of the image than is available to the naked eye" (Thomas 2007, p. 200). In the Dickens context, these and other potential, future digital applications could be used to analyse previously unperceived details and interconnections within the rich visual archive that surrounds the Inimitable's works, and in so doing, to extend the critical conversation beyond the familiar association of the words of Boz with the drawings of Phiz.

References

Allingham, Philip V. (Ed.) (n.d.). *The Victorian Web*. Retrieved from www.victorianweb.org/

Allingham, Philip V. (2012). "Reading the Pictures, Visualizing the Text": Illustrations in Dickens from *Pickwick* to the *Household Edition*, 1836 to 1870, Phiz to Fred Barnard. In Paul Goldman & Simon Cooke (Eds.), *Reading Victorian Illustration, 1855–1875: Spoils of the Lumber Room* (pp. 159–178). Farnham: Ashgate.

Andrews, Malcolm (2008). Illustrations. In David Paroissien (Ed.), *A Companion to Charles Dickens* (pp. 97–127). Oxford: Blackwell.

Barnard, Fred (?1866–1869, January 25). [Letter to Harold Faraday]. The Getty Research Institute Digital Collections. Retrieved from http://hdl.handle.net/10020/860601

Barnard, Fred (1876, July 25). [Letter to Dalziel Brothers]. The Henry W. & Alfred A. Berg Collection of English and American Literature (Berg Coll MSS Dickens, Manuscript box H). The New York Public Library.

Bolton, H. Philip (1983). Bleak House and the Playhouse. *Dickens Studies Annual*, 12, 81–116.

Broadley, A.M. (1910). *Chats on Autographs*. London: T. Fisher Unwin.

Calè, Luisa, Goodman, Michael, Thomas, Julia, et al. (2015). Lost Visions: An Interview with Julia Thomas. *19: Interdisciplinary Studies in the Long Nineteenth Century*, 21. Retrieved from https://www.19.bbk.ac.uk/articles/10.16995/ntn.752/

Cohen, Jane Rabb (1980). *Charles Dickens and His Original Illustrators*. Columbus: Ohio State University Press.

Cooke, Simon (2010). *Illustrated Periodicals of the 1860s: Contexts and Collaborations*. London: The British Library.

Dalziel, Edward, & Dalziel, George (1901). *The Brothers Dalziel: A Record*. London: Methuen.

Dickens, Charles (1873). *Bleak House*. Household Edition. London: Chapman and Hall.

Dickens Journals Online (n.d). Buckingham: University of Buckingham. Retrieved from www.djo.org.uk/

Elliott, Kamilla (2003). *Rethinking the Novel/Film Debate*. Cambridge: Cambridge University Press.

Felluga, Dino Franco (2015). The Eventuality of the Digital. *19: Interdisciplinary Studies in the Long Nineteenth Century*, 21. Retrieved from https://www.19.bbk.ac.uk/articles/10.16995/ntn.742/

Goldman, Paul (2012). Defining Illustration Studies. In Paul Goldman & Simon Cooke (Eds.), *Reading Victorian Illustration, 1855–1875: Spoils of the Lumber Room* (pp. 13–32). Farnham: Ashgate.

Goodman, Michael John (n.d.). *Victorian Illustrated Shakespeare Archive*. Cardiff: Cardiff University. Retrieved from https://shakespeareillustration.org/

Grego, Joseph (1899). *Pictorial Pickwickiana: Charles Dickens and His Illustrators*. 2 vols. London: Chapman and Hall.

Halliday, Andrew (Ed.) (1867). *The Savage Club Papers*. London: Tinsley Brothers.

Holterhoff, Kate (Ed.) (n.d.). *Visual Haggard*. Retrieved from www.visualhaggard.org/

Kitton, F.G. (1899). *Dickens and His Illustrators*. London: George Redway.

Leighton, Mary Elizabeth, & Surridge, Lisa (2008). The Plot Thickens: Towards a Narratological Analysis of Illustrated Serial Fiction in the 1860s. *Victorian Studies*, 51(1), 65–101.

Louttit, Chris (2014). "A Favour on the Million": The Household Edition, the Cheap Reprint, and the Posthumous Illustration and Reception of Charles Dickens. *Book History*, 17(1), 321–364.

Lydon, Jane (2015). "The Colonial Children Cry": Jo the Crossing-Sweep Goes to the Colonies. *Journal of Victorian Culture*, 20(3), 308–325.

Patten, Robert L. (2006). Publishing in Parts. In John Bowen & Robert L. Patten (Eds.), *Palgrave Advances in Dickens Studies* (pp. 11–47). Basingstoke: Palgrave Macmillan.

Patten, Robert L. (2002). Serial Illustration and Storytelling in *David Copperfield*. In Richard Maxwell (Ed.), *The Victorian Illustrated Book* (pp. 99–128). Charlottesville: The University Press of Virginia.

Project Boz (n.d.). Digital WPI. Worcester, MA: Worcester Polytechnic Institute. Retrieved from https://digitalcommons.wpi.edu/dickens-novels/

Pugh, Edwin (1908). *Charles Dickens: The Apostle of the People*. London: The New Age Press.

Saunders, Mary (1989). Lady Dedlock Prostrate: Drama, Melodrama, and Expressionism in Dickens's Floor Scenes. In Carol Hanbery MacKay (Ed.), *Dramatic Dickens* (pp. 68–80). New York: St Martin's Press.

Skilton, David (2007). The Centrality of Literary Illustration in Victorian Visual Culture: The Example of Millais and Trollope from 1860 to 1864. *Journal of Illustration Studies*, 1. Retrieved from http://jois.uia.no/issues.php

Smith, Julianne (2014). *Bleak House* on London's East End Stage, 1853: George Dibdin Pitt and Dickens at the Royal Pavilion Theatre. *Nineteenth-Century Theatre and Film*, 41(1), 2–20.

Stevens, Bethan (Ed.) (2016). *Woodpeckings: The Dalziel Archive, Victorian Print Culture, and Wood Engravings*. Brighton: University of Sussex. Retrieved from http://www.sussex.ac.uk/english/dalziel/

Stretton, Hesba (1873). *Lost Gip*. London: H.S. King and Company.

Thomas, Julia (2004). *Pictorial Victorians: The Inscription of Values in Word and Image*. Athens: Ohio University Press.

Thomas, Julia (2007). Getting the Picture: Word and Image in the Digital Archive. *European Journal of English Studies*, 11(2), 193–206.

Thomas, Julia (Ed.) (2011). *Database of Mid-Victorian Illustration*. Cardiff: Cardiff University. Retrieved from https://www.dmvi.org.uk/index.php

Thomas, Julia (2017). *Nineteenth-Century Illustration and the Digital*. Basingstoke: Palgrave Macmillan.

Part III

Resetting Dickens

9

Speculation and Silence

Reading Dickens by Instalment in Time, at the Time and for Our Time

Pete Orford

Reading Dickens in instalments clearly offers a different experience from the way most readers consume his work in the twenty-first century. While the serial publication of most of his fiction is widely recognised, and his is "the name most closely associated with the serial form," the idea of each book as a series is nonetheless still treated predominantly in an historical context (Hughes & Lund 1991, p. 150). Today, when purchasing copies of Dickens's work, general readers and academics alike will prefer a book over a series of instalments. Even with those editions that take the time in their prefatory material to note the original parameters of each monthly or weekly part, readers are still left with a complete unit in their hands, and the certainty that the text is secure and laid out in front of them. It is thus questionable whether they truly appreciate the ambiguity and uncertainty of the text as it was first presented to Dickens's original audience. Readers nowadays might consider themselves as victims of their place in history; thus they might be led to believe that works like *David Copperfield* or *Oliver Twist* are only available to them as completed tales, with no room for deviation from the fixed plot.

The nature of serial reading, in contrast to serial writing, is an area of particular interest. The author composing in instalments may yet have that projection in mind of where the story is heading; but readers are without an accurate compass as they embark on each new serial, even though they might have an ostensible guide, like the illustrated monthly wrapper, which was meant to feature incidents from the text (see Cohen 1980, p. 205). In order to delve more deeply into the nature of reading in instalments, a number of recent online reading projects involving nineteenth-century texts (three of which are by Dickens) have been conceived. The texts considered were Dickens's *A Tale of Two Cities*, *Our Mutual Friend* and *the Mystery of Edwin Drood*, as well as Wilkie Collins's *No Name*. Research issues emerging from these initiatives include the effect of the enforced break between instalments; the elongated time frame of the reading experience;

Reading Dickens Differently, First Edition. Edited by Leon Litvack and Nathalie Vanfasse.
© 2020 John Wiley & Sons Ltd. Published 2020 by John Wiley & Sons Ltd.

and, most interesting of all, the nature of the community that developed and thrived between readers, as they shared their thoughts and speculations about the unfolding text. An online reading group today can facilitate an understanding of reading Dickens in parts, and can highlight the distinct contrasts between a modern manifestation of this reading practice and the original experience of consumption in the nineteenth century. Such an investigation can offer particular assistance in decoding *Edwin Drood*, the serial novel envisaged as emerging in 12 monthly parts, but of which only six were written by the time Dickens died in June 1870. Such reflections can also illuminate how the process of reading an unfolding narrative (rather than a concluded one) affects our understanding of plot, tone and character.

The launch of *Dickens Journals Online* (n.d.) in 2012 to mark the bicentenary of Dickens's birth allowed unprecedented access to *Household Words* and *All the Year Round*; but offering content is only the beginning of a digital project: the second stage is to encourage readers to use that content. Accordingly, a reading group was established in 2012, to work through *A Tale of Two Cities* in its original weekly instalments (Drew et al. n.d.a). This was followed by a second project in 2013 involving Wilkie Collins's *No Name* (Drew et al. n.d.b), which also appeared in *All the Year Round* in weekly instalments. In 2014 two reading projects were launched, this time for monthly instalments: *The Mystery of Edwin Drood* and *Our Mutual Friend* (Curry & Winyard n.d.). *A Tale of Two Cities* and *No Name* were run by a group of scholars from the Universities of Buckingham and Leicester, with a core team running a blogpage in which weekly discussion was facilitated by way of an initial post from a member of the core team; other readers were encouraged to engage with this opening salvo, and to offer comment. The same principle was applied to the monthly readalongs of the latter two projects. The first of these, overseen by Orford as part of *The Drood Inquiry* (a website that explored the various solutions to *Drood*; Orford n.d.a), encouraged further interaction by asking the general public to vote for the ending they believed Dickens intended. The second project was run by another of the original central team, Ben Winyard, who administrated the readalong of *Our Mutual Friend*.

All four projects were run in synchronised "real time" – that is, to accord with the dates of the original publication; for example, the first part of *A Tale of Two Cities* was released online on 30 April 2012, in order to parallel the original publication on 30 April 1859. Reading Dickens and Collins in instalments prompted several findings, some confirming initial expectations, and others confounding them. Deborah Wynne notes how serialisation "involved enforced interruptions to the reading process, making specific demands on readers in terms of curbing the pace of reading and denying them the freedom to curtail suspense by turning to the end to discover the outcome of a novel" (2012, p. 23). Such an assumption was generally held by those on the project who anticipated that in the case of *No Name* especially, it would prove particularly suspenseful to read in instalments, given Collins's reputation for sensation fiction and cliffhangers; however, in this specific case the experience of reading his story in short weekly bursts was frustrating, and worked against the momentum of the author's plot. Collins had already separated his story into several scenes, and the further breaking up of these into weekly sections often resulted in too little information each week, or too constrained a space to let the suspense build effectively. Leaving the audience wanting more each week was not a boon to reading, but rather a barrier, whereas Dickens, as Hughes and Lund note, "wanted each part to be self-contained – with a clear climax and resolution" (1991, p. 151). Thus reading *A Tale of Two Cities*, *The Mystery of Edwin Drood* or *Our Mutual Friend* inspired a greater sense of achievement and closure after each instalment (whether weekly or monthly), with the promise of more to come.

By far the most important aspect of each reading project was the discussion generated between instalments: the readers forged an online community and collectively agreed on where the story was going and what the key areas of interest were. Moments that might have been passed over, had they been read independently and in one sitting, were enlarged upon precisely because of the nature of reading collectively in instalments. For example, after an incidental description in the second week of *A Tale of Two Cities* of a "gaunt pier-glass" (*TTC* 1:4) behind Miss Manette, a long discussion followed in which questions were raised among the group about this curious object, which the *Oxford English Dictionary* defines as a "large tall mirror; orig[inally] one fitted to fill up the pier or space between two windows, or over a chimney-piece"; the group's fascination with the pier-glass led to an analysis and consideration of its symbolic meaning. The enforced hiatus of instalment reading, filled by discussion with others, prompted deeper reading of a moment which would otherwise have been overlooked.

Several shortcomings became evident in twenty-first-century online reading projects which attempted to recapture the spirit of nineteenth-century journal reading. As much as the one tried to emulate the other, there were always going to be marked distinctions: for example, the readers did not immerse themselves in nineteenth-century role-play or in re-enactments of historical events. Instead, the books became bound by a new context of twenty-first-century history. *A Tale of Two Cities* played out against the 2012 London Olympics, resulting in a marked rise in sporting metaphors during discussion of the book, not to mention the release of the film *The Dark Knight Rises*, which the director Christopher Nolan and screenwriter Jonathan Nolan openly admitted to have been inspired by Dickens's revolutionary novel (Goldberg 2012). If the reading experience was not authentic in responding to the original context, it remained true to the spirit of reading by instalment in identifying a new backdrop for the novel. One interesting potential for closer grounding in original context has subsequently been provided by the *Victorian Serial Novels* website, which uses as its catchphrase "Read like a Victorian" (Warhol n.d.). The site offers several "stacks" of serial works written at about the same time (for example, *Dombey and Son*, *Vanity Fair*, *The String of Pearls*, *La Cousine Bette* and *Tancred*, all from the period 1846–1848), and encourages readers not only to read *Dombey* in instalments, but to interweave this with other serials of the time.

The second failing arises from the distinctions raised between physicality and virtuality. For *A Tale of Two Cities* and *No Name*, the projects relied on digital scans of *All the Year Round*, made available via *Dickens Journals Online* (n.d.), with the intention that the readers would not only keep up with Dickens's story each week, but would also peruse the other articles in each issue, to see how this context enriched the experience. Similarly, a full scan was made available of *The Mystery of Edwin Drood* in its original monthly numbers, including all the advertising material which accompanied each part, so that readers could see the text in context, and link the story itself to the surrounding commercial context. In practice this seldom happened, and tended to be forced when it occurred. For Dickens's contemporary readers with a physical copy of each issue in their possession, the ease of reading, rereading and browsing was patently evident, especially when compared to the experience of logging on to access a website. The twenty-first-century reading was inherently more focused on the job at hand, and missed the opportunity for casual browsing in quiet moments of boredom or restlessness. As much as the novel became absorbed into readers' weekly routines, it did not approach the full saturation that a physical copy of each instalment might have achieved.

The final unavoidable shortcoming was that of foreknowledge: a reader in 1859 could not have read the story before; but the reading community involved in the 2012 project most decidedly had read – or had at the very least known something of – *A Tale of Two Cities*. This initially resulted in accidental slips that were picked up on by those few who were reading it for the first time. For example, Lucie Manette is not identified by her first name until the seventh weekly part of the narrative (*TTC* 2:4): in the opening instalments she is merely "Miss Manette." When the moderator unthinkingly referred to her as Lucie during these early stages he was leapt upon for this transgression. "That's cheating" warned one, while another wailed "Oh no! Spoilers." The revelation of Miss Manette's name might seem insignificant and of little import to the story as a whole; but the sensitivity of readers trying to achieve an authentic experience made the organisers overly cautious thereafter, in order to avoid a repeat occurrence. This scrutiny became more difficult as the book's dramatic ending approached; the increasingly obvious hints surrounding Sydney Carton's intentions had to be wilfully ignored by the project team. In effect, the aim of being authentic created an even more artificial response of feigned blindness: the project designers were not free to anticipate as genuinely as Dickens's contemporary readers would have done.

The choice of *No Name* for the follow-up project was largely determined by the quest for a less familiar work, though this in turn called for a leap of faith on the part of Orford (one of the project directors) as the only member of the central team of bloggers not to have read the novel before. Orford was thus required to publish his thoughts about the book without having read it all. This "blind" facilitation led to a number of utterly incorrect interpretations, especially about Captain Wragge, who might have been seen as the book's villain. After the group had read the fourth weekly instalment, Orford had to confess that "I feel none the wiser as to whom our sympathies are supposed to be with"; nor was he alone. This revelation emphasised the misdirection that Collins employed; it also captured the way in which readers could be led astray – something that is lost from the secure position of analysing a story only after the end has been reached. Thus in order to appreciate the serial reading experience, a revision of the concept of a book's structure is required. Readers inherently find a novel's ending to be its crowning moment, in which (at least, in the majority of Victorian fiction) all is explained: they look to the conclusion to confirm suspicions and clarify impressions of the story. Yet they rarely read books in one sitting, and even if they were to do so, there still remains that time before the end is reached when the book is open to possibilities. It is precisely this moment of uncertainty and wider possibility which is best captured by serial reading, and the speculation engaged upon during the enforced break between numbers, when the reader's voice fills the void of the author's temporary silence. When scholars research contemporary responses to nineteenth-century novels, they invariably turn to reviews of the entire work, and dismiss earlier reviews, written before the conclusion, as less-informed; however, those developing thoughts offer just as much insight into how a work was received and understood. For example, John Forster reviewed *Oliver Twist* in *The Examiner* in September 1837, when only seven of the 24 parts had been published:

> We leave Oliver Twist, at a trying point of his story, once more in the haunt of thieves. We leave him most reluctantly, and so will every reader who has any capacity to see and feel whatsoever is most loveable, hateful, or laughable, in the character of the every-day life about him. We feel as deep an interest in little Oliver's fate, as in that of a friend we have long known and loved. ([Forster] 1837, p. 582)

Such sentiments were taken into account in Orford's development of a third, more distinctive reading project, focusing on *The Mystery of Edwin Drood* (Orford n.d.b). Because that novel was famously left unfinished at the time of Dickens's death, its reviews are more akin to those part-reviews of early instalments, rather than the preferred model of a fully informed judgement after the book's close. The preservation of *Drood*'s uncertainty between instalments presents scholars with an opportunity to understand more fully the experience of reading a Dickens novel serially.

While it is known that Dickens's readers talked about the stories in between monthly numbers, little detail survives of what was actually discussed. There are several anecdotes concerning people reading aloud to groups and sharing that moment. There are also instances of changes Dickens imposed to his text in reaction to popular opinion, such as the enhanced role of Sam Weller in *Pickwick Papers*, and the swift disappearance, and subsequent character change in *David Copperfield*, of the villainous Miss Mowcher, who strongly resembled Mrs Jane Seymour Hill (who had threatened Dickens with legal action; see *Letters* 5:674–675, 679; 6:35). While there are many anecdotes concerning Dickens's readers' actively engaging with the narrative, the very nature of verbal communication means it does not last: we know they talked, but we do not know what they said. Discussions in print were limited; most reviewers preferred to wait until the publication of the final instalment before reviewing a book, thus denying us that chance of capturing the conversation in development.

Some of this problem is, however, of readers' and reviewers' own making. Shorter reviews and brief contemporary comments do exist; but they have not received as much critical attention as the longer, final reviews. These fleeting moments in print may not offer the same critical insight into the text, but they do shine a light upon contemporary reactions. On 9 April 1870 the journal *John Bull* published this short comment on *Drood*'s merits: "The Mystery of Edwin Drood! Of course it did, a work from the pen of Boz is always sure to draw. Please alter: 'The mystery of Edwin *drew*'" (p. 53). The first monthly number had gone on sale on 31 March 1870; this comment appeared just 10 days later. On 21 May 1870 *Punch* included a satirical critique of Parliament, which featured a discussion on opium – a major feature of the plotting of the novel:

> We own that we think a more elegant way out of the difficulty was open. A resolution should have been carried to the effect, that it would be disrespectful to the greatest of living novelists to enter into the opium question at all until the *Mystery of Edwin Drood*, so far as it affects *Mr Jasper*, should be solved ("Punch's Essence of Parliament" 1870, p. 202).

The effect of this observation relies upon the reader's understanding the reference (thus assuming knowledge of the story so far), and teases at the idea of uncertainty of ending and an unwillingness to know too much, or make too strong an assertion, before the book's conclusion.

Elsewhere the passing comments were more linguistically focused. An entry in the "Notes and Queries" section of *Judy* on 4 May 1870 notes that Dickens's phrase "oppressively respectable," used in the first monthly number of *Drood*, "was used six months since in the introduction to Mr Hotten's little volume 'The True Story of Lord and Lady Byron'" (p. 19). The comment is intended to generate further discussion, as "The Writer asks whether any earlier use of the expression can be pointed out." Even before the full plot is unravelled, readers are engaging with the text on a critical and linguistic level, seeking out precedents and influences and treating it not simply as a story, but as a body of writing, replete with intertexts, to be probed and analysed. The passing comments above on language and political analogy divulge little about *Drood*, but reveal a great deal about the way Dickens's works embedded themselves into contemporary culture and became common currency in conversation. In both the Parliamentary sketch and the note of borrowed phrases, the writers either assume that readers know what is being talked about, or that they will have opinions that they want to share. Dickens's novel is thus not simply read within the pages of each monthly number, but is woven into the pattern of daily life, as small references accumulate, consequently positioning the work at the forefront of common consciousness.

Though most publications preferred to wait until the final number to review a novel, some did offer regular reviews after each instalment. The *Illustrated London News* (*ILN*), in a section of the publication devoted to discussion of developing stories, reviewed each of the six monthly parts of *Drood*. Yet these reviews can be frustratingly cursory and obscure; for example, the review published on 21 May 1870 (pertaining to the second monthly number) is here quoted in full, to convey the idea of its extreme brevity:

> This number will sustain Mr Dickens's reputation, and even increase it, from the novelty and variety of the scenes and personages introduced. There is plenty both of humour and more serious interest, and both are excellent in their way (p. 538).

The *ILN*'s commitment to publishing regular reviews of a range of serials makes it likely that its purpose was as much to recommend these publications to readers as it was to critique their contents, and in the case quoted above it is unclear whether the reviewer even read the monthly instalment. Nevertheless, the fact that the summary avoids exact description might suggest that nineteenth-century readers were no different from twenty-first-century bloggers in their fear of introducing spoilers. Instead the *ILN* reviews focus on congratulating the depiction of particular characters (Durdles receives special mention in the first number) or on commending the quality of the writing. In the review of the fifth monthly number on 13 August 1870, it is noted that "The most remarkable passage is one in which the author, through the mouthpiece of Mr Crisparkle, delivers himself with considerable energy on the subject of one of his old antipathies, the political and religious platform" ("The Magazines" 13 August 1870, p. 167). Like the previously cited query regarding "oppressively respectable," here is yet another case of readers' approaching the novel for its literary merits over and above its plot. One of the curious effects of reading in instalment is that rather than urging the reader always to look ahead to the next part, this strategy instead encourages closer reading, and rereading, of an individual part. With a whole month to wait, it increases the opportunity to revisit and ponder over the text. Robert Patten speaks of the "views of Victorian serials as forward-looking and time-specific," and suggests there should be added "a third perspective: looking backward" (1995, p. 124). He argues that looking backward "is a way of reading, possibly the way of reading" (p. 131): we pay more heed to what has come before than we do to anticipating what is coming next.

The reviews in the *ILN* provide some insight into ways of discussing the text; but their brevity curtails speculation on reactions to the novel as it first appeared. In the specific case of *Drood*, though, there is an important external factor which prompted larger and fuller reactions to the book in progress, rather than the completed tale: the author's premature demise. Dickens died on 9 June 1870, at which point only three of the instalments of *Drood* had been published. As a consequence, in among the obituaries and numerous outpourings of grief, admiration and reminiscence in the press, there are further insights into *Drood*, not at its conclusion, not even at the half-way point that was eventually reached in September 1870, but a mere quarter of the way into the story. Of course the context of these reviews is often subjective, and considerations of the tale's merits are heavily influenced by the sorrowful tone that pervaded at the time of the author's death. The *Examiner* verged on the poetic in its summary of the book as "a broken pillar of letters, not of marble, carved by himself, which we have only to preserve over his grave" ("Charles Dickens" 1870, p. 387). Other commentators were happy to praise the early works of Dickens at the expense of his later writing: on 18 June 1870 *The Spectator* attacked "How little of a realist Dickens actually was in his creations of character" by drawing attention to several "deplorable failures" including "the worthy minor Canon in 'The Mystery of Edwin Drood' [who] promised to be so too" ([Hutton] 1870, p. 750). Singling out Crisparkle was not unique; a six-stanza poem in *The Period* in June 1870, which pitifully lamented the author's death ("Dickens is dead. Who has not lost a friend?/Far, far too early seems this sudden end"), drew attention to just three of the characters in *Drood*: "Latest, to move our wonder,/Crisparkle, Honeythunder" the poet writes, before proceeding to an entire stanza devoted solely to Rosa Bud ("The Late Charles Dickens" 1870, p. 84). There is no mention of John Jasper, who was universally recognised as the novel's protagonist (or at the very least, antagonist); there is not even a mention of the novel's title character. The reasons why they might here be overlooked in favour of Rosa, Crisparkle and Honeythunder provide fertile ground for speculation on initial reception of the text. Dickens's heroine seems to have stolen at least one heart (the poet's), and Crisparkle can lay claim to being a hero of a sort in the text; but of the three it is the special acclaim given to the minor character of Luke Honeythunder which seems most incongruous. The hypocritical philanthropist is by no means central to the plot, but does offer comic relief in those few scenes in which he appears; it is this which appears to justify the early praise he receives.

The contemporary focus upon the comic elements in *Drood* can be further seen, and perhaps better understood, by returning to the publication of the first number in April 1870, and exploring the immediate reviews. As much as Dickens's death has come to overshadow *Drood*, an equally important event that shaped reaction to the text was Dickens's return to novel publication after a gap of nearly five years. The hiatus between publication of *Drood* and the preceding novel, *Our Mutual Friend* (1864–1865), is the longest in Dickens's career. The break was due in part to Dickens's reading tours in the UK and United States, which allowed him to be simultaneously absent as an author and present as a reader, thus raising his profile and generating anticipation for his return to the page. The *ILN*'s brief review on 9 April 1870 notes that "all the world is eager to welcome Mr Dickens back to the domains of serial fiction, and so far as we can judge from the first number of his work, public expectation is not likely to be disappointed" ("The Magazines" 9 April 1870, p. 383); indeed such was the public eagerness that the first number received a higher degree of attention in the press than usual: most of this was not only anticipating the story to come, but joyfully remembering all other stories that had gone before. As Patten suggests of Dickens's novels, the readers are looking backwards while the text is "articulating a nostalgia for previous modes" (1995, p. 124). Accordingly, the remarkably long review on 2 April 1870 in the *Times* – a full page – echoed the *ILN*'s keen tone; the paper noted:

> The novel-reading world have been on the tip-toe of expectation since the announcement of a new work by their favourite author. We have perused the first instalment, and venture to express the public pleasure, and to thank Mr. Dickens for having added a zest to the season (p. 4).

The *Athenaeum* also dedicated a page to the first instalment of *Drood*, on 2 April. In contrast to the short, enigmatic, uninformed reviews of the *ILN*, this was a much fuller and more explicit discussion of characters and plot, published just three days after the release of the first number. Not only was the *Athenaeum* expecting everyone to be reading *Drood*, but to have read it straightaway. As in the other reviews of April 1870, nostalgia is rife: the reviewer John Doran notes: "it is a positive pleasure to see once more the green cover in which the world first beheld Mr Pickwick" (1870, p. 443). Like the poem that would later appear in *The Period*, the review also praises Rosa Bud; but most of the allotted space is taken up with praise of Sapsea and Durdles, with Jasper getting only a brief mention. Once more, comic characters merit the most attention.

The awareness of previous works of Dickens is also evident in attacks on *Drood*. On 13 April 1870 the first instalment was mercilessly lampooned in *Judy* as "The Mysterious Mystery of Rude Dedwin"; the main thrust of this piece is retrospective, but here the backward glance is critical: the reviewer accuses Dickens of simply rehashing old characters. Hence Sapsea, or "Papsy," introduces himself:

> My own name ... is not Pecksniff, as at first you might imagine, but Papsy. I chose it because it was funny (1870, p. 240).

The claim throughout the parody is that it has all been seen before, and is often comic just for the sake of being comic. Whether lampooning or praising *Drood*, these early responses share a tendency to emphasise the comedy of the book – a reaction that is notably absent from the bulk of reviews and analyses of the novel ever since. It is interesting to note the *ILN*'s judgement on 9 April, that the "most successful of the character portraits is Durdles" ("The Magazines" p. 383); the *Times* likewise praised the stonemason on 2 April as "a thoroughly original conception" ("The Mystery of Edwin Drood" 1870, p. 4). The marked difference between readers in April 1870 and readers of later generations in interpretative tone is dictated by more than just the former's preference for Dickens's earlier comic works. It is also shaped by the shifting perspective of the whole narrative, which evolves with each new instalment.

While the special attention paid in contemporary reviews to Durdles, Sapsea and Honeythunder can be explained in part by their comic potential, it is equally important to consider structure and the cumulative significance of characters. Figure 9.1 features a simple calculation of character presence in the six extant monthly numbers. If a character appears in a chapter, he/she is awarded one point; if the character does not appear but is talked about, he/she scores half a point. The results indicate the extent to which characters are brought to the reader's attention as the narrative progresses. Unsurprisingly, Jasper emerges as a regular presence in every chapter: he appears in all but five (and even then is still mentioned in those chapters). Edwin too maintains a hold in the reader's consciousness even after his disappearance, thanks to the extent to which other characters continue to recall him. Figures 9.2, 9.3 and 9.4 convert these figures into percentages by considering each character score as a fraction of the maximum possible appearance (that is, appearing in every single chapter). Thus in Figure 9.2, which covers the first number, their appearances are shown as a percentage of five chapters. In Figure 9.3, which considers the first three numbers, these appearances are shown as a percentage of the cumulative total of 11 chapters. Figure 9.4 charts the appearances by the close of the last surviving instalments, when the total number of chapters climbs to 23. Even a cursory glance at these graphs demonstrates how each successive number becomes increasingly complicated, as more characters begin to compete for the reader's attention. While major characters such as Jasper and Edwin maintain their hold regardless, it is the peripheral characters who are most affected. At the end of the first number, Durdles scores 2 out of a potential 5 – 40% of the number – having appeared in two of the five chapters in that number. By the end of the third number that has reduced to 3 out of 12 – 25% of the three instalments – as more characters are introduced and less space is afforded him. What might have been assumed to be a major role in April 1870 is shown to be a supporting part by June. By the time the final instalment is published in September, Durdles's score is down to 21%.

The perceived importance of a character can be equally explained by the absence of others. Crisparkle maintains his prominent position throughout the novel as published; yet in subsequent years, since the sixth number appeared, he has played second fiddle to the more enigmatic Datchery (*MED* 18, 23), and the more obvious romantic lead, Tartar (*MED* 17, 21, 22). The praise afforded to

Character	Monthly Numbers and Chapters																							TOTAL
	No. 1					No. 2				No. 3			No. 4				No. 5				No. 6			
	Ch. 1	Ch. 2	Ch. 3	Ch. 4	Ch. 5	Ch. 6	Ch. 7	Ch. 8	Ch. 9	Ch. 10	Ch. 11	Ch. 12	Ch. 13	Ch. 14	Ch. 15	Ch. 16	Ch. 17	Ch. 18	Ch. 19	Ch. 20	Ch. 21	Ch. 22	Ch. 23	
John Jasper	1	1	0.5	1	1	1	1	1	1	1	0.5	1	1	1	1	1	1	1	1	0.5	0.5	0.5	1	20.5
Princess Puffer	1	0	0	0	0	0	0	0	0	0	0	0	0	1	0	0	0	0	0	0	0	0	1	3
Mr Tope	0	1	0	0.5	0	1	0.5	0	0	0	0	1	0	1	0	1	0	1	0	0	0	0	1	8
The Dean	0	1	0	0	0	0	0	0	0	0	0	1	0	0.5	0	1	0	0.5	0	0	0	0	0.5	4.5
Septimus Crisparkle	0	1	0	0	0	1	1	1	1	1	0	1	0	1	1	1	1	0	0.5	0.5	1	1	1	15
Edwin Drood	0	1	1	0	1	1	1	1	0.5	0.5	1	0	1	1	0.5	0.5	0.5	0.5	0.5	0.5	0.5	0.5	0.5	14.5
Rosa Bud	0	0.5	1	0	0	1	1	0.5	1	0.5	0.5	0	1	0.5	0.5	0.5	0	0	1	1	1	1	0.5	13
Mrs Tope	0	1	0	0	0	0	0	0	0	0	0	0	0.5	0.5	0	1	0	1	0	0	0	0	1	5
Edwin's father	0	0.5	0	0	0.5	0	0	0.5	0.5	0	0	0	0	0.5	0	0.5	0	0	0	0	0	0	0	3
Miss Twinkleton	0	0	1	0	0	1	1	0	1	0	0	0	1	0.5	0	0	0	0	0.5	0.5	0.5	1	0	8
Mrs Tisher	0	0	1	0	0	0	1	0	1	0	0	0	1	0	0	0	0	0	0.5	0	0	0	0	4.5
Mr Sapsea	0	0	0	1	0	0	0	0	0	0	0	1	0.5	1	1	1	0	1	0	0	0	0	0	6.5
Mrs Sapsea	0	0	0	0.5	0	0	0	0	0	0	0	0.5	0	0	0	0	0	0	0	0	0	0	0	1
Durdles	0	0	0	1	1	0	0	0	0	0	0	1	0	1	0	0	0	1	0	0	0	0	0	5
Deputy	0	0	0	0	1	0	0	0	0	0	0	1	0	0	0	0	0	1	0	0	0	0	1	4
Rosa's parents	0	0.5	0	0	0	0	0	0	0.5	0	0.5	0	0	0	0	0	0	0	0	0.5	0.5	0	0	2.5
Mrs Crisparkle	0	0	0	0	0	1	1	0	0	1	0	0	0	0.5	0	0.5	0.5	0	0	0	0.5	0	0	5
Mr Honeythunder	0	0	0	0	0	1	0.5	0	0	0	0	0	0	0	0	0.5	1	0	0	0	0	0	0	3
Neville Landless	0	0	0	0	0	1	1	1	0.5	1	0	1	0	1	1	1	1	0	0.5	0.5	0.5	0.5	0.5	12
Helena Landless	0	0	0	0	0	1	1	0.5	1	1	0	0	0.5	1	0.5	0.5	0.5	0	0.5	0.5	0.5	1	0.5	10.5
Mrs Crisparkle's sister	0	0	0	0	0	0.5	0	0	0	0	0	0	0	0	0	0	0	0	0	0	0	0	0	0.5
Joe	0	0	0	0	0	1	0	0	0	0	0	0	0	0	1	0	0	0	0	1	0	0	0	3
Mr Grewgious	0	0	0	0	0	0	0	0	1	0	1	0	0.5	0.5	1	1	1	0	0	1	1	1	0.5	9.5
Bazzard	0	0	0	0	0	0	0	0	0.5	0	1	0	0	0	0	0	0	0	0	0.5	0	0.5	0	2.5
Tartar	0	0	0	0	0	0	0	0	0	0	0	0	0	0	0	0	1	0	0	0	1	1	0	3
Datchery	0	0	0	0	0	0	0	0	0	0	0	0	0	0	0	0	0	1	0	0	0	0	1	2
Billickin	0	0	0	0	0	0	0	0	0	0	0	0	0	0	0	0	0	0	0	0	0	1	0	1
Lobley	0	0	0	0	0	0	0	0	0	0	0	0	0	0	0	0	0	0	0	0	0	1	0	1

Figure 9.1 Characters' appearances in the monthly numbers and chapters of *The Mystery of Edwin Drood*. © Pete Orford.

178 | Pete Orford

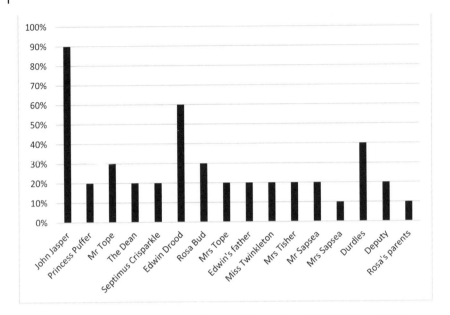

Figure 9.2 Character presence in the first monthly number of *The Mystery of Edwin Drood*. © Pete Orford.

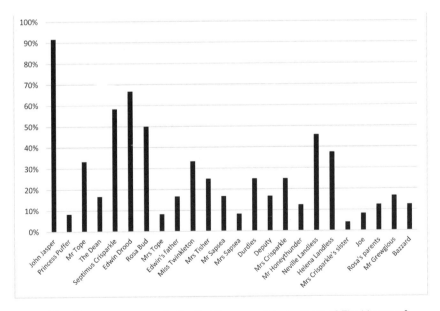

Figure 9.3 Character presence in the first three monthly numbers of *The Mystery of Edwin Drood*. © Pete Orford.

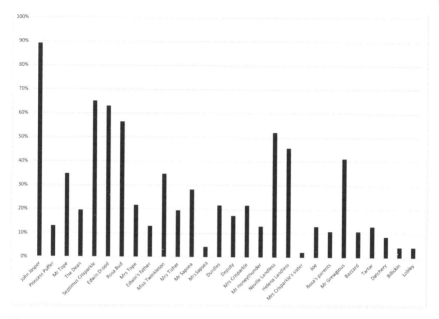

Figure 9.4 Character presence in the first six monthly numbers of *The Mystery of Edwin Drood*. © Pete Orford.

Crisparkle in contemporary reviews is therefore less an indication of how much he appears in the text and more of a reflection of how others fail to appear. In those early numbers he is the most obvious choice for hero (*MED* 2, 6, 7, 8, 9, 10, 12, 13, 14, 15, 16) until supplanted by the two later arrivals. Assigning a quantitative value to each character in this way offers some illumination; but the figures need to be treated as indicative rather than absolute. The table and graphs only consider the number of appearances, with no consideration given to the significance of those moments. The Princess Puffer, for example, barely features in the final graph (Figure 9.4): she has only appeared in three chapters of the first six numbers; yet she has become a figure of enormous interest to the enthusiastic army of Droodians attempting to solve the mystery, precisely because her appearances, though few and far between, are all ominous in nature, and offer particular insight into the character of Jasper. Archibald Coolidge notes how Dickens's novels contain not just one plot, but instead "each important character has a sort of plot of his own, which sometimes joins or crosses that of one or more other important characters" of which "the result is a sort of weaving in and out of several stories at once and a constant stopping of one plot and another" (1961, p. 180). Thus while Jasper and Edwin might seem to dominate the main plot of *Drood*, in fact their story is complemented by, and interwoven with, the individual stories of all the characters surrounding them – any one of whom might pique the interest of a reader.

Serial publication has too long been considered as an imposition on the author, with a prejudice forming in favour of the novel as the true form of the story. Thomas Carlyle's remark that serialisation meant serving the novel up in "teaspoons" (his term for a weekly number; see *Letters* 9:113) betrays this sense of frustration over enjoyment, of a story being denied its most effective form. Dickens's own ambitions early in his career to produce a triple decker as a status symbol belie the success he achieved as a writer of serials. It is often argued that Dickens transformed serialisation (see, for example, Tillotson 1954, p. 29); but it is equally valid to argue that serialisation shaped Dickens into the writer we now know. Joanne Shattock notes that "part publication instilled in Dickens a need for formal planning, and a corresponding sense of structure" (2012, p. 11). Far from being a form that constrained him, it was a method of publishing that sharpened his narrative powers and contributed positively to the quality of his work.

What serial publication highlights is the importance of challenging the aforementioned conception that true understanding of a book is only achieved at the end. While Patten argues that "Beginnings are determined by endings," that understanding of the beginning necessarily shifts as the ending continues to adapt with the publication of each fresh instalment (1995, p. 132). Hughes and Lund argue that "Modern studies of reading place great emphasis on narrative endings, resolutions that retrospectively validate patterns throughout a text": we understand the novel through its conclusion, and we retrospectively frame the narrative to suit that end and define its tone and genre (1991, p. 144). Celebrating the final work for its "organic unity" (Coolidge 1967, p. 5) assumes the work to be one complete whole, rather than several smaller sketches laid side by side; but a book need not be greater than the sum of its parts, and reserving judgement about a novel until after its close ignores the equally valid responses formed during the process of reading, before knowing how it is going to end.

This is where *Drood* offers a unique opportunity in challenging accepted reading practices, for the simple fact that it has no conclusion. Hundreds have stepped forward to propose an ending, maddened by the apparent lack of conclusion and the difficulty this presents in understanding what becomes, in their eyes, merely a "fragment." Yet others have stepped forward to recognise the merit in redefining the six existing numbers of *Drood* as complete. Roussel argues that its unplanned state of inconclusion perfectly reflects the quests of several characters, notably Jasper and Rosa, to break free of their own repetitive cycles, in order to achieve a sense of closure: "Both their stories are concerned with their attempts to realize their dreams and, in this sense, finish their stories" (1978, p. 384). Gerhard Joseph believes that the six numbers should be treated as complete, and the last chapter of the sixth instalment should be approached as the final one of the book: "the novel comes to a satisfactory close with what we now have in chapter 23: there is not, nor need there be, any more" (1996, p. 170). Roussel and Joseph successfully challenge the perceived dissatisfaction with *Drood*'s incomplete status: they encourage closer reading of the text which exists; yet there is merit in accepting its inconclusiveness rather than trying to repackage it as finished. *Drood* in its final state is an accidental freeze-frame of every Dickens novel in progress: it captures that moment which the end lays open before the reader, and defies both the comforting sense of closure and the culturally programmed approach to understanding novels from the end backwards. Instead, caution must be thrown to the wind in speculating about what happens next, in the knowledge that virtually any careful reader could be wrong or right.

Far from being frustrating, this openness can be immensely liberating. A completed plot can be represented by a single line; it starts at point A and progresses to point B, according to the author's wishes. But a novel half-written, or half-read, only maintains that single line to the point at which the reader has arrived. Everything remaining in the plot then expands outward into a myriad of possibilities: is Edwin alive? Whom will Rosa marry? Who might Datchery be? There are a number of potential directions in which the narrative might go, and that very multiplicity expands the range of both plot and characters, to make them more than what they ever could have been, had Dickens completed the novel. Instead of being limited to Dickens's plans, the characters exist in a multitude of opportunities. This in turn identifies and celebrates the experience of reading by instalment, and how it makes each character bigger and more multifaceted, without the restrictive – indeed permanent – bonds of the book's end, which would embed them within one plot, or one interpretation. Wynne notes that "serialization encouraged communal reading and offered the potential for a rapport between author and reader" (2012, p. 30); this rapport is best noted in *Drood* where readers have picked up the threads left by the author in order to continue that communication and project the story forward in their own image of what constitutes a Dickens novel.

Accordingly, the reading project involving *Drood* allowed for a far more frank and open exploration of plot and character than participants first realised: they could say what they thought without the mortifying experience of being proved wrong, and readers were directed to the website *The Drood Inquiry* (Orford n.d.a), where they were able to vote on the ending they thought was intended. Needless to say, opinion was divided. The open-endedness of *Drood* allows it to maintain that moment which other Dickens novels would have held during their original conception: when the author had yet to pen the ending and readers' premonitions still had the very real potential of being proved correct. Serialised reading thus elevates the reader to a position of fellow traveller, who speculates between publication of parts and projects forward numerous possibilities of plots, before finally adopting the one dictated by the author. It is little surprise that Dickens should be so celebrated for the vitality of his characters when his works were read in this way, when, for example, the young Oliver Twist (recalling the comments above from Forster's *Examiner* review) could occupy the reader's imagination and live a thousand lives before the close of the book.

This exploration of characters beyond the immediate confines of the page was best realised in the fourth project, for which the monthly reading of *Our Mutual*

Friend was accompanied by the launch of a Twitter account for each character, which an individual reader could adopt; thus they masqueraded as the *dramatis personae*, voiced their ongoing reaction to events and pondered on what was happening in between monthly parts. The incorporation of Twitter allowed for a much more fluid and dynamic interaction between reader and text than had previously been achieved in any of the other reading projects, allowing participants to react to each other as much as, if not more than, the text itself. This extra-textual freedom reached its zenith after the reading of the last instalment, when contributors were invited to imagine the counterfactual endings that their particular characters deserved. In one instance this meant a more modern reimagining of a suitable ending for the Mortimer Lightwood–Eugene Wrayburn relationship, in which they live in the hypothetical lighthouse Dickens has them discussing (*OMF* 1:12), with the reader who adopted the Twitter handle "@OMF_Mortimer" wondering "why choose between best pal and best girl when a comfortable harmony is so easy to attain?" (Figure 9.5). Dickens's characters were adapted to contemporary sensibilities in order to achieve the endings the readers wanted, rather than those that the author envisaged.

Such speculation need not, and can not, be reserved until the end of the book; rather it is a continual process of anticipation throughout the serialised reading

Figure 9.5 Twitter feed for Eugene Wrayburn (@OMF_Eugene), from *Our Mutual Friend Reading Project*. Retrieved from https://twitter.com/OMF_Eugene. By kind permission of Pete Orford.

experience. The enforced breaks are just as important as the text itself: each pause gives room for thought, and each thought enlarges the scope and realm of the story and its characters. The silence each month, or week – far longer than the time taken to read the instalment – leaves a gap for readers to fill with their own voices and views.

The new possibilities which these reading projects offer for Dickens's characters and text can be dismissed as frivolous and beside the point; but the tradition-bound tendency to favour the possession of all the facts before forming an opinion has blinded readers and scholars to the thrill and enjoyment to be had from speculation. The bias towards discussing only the completed story, originating in the idea of the writer as architect, whose work is best understood in full, ignores the dialogue that springs up between reader and author, and the richness this can bring to the novel in its potential for deeper immersion in the world of the story. Formal, linear study of texts teaches readers to gather all the facts before reaching a conclusion; but an essential element of being human is the need to prompt and inspire further discussion, rather than to arrive at stark, closed resolutions. It is understandable – even natural – to crave the comfort of a definite conclusion; but what these reading projects have demonstrated is the expanded range of possibilities offered for readers of Dickens when closure is dismissed, and open-endedness embraced.

References

Charles Dickens (1870, 18 June). *The Examiner and London Review*, 387.
Cohen, Jane Rabb (1980). *Charles Dickens and His Original Illustrators*. Columbus: Ohio State University Press.
Coolidge, Archibald C. (1961). Dickens's Complex Plots. *Dickensian*, 57, 174–182.
Coolidge, Archibald C. (1967). *Charles Dickens as a Serial Novelist*. Iowa City: Iowa State University Press.
Curry, Emma, & Winyard, Ben (Eds.) (n.d.). *Our Mutual Friend Reading Project*. London: Birkbeck University of London. Retrieved from https://dickensourmutualfriend.wordpress.com
Dickens Journals Online (n.d.). Buckingham: University of Buckingham. Retrieved from www.djo.org.uk/
[Doran, John]. (1870, 2 April). Literature: The Mystery of Edwin Drood, No. I. *Athenaeum*, 443–444.
Drew, John, et al. (Eds.) (n.d.a). *A Tale of Two Cities Reading Project*. Leicester: Victorian Studies Centre; Buckingham: Dickens Journals Online. Retrieved from https://dickensataleoftwocities.wordpress.com
Drew, John, et al. (Eds.) (n.d.b). *No Name Reading Project*. Leicester: Victorian Studies Centre; Buckingham: Dickens Journals Online. Retrieved from https://collinsnoname.wordpress.com

[Forster, John] (1837, 10 September). The Literary Examiner: Bentley's Miscellany. February to September. *Oliver Twist*, by Charles Dickens, Esq. Bentley. *The Examiner*, 581–582.

Goldberg, Matt (2012). Christopher and Jonathan Nolan Explain How A TALE OF TWO CITIES Influenced THE DARK KNIGHT RISES. *Collider.com*. Retrieved from http://collider.com/dark-knight-rises-tale-of-two-cities/

Hughes, Linda K., & Lund, Michael (1991). *The Victorian Serial*. Charlottesville: University Press of Virginia.

[Hutton, Richard Holt] (1870, 18 June). The Genius of Dickens. *The Spectator*, 749–751.

Joseph, Gerhard (1996). Who Cares Who Killed Edwin Drood? Or, on the Whole, I'd Rather Be in Philadelphia. *Nineteenth-Century Literature*, 51(2), 161–175.

The Late Charles Dickens (1870, June). *The Period*, 84.

The Magazines (1870, 9 April). *Illustrated London News*, 383.

The Magazines (1870, 21 May). *Illustrated London News*, 538.

The Magazines (1870, 13 August). *Illustrated London News*, 167.

The Mysterious Mystery of Rude Dedwin (1870, 13 April). *Judy, or the London Serio-Comic Journal*, 240.

The Mystery of Edwin Drood (1870, 2 April). The *Times*, 4.

Notes and Queries (1870, 4 May). *Judy, or the London Serio-Comic Journal*, 19.

Orford, Pete (Ed.) (n.d.a). *The Drood Inquiry*. Buckingham: University of Buckingham. Retrieved from http://droodinquiry.com/home

Orford, Pete (Ed.) (n.d.b). *The Mystery of Edwin Drood Reading Project*. Buckingham: University of Buckingham. Retrieved from https://cloisterhamtales.wordpress.com

Oxford English Dictionary. Retrieved from www.oed.com

Patten, Robert L. (1995). Serialized Retrospection in *The Pickwick Papers*. In John O. Jordan & Robert L. Patten (Eds.), *Literature in the Marketplace: Nineteenth-Century British Publishing and Reading Practices* (pp. 123–142). Cambridge: Cambridge University Press.

Punch's Essence of Parliament (1870, 21 May). *Punch, or the London Chiarivari*, 202.

Roussel, Roy (1978). The Completed Story in "The Mystery of Edwin Drood." *Criticism*, 20(4), 383–402.

Shattock, Joanne (2012). The Publishing Industry. In John Kucich & Jenny Bourne Taylor (Eds.), *The Oxford History of the Novel in English: Volume 3: The Nineteenth-Century Novel 1820–1880* (pp. 3–21). Oxford: Oxford University Press.

Tillotson, Kathleen (1954). *Novels of the Eighteen-Forties*. Oxford: Clarendon Press.

Warhol, Robyn (Ed.) (n.d.). *Victorian Serial Novels*. Columbus: Ohio State University. Retrieved from http://victorianserialnovels.org/

What the Dickens Next? (1870, 9 April). *John Bull*, 53.

Wynne, Deborah (2012). Readers and Reading Practices. In John Kucich & Jenny Bourne Taylor (Eds.), *The Oxford History of the Novel in English: Volume 3: The Nineteenth-Century Novel 1820–1880* (pp. 22–36). Oxford: Oxford University Press.

10

Dickens Touches the Sky

Urban Exploration and London's Greatest Author

Gillian Piggott

In his study of recreational trespassing in the built environment, Bradley Garrett observes:

> The desire to explore for the sake of exploring, to take risks for the sake of the experience, with little thought to the 'outcome' is something that flows deeply through us as children. Urban explorers are in a sense rediscovering and forging these feelings of unbridled play; staying up all night, wandering, plotting, having significant conversations during spontaneous encounters ... being playful in the city stands in contrast to the importance of 'work and construction.' (2014a, p. 89)

The marginal and subcultural activity of Urban Exploration (otherwise "Urbex," "Place-Hacking" or "UE," as it will be designated in this chapter) evolved between the 1970s and 1990s, but was fairly invisible until about the early 2000s (see Garrett 2014b, p. 7). The activity of the urban explorers (or "Urbexers"), those seemingly crazy young men – and it is mostly young men – who traverse the city by scaling skyscrapers, scrambling across bridges, traversing crane counterweights or delving into the sewer and transport systems of the world's big cities, is now a staple of popular culture. Not only do urban explorers feature on daytime television and in the mainstream press (see Macfarlane 2013; Self 2014; Moss 2016), they have also starred in full-blown documentaries and films about the activity (see Channel 4 Urban Explorers n.d.). Visual media are influenced by the Urbex aesthetic; the films in the James Bond franchise are outstanding examples (Wilson et al. 2006, 2012). Numerous websites have sprung up, and have become integral to the scene, giving space to the discussions and presenting stunning photographs of the Urbexers' adventures (see 28 Days Later n.d.; HK Urbex n.d.). In the gaming world, Urbex serves both as the title of individual products and as the inspiration behind digital adventures and mobile augmented reality games (see Heath &

Reading Dickens Differently, First Edition. Edited by Leon Litvack and Nathalie Vanfasse.
© 2020 John Wiley & Sons Ltd. Published 2020 by John Wiley & Sons Ltd.

Potter 2005; *Urbex* 2013; EA Digital Illusions 2008–2012; Fowler et al. 2008, 2013; Nomura 2013, 2016). Urban explorers, then, not only undertake UE, putting themselves at risk physically and legally, they also record their activities photographically and textually. Glamorous, incongruous and unique perspectives on our cities – the manna of Urban Exploration – have become a powerful presence in the stories we tell ourselves about modernity and our urban life.

Urban Exploration is an activity in which participants engage in "recreational trespass" in the built environment; indeed the adjective "recreational" is often paired with the term "infiltration" or "place-hacking." UE, in other words, is seen by many, and by practitioners themselves, as a transgressive activity; it is, among other things, dependent upon determining rights to urban spaces. It is an act involving the redrawing of boundaries and re-appropriating public space. Examples include climbing unfinished skyscrapers or abandoned buildings; scrambling through construction sites; and burrowing in off-limits tunnels and abandoned parts of London's Underground network. Their infiltration amounts to taking possession of forbidden space, in opposition to what is seen as an increasingly prevalent privatisation of public space. This is fast becoming a political issue (see Shenker 2017, 24 July, 25 July; Garrett 2017); the press, homing in on the sensational daredevilry and stunning images propagated by UE, tends to represent the activity as an ongoing cat-and-mouse game between Urbexers and officialdom: the police, security guards and organisations running infrastructural spaces, such as Transport for London.

There is something of the "cyberpunk" aesthetic about Urban Exploration; this subculture focuses on post-industrial urban landscapes, and examines the impact of technology, drug culture and the sexual revolution upon metropolitan life, relationships and human emotions (see Lindsay 2010). It depicts a near future in which high-tech advances such as cybernetics and artificial intelligence exist alongside a devastated post-industrial world, where the social and political order have broken down, and widespread poverty and inequality have taken hold. It could be suggested that our own age, with its shiny supercities, influential billionaires and global corporations, sitting alongside political instability, economic uncertainty and social unrest, is not so far removed from such a state of affairs. Urbexers themselves, armed with their cybernetic enhancements (headcams, smartphones, masks and quadcopter drones) can be seen to resemble gothic cyborgs, marauding the cityspace. Their interest in ruins and abandoned spaces (with UE's aim to "cartographically and photographically preserve the decay and dilapidation of old buildings and by extension, the period they represent") means they emerge as "guerrilla preservationists," who break down barriers not only of space, but of time, travelling between the past and the present, between memories of former lives and the present's decaying fragments, "between the living and the dead," as they examine the present with an attachment to the past (Lindsay 2010).

Bradley L. Garrett has become the unofficial spokesman, or theorist-in-chief, of the activity over the past few years, and is himself a practitioner as well as an academic (see, for example, Garrett 2014a, 2014c; Garrett et al. 2016). He argues that UE is an alternative reading of urban space; it functions as a "haptic placemaking process," that allows the embodied "forging of furtive yet intimate connections with the city" (Kindynis 2017, p. 985). In the course of his research of the London Consolidation Crew (a UE collective), he immersed himself in the topic, risking life and limb by scaling the heights of the Heron Tower and Canary Wharf, among other edifices; this experience led to a number of publications and opened up a stable academic career for him in geography (for an image of Garrett atop London's Shard see Self 2014). Garrett has cited Dickens, among other nineteenth- and twentieth-century "inspirational figureheads" for developing an understanding of UE (2014a, p. 16).

The above prefatory discussion raises the question of what Urbex has to do with Dickens. At first, one would imagine, the connections are tenuous: if UE can be seen as part of a vibrant contemporary urban culture, with rhythms, ideas and sensations expressed (amid twenty-first century skyscrapers of glass and steel) through rap, hip hop, grime, skate boarding, graffiti and even gaming and fantasy (see Miéville 2009; Jordan 2011), then surely Dickens cannot be anywhere in the mix? Yet the Victorian author's imagined city, and his London meanderings, which have attracted so much critical attention, must have some bearing upon UE, not least because, as G.K. Chesterton put it, "Dickens Dickensized London" (1917, p. 42). If, as Urbexers fully accept, the city is a palimpsest whose layers are constantly re-inscribed in the chronological movement of history, then Dickens's iteration must be part of the Urbex experience. As one Urbexer put it, spaces in the city "become like a drug for some reason … get you high, a combination of the history, the architecture, the light moving through, the smell of one hundred years … you are just another layer in the history of the place" (Garrett 2014a, p. 38).

An additional factor in Dickens's favour is his ability to create incessant movement and variety: the visual, aural and even moving images he conjures up in his fiction; his obsession with representing the vertiginous experience; his descriptions of speed; the delineation of urban space with all its strange enigmatic points of connection and disconnection; and his re-enchantment of the everyday. All of these are inspired by his own extraordinary mode of imaginative conception – especially his obsession with walking/writing the city. His intense engagement with the urban, and the fiction and journalism that emerge from it, are energised and animated by bodily rhythms and the sensations of metropolitan life, as he experiences them through his walking and delving into the cityscape.

UE can be viewed as part of a tradition going back hundreds of years, of writers and artists as walkers, feeding from, and representing, the city; Dickens is one of the most complex and interesting of possible examples (see Beaumont 2015). It is well known that he obsessively walked in London and in other cities; in Lausanne, for example, he complained of writer's block without the "magic lantern" of the streets and crowds around him (*Letters* 4:612–613). Excessive energy seems to have been a factor in his metabolism; walking relieved a restlessness in him, as he intimated to Forster in 1854: "If I couldn't walk fast and far, I should just explode and perish" (*Letters* 7:429). He also declared that writing all day brought on an "extraordinary nervousness" that only an encounter with the streets could cure (*Letters* 4:579). Perambulation was a habit that continually increased his level of fitness – something of which he (in the guise of the Uncommercial Traveller) was proud and about which he was jocular:

> So much of my travelling is done on foot, that if I cherished betting propensities, I should probably be found registered in sporting newspapers under some such title as the Elastic Novice, challenging all eleven-stone mankind to competition in walking. ([Dickens] 26 May 1860, p. 155)

Walking companions spoke of Dickens's capacity to travel at particularly high speed; according to how the author referred to his walks, his companions knew that they could be in for either a "breather" (a relatively short walk) or a "buster" of eight miles or more (see *Letters* 12:54; Dolby 1887, pp. 255–256). The author's ambulatory stamina was impressive; but what is more notable is the fact that his creative process is inextricably caught up with his body and its physical needs. In a letter to Cornelius Felton he remarked (in the third person) of his writing *A Christmas Carol* that he "wept and laughed, and wept again, and excited himself in the most extraordinary manner, in the composition: and thinking whereof, he walked about the black streets of London, fifteen and twenty miles, many a night when all the sober folks had gone to bed" (*Letters* 4:2). Here a huge energy and emotion spills out of his being in the heat of creativity; it results in an overwhelming need to walk for immense distances in the city at night. But the creative process did not end there: if anything, it escalated and expanded during the walking. The city's kaleidoscopic material provided manna for his imagination, and characters grew out of his walking experience; as Forster noted, "The first conceiving of a new book was always a restless time ... the characters that were growing in his mind would persistently intrude themselves into his night-wanderings" (Forster 1928, p. 388).

It was a chicken-and-egg conundrum: it is debatable whether Dickens's creativity required exercise/walking or whether walking determined fluent creativity and writing. A connection with the energy of the crowd – what Baudelaire called its "enormous reservoir of electricity" (1996, p. 139) – was what Dickens most needed; he craved a boost of energy or blood to engorge and exercise his ideas. The people, he said, "supplied something to my brain, which it cannot bear, when busy, to lose" (*Letters* 4:612). Dickens's production could even be viewed as "embodied writing" or "embodied creativity": it amounts to a collapse of the Subject/Object divide. His mode of production involved strolling, absorbing, thinking, reviewing, dreaming and writing fiction (see Litvack 2007). His constitution involved a conflation of the mental and physical: mind and body, particularly in walking, are for him one and the same, in contrast to any conventional mind/body dualism. Dickens himself illustrates this intriguing elision of thought and the physical self-in-motion, in urban space, in his delineation of his character Sidney Carton: "From being irresolute and purposeless, his feet became animated by an intention, and, in the working out of that intention, they took him to the Doctor's door" (*TTC* 2:13).

It could be suggested that Dickens's narrative comes close to a dancer's view of the self – that is, the self as embodied. It is certainly an urban perspective (a glimpse or sketch from an external gaze) of an embodied self who inhabits and re-inhabits space, revisits locations, and rethinks and reconfigures – with new steps and physical traces – old memories, old footprints and spaces. This idea can also be applied to Dickens's relationship to the city as a walker/artist. It suggests an intimacy with the city, as if the urban environment were an integral part of the self's existence and body, or in an immanent relationship with it – or, to put it another way, with a Heideggerian spin, it suggests that the nature of one's being-in-the-world is an opening onto the city, a practical relationship to it that is fundamental, and which is prior to the subject/object divide (see Heidegger 1993; Cooper 1990, p. 103). In Dickens's description of Carton's love for Lucie Manette, expressed in terms of urban space, there is a similar suggestion of an embodied self as well as an intimacy/identity between body and city: "He did care something for the streets that environed that house, and for the senseless stones that made their pavements. Many a night he vaguely and unhappily wandered there" (*TTC* 2:13). Here a character's perspective points to a fundamental relationship to the city that precedes the subject/object divide, and again sets up the idea of an embodied self. Carton exercises/exorcises/expresses love by walking, opening up onto the city, with his embodied self depicted as spatial, identical with proximity and space. The narrative describes Carton's psycho-empathetic working out of the proximity of his lover in the city; it is a physical enactment, and a measuring out, of his opportunity to be near her. The streets resemble an embracing body caressing Lucie's home, her intimate space; he caresses, approaches, is intimate with it, as he is familiar with the "senseless stones" of the pavement. His body/love will touch and inhabit and re-touch and re-inhabit the space, as he wanders and revisits the neighbourhood/body of Lucie.

Even if a Heideggerian framework seems stretched when considering the work of Dickens and UE theorists, Kindynis, in his analysis of Urbex, adduces a productive, creative physical interstitial relationship between the body and the city in UE activity:

> Of central importance here is that the meaning created by trespassers in forbidden spaces is generated neither 'by ... subject or object but in the space between them'... It is perhaps for this reason that in occupying those junctures at which body and city temporarily converge, trespassers sometimes feel a connection – an almost profound metaphysical sense of oneness – with the city. (2017, p. 985)

For Garrett, similarly, "[Urban explorers] simply want to actively engage with their environment ... creating new 'sensuous dispositions', porous encounters of bilateral exchange between body and city that inscribe the urban environment with new stories" (2014b, p. 7). Like Dickens, urban explorers emerge as not only creative readers of the palimpsestic city, but as productive writers of it too, "inscribing" urban space with their (physical) traces during each re-visitation. The UE motto is "Take nothing but photographs. Leave nothing but footprints." Urbexers are re-visiting and re-configuring known areas of urban space which are often familiar, but are usually viewed and experienced in a determined, ordered and preordained way.

The Urbexers' allusion to a body/city convergence is interesting in view of Dickens's own experience of the city as a topographical site of memory, which generates intense emotions in the author and in his writing. For example, in his autobiographical fragment, Dickens depicts his childhood experience of entering a coffee shop, looking at the window and seeing "MOOR-EEFFOC" on the glass (Forster 1928, p. 28). This opens up a chilling moment of the uncanny for the young Dickens: the strangeness of the everyday and the familiar suddenly rears its head. Dickens's body, its inhabiting of a particular space, and later in life, the re-inhabiting of it, causes this intense feeling to return again and again. Space, the topography of the metropolis, inheres in the narrative of the city dweller's subjectivity, which periodically discloses itself in the most dramatic way, coming about through the convergence of the embodied self and the city. The habit of urban walking means that where the body is, the site it inhabits, and re-inhabits, prompts a meeting with a younger self, and with old feelings, memory and an awareness of time's ravages. Walking in the city, for Dickens, is about experience, repetition and revision or reconfiguration. He tells Forster that in order to prepare for writing the autobiographical fragment (which preceded his fictional *David Copperfield*), he re-visited the blacking factory part of town (the north side of the Thames at Old Hungerford Stairs, where he was forced to labour as a child): "In my night walks I have walked there often, since then, and by degrees, I have come to write this" (Forster 1928, p. 35).

There is something even more intriguing about Dickens's walking: he appears to have need not only of movement in the city, but also of immersion and interactivity as a part of his creative process. His own description, in an "Uncommercial Traveller" essay, of his movement around the city conjures up the image of the gamer wearing a headset that provides augmented perceptual information (or augmented reality) across multiple sensory modalities: "I fell asleep to the monotonous sound of my own feet, doing their regular four miles an hour. Mile after mile I walked, without the slightest sense of exertion, dozing heavily and dreaming constantly" ([Dickens] 26 May 1860, p. 155). In this description of Dickens's 30-mile walk from his London office to Gad's Hill, his home in Kent (at 2 a.m.), he walks in a space – both city and country – overlaid by his imagination and his dreaming, as if he is immersed in, and interacting with, an augmented form of reality. He continues: "It was only when I made a stumble like a drunken man, or struck out into the road to avoid a horseman close upon me on the path – who had no existence – that I came to myself and looked about" (26 May 1860, pp. 155–156). This mention of the horseman seems to indicate that augmented perceptual information (not generated by a computer, of course, but by Dickens's vivid imagination) seamlessly overlays objects residing in the real world. It also appears that the author's immersive and interactive experience involves senses other than the purely visual: the auditory (presumably, he "hears" the approach of a horseman), the haptic (he seems to "feel" the splash of mud as he gallops by) and the somatosensory (he senses the rhythm of the hooves on the path behind him, which wakes him up).

This phenomenon of "overlaying" reality with imaginative input, or experiencing the city through an "augmented" lens, is what drives "Gone Astray," Dickens's 1853 fictional account of getting lost in London as a boy. His eight-year-old self overlays the city in which he is cast adrift with his childhood reading: he himself becomes Dick Whittington, pursuing his fortune in the city of London. The huge statues of Gog and Magog adorning the Guildhall are to him "giants"; Mansion House holds the Lord Mayor of London, a fairy-tale character whose princess daughter will see young Dickens out of the window, take pity on him and call him in; and a hungry dog is a comic character called Merrychance, an ostensibly friendly fellow and a potential companion on the boy's Whittingtonian adventures (he actually turns out to be a rather sharp and bullying dog, who runs off with the only meal the boy has). Having fallen asleep, the narrator is awoken by the city's loud din, or, as Dickens put it, "I thought the giants were roaring, but it was only the city" ([Dickens] 1853, pp. 553, 555, 554); this functions as a kind of auditory augmentation, that overlays the boy's experience of the city and then reverts to "reality."

An encounter between Dickens and his son Charley at the offices in Wellington Street in May 1870 conjures up the potency of Dickens's imagination and its apparent power to envelop him and overlay reality completely:

> The door of communication between our rooms was open, as usual, and, as I came towards him, I saw that he was writing very earnestly. After a moment I said: 'If you don't want anything more, sir, I shall be off now,' but he continued his writing with the same intensity as before, and gave no sign of being aware of my presence. Again I spoke – louder, perhaps, this time – and he rested his head and looked at me long and fixedly. But I soon found that, although his eyes were bent upon me and he seemed to be looking at me earnestly, he did not see me, and that he was, in fact, unconscious for the moment of my very existence. He was in Dreamland, with Edwin Drood, and I left him for the last time. (Dickens Jr 1934, pp. 30–31)

Dickens needs to immerse himself in, and interact with, the city space, its stimulants and the "augmented reality" that results from this process, in order to achieve creative momentum. Such an analysis of the author's inspiration makes the process seem like a nineteenth-century version of the augmented reality mobile game *Pokémon Go*, which uses a mobile device's Global Positioning System (GPS) to locate, capture, train and wage war against virtual creatures, called Pokémon, which appear as if they are in the player's real-world location (Nomura 2016). The characters who appear to Dickens are not, of course, computer-generated, but rather Dickens's own characters from his novels that he has set about "finding" or communing with in the city during a walk, and which he hopes to develop more clearly and fully during exercise. Charley Dickens recalls the vividness with which Dickens communed with characters while he walked:

> He lived, I am sure, two lives, one with us and one with his fictitious people, and I am equally certain that the children of his brain were much more real to him at times than we were. I have, often and often, heard him complain that he could *not* get the people of his imagination to do what he wanted, and that they would insist on working out their histories in *their* way and not *his*. I can very well remember his describing their flocking-round his table in the quiet hours of a summer morning when he was – an unusual circumstance with him – at work very early, each one of them claiming and demanding instant personal attention ... Many a mile have I walked with him thus – he striding along with his regular four-miles-an-hour swing; his eyes looking straight before him, his lips slightly working, as they generally did when he sat thinking and writing; almost unconscious of companionship. (Dickens Jr 1934, p. 25, emphasis original; see also Litvack 2007, p. 8)

It is interesting to note that Dickens's characters craved the city – just as he did; he maintained, in a letter to Forster, "*My* figures seem disposed to stagnate without crowds about them" (*Letters* 4:612–613; emphasis original).

Dickens's embodied, immersive mode of production may be readily explained by reference to twenty-first-century models of augmented reality and speedily moving images; yet in some of his own descriptive passages he can only fall back upon the visual technology of his day. There is something of the cyborg about his description of himself as "a sort of capitally prepared and highly sensitive photographic plate" absorbing images during his perambulations (Letters 8:669; see also Litvack 2017, p. 98). Yet Dickens's choice of the photography metaphor fails to capture the synaesthetic quality, with multiple modalities involved, in Dickens's walking experience and in the fiction and journalism that result from it. It also fails to capture the sense of movement that walking necessitates. Perhaps a better idea of what he absorbs from perambulation is conveyed in his description of London as a "magic lantern" (*Letters* 6:412); this form of popular entertainment was not limited to static images: the operator could give the impression of movement by manipulating a "slipping-glass" alongside a fixed slide (see Marsh 2009). Dickens uses another moving image technology to describe walking in the French capital:

> I have been seeing Paris – wandering into Hospitals, Prisons, Dead-houses, Operas, Theatres, Concert Rooms, Burial-grounds, Palaces, and Wine shops. In my unoccupied fortnight of each month, every description of gaudy and ghastly sight has been passing before me in a rapid Panorama. (*Letters* 5:19)

This form of popular entertainment (see Plunkett 2013) fascinated Dickens, who conceived of a panoramic enthusiast, Mr Booley, the "roving spirit" who visits Australia, New Zealand, the United States, Egypt, India and the Arctic – all by means of frequenting the panoramas on display in London. The author emphasises the innovations in visual technology which facilitate Booley's expanded knowledge of the world:

> 'It is very gratifying to me,' said he, 'to have seen so much at my time of life, and to have acquired a knowledge of the countries I have visited, which I could not have derived from books alone. When I was a boy, such travelling would have been impossible, as the gigantic-moving-panorama or diorama mode of conveyance, which I have principally adopted (all my modes of conveyance have been pictorial), had then not been attempted. It is a delightful characteristic of these times, that new and cheap means are continually being devised, for conveying the results of actual experience, to those who are unable to obtain such experiences for themselves; and to bring them within the reach of the people. ([Dickens] 1850, p. 77)

This piece, entitled "Some Account of an Extraordinary Traveller," offers something akin to modern-day virtual reality (VR) experiences – a phenomenon in which UE is at the cutting edge. 360° video is becoming an established part of Urbexers' documentation of their exploits; these uploads, available on YouTube and elsewhere, allow viewers with VR glasses (such as the Oculus Rift or Oculus Go) and a compatible mobile phone to appreciate an entire UE expedition from every possible angle and elevation, as the participants push themselves to the edge (see HK Urbex 2015; Halloran 2016).

In considering UE in relation to Dickens, it is important to note that the Urbex view of the city as a playground for immersive exploration and a space for "hacking" (with all of the humour, playfulness and radical resonance of that term) is, as noted above, part of the subculture's framework of ideas. Many digital games draw upon Urban Exploration and a cyberpunk post-apocalyptic aesthetic (see Walker-Emig 2018; Pondsmith 1990, 2020). The Urbexers' notion of play is to take it seriously, and to see it as a form of political radicalism (see Garrett 2014a, p. 89). Aside from its playful effects, what brings UE into an intriguing relationship with Dickens is energy and embodiment, and the channelling and experiencing of heightened and intense emotion through the exertion of the body. Kindynis comments on the guiding of powerful, instinctive feelings, such as fear, while immersed in daring and unusual encounters with the city:

> The corporeal sensations, physical challenges and affective-atmospheric impressions … encountered within off-limits spaces are central to practitioners' experiences of, and reasons for engaging in, recreational trespass. Immersion in the city's secret and surreal sensescapes; revering and revelling in the uncanny ambience and awe evoked by cavernous subterranean chambers; and relishing the giddy 'fluttery' feeling in one's stomach. (2017, p. 985)

Urbexers use their bodies to interact with the landscape; their activity also allows for experiencing their bodies anew. Kindynis captures this feeling:

> Certainly, for myself and many of those who I have trespassed with, a significant part of the attraction to this form of voluntary risk-taking is that our experiences in off-limits spaces often feel 'much more real than everyday existence.' (2017, p. 986)

It could be argued that what urban explorers are attempting to shape is a kind of "augmented" reality, or a re-coding of it, in viewing the physical city as a playground to explore (see Kindynis 2017, p. 986). They "overlay" the controlled and often off-limits physical environment in which one lives and works with an enchantment or enhancement that perceives physical structures such as skyscrapers as mountains to climb, or underground or derelict urban spaces as adventurous caves to be explored.

The sheer energy and exertion of the Uncommercial Traveller's walking out of London to Kent elevates the power of Dickens's experience of "augmented reality," and, like the Urbexers, the overwhelming urge is to start climbing mountains:

> I could not disembarrass myself of the idea that I had to climb those heights and banks of clouds, and that there was an Alpine Convent somewhere behind the sun, where I was going to breakfast. This sleepy notion was so much stronger than such substantial objects as villages and haystacks, that, after the sun was up and bright, and when I was sufficiently awake to have a sense of pleasure in the prospect, I still occasionally caught myself

looking about for wooden arms to point the right track up the mountain. ([Dickens] 26 May 1860, p. 156)

Urbexers freely admit to nurturing the sensibility of the child, in their attempt to re-code the city as an adventure playground for exploration; in "Gone Astray" such elements as the preponderance of fairy tale in Dickens's childhood reading, and the intense quality of the child's view of the world (including the emotions that buoy up the young Dickens and drive him from pillar to post), pick up on the idea of enchantment about the city; thus for the author this is a view of the metropolis that is more real, more dominant than everyday reality. The child, like the Urbexer, must improvise: he must act upon a flood or rush of emotion. He moves, as Dickens writes, from hope – "my heart began to beat with hope that the Lord Mayor ... would look out of an upper window" – to fear: "'Cut away, you sir!' which frightened me so" ([Dickens] 1853, p. 555); thus he is propelled from one intense emotion to another, from one place to another and from one adventure to another. It should be noted that the very structure and (at times) sensational tone of Dickens's writing exudes embodied creativity, intense energy and vitality. The sheer narrative intensity and drive, his complex sentences with their many clauses and habitual poetic examples of anaphora: such techniques point to Dickens's pen running away with itself, powered by the author's walking exertions and accelerated metabolism. An example of this tendency occurs in chapter 10 of *Oliver Twist*:

> 'Stop thief! Stop thief!' There was magic in the sound. The tradesman leaves his counter, and the carman his waggon; the butcher throws down his tray, the baker his basket, the milkman his pail, the errand-boy his parcels, the school-boy his marbles, the paviour his pick-axe, the child his battledore. Away they run, [...] knocking down the passengers as they turn the corners, rousing up the dogs, and astonishing the fowls: and streets, squares, and courts re-echo with the sound.
>
> 'Stop thief! Stop thief!' The cry is taken up by a hundred voices, and the crowd accumulate at every turning. Away they fly. (*OT* 10)

The other "play" element worthy of mention in Dickens, and which is also present in the sensibility of Urbexers, involves making oneself vulnerable to dangers both known and unknown, or indeed unimaginable. Throughout "Gone Astray" the young boy contends with a lurking undercurrent of fear, which is mostly repressed, but occasionally bursts out in fits of weeping. The intense emotion of being close to tears, and fearfully "astray" in a crowded city, often expresses itself in a wide openness, and an almost perverse joy, in confronting the magnitude and fearsomeness of the city. In front of Temple Bar, the awestruck Dickens states: "it took me half-an-hour to stare at it, and I left it unfinished even then." There is also a tendency to cling on determinedly to delusions in the face of formidable obstacles: "It made me tremble all over to think of the possibility of my good fortune"; here the trembling is evidence of how hopes and imagination hold out against adversity ([Dickens] 1853, pp. 554, 556). This idea of being perversely and joyfully open to all eventualities, due mostly to emotional and physical exertion and exhaustion, and the resulting childlike powerlessness in relation to urban life and its dangers, is one that is wholly embraced and even fetishised in Urban Exploration; Kindynis observes:

> The attraction to such places cannot be separated from the risky – and, it goes without saying, *embodied* – practice of accessing them illicitly and illegally: an intoxicating cocktail of materiality, corporeality, atmosphere and affect; sweat, pigeon shit and concrete dust; the rushing lights of passing trains; echoes reverberating through subterranean tunnel networks; and the imminent threat of arrest, injury or death. Only through their physical, embodied occupation are forgotten and forbidden spaces recoded as realms of adventure and imagination. (2017, p. 986; emphasis original)

The idea of entering a place illegally and illicitly, of experiencing dust and sweat – the messy materiality of a space – is fully present in Dickens's "Uncommercial Traveller" piece that was later retitled "Night Walks," when he gains entry to the Royal Victoria Theatre:

> In one of my night walks, as the church steeples were shaking the March wind and rain with the strokes of Four, I passed the outer boundary of one of these great deserts and entered it ... I groped my well-known way to the stage and looked over the orchestra [...] into the void beyond ... A ghost of a watchman carrying a faint corpse-candle, haunted the upper gallery and flitted away ... my sight lost itself in a gloomy vault ... methought I felt much as a diver might, at the bottom of the sea. ([Dickens] 21 July 1860, p. 349)

Here the Uncommercial is indulging in recreational trespass, and, like the Urbexers, he enjoys the cloak of night, which transforms buildings into dark, impressive and frightening monoliths. Also, like his twenty-first-century inheritors, he masters space: he freely utilises strange perspectives and either expands or shrinks scale in a phrase or moment; hence, looking over the edge of the stage is a case of looking into an "abyss." After rapidly shifting focus to the ghostly light in the upper gallery, he follows with an elevated perspective across the whole of the dark theatre, which resembles the diver's fathomless and surreal experience of the seabed.

Urbexers also attempt to master space. By voluntarily taking death-defying risks, and pushing their bodies to the limit to overcome spatial barriers, they re-exert control over a reality they view as banal. For them, the cyberpunk urban norm is overly determined, inhuman and, paradoxically, precarious; Hayward notes:

> Importantly, the ostensibly reckless and irrational activities of recreational trespassers – hanging from crane jibs, running down metro tunnels and exploring storm relief drains – can, according to this framework, be understood as 'an attempt to achieve a semblance of control within ontologically insecure social worlds'. (2002, p. 86)

The need for the urban explorer to revel in a situation that affords an abnormal potential for personal injury or death is both puzzling and fascinating. Garrett's account of urban explorer "Dan" is representative of this motivation:

> After balancing for a photograph on a girder in an icy wet wind atop London's Heron Tower at 1 a.m. with a deadly two-hundred-metre drop below him, Dan wrote on his blog: 'Sometimes I just desire the edge. It's not about adrenaline or ego or any of that bullshit; it just happens, as if drawn by the reins held by some deeper level of consciousness'. (Garrett 2014a, p. 89)

The Urbexer describes the phenomenon of finding himself at the edge (of a precarious precipice), as if his body simply takes him there, without the intervention of a rational procedure. The body reacts to what the he calls "desire" – or perhaps it is closer to "addiction," as if the body were an extension of, and identical to, what "Dan" calls a "deeper level of consciousness." There is no mind/body dichotomy, and an intense feeling, or desire, inspires the body's risky movement towards the edge. Dickens's version of this activity – in an adaptation of a description applied to Sydney Carton (*TTC* 2:13) – would be: "his feet became animated by an intention, and, in the working out of that intention, they took him to the edge."

This notion of intentionally creating a state of affairs in which one mindfully contemplates a confrontation with death is crystallised in the moment when Urbexers arrive at the top of a skyscraper or a crane, or run along a railway or tube line when they know a train is approaching. Urban explorers describe how they cannot help but make their way to a dangerous height, risking their lives, desiring the edge. This moment is so important, yet so ephemeral and elusive, that Urbexers often record the event on devices and upload the images, just to provide themselves and their peers with evidence that they were really there. The descriptors they use when confronting these dangers include "intoxicating"; a "high," a "drug" or "desire." This contingent temporal fragment represents a coming together, an opening up, and even a conquering of time and space.

The role of emotions in Urban Exploration – the predominance of fear, and the conquering of it – is difficult to assess accurately. Floods of adrenaline produce a rush which Urbexers seem to manipulate into a positive, joyful mental attitude and a balanced approach, thus facilitating their attacking and completing their physical tasks. The idea is that the city is a huge game to be played. Adrenaline produces a numbing effect concerning the stakes involved at the crucial moment of danger; this allows Urbexers to traverse dangerous gaps, and psychologically reduce scale, height and distance through physical prowess and a ludic mental attitude. In other words, adrenaline works as an obscurer of the true scale of the heights, depths or distances to be traversed. Kindynis describes this unique state:

> The giddy 'fluttery' feeling in one's stomach that comes with standing on the edge of a skyscraper: these experiences emerge at the intersection of bodies and spaces – or, more precisely, bodies 'out of place' … In my own experience, the visceral thrill of a night of trespassing would reverberate for days afterwards: the following morning, I could sometimes still feel the residual sensation of my skin tingling from the previous nights' rushing adrenaline. (2017, p. 985)

On the face of it, the experience comes close to a version of the Kantian notion of the Sublime: a state in which imagination, so overwhelmed by the scale of the incredible vision before it, cannot adequately encompass it. This "failure" of imagination causes the subject to experience pain/terror/horror; but in reason's resolution of this, a feeling of overwhelming pleasure ensues (Kant 1951, pp. 82–181).

Dickens depicts his own version of the urban sublime in describing rail travel in "A Flight." The experience he maps there comes close to this Urbexer's experience of embodied risk coupled with a strange euphoria or pleasure. As Wolfgang Schivelbusch argues, the new technology of railway travel was a huge source of anxiety to the Victorians (1980); but Dickens realised that adapting to the confusion, upset and alarm of modern transport, as well as to the noise, confusion and abrupt transitions characteristic of the modern city, could sometimes generate pleasure (see Benjamin 1985, pp. 83–107, 162–196, 197–210; Piggott 2012, 87–142). As he notes in "The Last Cab-driver and the First Omnibus Cad" from *Sketches by Boz*, while crashes are numerous, "in these days of the derangement of the nervous system … people are content to pay handsomely for excitement" (Dickens 1995, p. 172).

In "A Flight" Dickens describes how the overwhelming power of steam and steel entirely disrupts time and space, thus producing fascinating effects upon the body. He notes, for example, "I wonder why it is that when I shut my eyes in a tunnel I begin to feel as if I were going at an Express pace the other way?" He sets up the idea of what a wonder it is to not exert any effort at all, yet paradoxically to be travelling with incredible speed:

> 'there's no hurry.' No hurry! And a Flight to Paris in eleven hours! … I can fly with the South Eastern, more lazily, at all events, than in the upper air. I have but to sit here thinking as idly as I please, and be whisked away … and away I go. ([Dickens] 1851, pp. 530, 529)

Dickens's language evokes the physical – both aural and perceptual – rhythms of railway travel. In one passage, he gradually reduces phrase length, eventually clipping his material to a two-word phrase, delineating the rapid shortening of the span of a perception and the mental processing of it, hence simultaneously evoking the growing speed of the train. This experience is a mixture of the exciting, the overwhelming, the anxious and the pleasurable:

> Whirr! The little streets of new brick and red tile, with here and there a flagstaff growing like a tall weed out of the scarlet beans, and, everywhere, plenty of open sewer and ditch for the promotion of the public health, have been fired off in a volley. Whizz! Dustheaps, market-gardens, and waste grounds. Rattle! New Cross Station. Shock! There we were at Croydon. Bur-r-r-r! The tunnel. (1851, p. 530)

Here Dickens seems to anticipate the film *Night Mail* (1936), which features the text of W.H. Auden's poem, and attempts to recreate the experience of rail travel, through the use of regular and syncopated rhythms. While Dickens does not wish to achieve such a regular metrical pattern, he does depict speed through a quickening pulsion, which has a visceral effect. The onomatopoeic series of sounds he introduces recalls the noises at a fairground: "Whirr!" "Whizz!" "Rattle!" "Shock!" "Bur-r-r-r!" all hint at the physically pleasurable instability and danger of the technology, and the body's fragility and utter powerlessness before it; yet, Dickens observes, "There is a dreamy pleasure in this flying. I wonder where it was, and when it was, that we exploded, blew into space somehow." Along with the spatiotemporal disorientation there exists a potency in the image of the body exploding and being torn to shreds. Another example is the line "Bang! We have let another Station off, and fly away regardless. Everything is flying" (1851, p. 530). These descriptions come very close to the Urbexers' "giddy 'fluttery' feeling" of physical pleasure, described above.

There is a darker, death-wish side to the idea of flying, that converges with the idea of falling and of the body's being obliterated by technology. This is both the ultimate anxiety of impending death and yet, simultaneously, something that might be considered aesthetically beautiful, albeit in a disturbing way. The tragic – perhaps amoral – image entitled "The Falling Man," taken by Associated

Press photographer Richard Drew, of a victim of the 9/11 terror attack on the World Trade Center, comes close to this idea (see "Richard Drew" 2011). The death of Carker, who falls under a train when he spots the man from whom he is fleeing, merits exploration in relation to these ideas; Dickens writes:

> In the quick unsteadiness of the surprise, he staggered, and slipped on to the road below him. But recovering his feet immediately, he stepped back a pace or two upon that road, to interpose some wider space between them, and looked at his pursuer, breathing short and quick.
>
> He heard a shout – another – saw the face change from its vindictive passion to a faint sickness and terror – felt the earth tremble – knew in a moment that the rush was come – uttered a shriek – looked round – saw the red eyes, bleared and dim, in the daylight, close upon him – was beaten down, caught up, and whirled away upon a jagged mill, that spun him round and round, and struck him limb from limb, and licked his stream of life up with its fiery heat, and cast his mutilated fragments in the air. (*DS* 55)

The author stages Carker's fall as a rapid-fire series of thoughts and sensations, paralleling the hyper-intensity and rhythm of urban experience, and perhaps the sensation of crisis as one approaches death. The overall tone in representing the ultimate iconic fear – the vulnerable body being chewed up and spat out by industrial machinery – is one of anxiety, resonant in the breathless brevity of the sensations/phrases, and in the vision of the train as a fiery dragon inexorably grinding the body to fragments and devouring it. Yet, like the photographic representation of "The Falling Man," Dickens lingers upon this image of death, raising it to another level. He slows down a concatenation of events into a sequence resembling a stop-motion animation technique, so that it becomes a staccato performance of Carker's fall under the wheels. Each phrase is a simple statement of what occurs next, conveyed with a matter-of-factness that often cuts against the content of the phrase, as in "struck him limb from limb," which increases the anxious feeling of inevitability and the power of the train's destructive forces.

This idea of the art or the stylisation of death in the city is particularly important when considering Urban Exploration, with its dependence upon iconic images of "high stuff" (that is, photographic material from climbs; see 28 Days Later n.d.), "edgework" and sensational moments captured while teetering on the brink of death. At times, Urbex attracts live audiences in the streets down below; they gaze up at a death-defying feat as if spellbound by a high-wire act or other circus performance. The risk of the demise of the performer (see Lyng 1990) is part of the dark underbelly of what Forster called the "attraction of repulsion" (1928, p. 11). Carker's death is relevant to Urbex in two ways: it rehearses the ultimate Urbex catastrophe – "the fall" – here with the victim's anxious mental state culminating in his/her inevitable destruction; it also replicates the Urbex fear of being run down by a train, or buried under steel and brick. Carker's death is thus a fascinating anticipation of these UE "fantasies."

In the more refined and performative versions of Urban Exploration, there is an element of Romantic beauty and aesthetics at play – at least as it is represented in popular culture. The photographs and other footage of "high stuff" often consist of compositions of a breathtaking, panoramic vision (increasingly available in 360° format) of the city seen from an incredible height, with an awestruck observer at the margins, struck dumb and entranced by the immensity and immediacy of it all. There is a poetic and even a transcendent quality to some of the Urbexers' climactic moments. This is clearly evident, for example, in the film *Man on Wire*, which focused upon one of the earliest and most high-profile cases of urban trespass, featuring the incredible tightrope walker Phillippe Petit (Chinn & Marsh 2008). He performed stunts 1,780 feet above ground, on a 200-ft-long tightrope erected between the World Trade Center's twin towers, in August 1974; his feat was entirely unauthorised, and was treated as criminal trespass. He said of his adventure, "I had a sense of dancing on top of the world. I had a sense of having a communion with the city of New York ... I had a sense of having stepped in otherworldly matters." His colleagues called his performance on the wire "profound" and "magical," using terms referring to the act's resonant symbolism and metaphoric possibilities, as well as to Petit's physical skills, concentration and ability to deal with fear. Petit called himself a "poet conquering beautiful stages." He exuded a sense of the experience's being metaphysical, or even sacred or ineffable, even though his euphoria also resembles, in psychological terms, a hyper-manic episode or a drug-induced "high." He was, he claimed: "living more than 1000 per cent" while he walked on the rope, adding: "I was happy, happy, happy"; he remembered thinking before he stepped out on the wire: "It was impossible. If I die, what a beautiful death. It is fate now. This is probably the end of my life. Death is very close. Life should be lived on the edge" (Chinn & Marsh 2008).

The gothic aspect of dicing with death in the city is widely evident in Dickens's fictional cities, as is a perverse obsession with or attraction to it. A suggestive death in this regard is the accidental hanging of Bill Sikes who, to defy the baying mob, climbs high up onto a roof and, haunted by the eyes of the lover he murdered, loses his balance, and in the process wraps a noose round his own neck. As Petit might have done had he fallen, Sikes gets caught in his own equipment – an unimaginably grotesque event, luridly described by Dickens (*OT* 50). The mob's attraction to watching events high up, and their anticipation that things could go wrong, is present both in Petit's display and in the dramatic scene from *Oliver Twist*. In the case of Sikes, Dickens suggests that there is an extra dimension, an ethical one, to his fall: if one is immoral or has committed an evil act, he is off balance, and will surely plummet.

Dickens's immersion in the city may not amount to climbing buildings and transgressing transport systems, but there are dramatic narrative sweeps and angles, as well as emotions and bodily exertions and an attraction to high perspectives in his writings that are relevant to this discussion. Like the Urbexers, Dickens is intent upon viewing the city, and representing it, from every possible, enchanting angle. In his scheme for *Household Words*, he imagines

> a certain SHADOW, which may go into any place, by sunlight, moonlight, starlight, firelight, candlelight, and be in all homes, and all nooks and corners, and supposed to be cognisant of everything, and go everywhere without the least difficulty. (*Letters* 5:622)

Here he describes his editorial perspective on urban life and politics as one that takes him everywhere, invading space with ease at every level. While a huge physical effort is required for all UE activities, the idea that one can go "everywhere without the least difficulty" (or at least should be allowed to do so legally) is undoubtedly a sensibility, an ideal, that Urbexers share with Dickens. The panoptic perspective that Dickens cites is undoubtedly that of the investigative journalist, burrowing into every area of life at street level and behind closed doors; it also alludes to the perspective of Asmodeus, who offers a Godlike aerial view of the nineteenth-century city (Murais & Thornton 2017, p. 57; see also *DS* 47). Hence if, like the urban explorers, Dickens sometimes wants to get beyond street level and see things from above, one can easily find this in his narratives, as in the opening chapter of *Bleak House*, where he depicts "Chance people on the bridges peeping over the parapets into a nether sky of fog, with fog all round them, as if they were in a balloon, and hanging in the misty clouds" (*BH* 1). There is also the beautiful, panoramic scene in *A Christmas Carol*, where Scrooge's horizons are literally expanded by the Ghost of Christmas present, as he flies him to witness how workers – miners, lighthouse keepers and sailors braving thunderous waves – are folk with far, far lighter hearts than his (*CC* 3).

By examining aspects of Dickens's urban writings through the lens of the ultra-contemporary activity of Urban Exploration, new perspectives may be offered concerning the centrality of space, of movement and of the body within the author's productions. Like the Urbexer, Dickens is intent upon seeing things from an innovative, unique perspective; his narratives take him from street level to the lofty heights in a sweeping phrase. The whole world is open to him, in terms of going anywhere at any time, into areas never before seen or accessed. He breaks down and reconfigures spaces and boundaries in the city, not just for the sake of his own multi-layered experience, or for special, enlightened moments, but also for the sake of intrepid searching for the truth about human experience. While Urbexers are passionate about "discovering dangerous, precarious, incongruous and absurd urban spaces" (Garrett 2014a, p. 16), Dickens too succeeded in negotiating with feeling this complex process of discovery and representation.

References

28 Days Later (n.d.). [Urban Exploration website]. Retrieved from www.28dayslater.co.uk/

Baudelaire, Charles (1996). The Painter of Modern Life. In Lawrence Cahoone (Ed.), *From Modernism to Postmodernism: An Anthology* (pp. 136–144). Oxford: Blackwell.

Beaumont, Matthew (2015). *Nightwalking: A Nocturnal History of London*. London: Verso.

Benjamin, Walter (1985). *Illuminations*. Trans. Harry Zohn. New York: Schocken Books.

Channel 4 Urban Explorers (n.d.). [Urban Exploration videos]. Available from https://www.channel4.com/programmes/urban-explorers

Chesterton, G.K. (1917). *Charles Dickens* London: Methuen & Co.

Chinn, Simon (Producer), & Marsh, James (Director). (2008). *Man on Wire* [Motion Picture]. USA: Magnolia Pictures.

Cooper, David E. (1990). *Existentialism*. Oxford: Blackwell.

[Dickens, Charles] (1850, 20 April). Some Account of an Extraordinary Traveller. *Household Words*, 1, 73–77.

[Dickens, Charles] (1851, 30 August). A Flight. *Household Words*, 3, 529–533.

[Dickens, Charles] (1853, 13 August). Gone Astray. *Household Words*, 7, 553–557.

[Dickens, Charles] (1860, 26 May). The Uncommercial Traveller. *All the Year Round*, 3, 155–159.

[Dickens, Charles] (1860, 21 July). The Uncommercial Traveller. *All the Year Round*, 3, 348–352.

Dickens, Charles (1995). *Sketches by Boz*. Ed. Dennis Walder. London: Penguin.

Dickens, Charles, Jr (1934). Reminiscences of My Father. *Windsor Magazine*, 79 (Christmas Supplement), 7–31.

Dolby, George (1887). *Charles Dickens as I Knew Him: The Story of the Reading Tours in Great Britain and America (1866–1870)*. London: T. Fisher Unwin.

EA Digital Illusions CE (Creator) (2008–2012). *Mirror's Edge* [Action adventure video game]. Redwood City, CA: Electronic Arts.

Forster, John (1928). *The Life of Charles Dickens*. Ed. J.W.T. Ley. London: Cecil Palmer.

Fowler, Adam, Roger, Alexander, & Vermeij, Obbe (Creators) (2008). *Grand Theft Auto IV* [Action adventure video game]. New York: Rockstar Games.

Fowler, Adam, Roger, Alexander, & Vermeij, Obbe (Creators) (2013). *Grand Theft Auto V*. [Action adventure video game]. New York: Rockstar Games.

Garrett, Bradley L. (2014a). *Explore Everything: Place-Hacking the City*. London: Verso.

Garrett, Bradley L. (2014b). Undertaking Recreational Trespass: Urban Exploration and Infiltration. *Transactions of the Institute of British Geographers*, 39(1), 1–13.

Garrett, Bradley L. (2014c). *Subterranean London: Cracking the Capital*. Munich: Prestel.

Garrett, Bradley L. (2017, 25 July). These Squares Are Our Squares: Be Angry about the Privatization of Public Space. *The Guardian*. Retrieved from https://www.theguardian.com/cities/2017/jul/25/squares-angry-privatisation-public-space

Garrett, Bradley L., Moss, Alexander, & Cadman, Scott (2016). *London Rising: Illicit Photos from the City's Heights*. Munich: Prestel.

General Post Office (Producer), Watt, Harry, & Wright, Basil (Directors) (1936). *Night Mail*. UK: Associated British Film.

Halloran, Corinna (2016). Feel Like You're on the Ledge of a 100m Building [Virtual Reality video]. Red Bull videos. Retrieved from https://www.redbull.com/gb-en/360-video-red-bull-tv-urbex

Hayward, Keith J. (2002). The Vilification and Pleasures of Youthful Transgression. In John Muncie, Gordon Hughes & Eugene McLaughlin (Eds.), *Youth Justice: Critical Readings* (pp. 80–94). London: Sage.

Heath, Joseph, & Potter, Andrew (2005). *The Rebel Sell: How the Counterculture Became Consumer Culture*. Chichester: Capstone.

Heidegger, Martin (1993). The Origin of the Work of Art. *Basic Writings: Martin Heidegger* (pp. 83–140). Ed. David Krell. London: Routledge.

HK Urbex (n.d.). [Hong Kong Urban Exploration website]. Retrieved from https://www.facebook.com/hkurbex/

HK Urbex (2015). 360° Virtual Reality Urban Exploration [Virtual Reality video]. Retrieved from https://www.youtube.com/watch?v=VpISqa4cSxk

Jordan, Justine (2011, 14 May). A Life in Writing: China Miéville. *The Guardian*. Retrieved from https://www.theguardian.com/books/2011/may/14/china-mieville-life-writing-genre

Kant, Immanuel (1951). *The Critique of Judgment*. Trans J.H. Bernard. New York: Hafner Publishing.

Kindynis, Theo (2017). Urban Exploration: From Subterranea to Spectacle. *British Journal of Criminology*, 57(4), 982–1001.

Lindsay, Stewart (2010). Urban Exploration and the Gothesization of Reality. University of Stirling Gothic blog. Retrieved from www.gothic.stir.ac.uk/blog/urban-exploration-and-the-gothesization-of-reality/

Litvack, Leon (2007). *Dickens's Dream* and the Conception of Character. *Dickensian*, 103, 5–36.

Litvack, Leon (2017). Dickens Posing for Posterity: The Photographs of Herbert Watkins. *Dickens Quarterly*, 34(2), 96–158.

Lyng, Stephen (1990). Edgework: A Social Psychological Analysis of Voluntary Risk Taking. *American Journal of Sociology*, 95(4), 851–856.

Macfarlane, Robert (2013, 20 September). The Strange World of Urban Exploration. *The Guardian*. Retrieved from https://www.theguardian.com/books/2013/sep/20/urban-exploration-robert-macfarlane-bradley-garrett

Marsh, Joss (2009). Dickensian "Dissolving Views": The Magic Lantern, Visual Story-Telling, and the Victorian Technological Imagination. *Comparative Critical Studies*, 6(3), 333–346.

Miéville, China (2009). *The City and the City*. London: Pan Books.

Moss, Stephen (2016, 10 November). Politics, Thrills or Social Media: What Drives the New Breed of Urban Explorers? *The Guardian*. Retrieved from https://www.theguardian.com/cities/2016/nov/10/urbex-politics-thrills-social-media-new-breed-urban-explorer

Murais, Estelle, & Sara Thornton (Eds.) (2017). *Dickens and the Virtual City: Urban Perception and the Production of Social Space*. London: Palgrave Macmillan.

Nomura, Tatsuo (Creator) (2013). *Ingress* [Location-based, augmented reality mobile "exergame"]. San Francisco, CA: Niantic.

Nomura, Tatsuo (Creator) (2016). *Pokémon Go* [Augmented reality mobile game]. San Francisco, CA: Niantic.

Piggott, Gillian (2012). *Dickens and Benjamin: Moments of Revelation, Fragments of Modernity*. Farnham: Ashgate.

Plunkett, John (2013). Moving Panoramas c. 1800 to 1840: The Spaces of Nineteenth-Century Picture-Going. *19: Interdisciplinary Studies in the Long Nineteenth Century*, 17. Retrieved from https://www.19.bbk.ac.uk/articles/10.16995/ntn.674/

Pondsmith, Mike (Creator) (1990). *Cyberpunk 2020* [Role-playing video game]. Renton, WA: R. Talsorian Games.

Pondsmith, Mike (Creator) (2020). *Cyberpunk 2077* [Role-playing video game]. Warsaw: CD Projekt Red.

Richard Drew (2011, 5 September). [Video interview]. *The Telegraph*. Retrieved from https://www.youtube.com/watch?v=allrsaspucA

Schivelbusch, Wolfgang (1980). *The Railway Journey: Trains and Travel in the Nineteenth Century*. Trans. Anselm Hollo. Oxford: Blackwell.

Self, Will (2014, 25 April). Will Self: Give the Freedom of the City to Our Urban Explorers. *Evening Standard*. Retrieved from https://www.standard.co.uk/comment/will-self-give-thefreedom-of-the-city-to-our-urban-explorers-9286780.html

Shenker, Jack (2017, 24 July). Revealed: The Insidious Creep of Pseudo-Public Space in London. *The Guardian*. Retrieved from https://www.theguardian.com/cities/2017/jul/24/revealed-pseudo-public-space-pops-london-investigation-map

Shenker, Jack (2017, 25 July). Corbyn Joins Calls to Reclaim Pseudo-Public Space from Corporate Owners. *The Guardian*. Retrieved from https://www.theguardian.com/cities/2017/jul/25/corbyn-joins-calls-reclaim-uk-public-space-from-corporate-owners

Urbex (2013). [Online adventure game]. Irvine, CA: Armor Games.

Walker-Emig, Paul (2018, 16 October). Neon and Corporate Dystopias: Why Does Cyberpunk Refuse to Move on? *The Guardian*. Retrieved from https://www.theguardian.com/games/2018/oct/16/neon-corporate-dystopias-why-does-cyberpunk-refuse-move-on

Wilson, Michael G., Broccoli, Barbara (Producers), & Campbell, Martin (Director) (2006). *Casino Royale* [Motion Picture]. USA: Columbia Pictures.

Wilson, Michael G., Broccoli, Barbara (Producers), & Mendes, Sam (Director) (2012). *Skyfall* [Motion Picture]. USA: Columbia Pictures.

11

Dickens as Icon and Antonomasia in *Assassin's Creed*: Syndicate

Francesca Orestano

Icon and antonomasia – two key words, denoting "image" and "name" – point to the figural and the verbal, but concentrated to a zero-degree of signification, because the object therein ensconced is powerful enough to radiate a whole panorama of suggestions, and a polyphony of different voices. In the case of the video game at the centre of this essay, *Assassin's Creed: Syndicate*, these suggestions relate to a twenty-first-century response to, and appropriation of, Dickens's image and work, as well as to contemporary re- and de-constructions of his times and culture. The interaction with a literary text or figure in a ludic context recalls "The Ivanhoe Game," which arose out of a dissatisfaction with the limitations inherent in received forms of interpretation; it consists of interventions, changes, additions and commentaries in the field of discourse of an imaginative work like Walter Scott's romance *Ivanhoe*. In the game (originally played by way of email exchange), the text is imagined as a field of interrelated textual, visual, cultural and critical artefacts; players construct a digital writing space, in which every "move" involves the production of text as a performative act of interpretation. The aim of the creators was to develop a more imaginative critical methodology: a form closer in spirit and method to original works of poetry and literature (McGann & Drucker 2003; Kingsley 2014). *Assassin's Creed: Syndicate* also involves such interventions by the players, and, as an interactive video game, chimes with the manifold cultural practices described as neo-Victorian discourse. These creative engagements in a dynamic space also serve to reinforce the Dickensian core, and enhance the reception of historical and archival material.

Icon and antonomasia thus jointly thrive upon the peculiar concentration of meaning that concerns cultural stereotypes and their embedded load of connected notions. The name "Charles Dickens" functions as a verbal synecdoche; yet at a higher level of concentration and by sheer antonomasia, it suggests the entire Victorian cultural milieu generated by Dickensian discourse, and is endowed with

Reading Dickens Differently, First Edition. Edited by Leon Litvack and Nathalie Vanfasse.
© 2020 John Wiley & Sons Ltd. Published 2020 by John Wiley & Sons Ltd.

all the shades of darkness and light, despair and hope, poverty and wealth that we are wont to attach to it. Consider the opening line of *A Tale of Two Cities*: "It was the best of times, it was the worst of times" (*TTC* 1:1): a simple image and a name are charged with such energy as to empower manifold associations about an age that is no more, about a writer whose voice we cannot hear, and whose face we can only trace in the photographs in which he is posing for posterity (Litvack 2017).

The iconic focus in *Assassin's Creed: Syndicate* is Dickens's face; his physical presence is familiar from many contemporary visual images. The portrait of the great Victorian writer is everywhere recognisable today, and is institutionalised by such images as that which appeared on British £10 banknotes between 1993 and 2003 (John 2010, pp. 240–241). The celebrations of the bicentenary of the author's birth in 2012 facilitated the global dissemination of the portrait of a young Dickens, through an image taken from the "Nickleby" portrait by Daniel Maclise (Litvack 2008, pp. 120–121), and adopted into the logo for "Dickens 2012." In the *Assassin's Creed* video game, Dickens undergoes an ulterior kind of resuscitation that is typical of mass culture and of today's technologically advanced intermediality (Bolter & Grusin 1999).

Movies and neo-Victorian novels have ferried the cultural response and the discourse about Dickens – whether visual or verbal – towards the present day. Despite being grounded on the reduction, adaptation and abridgement of his actual texts, of his letters, of the genuine primary documents fostering scholarly research and achievement, the result, in cultural terms, amounts to enlargement, expansion and dissemination. For instance, the film *The Invisible Woman* (2013, directed by Ralph Fiennes and based on the biography of Ellen Ternan; see Tomalin 1990) turns Dickens (who is played by Fiennes) into a cinema character, and his complex and crowded biography is transformed into script and action. The specific Victorian setting – a realistically detailed, largely urban environment – furnishes the many colours of a world and age that are labelled "Dickensian." Adaptations and other subsequent texts based on Dickens's originals expand creatively on the rich documentary material offered by the Victorian author's correspondence and creative work; a case in point is the weighty and magnificently baroque *Drood, A Novel* (Simmons 2009). Neo-Victorian fiction, with its manifold discourses, allows contemporary readers to "meet" Dickens in person, and to experience the character of his age with a mass of substantial – archival – evidence. But it requires the storm of neo-Victorian fashion, the modern format of a video game, and the highly sophisticated realistic standard of its realisation, to resuscitate Dickens by means of the meagre, scanty evidence provided by icon and antonomasia – that is, just a face and a name.

Dickens's resuscitation takes place within an episode of *Assassin's Creed* set in 1868 – that is, two years before the author's death, and a year that saw him frequently engaged with public readings, despite his declining health, and committed to his second journey to the United States (Slater 2009, pp. 561–584). In the same month as the launch in 2015, Ubisoft held an event at Milan State

University in Italy; it was attended by hundreds, young and old, students and members of the public, most enthusiastic fans of the game. In addition to the previews of the video game, Ubisoft offered cards, posters and many other collectible items. Such an event represents a shifting ground, where a storyline metamorphoses into a game, gadgets and collectibles. The poster for the event advertised "a plunge into the past, to discover the mysteries of Victorian London" (or, in the original Italian, "Un tuffo nel passato, per scoprire i misteri della Londra Vittoriana").

The game features episodes that provide players with a series of adventures set in different centuries and countries; it stages the fight for global power between two secret societies: the Knights Templar and the Assassins. The story opens in 2012 when Abstergo Industries (the modern version of the ancient Knights Templar) kidnaps Desmond Miles, who descends from the Assassins' lineage, in order to penetrate his ancestral memory through a machine called the Animus. Abstergo wants to locate the "Pieces of Eden" – that is, artefacts, tokens or talismans that could allow them to rule over humankind. Desmond has on his side a group of allies: the modern-day Assassins. The episodes of the game stage the different journeys into the past, and feature the various conspiracies and battles between the evil Knights Templar and the good Assassins (see Assassin's Creed n.d. [promotional website]). In the Victorian episode, where Dickens is resuscitated, the "good" heroes are Jacob Frye and his sister Evie (Figure 11.1). These twins are a new departure for the series; their presence allows players to identify with different gender identities and roles; Jacob is headstrong, while Evie is tactical. Here the characteristics are indeed strategic: the one who is more frequently engaged in fights is Jacob, who was raised by Assassins. Like the heroes of antiquity, Jacob is equipped with a special suite of weapons: a kukri (the Nepalese blade), hallucinogenic darts and a rope launcher, which allows him to fire a bolt into the distance and shoot up to the top of a building or even create a zip line, thus facilitating the jumping between rooftops. The style of their outfits could be described as neo-gothic: their black leather coats, hoods, boots and gloves shield them like dark armour. The twins are protagonists in dangerous encounters with enemy gangs. Their allies are the gang of the Rooks; their foes are the Templars. Jacob and Evie are followed and ambushed in the darkest corners of London; they are involved in perilous chases at breakneck speed, and are shown skipping among rooftops and running across spooky, derelict settings haunted by devils and ghosts. This infusion of spectacular action allows players to use the joystick and enter the game in search of the magic Pieces of Eden, side by side with the two heroes.

The episode set in Victorian London offers a fascinating representation of the capital that is at once detailed, recognisable, picturesque and fascinating (Figure 11.2). Under a dramatic sky, the London of the game is a city of magnificent buildings and rotten rookeries, slums and old pubs, gothic railway stations, bridges and barges floating on the dark stream of the Thames; indeed, it is a

Figure 11.1 The Twins Jacob and Evie Frye, from *Assassin's Creed: Syndicate*. © Ubisoft Entertainment. All rights reserved. Assassin's Creed, Ubisoft and the Ubisoft logo are trademarks of Ubisoft Entertainment in the U.S. and/or other countries.

Figure 11.2 Thames River prospect, at Westminster Pier, from *Assassin's Creed: Syndicate*. © Ubisoft Entertainment. All rights reserved.

veritable "Victorian Babylon" (Nead 2000). A trailer for the Victorian episode whets the appetite of potential purchasers/players by presenting a vivid image of London, at once foggy, dark and roaring but also powerfully mechanised with modern technology (Assassin's Creed Syndicate (n.d.) [video trailer]); this brief taster also emphasises the moral overtones connected with the game: the good characters fight on behalf of the poor and the destitute, and against brutal exploitation and greedy capitalism.

Dickensians will wonder about the active role taken by the persona of the author in this episode, especially given that in the year 1868 he spent a few months in the United States, and when in England he was often staying at Gad's Hill, his country home in Kent. The author's health was rapidly declining, and the fatigue of the "Farewell" series of public readings was immense (Slater 2009, pp. 589–599). Yet despite these marks of increasing debilitation, he was still a figure so relevant, so topical, so central to the notion of the adjective "Victorian," and to the image of the nation's capital, that to evoke Dickens and to ensconce his living presence within the video game adds a strong injection of realism to a platform that claims to offer its players an extremely reliable reconstruction of the past, as the background to the Assassins' adventures (see Notre Dame 2019).

To ensure historical verisimilitude, Ubisoft employed the designer Jean-Vincent Roy, a military historian and expert in military maps. In the Milan Masterclass referred to above, Roy described the process that led to his impressive reconstruction of Victorian London; he explained that they had used nearly 40 different maps of London that were produced between 1830 and 1870. The maps were the basis of an accurate rendering of the streets and squares, of the monuments, prominent buildings, houses, bridges, yards and other features of the city, which Roy wished to evoke with the greatest precision, from all perspectives, including from high elevation (Figure 11.3). Ubisoft designers also used the Gustave Doré engravings from *London: A Pilgrimage* (Jerrold 1872), and some old photographs of the city. Henry Mayhew's *London Labour and The London Poor* (1861–1862) provided images of people of different callings: street-vendors and pedlars, butchers and chimneysweeps, each with his or her specific attire. Lee Jackson's *Dirty Old London* (2015), and his website, *The Victorian Dictionary* (n.d.), provided the software developers with reliable accounts of the material condition of the city, which buttressed the visual evidence of the game. *Assassin's Creed* is further enlivened and historically grounded through the presence of other eminent personages, including Charles Darwin, Florence Nightingale, Karl Marx, Alexander Graham Bell and Queen Victoria herself. Their roles in *Syndicate* are minor, although they are always pitched on the side of the good; indeed, they act as beneficent landmarks in the fields of science, medicine and nursing, political theory and technology. Apart from these cameos, the greater part of the game consists of action, involving running, fighting, skipping across barges on the river, confronting gangs of enemies in bodily combat, chasing enemies at full speed on carts and coaches launched along the perilous crowded thoroughfares of London,

Figure 11.3 Palace of Westminster from high elevation, surveyed by Evie (L), and Jacob (R), from *Assassin's Creed: Syndicate*. © Ubisoft Entertainment. All rights reserved.

and jumping from rooftops. As far as the player's experience goes, there is not much to be derived from reading; but there is much to see, and to enjoy, by actively participating in the adventure. The visual element in such games largely supersedes the verbal plot or even the script, which is left to pit the forces of good against those of evil, the poor against the rich, and heroes against criminals.

Thus *Assassin's Creed: Syndicate* was launched as an historically valuable piece of entertainment, offering authenticity and historical awareness, together with the dramatic action that players enjoy. Such a strategy is not entirely new: in *Dungeons & Dragons* (the best-known fantasy role-playing game, developed in the 1970s) a quest into the past (often the Middle Ages) provides the backbone of the story, which is enhanced through the use of modern weaponry. The game master, who acts as the "author" of the episodes, assigns each player a character, and equips each one with adequate weapons and abilities to deflect the dangers encountered in the game. In addition to these features, multi-sided dice-casting adds the element of unpredictability, as events and encounters are influenced by chance at each stage of the adventure plot.

The game master role in *Assassin's Creed: Syndicate* is occupied by Abstergo Industries, which is behind the entire conspiracy. The character of Desmond Miles (whose memories are accessed in order to locate the Pieces of Eden) provides the script for the different adventures. Characters are defined at this stage – both the good ones, descending from the Assassins, and the evil ones, originating in the Templars. There is little dialogue: the action is accompanied by noises underlying the violence of the combats – the shrill passage of trains, the rolling of the horse-drawn coaches – to heighten the impact of the action; the episodes are often underlined by a dramatic musical score. In this game Dickens can indeed be read differently: as icon, owing to his physical presence in some side episodes, and, through the mechanism of antonomasia, as a figure of speech close to an eponym, and an epithet.

To evoke Dickens as icon is not a new consideration. During his lifetime, paintings, engravings and photographs made him a well-known iconic figure. His features were also familiar as a result of the presence of his effigy in Madame Tussauds Wax Museum, in London, since 1873 (Figure 11.4; see "Whitsuntide" [1873], p. 4). It is interesting that Dickens himself was fascinated by Madame Tussauds. In *The Old Curiosity Shop*, he based the portrayal of Mrs Jarley, the wax salon owner where Little Nell is briefly employed (*OCS* 27), on Madame Marie Tussaud (Bloom 2003, pp. 191–201). In "History in Wax," published in Dickens's *Household Words*, Dudley Costello provided a detailed account of his visit to the

Figure 11.4 Dickens wax figure at Madame Tussauds, London. By kind permission of Merlin Entertainments Group.

attraction, admitting that he was struck by the visible presence of the great men whose statues were on display:

> the greatness of which I had all my life been dreaming, was there in visible presence: not merely sculptured in marble, or pourtrayed [sic] on canvas, but actually wearing the habit in which it lived; a thing to be walked close up to and examined; to be looked at behind and before; to be handled – no, that was a mistake of mine, as I afterwards discovered; to be face to face with, and yet, not altogether to be borne down. ([Costello] 1854, p. 18)

The eerie feeling of being in front of great historical figures, and yet sensing their physical presence as representation, as a make-believe – albeit obtained with the greatest theatrical skill of costume and three-dimensional realism – is what affects us today when confronted with Dickens's bodily presence in *Assassin's Creed: Syndicate*. A comment in "History in Wax" seems relevant to this kind of fiction:

> The truth is, that although a 'plain man in black' may pass muster very well in real life, a man of wax is all the better for a little gilding. The rouged cheek, the glittering eye, the well-arranged hair, which are the universal characteristics of the waxen race, do not harmonise well with simple black and white; they require to be sustained by rich colours, bright ornaments, and flowing draperies. ([Costello] 1854, p. 18)

The passage unmasks the nature of the iconic object, in terms that accord with Jean Baudrillard's *Simulations and Simulacra* (1994). This is exactly the kind of manifestation of simulacra evident not only in Dickens's figure in wax, but in his Ubisoft avatar. At Madame Tussauds the author is indeed wholly recognisable – especially if visitors recall the 1859 portrait by William Powell Frith (now in the Victoria & Albert Museum), and notice that the chair in which he is sitting at Tussauds is modelled on the one in the oil portrait (Litvack 2017, pp. 130–131, 144–146).

Dickens's visual representation in *Assassin's Creed: Syndicate* (Figure 11.5) establishes undeniable claims to being recognised, and recognisable. His clothes are expensive and in fine condition; though slightly on the sombre side, they tell of an affluent middle-class figure. The coat, cravat and shirt are based on the clothes he wore for the photographic session with Benjamin Gurney in New York, in early December 1867; thus the clothes match the year in which the game is set: 1868. The Ubisoft Dickens is endowed with movement, a few changing facial expressions and a voice. While he has the telling greying hair and wrinkles, his teeth are remarkably white and regular, and give the appearance of being prosthetic. Bloom recalls that the authenticity effect generated by wax figures often amounts to a display of inanimate objects closer to corpses than to living creatures (2003, p. 203). Actually the higher the degree of realism achieved in the effigy of Dickens, the stranger the resuscitation of his corpse, with an effect described by John Carey as that of

Figure 11.5 Visual representation of Dickens, from *Assassin's Creed: Syndicate*. © Ubisoft Entertainment. All rights reserved.

Dickens's necropolis (Carey 1979, p. 101); but in the video game Dickens is indeed what we expect him to be: he belongs to the race of simulacra.

In contemporary – eminently visual – culture, Dickens's face is fully and immediately recognisable, insofar as the Dickensian note – that is, the Victorian note – chimes in with the semiosphere in which neo-Victorian movies, gadgets, theme parks and games are also produced. Yet the immediacy of the recognition, the visual "reading" of his features, whilst adding unquestionable glamour to the Victorian episode of the game, does not compensate for the loss of reading his works. The other way of "reading" Dickens today – and especially in the context of a video game – is through the rhetorical device of antonomasia, which uses the name of a famous person, or character (often a hero), to suggest by extension an outstanding and specific quality, a virtue or prerogative that characterises this figure. Antonomasia also points toward a period, a topicality or a cultural context affixed to the very name, which thus becomes an epithet, and insofar as containing a characteristic quality, it propagates such quality to situations or characters defined in the same guise: Hercules, for example, suggests the nature of a strong man; Methuselah is emblematic of old age; Penelope is the image of faithfulness. "Dickens" – not only in video games but also in recent fiction – is the name that replaces, or carries the weight of, the entire Victorian era, of the metropolitan centre of the British Empire, London, and of its streets, river, bridges and slums. Dickens thus epitomises the Victorian way of life; his voice is the articulation of the social issues of the period; his name is almost synonymous with notions of prisons and workhouses, schools, factories and other iconic nineteenth-century institutions.

A good example of the antonomasia effect is to be found in Tahib Khair's neo-Victorian novel *The Thing about Thugs* (2010), in which the novelist is simply evoked as a name, or as a book. This occurs when one of the narrators sits in his grandfather's library "reading about the damp, dark streets of London in Dickens or Collins":

> when I was a teenager ... I slowly unravelled the stories I am threading into a book here, unravelled them in Dickens, Collins, Mayhew, as well as in smudged snippets of paper, a mouldy notebook in Farsi, and many other fragments of text and language that were to follow. (Kahir 2010, pp. 66, 117)

These figures are named in order to imbue the novel with flavour, and to build the whole setting of a story that unfolds in the dark of Victorian London. While present in the game with his recognisable physique, against a carefully crafted realistic background, "Dickens" is also a name that functions through the mechanism of antonomasia. As such, his name resounds like a magic mantra, embodying a whole universe of ideas and themes related to his fiction, his journalism and nineteenth-century society in general.

The first episode of *Assassin's Creed: Syndicate* in the London Stories, under the subheading "Dickens Memories," is entitled "Spring-heeled Jack." Here the writer meets Jacob and Evie, dressed in their full warlike attire. Dickens asks their names; there follows a brief dialogue, which introduces the mission that the twins are about to undertake:

DICKENS: Alas, these days stupidity is all too prevalent! The question is: Do you believe in ghosts? I am skeptical myself. Here we are in the world's most advanced city, yet its citizens are so in thrall to the supernatural that they leave themselves vulnerable to charlatans. This is why I joined the Ghost Club, the first society to look systematically at the phenomenon. Because truth, like a spirit, must be cajoled before it will reveal itself. Will you join us?

Jacob and Evie agree to join the Ghost Club mission in its campaign against charlatans and superstition.

DICKENS: Splendid. I have a case for you. There's been some disturbing report in Lambeth. People claim they have been attacked by an age-old demon, Spring-heeled Jack. The fiend is no doubt on the prowl as we speak. It's up to you to find him!

The twins hasten toward their destiny – that is, to unmask the evil conspiracy. They are consequently involved in numerous battles, and have the opportunity to deploy their arsenal of weapons. This is where the player comes to the fore in the action, directing the movements of the lead characters, and receiving rewards for successful conquests. What follows, after the brief encounter with Dickens, coincides with the bulk of the action in the episode. The hero of this mission is Evie, who runs through the dark streets of Lambeth where the ghost has been spotted. She leaps from roof to precipitous roof, and at last, having killed the ghost, returns to Dickens; the author congratulates her. Having unmasked the ghost, she supports the rational attitude of the Ghost Club against the prevailing superstition of the age; they then toast their victory. It seems in this episode that the role of Dickens the writer, while characterised by his unquestionably authoritative attitude, is that of a wise, well-informed commander who sends his troops – or his secret agents – on dangerous missions, as in a James Bond film. The bulk of the episode consists of running and chasing the enemy everywhere in London; it also focuses on the fights that inevitably follow. The total time allotted to Dickens is not much more than a minute.

The same pattern characterises the other London stories (entitled "Hell's Bells"; "Recollection"; "50, Berkeley Square"; "Dead Letters"; and "The Terror of London"), which are also part of Charles Dickens's memories. In these scenarios Dickens sends either Evie or Jacob on missions in parts of London where ghosts have been spotted, and robberies or other crimes have been committed. "Spring-heeled Jack" is particularly interesting because this character, rather than simply being another urban ghost, has a unique claim to fame within Victorian urban culture: Jack became part of the city discourse in the 1830s, owing to the popular dissemination of the penny dreadfuls (see *The Apprehension* 1838; *Authentic Particulars* 1838). According to Bell, Spring-heeled Jack's "migratory appearances" both north and south of the Thames, "can be read as a bizarre reflection of contemporary urban explorers"; he continues:

> Spring-heeled Jack became a means of mapping a heterogeneous city through stories, generating small anecdotal vignettes of knowableness, that were made all the more memorable by their association with the bizarre and the supernatural. In form, although not in content, they were akin to the accounts provided by Dickens in *Sketches by Boz* and in the journalistic investigations that eventually evolved into Henry Mayhew's *London Labour and the London Poor*. (Bell 2012, p. 126)

This character, acting as a part of the literary and artistic language of London, is relevant to a tradition of urban discourse, or "urban marginalia," to which Dickens, whom Bell calls "one of the most verbose among its early Victorian articulators" (Bell 2012, p. 124), greatly contributed throughout his career as a novelist and journalist.

Reviews of *Assassin's Creed: Syndicate* were not always positive. Just after the launch of the Victorian episode, Sam White commented in his *Guardian* review (2015):

> Syndicate's romanticised rendition of 1860s London is certainly impressive ... Each district, from the grimy slums of Whitechapel to the stately grandeur of Westminster, feels distinct – visually, at least – and London has a dank sheen that does look glorious under a cloud-covered rainy evening ... In story terms, the narrative fog swirls around Crawford

> Starrick, the latest Head of the Hydra that is the Templar regime; longtime enemies of the Assassins … Starrick himself – shallow, softly spoken, [is] clearly torn straight from Ubisoft's Villain Handbook … This simplicity, of a bad guy with his henchmen poised in positions of power, plays perfectly into Syndicate's streamlined approach.

The reviewer admires the technical and visual realisation of Victorian London; but the simplistic, predictable "good vs. bad guys" plot does not earn equal praise. White also highlights the new feature of this episode: "the game's two new assassins – Jacob and Evie Frye – [who] act as two sides of the same coin, creating narrative dynamism and some of the series' best dialogue" (2015).

In other assessments, such as "a historian's view of *Assassin's Creed: Syndicate*," the episode has been described as "reductive, superficial, beautiful" (Nielsen 2015). For practical experience of the game, this *Guardian* review engaged Alana Harris, a social and cultural historian at King's College London, who found the game visually striking. She remarked on Ubisoft's policy of enlisting historical figures and anchoring the game's fictitious plot to an authentic setting; but, in her view, through the appearance of such historical figures as Karl Marx, "the game confirms common beliefs that the Victorian period was a time of class struggle" (Nielsen 2015). Harris also found fault with the presentation of poor children, who wander the London thoroughfares:

> Children run about the streets in Syndicate, often shoeless, searching through piles of rubbish. It is a familiar depiction of poverty in the 19th century city. The game seems to explore the Victorian cult of the innocent child – the Dickensian picture of innocent cherubs waiting to be saved. (Nielsen 2015)

Harris speculates: "the game has a very reductive understanding of what liberation for children might have meant in 1868 … 'If we're liberating these children, what are we liberating them to?'" (Nielsen 2015). There are also ways in which the Victorian London of the game is sanitised; according to Nielsen, it is "more of an adventure playground than a simulation" – a look and feel enhanced by a strong emphasis on architectural detail:

> 1868 is a very appropriate setting for this; the modern London we know has been constructed at this point, this is the year we have the Holborn Viaduct, we have Paddington Station, we have a whole raft of famous landmarks and sites that you can connect with. I guess that's probably been constructed with a mind to the international appeal of the game too, a way of connecting to London – a historical tourism.
>
> […]
>
> Syndicate is a fascinating example, then, of what we value in history and the issues of our own society reflected in our interpretations of the past.

> A few may sigh and drag out the old mantra of 'it's just a game' ... we're classing games lower than historical literature or film by refusing to examine them through the same lens. Games are the narrative medium of the digital age – they deserve to be taken seriously when they depict our world and heritage. (Nielsen 2015)

Games – the narrative medium of the digital age – do deploy a visual narration, closer to the cinema than the book; hence the reading skills, in this context, are bound to shrink to a minimum. Vita and Huguet recall the remarks of Dickens biographer Claire Tomalin ("Children Lack" 2012) concerning the author's readability:

> It is to be feared that Claire Tomalin's pessimistic diagnosis in an interview with the Press Association (5 February 2012), that [Dickens] is now 'beyond' children's reach, is unfortunately right: she decried the state of modern teaching for ill-equipping children nowadays with the attention span required to read his classic, but lengthy, books. Today's children, 'reared on dreadful television programmes,' lack ability for Dickens because, as she explains, they are not being educated 'to have prolonged attention spans and you have to be prepared to read steadily for a Dickens novel.' (Huguet & Vita 2016, pp. 22–23)

Levels of reading and education are important issues for the creation of a video game that counts among its users mainly young teenage players. Ubisoft reassures parents about the low level of violence, and dwells instead on the reliable amount of historical information offered by the game. Moreover, by avoiding such issues as prostitution and drug consumption, Ubisoft adopts a sanitising strategy, in order to ensure sales of the game. It is interesting to speculate on whether *Assassin's Creed: Syndicate* serves as a learning tool, promoting reading abilities and enticing young readers to engage with Dickens's novels; Harris is unconvinced: "In many ways there's a lot to it if you have a sufficient grounding to be able to decipher, unpack, augment and supplement what's here, but it works on a fairly superficial level of engagement" (Nielsen 2015).

It appears, then, that a reconsideration is necessary: Dickens needs to be read along the lines of an alternative communication. Rather than complaining alongside Tomalin, it is more productive to follow the hint offered by Harris, who argues that history is not confined to academic papers and the well-wrought documentary, but may indeed be vitally creative; as she notes, "There's a historical memory and the reprocessing and repackaging of it is ever present" (Nielsen 2015). The strategy is akin to heritage tourism, and the subjective experience provided by *Assassin's Creed: Syndicate* may augment and supplement the canonical body of knowledge about Dickens. To track this process of repackaging it is necessary to return to the concept of Dickens as icon and name, and observe that he appears in a game essentially structured around the good guys/bad guys opposition.

The two bands of Templars and Assassins are indeed like the Greeks and Trojans: their war is an epic war. Jacob Frye's weapons remind us of Achilles's suit of armour. Paul Innes, in his guidebook on epic, offers some useful insights on the question; besides analysing ancient classical epic, he suggests that today there are

> new kinds of entertainment that actively engage with the creative possibilities associated with aspects of the epic. These new media draw on existing cultural forms, resulting in computer game versions of the 'sagas' ... In these programs, players are given the opportunity to become personally involved in developing storylines that are built into the premise of each individual game. Epic narratives exist in various forms within the various genres of computer games ... The game reinvents the pivotal importance of the Homeric hero. (Innes 2013, p. 23)

This genealogy extends not only to Homer, but also to Dickens; Innes notes: "The line of descent is very clear: epic forms ... influenced modern literary writers, who in turn inspire the writers of these games." He adds that in role-playing games "It is now even possible for players to act out their roles in person ... this feature permits a form of post-modern performativity to appropriate the epic in especially distinct ways' (2013, pp. 23–24).

Thus modern audiences interact in fascinating new ways with old epic sagas. Innes perceptively comments: "Epic may no longer always be easily available to modern consumers in its traditional forms, but its components continue to resonate, even if they do so in relatively fragmented ways" (2013, p. 24). This is indeed the function performed by *Assassin's Creed: Syndicate*: it allows players to acquire creative potential, by experiencing their own epic productions. Innes considers this prerogative "a peculiar and appropriately post-modern return to the conditions of epic performance" (2013, p. 158).

Thus in this Victorian re-enactment of epic war in the classical mode, where bands, like ancient armies, confront each other, Dickens appears not only as the Victorian charismatic master, the moral anchor to which cultural values are attached, but indeed as the hero whose London associations are there to kindle young players' creativity, and to send them on many missions. If the author's imaginative works express the crisis of the hero in the Victorian age, his role in *Assassin's Creed: Syndicate* has reverted to that of the epic hero. If on the one hand his books are not so much read today, this posthumous development places this canonical writer at the source of great adventures in which we may participate side by side with him, as companions and players. In this sense Dickens's body and name, his material and immaterial entity, act as "lieux de mémoire" (Nora 1989), allowing us to read in them notions related at once to Victorian heritage and to our touristic present. Fragments of his books and looks are still with us, to inspire new generations and send them on their exciting quests.

References

Ansellem, Maya (Producer), & Fiennes, Ralph (Director) (2013). *The Invisible Woman* [Motion picture]. UK: BBC Films, Headline Pictures, Magnolia Mae Films and Taeoo Entertainment.

The Apprehension and Examination of Spring Heel'd Jack (1838). London.

Assassin's Creed (n.d.). [Promotional website]. Retrieved from https://www.ubisoft.com/en-us/game/assassins-creed/

Assassin's Creed: Syndicate (2015). [Video game]. Montreal: Ubisoft Entertainment.

Assassin's Creed Syndicate – The Twins: Evie and Jacob Frye Trailer (n.d.) [Video trailer]. Montreal: Ubisoft Entertainment. Retrieved from https://www.youtube.com/watch?v=zMjIUG8Nkaw

Authentic Particulars of the Awful Appearance of Spring-Heel'd Jack (1838). London.

Baudrillard, Jean (1994). *Simulation and Simulacra*. Trans. Sheila Glaser. Ann Arbor: University of Michigan Press.

Bell, Karl (2012). *The Legend of Spring-Heeled Jack: Victorian Urban Folklore and Popular Cultures*. Woodbridge: Boydell Press.

Bloom, Michelle E. (2003). *Waxworks: A Cultural Obsession*. Minneapolis: University of Minnesota Press.

Bolter, Jay David, & Grusin, Richard (1999). *Remediation: Understanding New Media*. Cambridge, MA: MIT Press.

Carey, John (1979). *The Violent Effigy: A Study in Dickens's Imagination*. London: Faber and Faber.

Children Lack Ability for Dickens, Says Biographer Tomalin (2012, 5 February). BBC News: Entertainment & Arts. Retrieved from https://www.bbc.co.uk/news/entertainment-arts-16896661

[Costello, Dudley] (1854, 18 February). History in Wax. *Household Words*, 9, 17–20.

Huguet Christine, & Vita, Paul (2016). Introduction: Unsettling Dickens. In C. Huguet & P. Vita (Eds.), *Unsettling Dickens: Process, Progress and Change* (pp. 20–29). Wimereux: Éditions du Sagittaire.

Innes, Paul (2013). *Epic*. Critical Idiom series. London: Routledge.

Jackson, Lee (2015). *Dirty Old London. The Victorian Fight against Filth*. New Haven, CT and London: Yale University Press.

Jackson, Lee (n.d.). *The Victorian Dictionary*. [Historical research website]. Retrieved from http://www.victorianlondon.org/index-2012.htm

Jerrold, William Blanchard (1872). *London: A Pilgrimage*. Illust. Gustave Doré. London: Grant & Co.

John, Juliet (2010). *Dickens and Mass Culture*. Oxford: Oxford University Press.

Khair, Tahib (2010). *The Thing about Thugs*. New Delhi: Fourth Estate.

Kingsley, Stephanie (2014, 2 September). Playing in the Classroom with the Ivanhoe Game. *Chronicle of Higher Education*. Retrieved from https://www.chronicle.com/blogs/profhacker/playing-in-the-classroom-with-the-ivanhoe-game/57713

Litvack, Leon (2008). Portrait of Charles Dickens. In Peter Murray (Ed.), *Daniel Maclise 1806–70: Romancing the Past* (pp. 120–121). Cork: Crawford Art Gallery.

Litvack, Leon (2017). Dickens Posing for Posterity: The Photographs of Herbert Watkins. *Dickens Quarterly*, 34(2), 96–158.

McGann, Jerome, & Drucker, Johanna (2003). The Ivanhoe Game. Retrieved from http://www2.iath.virginia.edu/jjm2f/old/IGamehtm.html

Mayhew, Henry (1861–1862). *London Labour and The London Poor: A Cyclopedia of the Condition and Earnings of Those that Will Work. Those that Cannot Work, and Those that Will Not Work*. 4 vols. London: Griffin, Bohn & Co.

Nead, Lynda. (2000). *Victorian Babylon: People, Streets, and Images in Nineteenth-Century London*. New Haven, CT and London: Yale University Press.

Nielsen, Holly (2015, 9 December). Reductive, Superficial, Beautiful – A Historian's View of Assassin's Creed: Syndicate. *The Guardian*. Retrieved from https://www.theguardian.com/technology/2015/dec/09/assassins-creed-syndicate-historian-ubisoft

Nora, Pierre (1989). Between Memory and History: Les Lieux de Mémoire. *Representations*, 26, 7–24.

Notre Dame: Assassin's Creed Unity Giveaway Praised (2019, 21 April). BBC Newsbeat. Retrieved from https://www.bbc.co.uk/news/newsbeat-48004285

Simmons, Dan (2009). *Drood: A Novel*. London: Quercus.

Slater, Michael (2009). *Charles Dickens*. New Haven, CT and London: Yale University Press.

Tomalin, Claire (1990). *The Invisible Woman: The Story of Nelly Ternan and Charles Dickens*. London: Vintage.

White, Sam (2015, 23 October). Assassin's Creed: Syndicate Review – A Historical Failure. *The Guardian*. Retrieved from https://www.theguardian.com/technology/2015/oct/23/assassins-creed-syndicate-review-failure

Whitsuntide Holidays (1873, 1 June). *Reynold's Newspaper*, 4.

12

From Movable Book to iPad App

Playing *A Christmas Carol*

Claire Wood

Adaptations of Dickens's *A Christmas Carol* (1843) take many different forms. There are film, television and radio versions; dramas, ballets and operas; graphic novels; board games and computer games. As Paul Davis argues, the story has been "adapted, revised, condensed, retold, reoriginated and modernized more than any other work of English literature" (1990, p. 4). Movable and pop-up books constitute a type of Dickens adaptation that has received relatively little critical attention, despite the growing number of titles produced in the late twentieth and early twenty-first centuries. Defined as a "book that incorporates one or more movable, manipulable, or three-dimensional elements," the pop-up features a range of devices, such as flaps, revolving discs, pull-tabs and repositionable figures, which add depth and motion to the printed page (Walkup 2010, p. 947). Such books place different demands on the reader; Jacqueline Reid-Walsh outlines how "to 'read' a movable book, a person has to engage with it in several ways; reading the words, as in a story, looking at the images, as in a picture book, and moving the components, as in a game" (2012, p. 164). Because movable books compel their readers to adopt a hybridised mode of engagement, the form seems particularly suggestive of novel or alternative modes of reading Dickens.

In many ways the *Carol* seems particularly appropriate for movable book adaptation. From the outset, Dickens's full title – *A Christmas Carol. In Prose. Being A Ghost Story of Christmas.* – indicates the tale's intermedia interests; the work's length and memorable set pieces also lend themselves to this form. Davis highlights the iconographic quality of the tale, which in memory and retelling turns from a "continuous narrative into a chain of remembered scenes, a series of visual stations along its narrative journey" (1990, p. 66). This is an apt description of the pop-up book format, with its lavish illustrated scenes (though limited in number). Furthermore, the extraordinary playfulness of Dickens's narrative has clear potentiality for movable adaptation. The *Carol* text reflects traditional festive pastimes: there are

Reading Dickens Differently, First Edition. Edited by Leon Litvack and Nathalie Vanfasse.
© 2020 John Wiley & Sons Ltd. Published 2020 by John Wiley & Sons Ltd.

numerous depictions of people at play, ranging from parlour games and practical jokes, to physically boisterous rounds of blind man's buff. J. Hillis Miller memorably noted the "inordinate linguistic exuberance" of the *Carol*, in which "a single adjective, example, or epithet will never do … Each thing calls forth another and then another, like the games that follow one another in the Christmas festivities at Scrooge's nephew's house" (1993, p. 193). Appropriately, this playfulness spills over into the inanimate world, so that even the buildings are described "playing at hide-and-seek" (*CC* 1). Play is thus a recurrent part of the surface action; but it is also crucial to Dickens's approach to the narrative, which exposes and unsettles established conventions of form and language. Chapters are designated "staves" in an extension of the titular *Carol* metaphor, and the digressions of the omniscient narrator repeatedly draw attention to gaps between language and meaning. The ludic qualities of the source text are well-served by the interactive form of movable books, which invite reader-interactors to explore the story by playing with it.

Chuck Fischer's pop-up (2010a) and app-based (2010b) versions of the "Carol" allow for an exploration of some of the ways in which movable adaptation can prompt fresh engagement with a familiar story, by enriching and disrupting the reading experience.[1] Featuring artwork by Fischer and paper engineering by Bruce Foster, the pop-up "Carol" consists of six double-page pop-up spreads: one for Marley's ghost and each of the spirits, bookended by London streetscapes. Two of these spreads incorporate secondary movable components in the form of pull-tab and lift-the-flap devices, but the main focus is the spectacular three-dimensional scenes that "pop up" when each page is turned. The interactive iPad app integrates illustrations from the pop-up "Carol" with parts of Dickens's text and overlays a series of special effects. Each of the 92 digital "pages" is enriched with enhancements such as an inset, watermarked or full-page illustration, a pull-quote, or an animation. Candles flicker, snow falls, dogs bark and iconic phrases are read aloud ("Bah, humbug!"; "God bless us, every one!"). In contrast to traditional movable books, the story is confined to two dimensions, and tactile engagement with cardboard flaps and tabs is replaced by tapping and swiping the iPad's touchscreen. Yet in line with Kathleen Walkup's definition, noted above, the app features numerous "movable, manipulable" elements and is strongly influenced by analogue movable devices. Tapping on an illustration of the two charitable gentlemen causes them to bow jerkily, as if operated by a pull-tab; an hour-glass can be turned like a volvelle (a rotating wheel); opening the shutters of Scrooge's house resembles a lift-the-flap technique; and tapping and dragging certain illustrations – such as Marley's ghost or the cab carrying the Cratchits' oversized turkey – enables them to be moved around the screen in the manner of figures in a toy theatre. The combination of digitally mediated interactions, sophisticated multimedia effects and movable-style devices helps to position the app as the latest stage in the long evolution of movable books (see Haining 1979).

Brief examination of cover designs and promotional materials for the pop-up book and app provides a sense of their positioning, both in the marketplace and in relation to Dickens's text. Retailing at $30 on initial release, the pop-up "Carol" continues the Christmas gift-book tradition in which the original *Carol* participated. The blurb on the back cover situates the pop-up as a deluxe edition of a "yuletide favourite," which offers readers the opportunity to "experience Dickens's beloved tale in an entirely new way," balancing fidelity to the source text with an appeal to novelty. On the front cover (Figure 12.1), Dickens's signature and the title are picked out in imitation gilt against a red background, along with small flourishes of holly. This helps to cultivate a luxury aesthetic and, perhaps, gestures towards the salmon-coloured binding and gilt wreath design of Dickens's first edition. The gilded subtitle, "A Pop-Up Book," draws the eye in appearing against

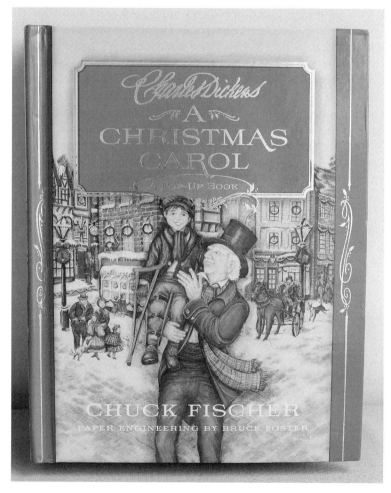

Figure 12.1 Cover image from Chuck Fischer's *A Christmas Carol: A Pop-Up Book* (2010a). By kind permission of Chuck Fischer. Photograph courtesy of Janet Wood, 2018.

a green background encircled by gold. The main focus, however, is Fischer's colourful full-page illustration, which depicts Scrooge carrying Tiny Tim upon his shoulder, in the foreground of a cheery Victorian street scene. Fischer is known for his meticulously researched architectural pop-ups, such as *Great American Houses and Gardens* (2003). Indeed, in a 2017 interview for the online platform *Best Pop-Up Books*, Fischer describes his process, noting that

> I like to travel and visit historic house museums, art museums, and libraries ... I did some research at the Charles Dickens museum in London before I started working on *A Christmas Carol* pop-up book. I also do a lot of research at libraries and on the internet. (Interview 2017)

Nostalgia, however, trumps historical accuracy in Fischer's production; this is a chocolate-box version of the past: the streets are clean, everyone is well-dressed and Tiny Tim's teeth are perfect. Fischer's own name is inscribed across this illustration in crisp white capitals, above that of Bruce Foster, who is specifically credited with the paper engineering. Neither Dickens nor Fischer stakes primary claim to this version of *A Christmas Carol* through direct attribution or the use of a possessive apostrophe; instead, in prominently featuring both names (albeit in different styles), the cover design suggests a collaborative endeavour. The app reproduces various elements of the pop-up book cover for its title screen, including the joint billing of Dickens and Fischer, although the illustration is cropped to focus on the figures of Scrooge and Tiny Tim. In both cases, the proleptic choice of cover image anticipates Scrooge's redemption and the tale's happy ending. Significantly, this scene does not feature in Dickens's *Carol*, where it is Bob Cratchit who serves as Tim's "blood horse" (*CC* 3). In the text, Scrooge and Tiny Tim never meet directly; the narrator states simply that Scrooge "did it all, and infinitely more" (*CC* 5); but here the visual substitution of Scrooge for Bob Cratchit depicts the reformed miser in practical fulfilment of his duties as the boy's "second father" (*CC* 5). Fischer's cover illustration, reproduced three-dimensionally in the final pop-up spread, epitomises his approach to the *Carol*: this family-friendly adaptation focuses on the individual and the family, rather than broader social concerns, and tends to subdue the more troubling aspects of the story. Whereas the initial pop-up version of this location (Figure 12.2) includes a shoeless child and a "party of ragged men and boys" (*CC* 1), gathered round a brazier at lower left, such figures are tacitly excluded from the cover; it is as if Scrooge's individual acts of charity have eradicated poverty entirely. Fischer's adaptations are not unduly bound to the letter of the text, as the invented scene on the cover (Figure 12.1), depicting Scrooge and Tiny Tim, indicates; but he does seek to translate the *Carol*'s spirit – albeit with an emphasis on the cosier and more sentimental aspects.

Promotional videos for the "Carol" pop-up book and app reinforce these values, while also highlighting the opportunity to experience the tale in new ways.

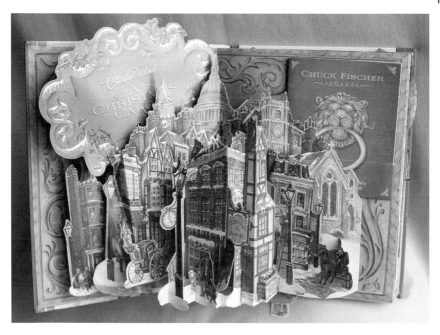

Figure 12.2 London street scene, from Chuck Fischer's *A Christmas Carol: A Pop-Up Book* (2010a). By kind permission of Chuck Fischer. Photograph courtesy of Janet Wood, 2018.

The enduring appeal of Dickens's text is central to the pop-up book video, produced in 2010 by Hachette Book Group, with the American voiceover reiterating its classic status ("a yuletide favourite for over a century and a half"; "a timeless fable"). Through Fischer's "dramatic paintings" and Foster's paper engineering, the voiceover continues, "this heart-warming fable is brought to life" (A Christmas 2010a). The ability of the pop-up form to vivify Dickens's story is suggested by the camerawork: the video starts with the book being opened slowly, before the camera zooms in on the pop-up streetscape. The ambient sound of horses' hooves, combined with the richly detailed three-dimensional illustrations, helps the viewer to imagine participating in the bustling scene. Several movable components are demonstrated, and the figures of Tiny Tim and the three spirits are animated in isolation from their respective tableaux, giving them a "life" beyond the book. Intriguingly, the interactive possibilities of the story are shown without depicting any direct human interaction, perhaps thus evoking the sense of magic associated with childhood experiences of movable books.

Promotion for the app also draws upon the idea of the movable book as magical, but makes technology the source of enchantment. When the iPad was announced 10 months earlier, in January 2010, Steve Jobs dubbed it Apple's "most advanced technology in a magical and revolutionary device." This fusion of magic and innovation was rooted in the "responsive high-resolution Multi-Touch display" that enabled users to "physically interact with applications and content" (Newsroom 2010). The novelty of the iPad platform is captured in the app's promotional video. At the start, an elderly gentleman wearing a top hat reaches for a physical copy of *A Christmas Carol*. Shot in black and white, the sequence is made to look and sound as if it is being shown on an old-fashioned projector, thus aligning the material book with older forms of technology (A Christmas 2010b). The film bursts into colour as the book is opened to reveal an iPad with the "Carol" app preloaded. This is followed by a series of close-ups, which are intended to show off the app's interactive features and to bring the tale to life through colourful animations and a prescribed – but nonetheless compelling – sense of responsiveness to the user's touch. In contrast to the pop-up promo, here it is important to see the interactor physically tapping and swiping the screen in order to explore the story-world. Today, the proliferation of sophisticated touchscreen devices makes it easy to forget the "magical and revolutionary" aspects of Apple's popularisation of touchscreen technology.

Fischer's "Carol" adaptations provide an intriguing case study for several reasons. First, both pop-up book and app retain authorised versions of the text. The former includes removable booklets that reproduce each "stave" of Dickens's text in full, as well as John Leech's woodcuts and coloured plates, thus allowing the original story to be read alongside or apart from the three-dimensional illustrations. The app is based upon Dickens's own adaptation of the *Carol* and uses the public readings text (*The Readings* 1868, pp. 3–53; Collins 1975, pp. 1–33). This strengthens the sense of dialogue between movable adaptation and source text. Second, the concurrent release of Fischer's pop-up and app-based "Carol" adaptations foregrounds intersections of tradition and technology. Also, the material/digital design of these adaptations affords different types of interaction with, and participation in, the story. Attention to these dynamics reveals three ways in which movable adaptation, in traditional and digital forms, can amplify aspects of the *Carol* story: blurred boundaries between life and death; a fusion of magic and mechanism; and an interest in drawing the reader into the story and prompting moral reflection through witnessing Scrooge's reform. Before moving to detailed analyses of these elements, it is helpful to foreground key ideas about interactivity and vivacity in relation to movable books that have important implications for the "Carol" adaptations.

Walter Benjamin's "A Glimpse into the World of Children's Books" (1926) captures the delight evoked by picture books. In part, the essay is about how children learn to read through imaginative engagement with words and images. Reflecting Benjamin's passions as a collector, it is also a celebration of the tactility and visual appeal of children's books. Like Dickens, Benjamin was interested in the way that children experience the world. The essay includes a vivid account of the child's ability to enter into a story:

> [T]he gazing child enters into those pages, becoming suffused, like a cloud, with the riotous colors of the world of pictures ... he overcomes the illusory

barrier of the book's surface and passes through colored textures and brightly painted partitions to enter a stage on which fairy tales spring to life. (2004, p. 435)

This gorgeous description shifts from a sense of the reader's immersion in the book ("suffused, like a cloud") to more active involvement, as the child becomes an actor on the story stage. Several figures that afford different levels of agency are used for the child's participation: he is the guest at a masquerade, in which words put on different costumes, and a "theater-producer who refuse[s] to be bound by 'sense'" (p. 435). The games that these books encourage children to play interest Benjamin. He refers to the ABC-book's "game in pictures" (p. 436) and the way that rebus books (which represent words or phrases by pictures or symbols) prompt readers to puzzle out connections between image and word. Benjamin also considers books in which "children's hands were catered to as much as their minds or their imaginations" (p. 437). This type of book is a "tangible narrative" that enables children to "play" with the story by physically engaging with various mechanical devices (Madej 2016, p. 22). Hidden mysteries can be discovered via "doors and curtains in the pictures" that "can be opened to reveal pictures behind them"; in another example a prince can be rescued "with the wave of a magic wand, by moving the strip at the side of the page" (Benjamin 2004, p. 437). Benjamin emphasises the fusion of magic and mechanism here, and draws attention to the role of the reader-interactor.

"A Glimpse" also engages with the play of life and death facilitated by movable books – a pertinent dynamic given the *Carol*'s ambivalence about mortal states. There is a poignant quality to the essay's reflections on childhood and its closing description of how "the eyes and cheeks of children poring over books are reflected in the glory of the [picture-book] sunset" (Benjamin 2004, p. 443). Suspension of this moment evades – but simultaneously evokes – the transience of childhood and the limited lifespan of some children's books. As Benjamin notes, "pull-out books" tend to "never last for long" (p. 437), due to the delicacy of their mechanisms. Yet Benjamin also observes the "life" contained within children's books. There is a telling allusion to Hans Christian Andersen's fairy tale "The Wild Swans" at the start. This story features a picture book in which "everything was alive. 'The birds sang, and people came out of the book and spoke.' But when the princess turned the page, 'they leaped back in so that there should be no disorder'" (p. 435). Benjamin's point is that "objects do not come to meet the picturing child"; instead the child enters into the story-world (p. 435); but the idea that stories can come to life through imaginative and tactile engagement is uncontested. Incidentally, the living picture book that Andersen describes, with singing birds and figures that emerge from and collapse into the book when the page is turned, anticipates several key developments in movable book history such as the introduction of the speaking picture book (with a mechanism consisting of string-pulls and tiny paper bellows) around 1895, and the emergence of the pop-up book in the 1930s (Haining 1979, pp. 136–138).

Several later commentators were more suspicious about the movable book's power to impart "life." As Hannah Field (citing an influential 1975 article by collectors Iona and Peter Opie) notes, for some "the mechanical evokes the exact reverse of life" (2014, p. 107). For the Opies, movable books are a form rooted in deficit:

> For a surprisingly long time now there have been firms ... who have sought to put life into their books by the crudest of all possible means, by representing life mechanically. The artists may not be able to depict movement, so the figures in their pictures are made to move in reality; they may not be able to convey the illusion of depth, so they produce pictures that are actually three-dimensional; they may be incapable of portraying a cow mooing, so a mooing noise is in fact contrived. (1975, p. 1055)

In contrast to Benjamin's fusion of magic and mechanism, movable books seem fundamentally lifeless here. These contrivances serve chiefly to cover for deficiencies in the writing and artwork, and provide no substitute for the animating power of the imagination.

Ultimately, whether a reader experiences mechanical animation as compellingly vivacious or disappointingly vacuous is subjective. Undoubtedly, the ingenuity and execution of individual designs are relevant; but the more interesting question is how these dynamics operate alongside other visual and textual elements. To demonstrate this point it is useful to recall the earliest Dickens movable that is readily available: *Stories from Dickens for Boys and Girls*, which dates from the 1930s and was published by Raphael Tuck & Sons. This title features a double-page "Come to Life" panorama, accompanied by 160 pages of letterpress, two full-colour plates and numerous black-and-white illustrations (M.A. Dickens et al. [1935]). Parts of the text, and some of Harold Copping's illustrations, come from previous Tuck & Sons productions, including Copping's artwork for *Character Sketches from Dickens* (1924) and Mary Angela Dickens's child-friendly retellings of her grandfather's works in *Dickens' Dream Children* (1926). A publisher's catalogue from 1937–1938 emphasises the "realistic" effect of Tuck's patented panorama technique and describes each book in the "Storyland Treasury" as "containing a beautiful coloured model cut out in stiff card which stands out and springs to life as the book is opened" (*Story Books* [1937], p. 16).

In the *Stories from Dickens* panorama (Figure 12.3), various characters are arranged across three rows, with the front two printed in full colour on cardboard and mounted to give depth to the illustration. The back row, rendered more simply in three colours, is printed directly onto the page. Viewed independently of the accompanying narrative, the static panorama presents a lively gathering of Dickens characters. The majority of the figures are based upon Copping's plates for *Character Sketches*, including David and Little Em'ly, Caleb Plummer and Bertha, and Mrs Gamp (in the original plate she is depicted with Betsey Prig,

Figure 12.3 "Come to Life" panorama from *Stories from Dickens for Boys and Girls* (1935). Front Row (L to R): Caleb Plummer and his blind daughter (from *The Cricket on the Hearth*), Trotty Veck and his daughter Meg (from *The Chimes*), Florence and Paul Dombey (from *Dombey and Son*), Mr and Mrs Harry Walmers, Jr (from *The Holly-Tree*). Second Row (L to R): Little Em'ly and David (from *David Copperfield*), Little Nell (from *The Old Curiosity Shop*), Mr Bumble and Oliver (from *Oliver Twist*), Sam Weller and his father (from *The Pickwick Papers*), Bob Cratchit and Tiny Tim (from *A Christmas Carol*), Mrs Gamp (from *Martin Chuzzlewit*). Back Row (L to R): Betsey Trotwood (from *David Copperfield*), The Little Kenwigses (from *Nicholas Nickleby*), The Fat Boy (from *The Pickwick Papers*), Mr Micawber (from *David Copperfield*), Fanny Squeers and Nicholas (from *Nicholas Nickleby*). Photograph courtesy of Janet Wood, 2018.

which explains why she appears to be talking to someone beyond the panorama; see Matz 1924, facing pp. 90, 134, 76). As in other character illustration composites, such as Robert William Buss's *Dickens's Dream* (1875), these characters have "become independent of their creator, and have acquired an autonomous existence" (Litvack 2007, p. 7). With the exception of Micawber's placement next to the Fat Boy, characters from different novels do not mingle; however, they do ostensibly inhabit the same verdant dreamlike space. Unlike *Dickens's Dream*, no authorial animating consciousness is pictured; instead, as the misspelt caption hints, we have entered into the story-world where Dickens's creations live, "In Dicken's [sic] Land."

The effects of the "Come to Life" panorama are enhanced when viewed within the broader context of the volume. The scene is concealed until the page is turned, surprising and delighting readers as they flip from the conclusion of the story of "Tiny Tim" (the top line reading "for Tiny Tim did not die – not a bit of it") to see

Tim among the characters "living on" in the panorama (M.A. Dickens et al. [1935], p. 71). At least one of the characters who does die in his particular story – Little Paul Dombey – is resurrected here (although others, including Smike and Jo, are not). Because most of the characters are drawn from illustrations for a different work, the panorama includes scenes which do not feature in this re-telling, such as Bumble's leading Oliver through the streets. Furthermore, Tony Weller, who features prominently in the centre of the middle row, does not appear in person, although the reader is assured "You will some day greatly enjoy reading all about Sam Weller and his father Tony Weller, a coachman; they are both delightfully comic characters" (*Story Books* [1937], p. 95). Part of the panorama's "Come to Life" effect, therefore, stems from finding characters in situations other than those described in the narrative, thus extending the story-world, and meeting "In Dicken's Land" characters whom the reader has not yet encountered.

Stories from Dickens uses a single movable feature to provide a visual index for some of the tales included in the collection. As a static, three-dimensional character composite, however, it does not take advantage of more dramatic opportunities to play with life and death, which are available when movable devices are used to support the telling of individual tales. This dynamic will be explored presently in Fischer's "Carol" adaptations. But first it is useful to reflect upon suspended animation as a facet of this play with life and death, with reference to the movable paper figures that prompted fear and fascination in the young Dickens. In an essay from *Household Words* entitled "A Christmas Tree" (1850), Dickens recalls a "cardboard lady in a blue-silk skirt, who was stood up against a candlestick to dance" and a sinister "cardboard man," operated by pull-string and rendered "ghastly" when "he got his legs round his neck (which he very often did)" ([Dickens] 1850, p. 289). The frightening aspects of this toy appear to reside in its unnatural range of movement and capacity for malfunction. This is the flipside of the wonder that Benjamin finds in the fusion of magic and mechanism. While the pull-string mechanism that imparts animation to this figure is clearly visible, there is a lurking suspicion that the cardboard man might have an independent life, beyond the manipulator's control: "he was ... not a creature to be alone with" (p. 289). Greater fondness is reserved for the toy theatre in "A Christmas Tree": although this plaything possesses a similar capacity for malfunction, with figures that are liable to "become faint in the legs, and double up, at exciting points of the drama" (p. 292), it lacks the cardboard man's sinister aspect. In part this may be due to the greater capacity for imaginative play afforded by this toy. In discussing the power that effigies possess in Dickens's imagination, John Carey notes that "an effigy can be counted on to repeat its gesture each time it appears, just like a person, and it has the strangeness and intensity that naturally adhere to something that only *looks* alive" (1979, p. 86; emphasis original). While the repetitive movement of the cardboard man aligns it with the mechanical life of effigy, the figures of the toy theatre – animated by imagination as well as manual manipulation – can conjure up "a teeming world of fancies" ([Dickens] 1850, p. 292).

It is interesting to see how the dynamics foregrounded here, in the play of life and death suggested by the "Come to Life" panorama in *Stories from Dickens*, and the tension between magic and mechanism in Dickens's engagement with paper toys, resonate in relation to later movables. The discussion above of the promotional videos accompanying Fischer's work highlights a couple of ways in which movable book adaptation attempts to bring stories "to life"; but in practice, the design and functionality of the pop-up book and app often tend towards a blurring of the boundaries between life and death, rather than straightforward vivification.

The adaptations reflect the source text in this respect. *A Christmas Carol* famously begins by insisting upon the fact of Marley's decease and establishing the possibility of his return: "Marley was dead, to begin with" (*CC* 1). Later, in the vision presented by the Ghost of Christmas Yet to Come, Scrooge (unknowingly) encounters his own shrouded corpse and observes Tiny Tim laid out (*CC* 4). Yet Tiny Tim is also only "dead, to begin with": the future is rewritten following Scrooge's promise to reform. The seeming open-endedness associated with mortality is reinforced at the level of the text. The opening passage makes reference to the official burial register, in which Scrooge's name is coupled with Marley's as a proof of the latter's demise. Several paragraphs later, the narrator notes that "Scrooge never painted out Old Marley's name. There it stood, years afterwards, above the warehouse door." As a result "Sometimes people new to the business called Scrooge Scrooge, and sometimes Marley, but he answered to both names" (*CC* 1). The two partners and their mortal states here become reversible.

In the app, the animations and interactions that accompany this passage wittily undermine the emphatic statement of Marley's death. A capitalised pull-quote proclaiming that "Old Marley was as dead as a door-nail" features prominently. On first navigating to the page, an inset illustration of a scroll unfurls automatically, revealing Marley's signed death certificate; at the same time, the word "dead" in the pull-quote starts to tilt downward, before falling to the bottom of the page and becoming inert (Figure 12.4). The animation enacts the word's meaning as a form of visual wordplay. This also leaves a conspicuous gap in the text – "Old Marley was as   as a door-nail" – which, in disrupting the idiomatic simile, prompts reflection upon the use of ready-made phrases. In the original text, the narrator goes on to muse, "Mind! I don't mean to say that I know, of my own knowledge, what there is particularly dead about a door-nail" (*CC* 1). This aside is cut from the public reading text, but the gap invites the reader-interactor to think independently about the fitness of the simile, and contemplate whether "dead" is the right or only word that could fill this space; this opens up the possibility that Marley could be many things other than deceased. Such animated wordplay occurs at other points in the app: "bang" slams sideways and "trembled" quivers. Such effects make visible the exuberance of Dickens's language and demonstrate the form's potential for bringing the author's prose to life, as well as his characters.

The app also plays with life and death by means of its interactive illustrations. While most of the animations are automatically triggered on navigation to the

234 | Claire Wood

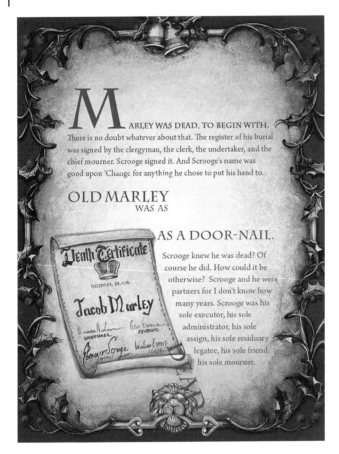

Figure 12.4 "Marley was dead"; screen capture from Charles Dickens's *A Christmas Carol: For the iPad* (2010b). By kind permission of Chuck Fischer.

relevant page, many can be reactivated, or reversed, by touch. For example, the first appearance of the Ghost of Christmas Past is the subject of a full-page animated illustration in which the Spirit emerges from a lit candle. But should the reader-interactor be of a mind, like Scrooge, to "see the Spirit in his cap" (*CC* 2), the ghost can be made to retract into the flame, either by tapping on the figure directly, or by tapping and dragging a candle snuffer. Importantly, this does not change the story or impede the progress of the narrative. While the app's design affords numerous opportunities for enlivening activity, interaction takes place within a carefully prescribed range, and the agency of the user is fundamentally limited (see Reid-Walsh 2012). The reader-interactor is not allowed to author an independent version of the *Carol*, in which Tiny Tim does die, because the Spirit is snuffed out before Scrooge has the chance to learn from his vision. Instead, the app focuses on making the reader-interactor a more active participant in the existing *Carol* story. Sometimes this is achieved through concealed animations and effects that are not automatically activated, thus encouraging tactile exploration of every inch of the screen. These effects can support and enrich the reading experience. For instance, the reader-interactor can tap upon an inset illustration of Marley's ghost to remove the bandage around his head, causing him to groan audibly as his jaw drops. The reader-interactor has the opportunity to catalyse an action performed by Marley in the text, but also experiences the same "horror" as Scrooge (*CC* 1), in seeing the ghost's face transformed. A more meditative way for the user to participate in the story is provided by the game-like design of three full-page illustrations, featuring Scrooge's counting-house (Figure 12.5), the spirits of those condemned to "walk abroad" (*CC* 1) and the Ghost of Christmas Present's feast. By means of a simple physics engine and the iPad's touchscreen and accelerometer, floating elements in the foreground (coins, ghosts and chains, various foodstuffs) can be made to move and bounce off one another by swiping

Figure 12.5 Scrooge in his counting-house; screen capture from Charles Dickens's *A Christmas Carol:* For the iPad (2010b). By kind permission of Chuck Fischer.

and tilting the screen. Intriguingly, these interactions are not scored or otherwise goal-orientated; however, in prompting users to linger upon these objects through prolonged tactile engagement, the app allows them to enter into the feelings of the protagonist, taking pleasure in handling the clinking coins, engaging more anxiously with the ghostly chains and perhaps pondering "the weight and length of the strong coil" (*CC* 1) they might carry, and savouring the variety and abundance of festive fare – as the Cratchits do later in Stave Three at a more sparing Christmas repast.

The primary way in which the pop-up "Carol" plays with life and death is through the dramatic manner in which the illustrations emerge from and collapse into the book, with the reader-interactor propelling the narrative forward and bringing it to life by turning the pages. In the case of "dead-to-begin-with" Marley, the nature of the paper engineering causes his vivification to be continually reversed and replayed. When the reader-interactor opens the pop-up spread that accompanies Stave One, Marley's ghost automatically bursts through the door to intercede with his former business partner (Figure 12.6); but when the page is turned, this process is reversed. Additional "come-to-life" effects are

Figure 12.6 Stave One pop-up, featuring Marley's Ghost, from Chuck Fischer's *A Christmas Carol: A Pop-Up Book* (2010a). By kind permission of Chuck Fischer. Photograph courtesy of Janet Wood, 2018.

created when the tableaux-based pop-ups are brought into dialogue with the linear narrative of Dickens's text, reproduced in the accompanying keepsake booklets. Moving between the text and the three-dimensional illustrations is one of the pleasures of this adaptation; users are able to appreciate correspondences between Dickens's description of Scrooge's chambers and Fischer's pop-up rendering, such as the Dutch tiles surrounding the fireplace and the disused bell. The three-dimensional environments also enable the reader-interactor to mimic actions described in the text, such as poking around every corner of Scrooge's room, as Scrooge himself does, and checking that there is "nobody under the table" (*CC* 1). However, the punctual art of the pop-up spreads also causes incongruities. The immediate appearance of Marley's ghost on opening the Stave One pop-up leaves the reader-interactor in no doubt that Marley is only dead "to begin with." Elsewhere, the subject of the Stave Four pop-up – Scrooge cowering in front of his own gravestone (Figure 12.7) – removes any sense of mystery regarding the identity of the "wretched man" who dies unmourned (*CC* 4), described in the accompanying booklet. These revelations are only ever a surprise to Scrooge; after all, Stave One is entitled "Marley's Ghost" and few could miss the irony of Scrooge's assumption in Stave Four that "the case of this unhappy man might be my own" (*CC* 4). Reading the text alongside the pop-up tableaux amplifies the *Carol*'s sense of dramatic irony. The process can also

Figure 12.7 Stave Four pop-up, featuring the Ghost of Christmas Yet to Come, from Chuck Fischer's *A Christmas Carol: A Pop-Up Book* (2010a). By kind permission of Chuck Fischer. Photograph courtesy of Janet Wood, 2018.

impress some unexpected truths; for example, the Stave One pop-up incorporates three key moments: the transformation of the door knocker, the confrontation between Scrooge and Marley's ghost and the revelation that outside the window "the air was filled with phantoms" (*CC* 1). As Figure 12.6 demonstrates, these events can be "read" from left to right, in the order in which they occur, although with the exception of the pull-tab operated door knocker (incorporated into the front cover of the booklet) these elements appear simultaneously. Whether intentional or not, the design serves to reinforce the fact that the ghosts in the background are always there, even if Scrooge can only perceive them at the end of the stave.

Dickens described his Christmas Books as "a whimsical kind of masque" in the Preface to the single-volume edition. This evokes a spectacular form dependent upon elaborate stage machinery for its rapid changes of scene and dazzling visual effects. Robert Tracy explores the influence of masques and pantomimes upon the Christmas Books, arguing that they "reproduce in prose the transformation techniques of contemporary stagecraft." Tracy notes that "mechanical transformations were usually presented as performed by magic" and tended to echo "the transformation of the principal character – Aladdin, Ali Baba – from rags to riches." The key difference, he observes, is that Dickens uses the transformation scene to "work a moral transformation, to make Scrooge a better man" (Tracy 1998, p. 121). There are suggestive parallels here between the masque's fusion of magic and mechanism and the movable book: for the reader-interactor the way that pop-up scenes spring to life seems magical; but these spectacular effects are predicated upon complex paper engineering beneath the surface of the page. The history of movable books is entwined with developments on the stage (Reid-Walsh 2012; Rahn 2011, p. 28). Fischer's pop-up "Carol" gestures towards this relationship – as well as the *Carol*'s own theatrical proclivities – through a number of design elements. In the first double-page pop-up spread (Figure 12.2), the paper engineering is reminiscent of a stage set in using scenery flats to create the impression of depth, while the theatre is evoked more explicitly through the baroque foliage and dominant red and gold colour palette. This theatrical inheritance is less evident in the app, although some visual echoes are carried over: a draped brocade curtain from the third pop-up spread is used as a background for the app's stave title pages, framing the action that follows as a stage drama. Transformation scenes – both in the sense of spectacular scenic transitions and Scrooge's personal transformation – are also well-served by the movable medium. In Fischer's pop-up book, for example, Scrooge's door knocker becomes Marley's face by means of a slat illustration technique. The second, third and fourth spreads (depicting encounters with Marley's ghost, and the Ghosts of Christmas Past and Present) all use Scrooge's chambers as a backdrop, creating the impression of a stage set that undergoes spectacular alterations as the reader-interactor turns from page to page. The third spread directly incorporates several scenic transformations in representing Scrooge's journey through his past. In a neat piece of design metaphor, a large fold-out panel conceals the neglected young Scrooge at school, thus suggesting the hidden dimensions of his character. When this flap is lifted, the adult Scrooge is drawn back in time, via the clock, as a witness. Two further scenes from Scrooge's past can be unfolded, revealing Fezziwig's ball and Scrooge's separation from his fiancée. After completing this journey through the miser's early life, the closing of the flap causes Scrooge to be drawn back to the other side of the clock, ready to extinguish the Spirit's light. Elsewhere, Dickens's description of how "the city rather seemed to spring up about them [Scrooge and the Ghost of Christmas Yet to Come], and encompass them of its own act" (*CC* 4) is reflected in the three-dimensional street scenes that pop up at various points.

The digital nature of the app renders the "stage machinery" invisible; in contrast to the labour of designing and assembling the pop-up book's paper mechanisms – still largely done by hand – the work of coding is imperceptible beneath the app's glossy surface. However, it too is invested in dazzling transformation scenes, using techniques such as fade, spin and mist-effect transitions to create a sense of wonder. In the app's rendering of Stave Three, for instance, the interactor is invited, by means of recorded speech, to touch the robe of the Ghost of Christmas Present. This action results in a burst of light that obscures the interior scene, before revealing a subsequent one in which Scrooge and the Ghost walk side by side through the streets of London as animated snow falls around them. This dramatically enacts the description in Dickens's text: "Holly, mistletoe, red berries, ivy, turkeys, geese, game ... puddings, fruit, and punch, all vanished instantly. So did the room, the fire, the ruddy glow, the hour of night, and they stood in the city streets on Christmas morning" (*CC* 3). Crucially, the pop-up and app-based version of Fischer's "Carol" do more than simply present these transformations in a dynamic and visually compelling way. Dickens stated that his "chief purpose" in presenting "a whimsical kind of masque which the good humour of the season justified" was to "awaken some loving and forbearing thoughts, never out of season in a Christian land." (*CC* Preface). In turning the pages and operating various mechanical devices, or performing particular interactions, reader-interactors are encouraged by these movable adaptations to become active participants in Scrooge's transformation and reflect upon their own capacity for change.

Contemporary commentators saw the *Carol* as a force for good. Lord Jeffrey proclaimed that it had "not only fastened more kindly feelings, but prompted more positive acts of beneficence ... than can be traced to all the pulpits and confessionals in Christendom, since Christmas 1842" (Collins 1971, p. 148). Thackeray dubbed it "a national benefit, and to every man or woman who reads it a personal kindness" (Collins 1971, p. 149). An American factory owner gave his workers another day's holiday; Thomas Carlyle was moved to order a turkey (Ackroyd 1999, p. 435). Underpinning these anecdotes is the sense that by witnessing

Scrooge's journey, the reader might undergo a similar transformation, as Audrey Jaffe suggests:

> In presenting Scrooge with images of his past, present, and future lives, Dickens's spectacular text seeks to awaken that character's sympathy and direct it to the world beyond representation ... such is also the implied effect of the reader's relation to the scenes of *A Christmas Carol*, given the text's explicit analogy between Scrooge's activity and the reader's. (1995, p. 255)

Scrooge's reflections are designed to prompt similar self-examination in the reader, who is offered a personal "spirit" guide in the form of the omniscient narrator, whose friendly, confiding tone makes it feel like we are participating in the text. For example, after the door-nail digression, the narrator responds as if in answer to the reader's question: "Scrooge knew he was dead? Of course he did" (*CC* 1). Later, at the arrival of the Ghost of Christmas Past, the reader becomes curiously embodied within the story-world:

> The curtains of his bed were drawn aside; and Scrooge, starting up in a half-recumbent attitude, found himself face to face with the unearthly visitor who drew them: as close to it as I am now to you, and I am standing in the spirit at your elbow. (*CC* 2)

The narrator is thus embedded in the reader's world as the scenes of Scrooge's transformation play out. But then the final half-sentence overlays the reader's world with the story-world, putting us in Scrooge's place: "I am standing in the spirit at your elbow" (*CC* 2). The pop-up adaptation captures aspects of this metafictional playfulness well. A small bust of Dickens, signifying the narrator's intrusive presence, features in Scrooge's lodgings (Figure 12.6). The analogy between Scrooge and the reader is strengthened by performing actions such as the transformation of the door knocker. Most strikingly, the design of the Ghost of Christmas Yet To Come pop-up has a similar effect to the "spirit at your elbow" aside: the interactor stands outside the scene and sees the Ghost pointing at the gravestone as Scrooge looks on aghast, while at the same time the Ghost's finger points beyond the text directly at the person operating the pop-up (Figure 12.7).

Fischer's pop-up and app-based versions of the "Carol" encourage the reader-interactor to become an active participant in the tale and continue the work of the *Carol* by prompting reflection upon personal reform, while simultaneously engaging in Scrooge's. Within prescribed limits, Fischer's adaptations offer a variety of interactive possibilities that serve to catalyse narrative action and enrich the reading experience by granting access to a three-dimensional version of the story-world, or adding animation and sound effects. While the platforms used oblige interactors to "read" Dickens in unfamiliar ways, the story remains a well-known one, with the affordances of the material and digital designs amplifying aspects of the source text – including Dickens's wordplay, his blurring of the boundaries between life and death, his interest in the fusion of magic and mechanism and his compulsion to draw the reader into the story-world.

Note

1 For ease of reference, double quotation marks are used to distinguish Fischer's movable book and app-based adaptations of the "Carol" from Dickens's *Carol*. Neither Fischer adaptation is paginated.

References

Ackroyd, Peter (1999). *Dickens*. London: Vintage.
Benjamin, Walter (2004). A Glimpse into the World of Children's Books. In Marcus Bullock & Michael W. Jennings (Eds.) *Walter Benjamin: Selected Writings Volume 1, 1913–1926* (pp. 435–443). Cambridge, MA: Belknap Press of Harvard University Press.
Carey, John (1979). *The Violent Effigy: A Study of Dickens' Imagination*. London: Faber and Faber.
A Christmas Carol by Charles Dickens, Chuck Fischer (2010a). [Video file]. Hachette Book Group. Retrieved from https://www.youtube.com/watch?v=eREyQRNrtJA
A Christmas Carol, Chuck Fischer for the iPad (2010b). [Video file]. chuckstudio1. Retrieved from https://www.youtube.com/watch?v=ZlAGJzW5zdE
Collins, Philip (Ed.) (1971). *Dickens: The Critical Heritage*. London: Routledge and Kegan Paul.
Collins, Philip (Ed.) (1975). *Charles Dickens: The Public Readings*. Oxford: Clarendon Press.
Davis, Paul (1990). *The Lives and Times of Ebenezer Scrooge*. New Haven, CT: Yale University Press.
[Dickens, Charles] (1850, 21 December). A Christmas Tree. *Household Words*, 2, 289–295.
Dickens, Mary Angela, et al. [1935]. *Stories from Dickens for Boys and Girls, Told by his Grand-daughter and Others*. Illust. Harold Copping. London: Raphael Tuck & Sons.
Field, Hannah (2014). Children's Movables and the Threat of the Mechanical Book. In Bridget Carrington & Jennifer Harding (Eds.), *Beyond the Book: Transforming Children's Literature* (pp. 101–111). Newcastle upon Tyne: Cambridge Scholars Publishing.
Fischer, Chuck (2003). *Great American Houses and Gardens*. New York: Rizzoli International Publications.
Fischer, Chuck (2010a). *A Christmas Carol: A Pop-Up Book*. With paper engineering by Bruce Foster. New York: Little, Brown and Company.

Fischer, Chuck (2010b). Charles Dickens's *A Christmas Carol*: For the iPad [iPad app]. Fort Lauderdale: Helium Creative.

Haining, Peter (1979). *Movable Books: An Illustrated History*. London: New English Library.

Interview: Chuck Fischer Pop-Up Book Creator (2017, 16 December). BestPopUpBooks.com. Retrieved from https://www.bestpopupbooks.com/interview-with-pop-up-book-creator-chuck-fischer

Jaffe, Audrey (1994). Spectacular Sympathy: Visuality and Ideology in Dickens's *A Christmas Carol*. PMLA, 109(2), 254–265.

Litvack, Leon (2007). *Dickens's Dream* and the Conception of Character. *Dickensian*, 103, 5–36.

Madej, Krystina (2016). *Interactivity, Collaboration, and Authoring in Social Media*. New York: Springer.

Matz, B.W. (1924). *Character Sketches from Dickens*. Introd. by Katie Perugini with illustrations by Harold Copping. London: Raphael Tuck & Sons.

Miller, J. Hillis (1993). The Genres of *A Christmas Carol*. Dickensian, 89, 193–206.

Newsroom: Apple UK (2010, January 27). *Press Release: Apple Launches iPad*. Retrieved from https://www.apple.com/uk/newsroom/2010/01/27Apple-Launches-iPad

Opie, Iona, & Opie, Peter (1975, 19 September). Books that Come to Life. *The Times Literary Supplement*, 1055.

Rahn, Suzanne (2011). *Rediscoveries in Children's Literature*. New York: Routledge.

The Readings of Mr. Charles Dickens as Condensed by Himself (1868). Boston, MA: Ticknor & Fields.

Reid-Walsh, Jacqueline (2012). Activity and Agency in Historical "Playable Media." *Journal of Children and Media*, 6(2), 164–181.

Story Books and Other Books 1937–38 ([1937]). [Raphael Tuck & Sons catalogue]. Retrieved from https://catalogues.tuckdb.org/items/9328

Tracy, Robert (1998). "A Whimsical Kind of Masque": The Christmas Books and Victorian Spectacle. *Dickens Studies Annual*, 27, 113–130.

Walkup, Kathleen (2010). Movable Books. In Michael F. Suarez, S.J. Woudhuysen & H.R. Woudhuysen (Eds.), *The Oxford Companion to the Book: Volume 2* (pp. 947–948). Oxford: Oxford University Press.

Index

Compiled by Leon Litvack.

Author names are indexed only where there is an in-text discussion of the individual and his/her work. Names of contributors to this volume are only indexed in cases where they have authored critical works discussed in the individual essays. Locators in **bold** indicate figures; those followed by *n* indicate notes. Charles Dickens is abbreviated as "CD." Locators for Dickens's individual works may be found in the main entry for "Dickens, Charles John Huffam."

a

"A.A."   39
Abrams, Philip   80, 87
Achilles   220
Ackroyd, Peter   96, 234
adaptation   150, 208, 232, 240 *see also* books, movable; iPad/iOS
   ballet   223
   digital   8, 225–228, 233–237, 239, 241
   film   208, 223
   graphic novel   223
   opera   223
   radio   223
   television   223
   textual   208
Adrian, Arthur A.   15, 19, 21
Adshead, Joseph   81, 87
Aeschylus
   Prometheus Bound   139
Albrecht, Delphine   5
Alderley House (Cheshire)   23 *see also* Stanley, Arthur Penrhyn
Aldworth House (Haslemere, Surrey)   22 *see also* Tennyson, Alfred
Alighieri, Dante   114
Allegory   133, 136, 144
Allingham, Philip   149, 160
   The Victorian Web (website)   160
America *see* United States
Andersen, Hans Christian
   "The Wild Swans"   229
Andrews, Malcolm   5, 149
animism   5, 120–122
Anker, Elizabeth S.   2
antonomasia   207, 208, 213, 215, 216
Arabian Nights, The (*One Thousand and One Nights*)
   Aladdin   238
   Ali Baba   238
archives
   Armstrong Browning Library   21
   digital   3, 6, 160–162
   government   70
   Internet Archive (website)   160

Reading Dickens Differently, First Edition. Edited by Leon Litvack and Nathalie Vanfasse.
© 2020 John Wiley & Sons Ltd. Published 2020 by John Wiley & Sons Ltd.

archives (cont'd)
  London Metropolitan Archives 83
  prison 4, 75, 81
  Westminster Abbey (Muniments) 19
Arctic 193
Armatage, Isaac (CD's page-boy) 15
Asmodeus 202
Assassin's Creed: Syndicate 207–220
  see also Ubisoft Entertainment
  Charles Dickens **213**
  Jacob and Evie Frye **210, 212**
  Palace of Westminster **212, 215**
  Thames River prospect **210**
Athenaeum, The 175
Athenaeum Club 18
Auden, Wynstan Hugh (W.H.) 199
Austin, Letitia (née Dickens; CD's sister) 17, 34
Australia 82, 87, 193 *see also* prisons: transportation
Avignon (Provence) 20

b

Bachrach, Fred G.H. 133
Baker, William 15, 32
Balzac, Honoré de 139
  La Cousine Bette 169
  Le Père Goriot 142
Barbier, Frédéric 2
Barnard, Fred 6, 150, 152–160
  Bleak House illustrations **155, 156, 157, 158**
  self-caricature 153, **154**
  theatre poster of Jo (*Bleak House*) **159**
Barrow, John Henry (CD's uncle) 63
Barrow, Thomas (CD's uncle) 135
Barthes, Roland 96
Baudrillard, Jean
  Simulations and Simulacra 214
Beard, Francis Carr (Frank; CD's doctor) 15, 16, 25, 34
Beckett, Samuel
  Murphy 121
  Watt 121

Bedford, Charles St Clare 33, 42*n*
Bedford, Earl of *see* Russell, John 1st Earl of Bedford
Bell, Alexander Graham 211
Bell, Karl 217
Benjamin, Walter 137–139, 141
  "A Glimpse into the World of Children's Books" 228–230, 232
Berkshire (county) 78
Best, Stephen 2, 3, 6
Billlingsgate Market (London) 134
biography 3, 4, 26, 39, 41, 49, 68, 80, 208 *see also* Dickens, Charles John Huffam: biography; Edel, Leon; Forster, John; reading
Blasselle, Bruno 2
Bleich, David 3
blog posts 168, 170, 171, 173, 197
Bloom, Harold 1
Bloom, Michelle E. 214
Bodenheimer, Rosemarie 52–53
Bonaparte, Napoleon 135
Bond, James (films) 185, 217
books *see also* reading
  digital 162, 167–183, 225–228, 233–235, 239, 240
  end of 1
  fragments 220
  history of 2
  materiality of 106–108
  movable ("pop-up") 8, 223–232, 236–240 *see also* Fischer, Chuck; Foster, Bruce
  picture 229
  rebus 229
  speaking picture 229
Booth, Wayne C. 108
Bourchier, Sir Humphrey 40
Boyle, Mary 17
Braddon, Mary Elizabeth
  Lady Audley's Secret 156
Bradford (Yorkshire) 96
Brighton (East Sussex) 153, 154

British Broadcasting Corporation (BBC)   117
British Museum   63, 162
Browne, Hablot Knight ("Phiz")   6, 55, 149–152, 157, 162
Buckinghamshire (county)   78
Buckingham, University of   168
Burial in Woollen Acts (1666–1680)   34
Burt, John   87

C

Calne (Wiltshire)   62, 63
Canaletto (Giovanni Antonio Canal)   128
Canary Wharf (London)   187
Canning, George   63
Canterbury (Kent)   119
Capri (Campania)   117, 120
Capuano, Peter   5, 114
Carey, John   214–215, 232
Carlyle, Thomas   4, 20, 22, 69, 71, 73, 180, 239
  "Model Prisons"   86
  "On History"   70
Carswell, Catherine   116–117
cartoons   161
Castiglia, Christopher   9
Cavallo, Guglielmo   2
Cavendish Square (London)   16
Cervantes (Miguel de Cervantes Saavedra)   126
Chambers, Jessie   113, 114
Chapman and Hall (CD's publishers)   55, 157
character presence (*The Mystery of Edwin Drood*)   176, **177, 178,** 179
Charing Cross Station (London)   36
Charles Dickens Museum   9, 226
Chartier, Roger   2
Chelsea (London)   134
Chesterton, George Laval   75–82, 84
  Revelations of Prison Life   81–83
Chesterton, Gilbert Keith (G.K.)   187
Christmas   1, 125, 145, 224, 225, 232, 239

Church, Roman Catholic   67–68, 103
Citton, Yves   1, 2
city   6, 8, 132, 134, 142, 144, 145, 154, 185–202, 217 *see also* London
civic disabilities, Jewish   62
class, social   17, 58, 62, 63, 65, 66, 85, 116, 118, 125, 127, 158, 214, 218
Clayton, Jay   3, 7, 111
Clerkenwell (London)   71, 75 *see also* prisons: Cold Bath Fields
Cockshut, A.O.J.   41
cognition   101, 102, 105–106
Cohen, Jane R.   149, 150, 154, 167
Cohen, William A.   100
Collins, Charles Allston   34
Collins, Jim   9
Collins, Katherine Macready (Katey; née Dickens; CD's daughter)   15, 17, 34, 35
Collins, Philip   75, 77, 80–82, 86, 87
Collins, (William) Wilkie   15, 18, 34, 216
  No Name   167–171 *see also* reading: online projects
Colman, George
  Broad Grins   135
comedy *see* humour
commedia dell'arte   119
Coolidge, Archibald   179, 180
Cooper, Dennis   96
Coover, Robert
  "The End of Books"   1
Copping, Harold   230
copyright   27
Costello, Dudley   213–214
Coutts, Angela Burdett   75, 81, 83, 84
Covent Garden (London)   132–136, 139
Crawford, William   77–78
Cresswell, Sir Cresswell   53, 54
Croydon (Surrey; now London)   199
Cruikshank, George   18, 143, 149–152
cyberformalism   3
cyberpunk   186, 194, 197
cyborg   186, 192

d

Dalziel, Edward 153, 162
Dalziel, George 153, 162
Damasio, Antonio 98
Dames, Nicholas 5, 95
"Dan" (Urbexer) 197
Danielewski, Mark Z. 96
Dark Knight Rises, The (film) 169
Darroch, Sandra Jobson 120
Darwin, Charles 105, 211
data sampling 7, 176–179
Davie, Neil 77, 78, 82, 87
Davis, Paul 223
Daylesford (Worcestershire) 37
Dean Street, Soho (London) 135
Dean's Yard (London) 36
death 126, 129, 130, 134–142, 145, 197, 199–201, 228, 229, 232, 233, 241 see also funeral customs; *see also under* Dickens, Charles John Huffam: biography
Deer, Samuel 33, 34, 42*n*
diachrony 2
dialect 118
Dickens 2012 (CD bicentenary celebrations) 208
Dickens, Alfred (CD's brother) 52
Dickens, Anna (née Weller; wife of Frederick Dickens) 48–54, 57, 58
Dickens, Catherine (née Hogarth; CD's wife) 17, 49–53, 58
Dickens, Charles Culliford Boz (Charley; Charles Dickens Jr.; CD's son) 15, 16, 21, 27–29, 34, 191, 192
Dickens, Charles John Huffam
  biography (chronological listing): Warren's Blacking 49, 61–62, 64; childhood reading 195; attends school 63; solicitor's clerk 63; shorthand reporter 63; reader at British Museum 63; Parliamentary reporter 4, 63–65, 68, 72; resides at Furnival's Inn 49; influenced by T.B. Macaulay 61, 62, 65, 68, 69, 70, 72–73; relationship with brother Fred 4, 49–54, 55, 56, 57, 58; 1st American visit 49, 76–77; sojourn in Italy 127; composes autobiographical fragment 64, 190; sojourn in Switzerland 64, 187; Urania Cottage 75, 81, 83–84; friendship with Frederick Locker 18; amateur theatricals 49; separation from Catherine Dickens 50, 51; "violated letter" 50; relationship with Ellen Ternan 15, 17, 28, 52, 54; public readings 5, 96, 126, 175, 208, 211, 228, 233; affection for France 54; Royal Literary Fund 38; 2nd American visit 96, 125, 129, 175, 208, 211; meetings with A.P. Stanley 17, 19–20, 29; last illness 15–17; telegram requesting urgent medical assistance 15, **16**; death 3, 6, 17, 21, 23, 125, 149, 168, 171, 174, 208; death certificate **36**; portrait after death (Millais) **35**; proposed burial sites (Strood, Shorne, Rochester) 23–25; burial in Poets' Corner, Westminster Abbey 3, 20, 21, 22, 23, 25, 26, 27, 29–37, 39, 41; grave **28**; funeral fee account **30**, **31**, 32–34; last will and testament 37–38; sale of domestic effects 24
  images of **35**, 208, **213**, 214, **215**
  works: *All the Year Round* 49, 53, 59, 168, 170; *American Notes* 72, 76–77, 81, 86, 129, 130; *Barnaby Rudge* 61, 68–72, 143; *Bleak House* 6, 62, 65, 114, 119, 125–127, 131–132, 133, 139, 142–143, 145, 149, 152–160, 202, 232; *The Chimes* 67; *A Christmas Carol* 8, 188, 202, 223–241; *The Cricket on the Hearth* 119, 230; *David*

Copperfield 72, 86, 96, 113–115, 119, 120, 127, 129, 136, 137, 167, 172, 190, 230, 231; *Dombey and Son* 6, 64, 96, 98–100, 114, 129–131, 142, 153, 154, 169–170, 200–201, 202, 232; *The Examiner* 82–83, 85; *Great Expectations* 6, 47, 63, 100–102, 106, 116, 132, 136, 139; *Hard Times* 125, 127; Household Edition 6, 149–160, 161, 168; *Household Words* 50, 75, 76, 84, 86–87, 119, 191, 193, 195–196, 198–199, 202, 213–214, 232; *Little Dorrit* 97–98, 126, 132, 136, 141, 142; *Martin Chuzzlewit* 96, 114, 119, 121, 129–130, 143, 230; *The Mystery of Edwin Drood* 7, 115, 167–181, 191; *Nicholas Nickleby* 96, 143, 232; *The Old Curiosity Shop* 127, 129, 142, 143, 213; *Oliver Twist* 108, 126, 127, 136, 143, 167, 171, 181, 195, 201, 231, 232; *Our Mutual Friend* 106–110, 118, 167–169, 174, 181–183; *The Pickwick Papers* 47, 64, 96, 117, 143, 172, 230, 232; *Sketches by Boz* 63, 77, 129, 198, 217; *A Tale of Two Cities* 4, 47–49, 52–59, 70, 102–106, 114, 167–169, 170, 189, 197, 208; "The Uncommercial Traveller" 136, 188, 190–191, 194–195, 196
Dickens, Edmund Henry (CD's nephew) 34
Dickens, Elizabeth Barrow (CD's mother) 62
Dickens, Elizabeth (Bessie, née Evans; wife of Charley Dickens) 34
Dickens, Frederick William (Fred; CD's brother) 4, 49–59
Dickens, Henry Fielding (CD's son) 17, 34
Dickens, John (CD's father) 49, 61
Dickens, Katherine Macready (Katey) *see* Collins, Katherine Macready
Dickens, Letitia Mary *see* Austin, Letitia
Dickens, Mary Angela (CD's granddaughter)
Dickens' Dream Children 230
Dickens, Mary ("Mamie"; CD's daughter) 15, 16, 19, 20, 23, 28, 34
Dijon (Bourgogne) 99, 129, 130
discourse, neo-Victorian 207, 208, 215
Disraeli, Benjamin
Tancred 169
Divorce and Matrimonial Causes, Court for 4, 49, 56, 57 *see also* law: divorce
Dixon, Edmund Saul 58, 119
Dixon, William Hepworth 86
Doctors' Commons (law court) 38, 63
Doran, John 175
Doré, Gustave
London: A Pilgrimage 211
Dorking (Surrey) 50–51
Dorset (county) 78
Douglas-Fairhurst, Robert 61
Douglas, Norman 120
drama *see* masque; melodrama; performance; theatricality
Drew, Richard
"The Falling Man" 199–200
Dungeons & Dragons 212

e

Eastwood Library (Nottinghamshire) 113
Ecclefechan (Dumfries and Galloway) 20
Eco, Umberto 3, 104
Edel, Leon 41
Eden, Garden of 133–134
Edward, Prince of Wales, later King Edward VII 23
effigy 150, 213, 214, 232
Egypt 23, 193
Eliot, George (Marian Evans) 115

Eliot, Thomas Stearns (T.S.)   114
Elliott, Kamilla   152, 160
Elliott, William   33, 42*n*
Elwin, Whitwell   37–39
Embankment (London)   133
Empire, British   215
energy
   imaginative   102, 129, 208
   physical   117, 187, 188, 194, 195
epic   8, 220
Essex (county)   78
Examiner, The   19, 82, 85–87, 171, 174, 181
exploration *see* Urban Exploration

f

fairy tale   191, 195, 229
Fall, the (Fall of humankind)   133
Faraday, Harold   153
Farsi (language)   216
Felluga, Dino   160
Felski, Rita   2, 9
Felton, Cornelius   188
Field, Hannah   230
Field, John   87
Fielding, Henry
   Tom Jones   113
Fiennes, Ralph   208
Fischer, Chuck   8, 224
   A Christmas Carol: A Pop-Up Book   224, **225**, 226, **227**, 228, 232, 233, **236, 237,** 238–240
   Charles Dickens's A Christmas Carol: For the iPad   225–228, 232, 233, **234, 235,** 239, 240
   Great American Houses and Gardens   226
Fish, Stanley   3
"F.N.B."   39
fog   117, 131–132, 134, 139, 202, 211, 217
Foord, John, & Sons   24, 25
Forster, John   3, 53, 59, 128, 129, 188, 192
   absence at time of CD's death   15, 23
   arranges CD's funeral and burial   21–23, 28, 34, 41
   arranges Edward Bulwer Lytton's funeral   39–40
   bids final farewell to CD   23, 35
   enlists aid of Whitwell Elwin for CD's funeral sermon   37–38
   forwards fee for CD's funeral   34
   The Life of Charles Dickens   3, 20, 26, 40–41, 62–64, 130–131, 135, 188, 190, 200
   meets A.P. Stanley to discuss CD's burial in Westminster Abbey   27–29
   reaction to CD's death   34, 38–39
   review of A.P. Stanley's *Life and Correspondence of Thomas Arnold*   18–19
   review of *Oliver Twist*   171, 181
   shapes narrative of CD's death and burial   15, 26, 41
Foster, Bruce   224, 226, 227
Foster, Christopher   32–34, 42*n*
Fourier, Joseph   119
Fowler, Charles   133
Fox, Charles James   63
Fraser's Magazine   69
Frey, James   96
Frith, William Powell   214
   Charles Dickens   214
   The Crossing Sweeper   157
Fuller, Loie   121
Fun   158
funeral customs   3, 32–35
Furniss, Harry   161

g

Gaddis, John Lewis   80
Gad's Hill Place (Higham, Kent; CD's country mansion)   15, 16, 23, 24, 29, 32, 35, 36, 54, 190, 211
games   3, 7, 106, 186, 198 *see also Assassin's Creed: Syndicate; Dungeons & Dragons;* Ivanhoe

Game; play; *Pokémon Go*; Urban Exploration
augmented reality   185–186, 192–194
board   223
digital (computer)   7, 8, 185, 187, 190, 192, 194, 207–220, 223, 225–228, 232–235, 239, 240
fantasy role-play   212
parlour   224
picture book   229
Garrett, Bradley   185–187, 190, 197 *see also* Urban Exploration
Garnett, David   117
George IV, King   63
Gibbon, Edward
Decline and Fall of the Roman Empire   106, 107
Gibson, Walker   108
Gilpin, William
Remarks on Forest Scenery   130
Giorgione (Giorgio da Castelfranco)   132
Glencoe (Highlands)   130–131
Global Positioning System (GPS)   192
Gog and Magog   191
Goldman, Paul   152
Goodman, Michael John
Victorian Illustrated Shakespeare Archive (website)   161
Good Words   152
Google Books (website)   160
Gordon Riots (1780)   70
Grant, Anthony   24
Grass, Sean   87
Greeks, ancient   220
Greenblatt, Stephen   9
Green, Charles   150
Grego, Joseph   153
Grey, Charles 2nd Earl Grey   64
Griffith, John, Vice-Dean of Rochester   24, 25
grime (music)   187
Grosvenor Street (London)   16
grotesque   117, 118, 126, 134, 143–145, 201
Guardian, The   217–218
Guildhall (London)   191
Gurney, Benjamin   214

h

Hachette Book Group   227
Haggard, Sir Henry Rider   161 *see also under* Holterhoff, Kate
Halliday, Andrew
The Savage Club Papers   157
Hamilton, Nigel   3, 41, 49
Hampshire (county)   78
Hand Court (London)   132, 134
Hansen, Adam   86
Harris, Alana   218–219
Hastings, Warren   37 *see also* Macaulay, Thomas Babington: *Warren Hastings*
Hayles, N. Katherine   3
Hayward, Keith S.   197
Hazlitt, William   139, 144
Heidegger, Martin   189
Heller, Tamar   54–55
Henderson, Heather   15, 35
Herbert, Henry John George 3rd Earl of Carnarvon (Lord Porchester)   67
Hercules (Heracles)   215
Heron Tower (110 Bishopsgate, London)   187, 197
Herschel, Sir John   20
Hertfordshire (county)   78
Hesperides, Garden of   133–134
Higham (Kent)   16, 17, 32, 36 *see also* Gad's Hill Place
Highgate (London)   119
Hillis Miller, J.   2
Hill, Sir Rowland   20, 21
Hine, George Henry   81
hip-hop (music)   187

historiography 26, 61, 69
history 4, 8, 95, 102, 103, 128, 140, 141, 167, 169, 187, 214, 226
 see also biography; reading: historical
 approaches to 4, 61–73, 80, 187, 211–212, 218–219, 226
 book 2, 229, 238
 creative 219
 cultural 29
 English 39, 61, 63–65, 67, 70, 72
 European 66, 137
 French 49, 54, 56, 73
 German 73
 military 211
 North American 66
 social 80, 87
 textual 161
Hoare, Samuel, Jr. 78, 80
Hogarth Club 158
Hogarth, Georgina (CD's sister-in-law) 15–17, 22, 25, 28, 34, 52
Hogarth, Mary Scott (CD's sister-in-law) 52
Hogarth, William 119
Holborn Viaduct (London) 218
Holland *see* Netherlands
Holland, Norman 3
Hollington, Michael 120
Holsworth, George 16
Holterhoff, Kate
 Visual Haggard (website) 161
Homan, Franklin George 23–25
Homer 220
homosexuality 120
Hotten, J.C. 172
House, Humphry 68
House of Commons 62, 63, 68, 72, 77–79 *see also* Parliament
Howitt, Mary 25
Hughes, Linda K. 167, 169, 180
Hughes, William R. 15–17, 23
Huguet, Christine 219

humanities 111
 curating 9
 digital 7, 160–162
humour 47, 107, 114, 120, 121, 129, 135, 145, 153, 173–176, 191, 193, 232
Hungerford Market (London) 134
Hungerford Stairs (London) 190
Hyde, Edward 1st Earl of Clarendon 69–70

i

icon 102, 107, 200, 207, 208, 213, 214, 219
Ilfracombe (Devon) 138
Illingworth, Edward 81, 84
Illustrated London News, The (*ILN*) 28, 173–176
illustration, book 5, 6, 55, 149–162, 223–239 *see also* Barnard, Fred; Browne, Hablot Knight; Copping, Harold; Cruikshank, George; Fischer, Chuck; Leech, John
 Anglophone 161
 digital resource 160–162
 interactive 233
 panorama 230–233
India 37, 193
infiltration 7, 186 *see also* Urban Exploration
Innes, Paul 220
inspiration, authorial 53, 188, 191, 192, 202
instalments, serial 7, 53, 152, 167–180
 see also reading: serial
intelligence, artificial (AI) 186
interdisciplinarity 2, 5
Invisible Woman, The (film) 208
iPad/iOS 8–9, 224, 226–228, 233–237, 239, 240 *see also* Jobs, Steve; Fischer, Chuck: Charles Dickens's *A Christmas Carol*: For the iPad
Iser, Wolfgang 3, 95, 101, 108
Ivanhoe Game, The 207

Index

j

Jackson, Lee
   The Victorian Dictionary (website)   211
Jaffe, Audrey   240
Jalland, Pat   17
James, Henry   41
James, William   98
Jauss, Hans Robert   3, 95
Jebb, Joshua   87
Jeffrey, Francis, Lord Jeffrey   239
Jerrold, Blanchard
   London: A Pilgrimage   211
Jobs, Steve   227–228, *see also* iPad/iOS
Jockers, Matthew   3, 7
John Bull   172
Jones, Inigo   133
Jones, Samuel Flood   33, 34, 42*n*
Jouve, Vincent   2
Jozsa, Pierre   3
Judy   172, 175

k

Kant, Immanuel   198
Kensal Green Cemetery (London)   39
Kent (county)   78, 130, 190, 194, 211
Kindynis, Theo   187, 189, 194, 196, 198
King's College London   218
Kirby, R.S.   107
Kitton, Frederick George (F.G.)   153
Knebworth House (Hertfordshire)   39
   see also Lytton, Edward George
Knight, Charles   18
Knight, George H.   24
Knights Templar   209, 220

l

La Spezia (Liguria)   115
Lambeth (London)   68, 216
landscape   129, 194
   artistic   6, 131, 139, 144
   fictional   6, 131, 138, 139
   physical   99
   urban   186

Lansdowne, Lord *see* Petty-Fitzmaurice, Henry
lantern, magic   187, 193
Latour, Bruno   2, 9
Launceton (Cornwall)   15
Laurie, Sir Peter (MP)   80, 82
Laurie, Peter Northall (magistrate)   80, 84–85
Lausanne (Vaud)   187
Lavater, Johann Kaspar   119
law   4, 25, 47, 48, 51–52, 66, 67, 69, 142, 172, 196, 202 *see also* Burial in Woollen Acts; Matrimonial Causes Act; Middlesex magistrates; Municipal Corporation Act; Poor Law Amendment Act; Reform Act; Test and Corporation Acts; trespass
   burial in linen   34
   criminal   82
   divorce   4, 53–54, 56–58
   English common   50
   Inns of Court   62
   penal *see* prisons
Lawrence, David Herbert (D.H.)   113–122
   Apocalypse   115
   "The Future of the Novel"   114
   Kangaroo   116
   The Lost Girl   5, 114–122
   Mr Noon   115
   reading habits   113, 115, 116
   "Smile"   114
   Sons and Lovers   113
   The White Peacock   114
Lawrence, Frieda   120
Ledger, Sally   48, 58
Lee, Jennie   159
Leech, John   228
Leenhardt, Jacques   3
Leicester, University of   168
Leighton, Mary Elizabeth   151–152
Lerici (Liguria)   115
Letissier, Georges   103

Index

Lincoln, President Abraham 20
Lincoln's Inn (London) 61–62
Linklater, Eric
   The Man on My Back 117
Lister, Martin 7
Little Red Riding Hood 109
Litvack, Leon 26, 63, 136, 188, 192, 208, 214
Livingstone, David 20
Locker, Frederick (later Locker-Lampson) 17–18, **19**, 21–23, 26–29, 36
Locker, Lady Charlotte Christian (née Bruce) 17
London 4, 6–9, 16, 17, 22, 49, 61–64, 66, 69, 75, 77, 83, 85, 87, 99, 109, 117, 129, 131, 132, 134–136, 139, 140, 142, 159, 169, 186–188, 190, 191, 193, 197, **210**, 211, **212**, 213, 215–218, 220, 224, 226, **227**, 239 *see also* city *see also names of individual locations*
London Bridge (London) 134
London Consolidation Crew 187
   see also Urban Exploration
London Society 152
London Underground 186
Longfellow, Henry Wadsworth 18
Louttit, Chris 149, 150
Lund, Michael 167, 169, 180
Lydon, Jane 157
Lytton, Edward George Earle Lytton Bulwer 1st Baron 18, 20, 39–40
   see also Stanley, Arthur Penrhyn: burial of Edward Bulwer Lytton
   Last of the Barons 40

m

Macaulay, Thomas Babington Macaulay 1st Baron 4, 40, 61–73
   History of England 72–73
   speeches 62–68
   Warren Hastings 37
Macé, Marielle 5

Mackenzie, Compton 117
Maclise, Daniel 128
   Charles Dickens 208
Macrone, John 49
Madame Tussauds 213–214 *see also* Tussaud, Marie
magic 195, 201, 216, 227–230, 232, 233, 238, 241
Magnus, Maurice 120
Magnússon, Sigurður Gylfi 3, 4, 41, 80
Mahoney, James 150
Mahr, Greg 99
Maiden Lane (London) 132–135
Man on Wire (film) 201
Mansfield, Katherine 120, 121
Mansion House (London) 191
Marcus, Sharon 2, 3, 6
Marx, Karl 211, 218
masque 238, 239 *see also* performance; theatricality
Matrimonial Causes Act (1857) 57, 58
Mayhew, Henry 216
   London Labour and the London Poor 211, 217
Maxwell, Richard 48
McKnight, Natalie 82, 86
media, social 7 *see also* blog posts; Twitter
melodrama 48, 96, 108, 111, 154, 156–157 *see also* theatricality
Melville, Herman 127
Merryweather, F. Somner 107
metafiction 240
Methuselah 215
Meuse River (Maas) 133
Miall, David S. 96–97
Middle Ages, the 212
Middlesex (county) 75, 77, 78
Middlesex magistrates 75–86 *see also* law
Milan State University 208–209, 211
Mill, John Stuart 20, 22
Millais, John Everett
   Charles Dickens After Death **35**

Milnes, Richard Monckton 1st Baron Houghton   18, 26–29
Milton, John   115
  Paradise Lost   130
mimicry   5, 104, 116–119, 121, 122, 237
Mirror of Parliament, The   4, 63, 65, 68
misers   106–108, 226, 239
Modernism   5, 116
Montfort, Nick   7
Monthly Law Magazine and Political Review   78–79
Moore, Wendy   9
Moretti, Franco   3, 7
Morgan, Capt. Elisha Ely (E.E.)   136
Morrissey, J.   33
Moynahan, Julian   100
mulcts   32–34, 42n *see also* Burial in Woollen Acts
Municipal Corporations Act (1835)   68
Murry, John Middleton   120

n

Napier, Macvey   72
National Temperance Society   82
nautical imagery   128–130, 133–141, 145 *see also* Turner, Joseph Mallord William
Nayder, Lillian   49, 50
Neele, Henry   69
Netherlands   133
neuropsychology   5, 101
New Cross Station (London)   199
New York City   201, 214
New Zealand   120, 193
Niagara Falls   129
Nielsen, Holly   218–219
Night Mail (film)   199
Nightingale, Florence   211
9/11 (September 11 2001 terror attacks)   199–200 *see also* World Trade Center
Nonconformists   23
Northumberland family *see* Percy family

Norton, Charles Eliot   125, 126, 143
Notre Dame Cathedral (Paris)   211

o

Oculus (headset)   193 *see also* games
Olympics, London (2012)   169
Once a Week   152
Opie, Iona   230
Opie, Peter   230
opium   172
Orford, Pete   170, 171
  The Drood Inquiry (website)   168, 181
Ouvry, Frederic (CD's solicitor)   17, 25, 34
Oxford English Dictionary   42n, 130, 141, 169
Oxfordshire   78

p

Paddington Station (London)   218
Palace, Crystal (Great Exhibition)   126
Palhaniuk, Chuck   96
Palmerston, Henry John Temple 3rd Viscount   20, 21
panorama, moving   193
pantomime   238
Paris   63, 73, 103, 193, 199
Paris Review   41
Parliament, British   4, 61–64, 67–68, 70, 73, 82, 172–173 *see also* House of Commons
Paroissien, David   49, 75, 77
Patoine, Pierre-Louis   5, 96
Patten, Robert L.   22, 61, 149, 150, 173, 175, 180
Peltonen, Matti   3
Penelope (wife of Odysseus)   215
penny dreadfuls   217
perambulation *see* walking *see also* reading: perambulatory
Percy family, Dukes of Northumberland   20–21

performance   117, 121, 157, 200, 201, 207, 220, 238 *see also* masque; theatricality
Period, The   174, 175
Petit, Philippe   201
Petty-Fitzmaurice, Henry 3rd Marquess of Lansdowne   62
"Phiz" *see* Browne, Hablot Knight
photography   157, 185, 186, 190, 192, 197, 199–201, 208, 211, 213, 214
physiognomy   4, 5, 118, 119
Picard, Michel   3
picturesque   130, 209
Piggott, Gillian   198
Pitt, George Dibdin   158
Pitt, William, the younger   63
place-hacking *see* trespass; Urban Exploration
Plantagenet, House of   66
play   7, 8, 64, 194, 195, 198, 207, 209, 211–212, 216, 218–220, 224, 229, 232–233, 240 *see also* games
plot resolution   168–183
Plymouth (Devon)   140
Pokémon Go   192
Poole, Henry, & Sons   33, 42*n*
Poor Law Amendment Act (1834)   68
Porchester, Lord *see* Herbert, Henry John George
Pound, Ezra   114
prisons   4, 48, 75–87, 97, 142, 193, 215
   Auburn (New York)   77
   Cold Bath Fields (Middlesex House of Correction; Clerkenwell Gaol)   4, 75–79, 81–87
   Eastern Penitentiary (Philadelphia)   76
   House of Correction (Boston)   77
   inspectors   76, 78, 79, 81–82, 86
   Marshalsea   97
   Millbank   75–76, 78, 79, 87
   Newgate   70
   Pentonville   75–76, 78, 79, 81, 86, 87

   regulations   83
   separate system   76–78, 80, 81, 86, 87
   silent system   77–78, 81, 86, 87
   Society for the Improvement of Prison Discipline   78
   Tothill Fields   75–77, 79, 81
   transportation (Australia)   75, 82, 87
Project Boz (website)   160
Prothero, Rowland   20, 21, 28, 39
Pugh, Edwin   150
Punch; or, the London Chiarivari   172

r

Radcliffe, Charles Bland   16
radicalism, political   48, 82, 158, 194
railway   16, 17, 22, 36, 80, 98–99, 130, 131, 141, 196–201, 209, 213
rain   130–132, 136, 139, 141, 154, 196, 217
Ramachandran, Vilayanur   101
rap (music)   187
ravens   5, 71–72, 119, 143
reader, classes of
   actual   3, 106
   creative   190
   empathetic   101
   general   167
   immersed   108, 229, 241
   implied   3, 101, 108
   interactive   224, 228, 229, 233–240
   intradiegetic   106
   mock   108
   model   108
   online   167–183
   postulated   108
   real   106, 110
   Victorian   150, 152, 168, 170, 171, 176
   woman   95
   young   219
reading   1–10
   addictive   95
   alternative   108, 187, 223
   biographical "turn"   2–4, 26, 41, 49

childhood 191, 195
close 97, 110, 173, 180
communal 7, 168–183
distant 3
eccentric 107
empathetic 5, 96, 98, 100, 101, 103, 108
hallucinatory 96
hermeneutical 5, 97, 111
historical 71
history of 3
hypnotic 99
immersive 108–111, 182–183, 193, 220, 227–229, 240, 241
interactive 7, 8, 168–183, 207–220, 223–241
interdisciplinary 5
interpictorial 4–6, 125–145, 149–162
intertextual 113–122, 151, 152, 160, 172
kinaesthetic 6, 100
literary 9
macroanalytic 7
meditation of 108
microhistorical 2, 3, 15–42, 47–59, 61–73, 75–87
Modernist 116
online projects: *Dickens Journals Online* 160, 168, 170; *The Mystery of Edwin Drood* 168–181; *No Name* 168, 170–171; *Our Mutual Friend* 168, 169, 181–183 *A Tale of Two Cities* 168–170; *Victorian Serial Novels* 7, 169–170
pace of 168
penological 2, 4, 75–87
perambulatory (walking) 8, 185–202
performative 5
phenomenology of 5, 108
practices 106–108
reader-response 5, 95, 96, 106
serial 7, 149, 152, 167–183
social 7
sociology of 3
somatic (physiological) 2, 4, 5, 95–111
spontaneous 2
surface 6, 7
symptomatic 6
technological (digital) 2, 6–8, 106, 160–162, 167–183, 207–220, 223–228, 233–241
transgressive 103
reality
 allegorical 145
 augmented 7, 185–186, 190–192, 194
 represented 8, 97–98, 101, 139, 144, 208, 211, 214, 216, 218
 social 62
 virtual 7, 193 *see also* Oculus
realist style 116, 144, 150, 152, 157, 191, 211, 214, 216, 218, 230
reception studies 3, 95, 97, 150, 160, 174, 207
Reform Act, First (1832) 4, 65, 67, 68
Reid-Walsh, Jacqueline 223, 234, 238
Rejlander, Oscar
 Night in Town 157–158
Religious Tract Society 42*n*
Renders, Hans 3, 26, 41, 49, 80
reviews (of CD's works) 72, 171–176, 179
Revolution, French
 1789–99 4, 54, 56, 67, 103, 105, 169
 1830 (July Revolution) 63
revolution, sexual 186
Reynolds, Frank 161
Reynolds, John Russell 1st Baronet 16–17, 25
Robinson, Thomas 24
Rochester (Kent) 16, 24, 25, 32
Rochester Cathedral 23–26, 39, 119
Rogers, Samuel
 Italy, A Poem 127
Rose, Hector 81
Rotch, Benjamin 80–87
Rotterdam 133

Routledge, George 18
Rowland, Peter 61
Rowlandson, Thomas 119
Roy, Jean-Vincent 211
Royal Academy 17, 20, 23, 128
Royal Victoria Theatre (The Old Vic, London) 196
ruin *see* wreckage
Rush, Walter 33, 42*n*
Ruskin, John 6, 125–145
  "Ariadne Florentina" 143
  "Fiction, Fair and Foul" 127, 142
  Fors Clavigera 130, 139
  "The Harbours of England" 134, 137
  inaugural lecture at Oxford 125
  "The Lamp of Truth" 144
  meets CD 126
  Modern Painters 126, 129, 143
  "Of Imagination Penetrative" 143
  The Seven Lamps Of Architecture 144
  "The Storm-Cloud of the Nineteenth Century" 132, 134, 139
  Unto This Last 127
Russell, John 1st Earl of Bedford 133
Russell, John 1st Earl Russell (Lord John Russell; Prime Minister) 64–68, 82
Russell, Whitworth 77, 78

S

St Paul's Cathedral (London) 8, 135
St Paul's Church, Covent Garden ("Actors' Church", London) 133, 135
Sala, George Augustus 23, 73
Sanders, Andrew 48, 53, 54, 56
satire 5, 114, 115, 121, 151, 157, 172
Saunders, Charles 35–36
Saunders, Mary 157
Savage Club 158
Savage, Henry 115
Schaeffer, Jean-Marie 2
Schivelbusch, Wolfgang 198

Schor, Hilary 55, 56, 58, 59
Scott, Sir Walter 113, 126, 142, 143
  Ivanhoe 207 *see also* Ivanhoe Game
seascape 129, 133–141, 144, 196
sensation, physical 4, 5, 95–100, 102–106, 110, 187, 194, 198, 200
  see also reading: somatic
Shakespeare, William 114
  Macbeth 139, 141, 142
Shard (London) 187
Shattock, Joanne 180
Shepherd, Alison 9
Shepherd's Bush (London) 84
Sheridan, Richard Brinsley 63
Shirley, Thomas 33, 42*n*
Shore, Daniel 3
Shorne (Kent) 23
Simmons, Dan
  Drood, A Novel 208
Skilton, David 151
Slater, Michael 55, 61, 85, 86, 135, 208, 211
Smith, Julianne 158, 159
Somerset House (London) 16
South Eastern Railway 36, 199
Spectator, The 174
Spring-heeled Jack 216, 217
Stanfield, Clarkson
  Venice from the Dogana 128
Stange, G. Robert 116
Stanley, Arthur Penrhyn, Dean of Westminster 17, **18**, 19–42
  burial of CD 21, 23, 25, 28, 30–34
  burial of Edward Bulwer Lytton 39–40
  Life and Correspondence of Thomas Arnold 19
  meets CD 19–20, 22, 23, 29, 41
  meets John Forster and Charley Dickens 27–28, 39
  memorial sermon for CD 28, 37–38
  Recollections 19–21, 25–27, 37, 39

Stanley, Lady Augusta (née Bruce)   20, 40
Stanley, Louisa   23, 25
Stebbing, William   34
Steele, Stephen   15–17, 25
Sterne, Laurence
  The Life and Opinions of Tristram Shandy, Gentleman   135
Stevens, Bethan
  Woodpeckings: The Dalziel Archive, Victorian Print Culture, and Wood Engravings (website)   162 *see also* Dalziel, Edward; Dalziel, George
Stonnell, Mary Anne   84
Strand (London)   16, 71, 133
Stratford de Redcliffe, Stratford Canning 1st Viscount   22
Stretton, Hesba (Sarah Smith)
  Lost Gip   157
  String of Pearls; or, the Barber of Fleet Street, The   169
Strood (Kent)   15, 23, 35, 36
sublime   129, 145, 198
Surrey (county)   78
Surridge, Lisa   151–152
Sussex (county)   78
Swift, Jonathan
  Gulliver's Travels   109

t

Tambling, Jeremy   75, 129
television   219, 223
Temple Bar (London)   195–196
Tennyson, Alfred 1st Baron Tennyson   18, 22, 23
Ternan, Ellen Lawless (Nelly; CD's lover)   15, 17, 28, 34, 52, 54, 55, 208
Test and Corporation Acts (1661, 1673)   67–68
Thackeray, William Makepeace   18, 39, 115, 239
  The Adventures of Philip   153
  Vanity Fair   153, 169

Thames Estuary   138
Thames River   61, 109, 110, 132–135, 139, 140, 190, 209, **210**, 211, 215, 217
Theatre Royal Edinburgh   **159**
theatricality   101, 103, 117, 127, 154–160, 212, 232, 236, 238 *see also* masque; melodrama; performance
Thomas, Julia   151, 160–161
  Database of Mid-Victorian Illustration   162
Thompson, Christiana (née Weller)   50, 52–54, 57
Thompson, Thomas James   50–54
Thomson, Helen   52
Thynne, John Charles   33, 42*n*
Thynne, Lord John   33, 34, 42*n*
Times, The (London)   17, 26–28, 36, 37, 39, 40, 49, 50, 53, 54, 133, 175, 176
Todorov, Tzvetan   1
Tomalin, Claire   15, 52, 55, 61, 96, 208, 219
totemism   5, 118–120, 122
tourism, heritage   219
Toussenel, Alphonse   119
toys, children's   224, 232, 233 *see also* games; play
Tracey, Augustus Frederick   77, 78, 84, 85, 87
Tractarianism   23
train *see* railway
transgression   54, 97, 186
Transport for London   186
trespass   7, 185, 186, 189, 194, 196–198, 201 *see also* Urban Exploration
Trojans, ancient   220
Trollope, Anthony   18
Tuck, Raphael, & Sons
  Stories from Dickens   230, **231**, 232–233
Turner, Joseph Mallord William   6, 125–145
  Bridge of Sighs, Ducal Palace and Custom-House, Venice: Canaletti Painting   **128**, 134

Turner, Joseph Mallord William (*cont'd*)
  CD's opinion of   128
  Dawn after the Wreck   140
  Entrance of the Meuse: Orange Merchantman on the Bar, Going to Pieces; Brill Church bearing S.E. by S., Masenluys E. by S.   133
  The Fighting Téméraire, tugged to her last berth to be broken up (*The Fighting Téméraire*)   138, **140**
  The Goddess of Discord Choosing the Apple of Contention in the Garden of the Hesperides   133–134
  meets CD   127
  Peace–Burial at Sea   140–141
  Rain, Steam and Speed   6, 130, **131**, 141
  Slavers throwing overboard the dead and dying–Typhon coming on (*The Slave Ship*)   6, 136, **137**, 139, 141, 145
  The Snowstorm: Steamboat off a Harbour's Mouth Making Signals in Shallow Water and Going by the Lead   136
  Staffa, Fingal's Cave   141
  War: The Exile and the Rock-Limpet   128
  The Wreck Buoy   6, **138**, 139
  The Wreck of a Transport Ship   139
Turner, William   135
Tussaud, Marie (Madame Tussaud)   213 *see also* Madame Tussauds
Tuttle, Erasmus P.   78
Twitter   9, **182**
Typhon   136

U

Ubisoft Entertainment   8, 209, 211, 214, 218, 219 *see also* Assassin's Creed: Syndicate
uncertainty, textual   167, 171, 172, 180–181, 183

United States   18, 49, 77, 81, 96, 119, 125, 175, 193, 208, 211 *see also under* Dickens, Charles John Huffam: biography
Urania Cottage *see under* Dickens, Charles John Huffam: biography
Urban Exploration ("Urbex")   7–9, 185–202

V

Venice (Veneto)   128, 132, 134 *see also* Turner, Joseph Mallord William: *Bridge of Sighs, Ducal Palace and Custom-House, Venice: Canaletti Painting*
  St Mark's Basilica   128, 135
Vesuvius, Mount (Campania)   141
Victoria & Albert Museum   56, 214
Victoria, Queen   211
Victoria Street (London)   19, 36
Virtual St Paul's Cathedral Project (website)   8
Vita, Paul   219

W

walking   187–196 *see also* reading: perambulatory
Walkup, Kathleen   223, 224
Wall, John N.   8
Walsh, John Benn 1st Baron Ormathwaite   66
Wapping (London)   135
Wardrip-Fruin, Noah   7
Warhol, Robyn   7
  Victorian Serial Novels (website)   169–170
Weller, Anna *see* Dickens, Anna
Weller, Christiana *see* Thompson, Christiana
Weller, Thomas Edmund   51, 54
Wellesley, Arthur 1st Duke of Wellington   64
Wellington Street (London)   136, 191

Westminster (London)   133, 217
Westminster Abbey   15, 19–21, 25, 26, 28, 29, 34, 36, 37, 41 *see also* archives: Westminster Abbey (Muniments)
Westminster, Palace of   4, 62, **212** *see also* House of Commons
White, Sam   217–218
Whitechapel (London)   217
Whitehaven (Cumbria)   133
Whittington, Dick   191
Wilkie, David   140
William IV, King   63
Wills, William Henry (W.H.)   50, 54, 56
Wilson, Edmund   115
Wiltshire (county)   62, 78
Winyard, Ben   168
Witheridge, John   21, 23, 28
Woloch, Alex   49
Woolf, Leonard
  Autobiography   115
Woolf, Virginia   116
Wordsworth, William   115
World Trade Center (New York)   201
  see also 9/11
World War I   150
Worthen, John   117
wreckage   6, 128, 129, 133–140, 186
Wynne, Deborah   168, 181

y
YouTube   193

z
Zoomify   162